Lotus

By the same author
The World Champions *(Leslie Frewin)*
Grand Prix Ferrari
Sports Car Championship
The Encyclopaedia of Motor Racing
(with Keith Davey)
Competition Cars of Europe
The Racing Sports Car
Porsche

THE MOTOR RACING MERCHANTS

The late Jo Siffert, one of the greatest sports car drivers of all time, with his Gulf-Porsche 908/03 in the 1970 Nürburgring 1000 Km race. (Nigel Snowdon)

THE MOTOR RACING MERCHANTS

ANTHONY PRITCHARD

A Review of Drivers,
Circuits, Stars and Cars from 1922 to date

LESLIE FREWIN of LONDON

First published in 1976 by
Leslie Frewin Publishers Limited,
Five Goodwin's Court,
Saint Martin's Lane,
London WC2N 4LL, England.

This book is set in Baskerville

Photoset, printed and bound by
Weatherby Woolnough, Sanders Road,
Wellingborough, Northants.

ISBN 0 85632 080 3

CONTENTS

*Was first published in *Autosport*

List of Illustrations

Page 6

15. The BRM team enjoyed consistent success during the years of the 1500 cc Grand Prix Formula. Here Graham Hill is seen on his way to second place in the 1964 British Grand Prix at Brands Hatch. (T C March)

16. Although the BRM team brought these new H-16 cars along to the 1966 Belgian Grand Prix, they relied on the older V-8s for the race. (Nigel Snowdon)

17. Jean-Pierre Beltoise scored a completely unexpected victory with the V-12 BRM in the rain-soaked 1972 Monaco Grand Prix. Here he leads team-mate Helmut Marko out of the Station Hairpin. (Nigel Snowdon)

Page 7

18. In 1954 Moss was leading the Italian Grand Prix when his Maserati 250F lost its oil pressure. He pushed his car across the line into tenth place. (Publifoto)

19. Two years later at Monza, Moss was in luck and he won the Italian Grand Prix with this Maserati – despite a leaking fuel tank. (Publifoto)

Page 8

20. There was a furious battle for the lead in the 1957 Italian Grand Prix and here Fangio (Maserati) holds a narrow lead over the Vanwalls of Brooks and Lewis-Evans. Number 6 is Jean Behra with the V-12 Maserati and Moss, the eventual winner, is at the tail of this group. (Publifoto)

Page 9

21. In the 1966 British Grand Prix, Gurney with the original Climax-powered Eagle leads Bob Anderson's Brabham. (Nigel Snowdon)

22. Dan Gurney and the All-American Eagle on their way to victory on the very fast, very beautiful Spa circuit in 1967. (Nigel Snowdon)

23. Gurney at the mist-enveloped Nürburgring in 1968. He took ninth place in this race after stopping for a wheel-change. (Nigel Snowdon)

Page 10

24. Autodelta was out of luck in the 1968 BOAC '500' race; this 33/2 coupé driven by Vaccarella and Attwood retired because of camshaft failure. (Nigel Snowdon)

25. The 3-litre Alfa Romeo 33/3 cars were superbly turned out at Le Mans in 1970, but all four were eliminated. This car was driven by Gregory and Hezemans. (Nigel Snowdon)

26. De Adamich and Hezemans drove this Tipo 33/TT car into third place in the 1972 Targa Florio. (Nigel Snowdon)

Page 11

27. The first of the breed: the Lea-Francis-engined sports Connaughts of McAlpine and Clarke at the Blandford circuit in Dorset in 1949. (Guy Griffiths)

28. At Goodwood in September 1952, Dennis Poore (A-series Connaught) leads Stirling Moss (G-type ERA). (Guy Griffiths)

29. Archie Scott-Brown drove this B-series 'Syracuse' Connaught into second place in the 1956 *Daily Express* Trophy race at Silverstone. (T C March)

Page 12

30. Colin Chapman in 1950 with the Ford-engined Lotus Mark 2. (Guy Griffiths)

31. Jim Clark and the monocoque Lotus 25-Climax on their way to victory in the 1963 British Grand Prix at Silverstone. (Nigel Snowdon)

32. Almost as revolutionary a design was the Ford-engined Lotus 49, seen here at La Source hairpin in the 1967 Belgian Grand Prix with Clark at the wheel. (Nigel Snowdon)

Page 13

33. Colin Chapman with Jochen Rindt, posthumous World Champion in 1970 following his death in practice at Monza. (Nigel Snowdon)

34. The experimental gas-turbine Lotus 56B Grand Prix car driven by Emerson Fittipaldi in the 1971 Race of Champions at Brands Hatch. (Nigel Snowdon)

35. Fittipaldi with the Lotus 72D in the 1971 French Grand Prix; the Brazilian finished third. (Nigel Snowdon)

Page 14

36. Alberto Ascari at the wheel of a Tipo 625 4-cylinder Ferrari in the 1954 Italian Grand Prix. He worked his way into the lead, but retired with engine trouble.

37. Ferrari dominated Grand Prix racing in 1961 with his V-6 rear-engined cars, but the following year these proved uncompetitive. Here Phil Hill is seen in the 1962 British Grand Prix at Aintree. (T C March)

38. Jacky Ickx with the 1970 flat-12 Ferrari 312B, derivatives of which are still being raced. Ickx is seen in the Monaco Grand Prix in which he retired with drive-shaft failure. (Nigel Snowdon)

Page 15

39. 1957 was Ecurie Ecosse's last year of great racing success. One of their braver, but less successful efforts was the entry of this D-type Jaguar in the Mille Miglia. Ron Flockhart rose to seventh place, but retired because of chassis problems. (Publifoto)

40. At Le Mans in 1957 Ecurie Ecosse scored their second successive victory with the ex-works 'long-nose' D-type driven by Flockhart and Ivor Bueb.

41. John Wyer devoted thirteen years to the development of Aston Martin cars and the most successful was the Sports Car Championship-winning DBR1. Here Carroll Shelby is seen at the wheel of the DBR1 he co-drove to victory in the 1959 Tourist Trophy.

Page 16

42. Jacky Ickx at the wheel of John Wyer's BRM-engined Mirage on its debut in the 1969 BOAC race at Brands Hatch. (Guy Griffiths)

43. Le Mans in 1969 witnessed its most exciting finish since the 'thirties. Eventual winner Jacky Ickx with the Wyer-entered Ford narrowly leads Herrman's Porsche as they lap a Ferrari 250 LM. (Guy Griffiths)

44. In 1970-1 John Wyer was running the team of works Porsche 917s. This 5-litre 917 was driven to victory at Spa in 1970 by Jo Siffert and Brian Redman. (Nigel Snowdon)

1

Sunbeam Supreme:
Grand Prix Cars from Wolverhampton

Few British *marques* of the pre-war years enjoyed such wide respect or experienced such a varied and checkered history as the Sunbeam. Conceived at the turn of the century, when public interest in motoring was gathering momentum, production continued right through the years when quality was the first consideration of the purchaser and, in post-World War One days, the make achieved Grand Prix successes that were not bettered by a British car for over thirty years. Today the name survives as the badge label of a specialised version of a mass-production design.

The father of the Sunbeam car was John Marston. Before becoming interested in the production of motor cars in 1899, he had, since 1859, been a manufacturer of japaned tinware and in later years he had built the famous Sunbeam cycle with its 'little oil-bath' chain-case. As an elderly and substantial businessman, many of his friends and associates thought that he would be very unwise to risk his reputation and fortunes on such a risky venture. He had been convinced by Thomas Cureton, who had originally been apprenticed to Marston, that a marketable car could be made for £70 and would sell at around £140. Although Marston trusted Cureton's judgement and gave him a free hand with early Sunbeam car designs, he proceeded very cautiously before sanctioning the start of production.

The first Sunbeam car was built in the works at Paul Street, Wolverhampton and every component including the radiator and sparking plugs were specially designed and made. The radiator was the first of many to be manufactured by John Marston, and eventually a separate company, now known as Marston-Excelsior Ltd and an ICI subsidiary, was formed for their manufacture. The first Sunbeam prototype had a 5 hp vertical single-cylinder engine mounted at the front, but the second car had the engine mounted horizontally with an exposed crankshaft and an engine speed of 700 rpm. Other features of this second car included a 2-speed and reverse gearbox, high-tension ignition, 28-inch front and 30-inch rear wheels and a dry weight of around 10 cwt. Neither these cars, nor a 6 hp twin-cylinder model exhibited at the 1901 Crystal Palace Motor Show, entered production.

When a Sunbeam car was finally offered to the public, it was not a model designed at the Wolverhampton works. This first production car was the Sunbeam-Mabley, the creation of ornamental ironwork designer Mabberley-Smith, who received a royalty for every one of these rather odd cars that was sold. The Sunbeam-Mabley had a driving wheel on either side and wheels at the front and rear extremities which turned simultaneously, although they were out of track with one another. In the early days of motoring there was a dread of skidding and the layout of the Mabley was intended to eliminate this possibility. In this it was no doubt a complete success – it was certain to overturn first!

The engine of the Sunbeam-Mabley was a 2¾ hp de Dion mounted at the front, with the driver seated at the rear and there was room for two passengers squeezed intimately into a narrow seat running length-ways. The price was £130 and between 1901 and 1904 some three hundred of these rather precarious devices were sold. Even by 1902 demand for the Sunbeam-Mabley had flagged and a great deal of development work had failed to produce a satisfactory successor. That year the company was joined by T C Pullinger, a very experienced engineer who was allegedly the inventor of the water-cooled cylinder head.

Pullinger urged that a separate company for car manufacture should be formed and suggested that it should make a car based on the French Berliet of which he had a very high opinion (and an additional advantage was that the Berliet was not being imported into the United Kingdom). Pullinger's advice was followed and a Berliet-based Sunbeam was exhibited at the 1902 Crystal Palace Show. This was priced at £512 and had a 4-cylinder 12 hp (80 × 120 mm) engine, a braced wooden chassis frame, chain drive and 3-speed gearbox. Chain-cases, similar to those used on the company's cycles, were later fitted and in this form a Sunbeam won a Silver medal in the 1000-mile Trial held in September 1903.

In the 1904 Scottish Automobile Club Reliability Trials, Pullinger drove an experimental 6-cylinder Sunbeam, still with cylinder dimensions of 80 ×

120 mm, and this was one of the first 6-cylinder engines to be built in Britain. For 1905 a new production model was a 4-cylinder T-head 2660 cc (84 × 120 mm) car, still largely based on Berliet designs.

The same year the Sunbeam Motor Car Company with an authorised capital of £40,000 was formed, but Pullinger declined a directorship to join Humber; he subsequently became General Manager of Arrol-Johnston. Sunbeam cycles and motor-cycles continued to be made by a separate company which remained under Marston's control.

Some embarrassment was caused by the fact that Berliet cars were now being imported, but Sunbeam had obtained the services of a very able engineer, Angus Shaw, who resolved their difficulties by producing an entirely new design for 1906. This was the 16/20 4-cylinder with the cylinders cast separately, the inlet and exhaust valves all on one side of the engine and a capacity of 3402 cc (95 × 120 mm). A wooden chassis was retained, and there was a leather-faced cone clutch and a 4-speed gearbox. The 16/20 had a claimed maximum speed of 40 mph and the company aimed at an output of 500 cars a year, a target that was almost achieved.

In 1907 Shaw produced a 6-cylinder car, the 25/30; this used the same cylinders as the 16/20 (giving a capacity of 5103 cc) and had side valves and twin carburettors. The 25/30 weighed 26 cwt, cost £800 and was claimed to be good for 16 mpg and 50 mph (but presumably not at the same time!). The 16/20 now had an increased capacity of 4503 cc (105 × 130 mm) and it was henceforth known as the Twenty. Lack of demand for the 25/30 resulted in its replacement for 1908 by a new 35 hp 6333 cc (120 × 140 mm) 4-cylinder car, but sales of this model, too, proved limited.

Angus Shaw was a competent designer, but he lacked that spark of genius needed to make the Sunbeam an outstanding car, as opposed to just another dull but reliable make. In 1908 he was replaced by Louis Hervé Coatalen who was of Breton stock, but had taken out British nationality. Coatalen had previously been Chief Engineer at Humber and he had been in partnership with William Hillman. His first design was the 14/20, introduced in 1909, which had a 3823 cc (95 × 135 mm) 4-cylinder engine cast in two blocks of two cylinders, with an L head and a power output of 54 bhp at 2300 rpm. Although the 14/20 (later known as the 16/20) had the option of chain drive or a live-axle bevel final drive, the 12/16 of 2412 cc (80 × 120 mm) produced later the same year was offered with only the latter transmission. An unusual feature of both cars was the overdrive top gear.

Coatalen was keen to embellish the company's reputation by racing at

Brooklands and elsewhere and over the winter of 1909-10 he built a competition single-seater to which he gave the name *Nautilus.* This car was powered by a special 4257 cc (92 × 160 mm) engine with four overhead valves per cylinder and had a very narrow body with wooden slats fitted on to hoops and tapering front and rear to 'points' on which polished brass cones were fitted. When this car appeared in practice at Brooklands for the Easter meeting in 1910, it was found to overheat badly. The front-mounted radiator was receiving an insufficient air supply through the small orifice at the front end and a supplementary radiator mounted behind the driver's seat was receiving no supply of air at all! Before the race most of the car's bodywork had to be removed. *Nautilus* and Coatalen were in third place in their race when the two leading cars collided and in taking evasive action Coatalen was forced along the straight instead of taking the proper course round the Members banking to the finishing line.

Nautilus had not proved an unqualified success, but Coatalen was not at all dismayed and for the 1911 season produced a much improved single-seater which was given the name *Toodles II.* Although this car had much more conventional bodywork, it was also much more interesting mechanically and its 3217 cc (80 × 160 mm) engine featured a single chain-driven overhead camshaft which operated the inclined overhead valves through rocking levers. *Toodles II* broke its crankshaft in practice for the opening meeting at Brooklands in March 1911, but it enjoyed a very successful season at the Weybridge track and won a total of twenty-two awards during the year.

For the 1911 Coupe de l'Auto race held at Boulogne, Coatalen constructed a special car using an engine based on the 12/16 production model, but with the stroke increased to 149 mm, giving a capacity of 2996 cc. This car was driven by T Richards and, although it was uncompetitive in comparison with Bablot's winning Delage, it ran well until the steering broke, fortunately on a straight stretch of road, and Coatalen was well pleased with its performance.

Another new model to appear in 1911 was a redesigned 25/30 6-cylinder with a capacity of 6105 cc (90 × 160 mm) and the 6-cylinder engine cast in two blocks of three cylinders. The 25/30 was given an auspicious introduction by a twelve-hour run at Brooklands with Richards and Coatalen himself sharing the wheel. The Sunbeam drivers covered a distance of 908 miles, thereby breaking by a comfortable margin Edge's 12-hour record with a Napier, set in 1907.

For 1912 both the 12/16 and 16/20 models were fitted with long-stroke monobloc engines similar to those used in the Coupe de l'Auto car. In January 1912 Coatalen became a director of the Sunbeam company and this brilliant engineer was planning both new production models and another foray into European motor racing. Although there was no model in the Sunbeam range fast enough to beat the Continental opposition in a straight fight, Coatalen knew that the course to be used for the 1912 Coupe de l'Auto (to be run simultaneously with the French Grand Prix at Dieppe) was exceptionally arduous and that staying power would be as important as speed. In addition the 12/16 had a capacity that exactly met the 3-litre capacity limit for the Coupe de l'Auto. The cars entered at Dieppe differed mechanically very little from the production models, but they had been prepared with exceptional care and close attention had been paid to improving the roadholding by replacing the three-quarter elliptic rear springs with semi-elliptics, engine components were lightened and the cars were fitted with narrow and very light bodies.

The race was run over a distance of 956 miles, divided into two days' racing and overnight the cars were impounded. Four Sunbeams were entered, but the car driven by Caillois retired after only seven laps with a host of mechanical problems that included a seized big-end bearing. Although the other three cars were not without their troubles, and that driven by Médinger lost time on the second day while a magneto was changed and caused great anxiety in the Sunbeam pits when it developed a fuel leak, they all made it to the finish in third, fourth and fifth places overall in the Grand Prix, first three places in the Coupe de l'Auto and won the team prize (which in itself was worth £400).

An interesting entry at Indianapolis in 1913 was a 30 hp 6-cylinder Sunbeam driven by Delage *pilote* Guyot. The entry received a great deal of publicity and was tipped as a likely winner, merely because it was a foreign entry believed to have heavy works backing, but in fact it was a two-year-old private car. Guyot, who was aiming to finish and never expected to win, led after the first twenty laps and although he was overtaken as the race progressed, he had a trouble-free run (apart from the necessity to change one tyre) and finished in a very commendable fourth place.

One rather suspects that Coatalen's success in the 1912 Coupe de l'Auto had gone to his head, for at the following year's French Grand Prix at Amiens there appeared, at vast expenditure, a full team of four Grand Prix Sunbeams driven by Caillois, Chassagne, Resta and K Lee Guinness. The

Sunbeams had 6-cylinder 4524 cc (80 × 150 mm) engines; they were not fitted with differentials (their absence was said to improve the roadholding) and they had roller blinds in front of thc radiators controlled from the cockpit by string so that the engines would always run at the optimum temperature.

This race was run on a rather odd fuel consumption basis which permitted a maximum consumption of 14.12 miles to the gallon, and it was held over a distance of 566 miles. The opposition included a very strong team of new Peugeots designed by Henry, and teams from Delage, Excelsior and Itala. When the race started the course was still enveloped in early-morning mist and visibility was less than a quarter of a mile. Boillot and Goux took the first two places for Peugeot and although their cars were vastly superior to the rest of the entry, including the Sunbeams, the Wolverhampton-built cars put up a good show. Chassagne drove a fine race to finish third ahead of the Delages and Resta, soaked with oil from a split tank, took sixth place; neither of the other Sunbeam drivers made it to the finish. Caillois retired because of a broken torque rod and Guinness had a lurid crash; the right-hand front tyre burst as he was entereing a corner, the car left the road, striking and killing a spectator, and smashed through the parapet of a bridge on to rocks in the river bed below. Remarkably enough neither driver nor riding mechanic suffered serious injuries.

In 1913 the Coup de l'Auto race was held in September and on this occasion the Sunbeams were unable to repeat their earlier success. The 4-cylinder Peugeots of Boillot and Goux took the first two places, K Lee Guinness finished third for Sunbeam, Hancock took fourth place with a Vauxhall and Rigal, who had still not fully recovered from a bad crash in the Spanish race earlier in the year, finished fifth with a Peugeot.

Although Sunbeam had suffered two major International defeats, Coatalen was determined to achieve as much kudos on the home scene as possible. At Brooklands one of the 4½-litre Grand Prix cars driven by Chassagne, Guinness and Resta covered 1000 miles at 90 mph. In all the car completed twelve hours' running for which period it averaged 89.85 mph, despite trouble with the return oil pump. In October a Sunbeam powered by a 12-cylinder aero engine and driven by Chassagne completed a standing start lap at Brooklands at 94.68 mph and went on to cover 150 miles at 105.51 mph. At this time Sunbeam held every world record from 50 miles to 1000 miles. The same car and driver combination reappeared at Brooklands the following March and despite tyre trouble covered a flying mile at 120.73 mph.

At Wolverhampton work was progressing steadily on a new team of Sunbeams to compete in the Tourist Trophy race to be held in the Isle of Man. Coatalen had acquired one of the previous year's Grand Prix Peugeots and had closely aped the design of this very successful French car. The new Sunbeams featured 16-valve, twin overhead camshaft 4-cylinder engines of 3255 cc (81.5 × 156 mm) and other features copied from Peugeot practice were the ball-bearing crankshafts and hemispherical combustion chambers. Three of the Wolverhampton cars were entered in the 600-mile race in Ireland and although K Lee Guinness scored a brilliant victory, the other two team drivers were out of luck. Sir Algernon Guinness was in close contact with his brother until a rear universal joint seized shortly before the finish and Dario Resta retired on the first lap because of a broken big-end bolt. Belgian Minerva cars took second and third places.

Very similar cars to those run in the Tourist Trophy, but with engines enlarged to 4441 cc (94 × 160 mm), were entered in the French Grand Prix held in July over a distance of 467 miles at Lyon. This was the famous race dominated by the new $4\frac{1}{2}$-litre Mercedes which took the first three places. Boillot who had led for Peugeot for the first 400 miles finished fourth and Resta took fifth place for Sunbeam; this was a very satisfactory performance in view of the strength of the opposition. The outbreak of war brought an end to Sunbeam works racing activities, but two very interesting Wolverhampton-built cars appeared in American races from 1916 onwards. These cars had a chassis similar to that of the 1914 Grand Prix model, but were fitted with 6-cylinder 4914 cc (81.5 × 157 mm) engines said to develop 140 bhp at 3000 rpm. Although these cars scored no outright victories they achieved a large number of good placings, including a third place at Los Angeles in April 1916, a second in the Coney Island Cup the following month and a fourth at Indianapolis.

During the war years the Sunbeam factory mainly concentrated on the production of aero engines. The 16 hp car continued in production, but construction was contracted out to the Rover company. This model was widely used as a staff car and after the war many of the War Department surplus Sunbeams were rebuilt and exported to Australia.

In 1919 the Sunbeam company was in a very strong position financially; the factory space had been greatly expanded during the war years and the company had received over half a million pounds from government contracts. Car production was soon under way again. The first post-war model was a revised version of the 16 hp called the *Armistice* – complete with silver plating. There was also a modified 25/30, now known as the 24 hp, with a smaller engine of 4524 cc.

John Marston had died in 1918 and the new Chairman was Thomas Cureton who was in far from good health. Although a more imaginative or able designer than Coatalen would have been hard to find, the company was lacking in top management. Accordingly, the offer of a merger with the Talbot-Darracq concern in 1920 seemed an excellent proposition. Henceforth the destinies of the three *marques*, Sunbeam, Talbot and Darracq were controlled by a new company known as STD Motors Ltd, but each retained its individuality to a far greater extent than is usual with mergers of this nature.

Coatalen was as anxious as ever to pursue Sunbeam's racing activities and he had in fact completed two new cars in time for the 1919 Indianapolis race. It seems that these cars were very similar to the 1916 models, apart from a slightly shorter wheelbase. The 6-cylinder engines were the same and surrounding these is one of the many mysteries of motor racing. During the years 1915-19 there was a 300 cubic inch (4915 cc) capacity limit at Indianapolis and it appears that in 1916 the cars were declared to have a capacity of 4708 cc (80 × 156 mm), ie well within the permitted limit. In 1919 similar engines were declared to have a bore of 81.5 mm, still within the permitted limit. Apparently the cars were rejected as being oversize, but it was also said that they were withdrawn because the engines suffered a bad vibration period. Subsequently they were raced at Brooklands with a stated capacity of 4914 cc. The real reason why the cars did not run in 1919 and the true capacity – in both 1916 and 1919 – remains a matter for speculation.

The first true post-war Sunbeam racing car appeared in 1920; this was a remarkable device powered by a 350 hp V-12 aero engine with a capacity of 18,322 cc. This was entered at the August Bank Holiday Brooklands meeting for Harry Hawker, test pilot of the Sopwith Aviation Company who lost his life the following year in an aircraft crash. In fact the new Sunbeam never had the chance to show its paces, for Hawker had the misfortune to stall the car on the starting line. Later in the year René Thomas drove this aero-engined monster at the Gaillon hill climb and set a new record of 109 mph. It was the first car ever to exceed 150 mph and with the intrepid Malcolm Campbell at the wheel broke the World's Land Speed Record in 1922, 1924 and 1925. Campbell had advertised this car for sale in 1924 at £1500 and at that time claimed that it was good for 168 mph.

In 1921 Coatalen announced a new Grand Prix car complying with the then current 3-litre Formula. At least four of these cars with 8-cylinder twin overhead camshaft, 32-valve 2973 cc (65 × 112 mm) capacity were built; the power output was said to be 108 bhp at 4000 rpm and a maximum speed of 110 mph was claimed. It was at this point that the history of Sunbeam Grand Prix cars becomes incredibly complicated for the same models were raced both as Sunbeams and as Talbots. Two cars were entered at Indianapolis and one, apparently wearing a Sunbeam badge, was driven into fifth place by Haibe. Just to confuse matters even further, a grand total of seven cars, three Talbot-Darracqs, two Talbots and two Sunbeams were entered in the French Grand Prix held at Le Mans on 26th July. Then all seven entries were scratched because, Coatalen complained, there had been insufficient time to prepare the cars since the Indianapolis race. The matter did not rest there; the drivers pressured Coatalen to get the cars ready in time and eventually four cars, two Talbots and two Talbot-Darracqs, appeared at the start. At Le Mans the cars were plagued by tyre troubles, and during the race the team switched to another make borrowed from an adjoining pit! American Duesenbergs finished first and third, French Ballots second and fourth and the best STD performance came from Boillot who drove his Talbot-Darracq across the line in fifth place. K Lee Guinness and Segrave finished seventh and eighth, with cars wearing the Talbot badge. It can safely be concluded that the four runners at Le Mans included the two Sunbeams that had run at Indianapolis and it is likely that these four runners were the only cars to be completed.

A number of changes were made to the production cars during 1921. The 16 hp and 24 hp models became available in sporting form with four valves per cylinder operated by a single overhead camshaft. In the autumn of that year the standard versions were fitted with push-rod overhead valve engines and now had monobloc engine castings. The 24 hp model, later known as the 24/60, was one of the most attractive touring cars of the early twenties, with good looks, good handling characteristics, smooth and quiet running and a very satisfactory performance.

For 1922 a new Grand Prix Formula with a maximum capacity of 2000 cc came into force and Ernest Henry, the very successful designer of Peugeot and Ballot cars, was persuaded to design a new racing car for the STD Group. The new cars appeared at the French Grand Prix at Strasbourg in

July, but in the meanwhile, in June, the team raced the 1921 Grand Prix cars in the Tourist Trophy race which had a capacity limit of 3000 cc. K Lee Guinness failed to start in the 302-mile race in the Isle of Man because of clutch trouble, but his team-mates kept the flag waving. Segrave set the fastest lap of the race at 57.7 mph from a standing start and led for the first five laps; unfortunately his magneto failed just 300 yards from the summit of the Mountain part of the course and if only he could have reached that point, he would have been able to coast all the way back to the pits. Jean Chassagne then took the lead with the third Sunbeam entry and won at an average 55.78 mph from Clement (Bentley) and Payne (Vauxhall).

Early in 1922 Coatalen had written firmly, '. . . the claims of the straight-eight are indisputable and solidly grounded' for Grand Prix racing, but he seemed perfectly content that Henry's new design for Sunbeam was a 4-cylinder, a type that he had cheerfully denigrated. The Henry design had a capacity of 1975 cc (68 × 136 mm), twin overhead camshafts, four valves per cylinder and a power output of 88 bhp at 4500 rpm. The maximum speed was approximately 100 mph. Three cars were entered at Strasbourg for Chassagne, Guinness and Segrave, but their performance was disappointing and all three retired with valve failure. Segrave was so disgusted with the poor turn-out of the body of his car that he arranged for it to be repainted in Germany at his own expense, while he practised with a spare car.

K Lee Guinness had a very luxurious boat described as a 'trawler-yacht' with a garage below decks. In September this vessel, *The Ocean Rover* with two Sunbeams and three Talbot-Darracq Voiturettes in the 'garage', left Southampton on a European motor racing cruise. The passengers included Guinness himself, Albert Divo and Segrave. The Sunbeams, which consisted of the 1921 Grand Prix chassis with the 1916 4.9-litre Indianapolis engine, were raced only in the Coppa Florio in Sicily where they were driven by Chassagne and Segrave. In this arduous 268-mile race held over the 70-mile Madonie road circuit, the Sunbeams performed magnificently and despite lubrication problems Segrave took second place to Boillot's Peugeot.

The production cars remained unchanged for 1923, apart from reduced prices, and Coatalen pressed on with his racing programme. Following the failure of the 1922 cars, Henry's services were quietly dispensed with. The most successful car that year had been the 6-cylinder Fiat which itself owed a great deal of its ancestry to the 1914 Mercedes. Coatalen was a firm believer in copying other people's ideas rather than pursuing his own, possibly abortive, line of development and Vincent Bertarione was persuaded to leave Fiat and design a similar car for Sunbeam (interestingly enough, only a year later Alfa persuaded engineer Vittorio Jano to join them from Fiat). Bertarione produced a 6-cylinder engine very similar to Fiat's, but he had the good grace to revise the cylinder dimensions from 65 × 100 mm to 67 × 94 mm (giving a capacity of 1988 cc). There was insufficient time to build a new chassis and those from the previous year were used with new Fiat-like bodies. The Bertarione-designed engine had a power output of 108 bhp at 5000 rpm and the 1923 cars were said to be good for 115 mph.

Three Sunbeams driven by K Lee Guinness, Albert Divo and Henry Segrave were entered in the French Grand Prix at Tours. The strongest opposition came from a team of the new 8-cylinder Tipo 805 Fiats, and the entry included teams from Bugatti, Rolland-Pilain and Voison. Guinness took the lead on the eighth lap after Bordino's Fiat had retired because the supercharger had sucked in grit, but, magnificent sight though it was to see a British car leading a Grand Prix, the Sunbeam's advantage did not last long; Guinness made a pit stop at the end of lap 11, rejoined the race with only the smallest of leads over Giaccone's Fiat and was passed a lap later. Both Guinness and Segrave were now slowed by slipping clutches and Guinness soon lost second place to Salamano. As the race progressed, Segrave's clutch problems cured themselves; a stop which had restricted the movement of the pedal sheared off, allowing the clutch to engage fully. Now Segrave, in fifth place, began to climb up through the field and by lap 18 (just short of half-distance) was in third place behind team-mate Divo.

Now Divo moved into the lead ahead of Salamano's Fiat, but after four laps the Fiat was back in front again with the Sunbeams of Divo, Segrave and Guinness second, third and fourth. Divo lost all hopes of victory on lap 30 when he stopped to refuel; in his haste he succeeded in jamming the filler cap of the main fuel tank, eighteen minutes were lost in futile efforts to force it open and the car eventually rejoined the race with only the reserve tank filled and the need to stop every lap to top this up. Giaccone's Fiat was already out of the race because of grit sucked in by the supercharger and now, just as Divo left the pits after his long stop, the leading Fiat of Salamano stopped out on the course. The driver believed that the car had run out of fuel and the mechanic rushed back to the pits to fetch a can. It was all to no purpose, however, for the Fiat had suffered the same fate as its stable-mates. Segrave went on to score what was Britain's first ever Grand Prix victory from team-mate Divo, with Guinness's Sunbeam in fourth place.

Fiat made no mistakes in the Italian race at which their cars were fitted with an improved type of supercharger and sailed home in the first two places. There is no doubt that if the Sunbeams had run at Monza they would have been soundly thrashed. For much of the rest of the season Coatalen concentrated his efforts on the 1500 cc Talbot Voiturettes, but in September Divo drove one of the Grand Prix cars in a 248-mile race at Sitges variously known as the Spanish Grand Prix and the Gran Premio de Automobiles (the latter being the correct title of the race). There was not much in the way of opposition, but Divo was led for most of the race by Count Zborowski with an American Miller and was lucky to gain the lead – and victory – when Zborowski was forced to stop for a wheel-change shortly before the finish.

A new 1598 cc (68 × 110 mm) 4-cylinder ohv 12/30 model was announced at the 1923 Motor Show, but this was made for only two years. Unlike the 24 hp, on which four-wheel brakes were standard, the 12/30 was offered with rear brakes only. In addition the 20/60 model with a 3181 cc 6-cylinder engine was introduced as a successor to the 24 hp. This new car was priced at £950, but it failed to achieve popularity and was withdrawn after two years. To add spice to this rather staid range an exciting 3-litre sports Sunbeam was introduced in May 1924. This was primarily aimed at the Bentley market, and it was much faster than the rival 3-litre from Cricklewood, but unfortunately production did not get under way until late in 1925. The twin overhead camshaft 2916 cc (75 × 110 mm) 6-cylinder engine was initially mounted in the 20/60 chassis.

For the 1924 French Grand Prix held at Lyon on 3rd August the Sunbeam team produced a trio of new cars that were based on the 1923 winner with a whole host of improvements, including supercharging. The superchargers fitted to the Sunbeams were mounted outside the carburettors and the 1924 cars were the first European cars to have a blower that compressed the petrol/air mixture instead of air alone. In this form power output was 138 bhp at 5500 rpm and maximum speed was 125 mph, making them not only the fastest cars in the race, but probably the fastest cars (record-breakers apart) running in Europe at the time. The chassis was longer and lower (again based on Fiat practice) and there were new 4-speed gearboxes. At Lyon the Sunbeam drivers were Guinness, Resta and Segrave.

On the eve of the race the Sunbeams were fitted with new Bosch magnetos after that company's representative had pointed out that the contact breaker covers of the original magnetos were badly burned because of their proximity to the cars' exhaust systems. This change proved Sunbeam's downfall. Segrave went straight into the lead at the fall of the flag, stayed in front for the first three laps and then pulled into the pits with a bad engine misfire. Both Segrave and Resta spent the remainder of the race in and out of the pits while the mechanics struggled in vain to cure the misfires. At no time did they suspect that the magnetos were the cause of the trouble, as, of course, these had only just been changed. . . . It was not until the race was long over that the fault was discovered. Guinness, whose car was not bothered by misfiring, was in second place when an engine bearing failed, Campari's Alfa Romeo P2 led home the Delage V-12s of Divo and Benoist, while Segrave struggled on to finish fifth. Resta was too far behind to be classified as a finisher. The only small consolations to be derived from this failure were Segrave's fastest lap at 76.25 mph and the fact that the Fiats had also failed.

In September, Segrave and Guinness competed with the 2-litre Sunbeams in the San Sebastian Grand Prix held on the Lasarte circuit. Despite opposition from Bugatti, Delage and Mercedes, Segrave did much to restore Sunbeam's prestige by winning this race at an average of 64.12 mph. Guinness had led away at the start of the race, but the circuit was in a terrible state with many of the corners thickly coated with wet clay. At one of these corners he lost control, hit a bank and overturned. Both Guinness and his mechanic, Barratt, were flung over telegraph wires and into a railway cutting. Barratt was killed instantly, but Guinness escaped with severe head and leg injuries.

Malcolm Campbell set a World Speed Record with the aero-engined car in September (this is discussed in a later chapter) and the same month Resta was killed during a record attempt at Brooklands with one of the Grand Prix cars.

Two of the 3-litre sports cars were entered at Le Mans in 1925, and these were driven by Segrave/Duller and Chassagne/S C H Davis. It was a poor year for British cars, as the Bentleys and one of the Sunbeams retired, but the 3-litre twin-cam driven by Chassagne/Duller covered 1343 miles, the second greatest distance, behind a French Lorraine-Dietrich.

Because 1925 was the last year of the 2-litre Formula no changes were made to the Sunbeam Grand Prix cars, three of which, driven by Segrave, Conelli and Masetti, were entered in the French Grand Prix at Montlhéry on 26th July. The race was marred by the fatal crash of Alberto Ascari and the rest of the Alfa Romeo team was withdrawn. This 621-mile race was won by the Delage of Benoist/Divo and the sole Sunbeam finisher driven by Masetti took third place.

At the 1925 Motor Show the first production 3-litre sports model was exhibited at a price of £1125 and the range was extended by the introduction of a new straight-eight model with the choice of 4825 cc or 5028 cc engines. The STD Group was beginning to get into deep financial waters and at the beginning of 1926 arrears of preference dividend amounting to over £300,000 were unpaid. It was announced that no new racing Sunbeams were to be built and that in future only Darracqs would compete in International events.

In fact it did not work out like this, as Coatalen was just completing a new 4-litre V-12 car based on two of the 2-litre Grand Prix cylinder blocks. With a single Roots-type supercharger, power output was 306 bhp at 5300 rpm and the dry weight was only 18 cwt. Segrave took the car to Southport sands in March 1926 to have a crack at the Land Speed Record which stood to Campbell's 350 hp Sunbeam at 150.87 mph. The 4-litre Sunbeam was plagued by constant supercharger failure and although 152.336 mph was achieved in one direction, the supercharger failed on the return run. Segrave then drove the car in the Spanish Grand Prix at San Sebastian, but retired because of a broken front axle after only six laps. In August he won the Boulogne Speed Trials with the 4-litre car at 140.6 mph and a month later he ran in the Italian Grand Prix, but retired with loss of oil from the gearbox. There were two of these 4-litre Sunbeams, and they were subsequently sold to Sir Malcolm Campbell who had the chassis rebuilt by Thomas & Taylor in 1932 to the design of Reid Railton.

Coatalen had realised that it would be impossible to extract much more power from the 4-litre cars and conceived the idea of constructing a fantastic record-breaker powered by two of the 500 hp 24-litre Sunbeam Matabele aero engines rescued from the speedboat Maple Leaf VII which had sunk while competing in the 1921 Championship of the Sea. In this way it was hoped to secure the maximum publicity at minimum cost by setting a new Land Speed Record of at least 200 mph. The engines were mounted front and rear, with a special 3-speed gearbox and enclosed chain drive to the rear axle encased by armour plate. The chassis was clad in a fully aerodynamic shell. Dunlop provided special tyres guaranteed to last for $3\frac{1}{2}$ minutes at 200 mph and Daytona Beach, Florida, was chosen for the run, as it offered 23 miles of sand, dead straight and a quarter of a mile wide. The attempt was a great success and Segrave achieved a mean speed for the two runs of 203.793 mph.

By now the Sunbeam branch of the STD group was beginning to stagnate; Segrave severed his connections with Sunbeam and was becoming increasingly interested in the Water Speed Record, which was to bring about his untimely death. Coatalen was showing disinterest in the production side of the company and indeed Sunbeam's star was beginning to fade. Subsequent Sunbeams were still first-class cars, but they lacked appeal and failed to match the developments of their rivals, especially their stable-mate Talbot.

In 1929 another contender for the Land Speed Record was built at Wolverhampton. This used two narrow V-12 engines mounted in tandem, with a total capacity of 48 litres and reputed to develop over 2000 bhp. The car was called the *Silver Bullet* and with Kaye Don as driver was taken to Daytona. The record attempt was a fiasco and was eventually abandoned. The financial instability of the company prevented the construction of any further special Sunbeams.

Early in 1931 the entire board of the STD group resigned as a result of strong criticism from independent auditors whose attack was aimed at the lack of co-ordination within the organisation. New models continued to appear and cars were sold in small numbers, but during 1934 petitions were presented in the Chancery Division of the High Court by the trustees for the holders of ten-year Guaranteed Notes issued by STD Motors Ltd in 1924. There were substantial arrears of interest and the appointment of a receiver was sought. New finance was found, the parties settled their differences and the Company managed to struggle on for a little longer.

In February 1935 Clement-Talbot Ltd was sold to Rootes Securities Ltd and a receiver was appointed for Sunbeam. Eventually, in July 1935, this company too was sold to Rootes who stopped production of all Sunbeam models. A prototype Sunbeam with a 4-litre Humber engine was exhibited in September 1936, but this failed to reach the production stage. From 1938 the Rootes-built Talbots were known as Sunbeam-Talbots. Although the products of this division of the Rootes Group had little in common with their illustrious ancestors but their name, Rootes' very active rallying efforts in the early 'fifties brought as much prestige as the racing victories of thirty years previously. Today the name Sunbeam is used for export versions of Hillman cars and for a higher-performance version of the Hunter saloon. A sad end for a name that brought Britain so much racing glory.

2

The Flying Mantuan:
A Portrait of Tazio Nuvolari

Tazio Giorgio Nuvolari, born at Casteldario in 1892, was unique amongst racing drivers. He was possibly the greatest of all Italian drivers, probably the greatest of all who raced before the second World War; above all he was unique for the tremendous courage with which he drove, his ability to fight against the heaviest odds, pushing from his consciousness the pain and torment that he was suffering from earlier accidents, racing regardless of broken bones and plaster casts. For much of his racing career Nuvolari had to make do with inferior cars and it was rare indeed for the great Italian ever to give up the fight, however many laps he was in arrears, and reconcile himself to defeat. All the while he raced Nuvolari maintained a constant conversation with himself and his car, grinning happily or furiously as the situation demanded, patting his car, coaxing it, talking to it, thereby encouraging it and himself to even greater achievements.

Like so many Italian drivers, Nuvolari started his racing career with motor-cycles in 1923, and within two years he was a member of the Bianchi motor-cycle works team and reserve driver for Alfa Romeo at the Italian Grand Prix at Monza. In practice at Monza the gearbox of his P2 car seized up and in the crash that followed Nuvolari was hurled through a wire fence. His injuries included a severely lacerated back and he was told that he could expect a stay in hospital of around a month. Such a prospect was totally unacceptable to Tazio whose whole life centred on racing and six days later he appeared, heavily swathed in bandages, astride his 350 cc Bianchi at the Grand Prix des Nations at Monza; he had to be push-started and despite terrible pain he duelled on a soaking wet track with Handley's Rex-Acme, going ahead to score a brilliant all-Italian victory after the British machine had failed shortly before the finish.

Nuvolari continued to race motor-cycles until 1929, by which time he was competing regularly in major International car races. He had taken third place with a Bugatti Type 35 car in the 1928 Italian Grand Prix and the following year he finished second with a private Alfa Romeo P2 in the 139-mile Coppa Ciano at Livorno. In 1930 Tazio sold his P2 back to the works and this was one of four of these old straight-eight cars rebuilt at Portello with modified suspension and slightly increased engine capacity. These rebuilt P2s were entered on behalf of the works by the newly formed Scuderia Ferrari and among the Ferrari drivers was 38-year old Tazio Nuvolari; the diminutive Nuvolari was almost lost in the roomy cockpit of the P2 and contemporary photographs show him dwarfed by fellow team drivers Borzacchini, Campari and Achille Varzi (his 'deadliest' rival).

Throughout the 1930 season the old P2 Alfas proved no match for the new 8C–2500 Maseratis and their only victories, scored by Varzi early in the season, were at Bordino and in the Targa Florio. The run of Maserati victories began at Rome in June on the debut of the 8C–2500 and in this race Tazio retired his P2. Off the circuits and on the hills Nuvolari and the P2 enjoyed rather more success and set fastest time of the day at the Trieste-Opicina, Cuneo-Colle Maddalena and Vittorio Veneto-Cansiglio hill climbs. Nuvolari was leading the Monza Grand Prix when his Alfa burst a tyre and he rounded off an unsatisfactory season by finishing third in the Czechoslovakian Grand Prix held on the Brno circuit; in this race he took over Borzacchini's car after his own had broken. Tazio's best performance had in fact been in the Mille Miglia sports car race at the beginning of the season and he had won this arduous event with a 1750 cc 6-cylinder Alfa at a record average of 62.42 mph.

Happily for supporters of the quadrifoglio, Vittorio Jano was planning several new cars for the 1931 season and his latest (and probably most successful) design, the 8C–2300 dominated the season's racing. This new straight-eight made its debut in the Mille Miglia in April, but in this race Scuderia Ferrari was out of luck. Both 2.3s were plagued by tyre troubles and Tazio finished a poor ninth after a crash. Shortly afterwards Nuvolari drove one of the new cars to victory in the Targa Florio in Sicily.

At the Italian Grand Prix at Monza in May Scuderia Ferrari raced both the new short-chassis version of the 2.3-litre car which afterwards became known as the Monza, and a rather improbable device powered by two supercharged 1750 cc supercharged sports car engines designated the Tipo A. In practice the twin-engined car was crashed by Luigi Arcangeli with fatal results, but this did not deter Enzo Ferrari from running it in the race and it was driven by the intrepid Nuvolari. After two hours of this ten-hour race the designer of the Tipo A, Vittorio Jano urged that it should be withdrawn (the reason why is far from clear) and Tazio switched over to one of the 2.3-litre cars which he shared with Campari. The Italian Monza drivers were in the lead by half-distance and went on to win the race at an average of 96.79 mph from another Alfa belonging to the same stable and driven by Minoia/Borzacchini. This was the first of three victories scored by the 'Flying Mantuan' in the Italian Grand Prix.

Later in the season Nuvolari and co-driver Borzacchini were leading the Belgian Grand Prix when their Monza was delayed by fuel starvation problems; after the trouble had been cured Tazio hurled the Alfa round Spa in desperate pursuit of the now leading Bugatti of Williams and Conelli, but he was unable to close the gap and had to settle for second place. Tazio scored victories with a Monza in the Coppa Ciano at Livorno and with a 1750 cc sports car in the Tre Provincie race at Bologna. The latter 80-mile race was run over a remarkably slow circuit and Tazio's winning speed was 40.33 mph; second place in this race went to Enzo Ferrari himself at the wheel of a 2.3-litre Alfa. Nuvolari rounded off his season with an almost unique accident in the Czechoslovakian Grand Prix by colliding with a bridge that had collapsed after it had been run into by Fagioli's leading Maserati. History repeated itself to a certain extent, in the mid-fifties when a bridge overloaded by spectators collapsed during a minor race in France and a driver who ran into the wreckage was killed.

Nuvolari suffered yet another crash in his first race of the 1932 season, the Mille Miglia. Team-mate Ghersi had misjudged his speed on the approach to the Piazza Michelangelo in Florence, skidded wildly and crashed into a post. Tazio arrived on the scene a few moments later, caught sight of the wreckage of his team-mate's car and as a result of a momentary loss of concentration went into a slide and crashed a few yards further along the road! Fortunately both drivers (and their co-drivers) escaped without injury. Soon afterwards Nuvolari more than compensated for this lapse by winning the Monaco Grand Prix with a Monza, three seconds ahead of German driver Rudolf Caracciola at the wheel of a similar car. In 1932 the Targa Florio road race in Sicily was run in oppressively hot conditions, but the diminutive Nuvolari seemed totally unaffected by the heat and, while many of his rivals sweated and strained, Tazio, looking cool and completely relaxed, pulled away to a clear victory with his 2.3 Alfa.

The Monza was a racing version of what might be termed a 'multi-purpose' Alfa Romeo design and at the 1932 Italian Grand Prix the Milan factory revealed their new 2.6-litre Monoposto car designed by Vittorio Jano. This design was derived from the Monza, but it was much more powerful and featured single-seater bodywork. Tazio was one of two Scuderia Ferrari drivers entrusted with the new model at Monza and he led throughout this 5-hour race to win at a record average of 104.09 mph. Another victory for the great Italian followed in the French race at Reims; Tazio made a poor start, holding eighth place early in the race, but he was through to the front with his Monoposto to take the lead from Caracciola by lap 11.

At the German Grand Prix at the Nürburgring, however, Tazio had to give best to Caracciola, who knew this 14.19-mile circuit intimately, and he finished second, thirty seconds in arrears. It was a matter of great annoyance to the fiery Italian that when he had stopped to refuel, the mechanics took 2 min 40 sec to tank up the Alfa, over a minute longer than Caracciola's refueling stop. Tazio argued, perhaps with some justification, that the mechanics had been instructed to dally over his pit stop so as to allow the German driver to win on home ground. Caracciola had a contract with the Alfa Romeo works, but raced as an independent. The unfortunate incident at the Nürburgring was soon forgotten in the thrill of later triumphs and Tazio went on to score three victories in quick succession at Livorno (the Coppa Ciano), Pescara (the Coppa Acerbo) and Avellino, all at the wheel of Monoposto cars. In only one race in 1932, the Czechoslovakian Grand Prix, were the Monopostos defeated and at the Brno circuit Tazio had to settle for third place behind Chiron (Bugatti) and Fagioli (Maserati).

Although the reason was not announced at the time, the Alfa Romeo works withdrew from racing at the beginning of 1933 because of serious financial difficulties. As a result of this decision Scuderia Ferrari was no longer allowed to race the Monoposto cars, but was forced to fall back on the old Monzas which, despite an increase in engine size to 2.6 litres, were no longer competitive compared with the latest products of Bugatti and Maserati. The season started well enough for Tazio, however, with a win in the rain-soaked Tunis Grand Prix and a fine victory with a 2.3-litre sports car in the Mille Miglia.

Thereafter Nuvolari's fortunes began to turn sour. At Monaco he fought a furious battle with his arch-enemy Achille Varzi (they disliked each other so much that they would not drive in the same team); the

Alfa and the Bugatti swapped the lead time and time again and they were still battling it out on the hundredth and final lap of the race. As the two cars ascended the hill from Sainte Devote to the Casino an oil pipe broke on Nuvolari's Monza and while Varzi's Bugatti roared on to victory, the Monza expired in a cloud of blue smoke. Tazio won the Bordino race in the absence of any serious opposition (Varzi's Bugatti failed to appear), but in the Tripoli Grand Prix he was beaten by Varzi by less than a car's length. Victories for Nuvolari followed in two minor races, the Eifelrennen at the Nürburgring and the Nîmes Grand Prix, but three failures in succession were to bring his dissatisfaction with the Monza to a climax. He retired with differential failure in the French Grand Prix at Montlhéry, finished fifth after carburation problems at Barcelona and retired yet again with differential failure in the Marne Grand Prix at Reims.

No longer was Nuvolari prepared to tolerate the unreliability and lack of speed of the ageing Monzas; he 'collected his cards', formed a private team with veteran driver Baconin Borzacchini and the following weekend appeared at the Belgian Grand Prix at Spa-Francorchamps with a private 3-litre Maserati. The full 3-litre version of the straight-eight Maserati had not appeared until the start of the 1933 season, and although it proved a match for the Monzas, its ancestry dated back to 1926, it lacked the technical sophistication of the Monoposto Alfa and it was slower; in addition the Maserati suffered excessively skittish roadholding characteristics. Nuvolari soon diagnosed part of the cause of the Maserati roadholding problems and after a brief practice session at Spa took the Maserati to the nearby Imperia car factory where he had the chassis braced to improve its rigidity. Nuvolari returned to the circuit to record second fastest practice time and to win the race from the Bugattis of Varzi and Dreyfus.

This switch of allegiance from Alfa Romeo to Maserati was to prove a wise move; 1933 was to be a successful year for Nuvolari and, taking into account the victories scored by other drivers, it was to prove one of the most successful in Maserati history. Nuvolari scored two more victories in his next two races, in the Coppa Ciano and in the Nice Grand Prix. At the finish of the French race Nuvolari was a minute and a half ahead of Dreyfus's Bugatti and, in the words of *Motor Sport,* at the end of his lap of honour, 'hundreds of blue jackets from the Italian fleet at Golf Juan tore Tazio Nuvolari from the seat of his winning Maserati, raised him shoulder high, and carried him, a white naval cap on his head, triumphantly along the

Promenade des Anglais – one of the most deliriously enthusiastic scenes ever witnessed in motor racing'.

As a direct result of the Maserati victories during 1933 the Alfa Romeo works released the Monopostos to Scuderia Ferrari once more in time for Luigi Fagioli to drive one in the Coppa Acerbo at Pescara on 13th August. Nuvolari took the lead on the first lap of the race and although Fagioli closed up on the 'Flying Mantuan', his chances of taking the lead seemed slim. Then trouble struck the race-leader. Tazio pulled into the pits where a seized universal joint was freed, and he resumed the race to finish in second place, two minutes behind the Alfa Romeo driver. Another failure followed at Marseilles where Nuvolari's Maserati broke its back axle whilst leading the race. In the Italian Grand Prix at Monza, a late stop for tyres cost Tazio the lead and he finished second to Fagioli's Alfa. Tazio's final race of the 1934 season was the Spanish Grand Prix at San Sebastian where he lost control and crashed after heavy rain falling on to the rubber-streaked track had turned the surface into a skating rink.

Nuvolari persisted with his role of Maserati privateer in 1934, but the Bologna team's chances of success were much diminished. Jano had developed a more powerful 2905 cc version of the Monoposto which was faster than the Maseratis at most circuits and, as the season progressed, the new and very advanced contenders from the German Auto Union and Mercedes-Benz teams improved in both speed and reliability. It was not until the very end of the season that Nuvolari, formerly a persistent wearer of the victor's laurels, scored his first win.

The first Grand Prix of the 1934 season was at Monaco and here Nuvolari drove a works 2.8-litre Type 59 Bugatti. In this race Tazio was never in contention for the lead and after a scrap with Taruffi's 4-cylinder Maserati (which retired with engine trouble on the last lap) he finished a none too satisfactory fifth. Next on the calendar was the Bordino Grand Prix, run in torrential rain that made the roads forming the 8-kilometre Alessandria circuit glisten blackly and lethally. Under these conditions the Maseratis were especially difficult to control and in one of the heats Carlo Pedrazzini was killed when he crashed on the approach to the bridge over the River Tanaro. In the final Nuvolari struck a tree at almost exactly the same spot and suffered severe injuries which included a broken leg. While he was in hospital recovering from this accident, a local gymnastic club presented him with a section of the tree into which he had crashed, bearing the inscription, 'To Tazio Nuvolari, intrepid ace of the wheel, as a record of the providential obstacle which, although preventing a sure victory, saved a precious existence.'

Broken bones meant little to the incredibly tough and determined Mantuan; the Alessandria race was on 22nd April and on 27th May Nuvolari appeared at the Avus circuit in Berlin, still swathed in bandages, his left foot in plaster and the clutch pedal of his Maserati moved closer to the central accelerator so that he could operate both with his right foot. Needless to say, Nuvolari was racing against the advice of his doctors and despite the entreaties of his wife; almost needless to say he finished the race, despite acute pain, persistent cramp and equally persistent tyre trouble. He finished fifth, one place behind fellow-Maserati driver Earl Howe who commented, '. . . it was one of the finest exhibitions of pluck and grit ever seen . . . by such men are victories won!'

Nuvolari's injured legs were still giving him terrible pain at the Penya Rhin Grand Prix at Barcelona in the middle of June. On the tortuous Montjuich Park circuit he led the field in the opening laps, but intense pain forced him to ease his pace and he was in fourth place when he retired with mechanical trouble. Nuvolari reappeared with a Bugatti Type 59 in the French Grand Prix at Montlhéry, but retired yet again; he retired with rear axle failure in the Marne Grand Prix at Reims and took fourth place at the Nürburgring. Nuvolari was usually to the fore in those two famous Italian races, the Coppa Ciano and the Coppa Acerbo; 1934 was no exception and he finished third at Livorno and second at Pescara. At the Italian Grand Prix at Monza he drove a new 6-cylinder 3.3-litre Maserati, but this car, the Tipo 34, was plagued by failing brakes and Tazio finished fifth, slowing the car on the gearbox for much of the race. It was only now that he scored his first victories of the year, both at the wheel of the 6-cylinder Maserati, in minor races at Milan and Naples.

It had been Tazio's intention to continue to race private Maseratis in 1935, but Mussolini was becoming increasingly dismayed at the Grand Prix successes of the two German teams and the comparative failure of Scuderia Ferrari; Nuvolari was persuaded that it was in the national interest that he should return to Alfa Romeo and drive once more for Scuderia Ferrari. In 1935 Ferrari was still racing the familiar Monoposto cars, in 3.8-litre form later in the year (although the more streamlined, fully independently sprung 8C–35 appeared at Monza in September) and these were no match for the German Auto Union and Mercedes-Benz entries; nevertheless 1935 represented something of an Alfa Romeo revival and Nuvolari in particular achieved unexpected successes. He was out of luck in the early races of the 1935 season and the monstrous twin-engined *Bi-motore* Alfa (capable of almost 200 mph on the straights) let him down both at Tripoli and Avus through its voracious appetite for tyres.

Tazio's first victory of 1935 was in June at the wheel of a 3.2-litre Monoposto in the minor Circuit of Biella which neither of the German teams entered, and later that month he set a new Class B (5000 – 8000 cc) record for the flying kilometre of 199.73 mph; the car used by Nuvolari for the record attempt was the *Bi-motore* and the scene was the Autostrada between Florence and Viareggio near Altopascio. In the French Grand Prix Tazio drove a 3.5-litre version of the Monoposto with great elan to take the lead at the start of the race and set fastest lap at 84.99 mph before retiring because of rear axle failure. Another minor victory for Nuvolari followed at Turin in July and then on the 28th of that month Tazio drove the new 3.8-litre version of the Monoposto in the German Grand Prix at the Nürburgring. In the opening laps of the race Nuvolari was in fifth position and then dropped back to sixth when he was passed by team-mate Louis Chiron. Then suddenly Nuvolari switched on, in the space of three laps his speed increased conspicuously and by lap 9 he had passed Rosemeyer (Auto Union), Chiron, von Brauchitsch (Mercedes) and Fagioli (Mercedes) to hold second place. On the next lap, just before the leaders stopped to refuel, Tazio snatched first place from Caracciola.

All five leading cars stopped to refuel at the end of lap 11 (half-distance) and while von Brauchitsch's stop lasted only 47 seconds (sufficiently slick to put him in the lead ahead of Caracciola and Rosemeyer), Nuvolari was stopped for all of 2 min 14 sec. The handle of the refuelling pump in the Scuderia Ferrari pit had broken and while the Monoposto was refuelled from churns, Tazio was prancing around the car in a frenzy of excitement and tension. The Alfa Romeo rejoined the race in fifth place and Nuvolari responded to this setback by driving at his hardest, obsessed with regaining as much time on the leaders as possible; within three laps he had passed Fagioli (slowed by shock-absorber trouble), Rosemeyer and Caracciola (who was feeling unwell) and was in second place. Although von Brauchitsch had been motoring very hard in the first few laps after his pit stop, he began to ease off, secure in the knowledge that Nuvolari could not catch him (even though the Italian was narrowing the gap at the rate of sixteen seconds a lap).

When the leader started his last lap, he still had an advantage of 35 seconds and von Brauchitsch's one and only cause for concern was that one of his tyres was showing the white breaker strip. Only seven kilometres from the finish the almost inevitable happened, the leading Mercedes burst a rear tyre and Tazio swept into the lead and to victory. Von Brauchitsch was nicknamed the *Pechvogel* (unlucky bird) and he was certainly out of luck on 28th July 1935. He struggled on to cross the line in fifth place and shed his tears of disappointment with Mercedes team-manager Neubauer's comforting arm round his shoulders. Despite the good fortune surrounding Nuvolari's victory in this race, it must be remembered that but for his protracted refuelling stop he would have almost certainly won the race in a straight fight.

Later in the season little success came Nuvolari's way and the German cars and drivers remained dominant. At the Italian Grand Prix at Monza Nuvolari appeared with the new 8C–35 Alfa Romeo and he was in second place with a little over half the race completed when his car burnt a piston. He took over team-mate Dreyfus's Monoposto to continue the chase after von Stuck's leading Auto Union, but this Alfa broke a valve and Tazio had to settle for second place, 1 min 41 sec behind the rear-engined car from Zwickau. All the Mercedes-Benz entries retired in this race. Nuvolari also took second place in the Czechoslovakian Grand Prix (a race which Mercedes did not enter).

Tazio Nuvolari remained with Scuderia Ferrari in 1936 and in the early part of the season the team had to make do with the new chassis, first seen at Monza in 1935, powered by the old 8-cylinder engine. Vittorio Jano's new 4.1-litre V-12 engine was not ready until the Tripoli Grand Prix in May. In the Monaco Grand Prix in April Tazio forced his way into the lead ahead of Caracciola's Mercedes and soon pulled out a lead of around 10 seconds. This tortuous 1.95-mile course was one of the few which were so arduous that a driver of a slow car could race on anything like even terms with the much more powerful German monsters and it was a situation of which Tazio took full advantage. Unfortunately the Alfa developed an engine misfire and lost much of its braking power, Tazio slipped back to second place behind Caracciola and was later passed by the Auto Unions of Varzi and von Stuck.

In practice for the Tripoli Grand Prix held on the very fast Mellaha circuit, Nuvolari was travelling at close to 125 mph with the new V-12 Alfa when he struck a marker stone; a tyre burst, the Alfa went out of control and rolled end over end into the sandy wastes bordering the track. Helpers rushed to the scene, but could find no trace of the driver in the shattered, smoking wreckage; it was only some ten minutes later that the unconscious Nuvolari was discovered lying in a pile of drying grass into which he had been fortunate enough to be flung as the car turned over. At hospital Nuvolari was discovered to have injured ribs and bad bruising and was immediately put in plaster. Despite the injuries, despite a plaster corset, Tazio insisted on driving in the race and brought another V-12 Alfa across the line in seventh place.

A month later Nuvolari scored another magnificent victory over the German cars in the Penya Rhin Grand Prix at Barcelona. Tazio took the lead at the start and not even Caracciola, perhaps the greatest of all German drivers, could match Nuvolari's cornering speed over the difficult Montjuich Park circuit. The German driver went ahead briefly when Nuvolari stopped to refuel, but Tazio soon repassed him and stayed in front despite another, unscheduled stop for tyres. In the Eifelrennen at the Nürburgring Tazio led with his V-12 car for three laps, but Rosemeyer (Auto Union) was dogging his wheel tracks; the German driver took the lead at the end of lap 6 and, despite thick banks of mist rolling across the circuit, steadily pulled away from the Alfa Romeo to win by a margin of two minutes.

Although the Alfa Romeos were only too obviously outclassed by their German rivals, Tazio trounced the Auto Unions in three races in quick succession. In the Hungarian Grand Prix held on 21st June over a tortuous 5-kilometre circuit Tazio took the lead at the start, was passed by Rosemeyer, clung grimly to the German's tail for twenty laps and then went ahead again to win by a margin of fourteen seconds. Remarkably enough all three Mercedes entries in this race retired. A week later Tazio met up with a solitary Auto Union driven by arch-rival Achille Varzi in the 97-mile Circuit of Milan race. This was not a race which Zwickau had intended to enter, for it was a very minor event and the tight, sinuous 1.6-mile circuit was ill-suited to Auto Union handling characteristics. Varzi, however, had been most anxious to compete and eventually the one car was sent to the Italian race. Nuvolari and Varzi battled throughout the race, Tazio won by nine seconds, but although the resulting publicity was bad for Auto Union, Varzi had in fact put up a very fine performance with an unwieldy, unsuitable car.

Tazio was in second place in the German Grand Prix held on 26th July when he retired with back axle trouble. Rosemeyer and von Stuck took the first two places for Auto Union ahead of Antonio Brivio's Alfa Romeo.

There were no Mercedes entered in the Coppa Ciano race at Livorno the following weekend, but both Alfa Romeo and Auto Union were out in strength. The German team had not entered this race until the last moment when, revelling in their triumph at the Nürburgring, they rushed three cars to the circuit without any proper maintenance work since their last race. Shortly after the start the rear axle failed on Tazio's V-12 Alfa and on his return to the pits Pintacuda (8-cylinder Alfa) was called in so that the 'Flying Mantuan' could rejoin the race. The mechanical trouble with his original car had thoroughly riled Tazio and he rejoined the race in a high dudgeon, driving at his most flamboyant and energetic, despite the fact that his chances of success were slim indeed. Tazio left the pits over a minute behind the leaders, but he had soon slashed the new lap record set by von Stuck with his Auto Union (this German driver had already retired) and began to close on the leaders so rapidly that the panic-stricken Auto Union pit hung out the 'faster' signal for their drivers. Because von Stuck was faster over this course, Rosemeyer was called in for his Austrian team-mate to take over and the order was now Varzi (Auto Union), Brivio (Alfa), Dreyfus (Alfa), von Stuck (Auto Union).

All Auto Union's efforts were to no avail. Tazio was driving at almost maniacal speed, slashing seconds off the leaders' advantage on every lap, gaining time at every corner by his unique technique of approaching the corner too fast, deliberately to encourage a slide, and with a quick flick of the wheel using that slide both to slow the car and set it up for the exit for the corner. The brakes on the Auto Unions had not been relined since the German Grand Prix, they weakened badly as the race progressed and one by one Nuvolari passed the cars in front to assume a commanding lead. Varzi retired and the finishing order was Nuvolari, Brivio, Dreyfus, von Stuck; Auto Union was thoroughly humiliated.

Rosemeyer and Zwickau gained their revenge a week later by winning the Coppa Acerbo at Pescara. Nuvolari retired in both this race and the Swiss Grand Prix held on 23rd August. One more success came Tazio's way before the end of the season, in the Italian Grand Prix which the Mercedes team did not enter. At Monza, Rosemeyer scored another brilliant victory for Auto Union, but Nuvolari took second place with his V-12 Alfa.

For the last year of the existing 750 kilogramme Formula, 1937, Mercedes-Benz produced a new model to replace their unsuccessful 1936 cars, but there were few changes among the other teams. Tazio Nuvolari stayed with Scuderia Ferrari which raced the same V-12 cars (a version with a lower chassis appeared at Pescara later in the year). Nuvolari's first race of the season was the Circuit of Turin on 18th April, but in practice on the eve of the race he rolled his 12-cylinder Alfa and was taken off to hospital from where he emerged three days later wearing his famous plaster corset. In this race there was no worthwhile opposition to Scuderia Ferrari and Alfa Romeos took the first four places. At Tripoli Nuvolari retired early in the race with an engine misfire and his first success of the year did not come until the Circuit of Milan held on 20th June. Once again a single Auto Union, driven by young bespectacled Rudolph Hasse, faced a strong team of 12-cylinder Alfas. Nuvolari led until he stopped at the pits for a plug-change, but soon fought his way back into the lead, lapping Hasse who had spun his Auto Union in his efforts to stay with the easier-handling Alfas over this difficult course.

An interesting race in 1937 was the second Vanderbilt Cup race held on 5th July at Roosevelt Raceway. Nuvolari drove a 12-cylinder Alfa, but retired with engine failure and the race was won by Rosemeyer's Auto Union. Tazio drove a fine race in the German Grand Prix at the Nürburgring, but the combination of the greater speed and reliability of the German cars proved too great a handicap and he had to settle for fourth place behind the Mercedes of Caracciola and von Brauchitsch and the Auto Union of Rosemeyer. Because of testing the new low-chassis V-12 Alfa Nuvolari missed the Monaco Grand Prix which was held later in the year than usual and he next appeared at Pescara where he was entered with the new model; the car ran very badly in the race and Tazio was in ninth place when he decided to call it a day and hand the V-12 over to Giuseppe Farina. In 1937 the Italian Grand Prix was held at Livorno, the circuit on which Tazio had defeated Auto Union the previous year, but on this occasion he could make no impression on the leaders and, as at Pescara, handed his Alfa over to Farina. At this stage in his career Nino Farina was very much the up and coming star of the Ferrari team. Nuvolari rounded off an unsuccessful season with a fifth place in the Masaryk Grand Prix. This result was not without significance, for it was the last occasion on which Nuvolari finished a race at the wheel of an Alfa Romeo.

For 1938 the existing 750 Kg Formula was replaced by a new Grand Prix Formula with a sliding capacity/weight scale up to maximum capacities of 3000 cc supercharged and 4500 cc unsupercharged. Tazio remained with Alfa Romeo in the early part of the season. The Milan team was now racing on its own behalf under the name 'Alfa Corse' and was fielding a mixed bag of cars with straight-eight, V-12 and V-16 engines. None of these cars proved competitive and racing remained an Auto Union and Mercedes-Benz benefit.

In fact Tazio's long-standing relationship with Alfa Romeo came to an abrupt end. The team's first race of the season was the Pau Grand Prix on 10th April and in practice for this race Nuvolari was in great form. Unfortunately the saddle fuel tank of his car had been rubbing against the scuttle and this caused a leak; the car caught fire and although Tazio succeeded in steering it off the road and into some shrubbery, the bushes caught fire and the Mantuan suffered burns on the face and to an arm and a leg. Nuvolari was greatly shaken by this accident (although he could endure broken bones, he had an almost pathological fear of fire); he threatened to retire from racing altogether and swore that he would never again drive an Alfa Romeo.

Once Tazio had recovered from this incident, he joined the Auto Union team to drive the latest rear-engined V-12 cars from Zwickau. At this time Auto Union desperately needed a top driver, for their greatest star, Bernd Rosemeyer, had been killed during a record attempt in the early part of 1938. Nuvolari was not fit to drive for Auto Union until the German Grand Prix on 24th July and it took some while to familiarise himself with the peculiar handling characteristics of these very potent rear-engined cars. At the Nürburgring Tazio spun off and damaged the tail of his car, putting himself out of the race on the second lap, and another retirement followed in the Coppa Acerbo at Pescara. At the Swiss Grand Prix held on the rain-soaked Bremgarten circuit Nuvolari was completely off-form and finished a poor ninth. Only now did the season begin to go right for Tazio and he scored two victories, in the Italian Grand Prix at Monza (Auto Union's first win of the season) and in the Donington Grand Prix.

The 1939 racing season was cut short by the outbreak of war in Erope and, in any case, the number of races in which Auto Union could compete was reduced by the decision that all races on Italian soil were to be held to 1500 cc Voiturette regulations. Auto Union did not compete in a race until the Eifelrennen in May (von Stuck had appeared at La Turbie hill climb) and Tazio drove a good but not outstanding race to finish second to Hermann Lang's Mercedes. In the tragic Belgian Grand Prix which cost the life of Dick Seaman, Nuvolari ran out of road at Stavelot corner and broke the chassis of his Auto Union. Another retirement followed in the French race and in the German Grand Prix at the Nürburgring Tazio's new twin-stage supercharged Auto Union blew up its engine. Nuvolari took fifth place in the Swiss Grand Prix on 20th August. A fortnight later Germany invaded Poland and the last race of the season, the Belgrade Grand Prix, started almost at the very moment at which France declared war on Germany. Nuvolari drove his Auto Union to victory ahead of the Mercedes of von Brauchitsch and Müller. This was the last occasion on which Nuvolari handled a competitive Grand Prix car.

Racing continued in Italy in 1940, but Tazio did not compete and his next race was not until 12th May 1946 when, at the age of 54, he drove a 1500 cc Maserati entered by Scuderia Milano in the Marseilles Grand Prix. Tazio set a lap record in his heat, but retired with valve failure in the final. In July he drove a Maserati to victory (his last) in the Albi Grand Prix. He competed in a couple of other races during the year, but failed to achieve any success.

By 1947 Nuvolari had retired from serious racing, but he still made the occasional appearance and during that year turned in one of the most heroic drives in his long career. Nuvolari entered the Mille Miglia at the wheel of an 1100 cc Cisitalia sports car and, despite a strong entry of Alfa Romeos, and torrential rain throughout the race, led a field of much younger and fitter drivers until his car expired with water in the ignition a mere 180 miles from the finish. After a long delay he rejoined the race to finish second, fifteen minutes behind Clemente Biondetti who commented, 'I did not win, I merely finished first'.

Nuvolari also drove the new V-12 Ferrari in a couple of events in 1947 and he appeared with one of Enzo's improved 2-litre cars in the following year's 1000-mile race. Nuvolari was leading the race on time with his stark, cycle-wing two-seater when he lost control near Livorno and crashed into a wall. The rear suspension was damaged, the bonnet had detached itself and was lost, but Tazio rejoined the race and battled on until the Ferrari's rear axle failed at Reggio. Later that year Tazio drove in his last Grand Prix, the French race in which he took over Villoresi's new Maserati 'San Remo' for a short spell and pronounced it the best Maserati that he had ever driven.

For several years Tazio had been plagued by ill-health resulting from lung trouble and indeed he had crossed the finishing line in the 1946 Circuit of Milan with a blood-stained handkerchief pressed to his mouth. He was invited to handle one of the new Jaguar XK 120s on their race debut in the Production Sports Car race at Silverstone in August 1949, but was too ill to take part. Nuvolari, one of the most exciting racing drivers ever to compete, survived another four years. A crowd of around 40,000 thronged to his funeral service at Mantua cathedral in August 1953 to pay homage to one of Italy's greatest heroes. On his tomb were engraved the words: You will travel yet faster along the highways of heaven.

3

English Racing Automobiles

For over thirty years, from the 2-litre Sunbeams of 1923-4 to the Vanwalls that won three World Championship races in 1957, there was no British car capable of winning a Grande Epreuve. During the 'thirties, however, when Grand Prix racing was dominated by the German Auto Union and Mercedes-Benz teams, another lesser, but still very important category of racing was proving a British benefit. The ERA cars built at Bourne in Lincolnshire were more than a match for the Italian Maseratis and reigned supreme in the Voiturette category (the pre-war equivalent of the modern Formula Two, limited to cars of up to 1500 cc supercharged) until the appearance of the straight-eight Alfa Romeo 158s in 1938.

In 1933 Raymond Mays, one of the leading amateur British drivers, had raced a much-modified Riley known as the 'White Riley' which had soon proved itself the fastest 1500 cc car in the country. Another enthusiast, Humphrey Cook, was so impressed by May's performances with the Coventry car that he wrote to Mays, offering to finance the construction of a new Voiturette with an engine based on the Riley unit. Mays was enthusiastic about the new project, he and Cook came to an amicable agreement and English Racing Automobiles was formed with Cook as managing director and principal shareholder and Mays and Peter Berthon (May's collaborator for many years) as directors, but with only a nominal shareholding. ERA moved into premises built on land adjoining May's home at Bourne and work was put in hand on the new car which, it was hoped, would do much to regain Britain's long-lost prestige in International single-seater racing.

Reid Railton of Thomson & Taylor of Brooklands, later responsible for John Cobb's Napier-Railton land speed record car, designed the chassis of the ERA, but he incorporated certain of Peter Berthon's ideas. The ERA was a simple enough design, traditional in concept almost to the point of crudity, although it was built at a time when racing car design was becoming sophisticated. There was a channel-section chassis frame and front and rear suspension was by rigid axles and semi-elliptic leaf springs.

The Riley engine was a 6-cylinder design with push-rod operation of the valves from twin camshafts mounted high on the cylinder block, and it was extensively modified for use in the ERA. As on the 'White Riley' there was an aluminium cylinder head designed by Peter Berthon, and Murray Jamieson evolved a new crankshaft and a Roots-type supercharger compressing at 16 lbs per square inch. The result was a power unit of considerable potential. The early cars were designated the A-type and the first to be completed was fitted with a 1488 cc (57.5 × 95.2 mm) engine which developed 150 bhp at 6500 rpm. Transmission was by an Armstrong-Siddeley Wilson-type preselector gearbox of the so-called 'self-change' pattern which required no clutch.

Like the rival 4-cylinder Maserati Voiturette, the ERA had blunt, uncompromising, square-rigged lines and it had the rather large frontal area of 13.5 square feet. With an unladen weight of 14.5 cwt, and starting-line all-up weight of around 18 cwt, the original 1500 cc A-type car had a maximum speed of around 125 mph. The cars were painted in a beautiful pale green known as Liberty green.

The original intention was that the ERA should make its debut with Mays at the wheel in the Mannin Moar race in the Isle of Man at the end of May 1934. In practice, however, the new car suffered from suspension problems and as it displayed every inclination to use the full width of the road plus rather more, there was no alternative but to scratch from the race. By the time the ERA made its next outing, in the British Empire Trophy race at Brooklands, new rear springs had been fitted, and slight modifications had been made to the steering. Because of a broken oil pipe the car joined the race five minutes late, a host of niggling faults caused it to spend much of the race in the pits and at the finish it had covered insufficient laps to be classified. The ERA's next outing was in the Dieppe Grand Prix where Mays ran well until the engine developed a misfire; this was traced to a broken rocker and resulted in the car's retirement.

By the meeting at Brooklands on August Bank Holiday Monday the team had completed a second ERA which was fitted with a 1084 cc (57.5 × 69.8 mm) engine developing 140 bhp. Cook drove the latest car to the *marque*'s first victory in a short handicap race and Mays with the original car finished second in another handicap. Later in the month both drivers and cars took International class records for the standing start kilometre and mile. Cook with the 1100 cc car set records in Class G of 79.75 mph for the kilometre and 88.91 mph for the mile, while Mays with the larger-capacity car achieved speeds of 85.35 mph and 96.08 mph over the same distances. These records were set on the Railway Straight at Brooklands which was a far from ideal venue as it was very bumpy and the use of this circuit necessitated fitting the notorious Brooklands silencers.

At Shelsley Walsh hill climb in September, Mays drove both the 1500 cc and a new 1950 cc (62.5 × 107 mm) car with a power output of 250 bhp at 6500 rpm. May's principal opponent was the young American Whitney Straight with a 3-litre supercharged Maserati, but the ERA driver, perhaps the finest of all British hill climb exponents, was at the peak of his form and with the 2-litre ERA snatched fastest time of the day by the narrow margin of a fifth of a second; the event was run in pouring rain and no hill records were broken that day.

The same month Mays scored the ERA's first important victory in the Nuffield Trophy, the first road race of any real length to be held in England; in this 1500 cc handicap 100-mile event Mays averaged 61.51 mph to win from the MGs of Seaman and Evans. A week later Mays was narrowly beaten by Straight with the Maserati in the Mountain Championship at Brooklands. Although the 1934 racing season was now over, ERA continued its battle with Maserati in another arena; before the year was out Mays with a 2-litre ERA had made a successful attempt at Brooklands on the world's standing start kilometre record which had only recently been set at 88.87 mph by Hans Ruesch with a 3-litre supercharged Maserati at the Montlhéry circuit near Paris. Mays achieved a speed of 89.73 mph and the ERA was the smallest capacity car ever to have held this record.

Cook and Mays, greatly encouraged by the promising performances of the ERAs in 1934, decided to tackle a number of Continental races during the coming season and to sell a number of cars to drivers with the ability to use them to good purpose. The first order came from Pat Fairfield, a South African with extensive racing experience with Riley cars; he was sold the fourth and last of the A-type cars in 1100 cc form (a 1500 cc engine was later fitted) and raced it in a smart white colour finish. All subsequent cars were to B-type specification which included extra cross-bracing of the chassis at a point under the driver's seat, different gear ratios and new rear springs giving a lower periodicity. Dick Seaman took delivery of the first of the B-type cars which he had painted black and later in the year Prince Birabongse of Siam (who raced as 'B Bira') acquired his first ERA chassis number R2B, which he christened 'Romulus'.

May's first outing of the season was at Shelsley Walsh hill climb where he broke the hill record with a 1500 cc car with a climb in 39.8 sec and later in the day reduced his own new record with a 2-litre ERA to 39.6 sec. ERA's first racing success of the 1935 season was scored in the 202-mile Mannin Beg race in the Isle of Man which Fairfield won at 67.29 mph. In this race Mays retired his 1100 cc car with a broken oil pipe and two days later he retired in the Mannin Moar race for larger-capacity cars with transmission failure. Shortly afterwards he scored a major victory in the 170-mile Eifelrennen Voiturette race at the Nürburgring, beating Ruesch's Maserati into second place. Another ERA, driven by Rose-Richards, finished third.

Fairfield scored a victory in the handicap Nuffield Trophy race at Donington Park and Fairfield and B Bira took the first places in the two-hour Voiturette race at Dieppe. ERA received an invitation to enter two cars in the German Grand Prix and responded by fielding two of the 2-litre models for Mays and German driver Ernst von Delius. In practice von Delius crashed into a tree and when he returned to the pits after the accident he was greeted by his friends with cries of, 'You're like a little dog, Ernst; you can't keep away from the nearest tree!' The surviving car was shared in the race by both drivers, but although it handled well over this particularly arduous circuit, it was outpaced by the 'pure' Grand Prix cars, it slowed because of plug trouble and loss of oil pressure finally caused its retirement.

Seaman's car now found its form and he scored a fine road-racing 'hat-trick' with victories in the Coppa Acerbo Voiturette race at Pescara, the Prix de Berne at Bremgarten (which he also won in 1934 with Whitney Straight's MG Magnette and in 1936 with his rebuilt Delage) and the Circuit of Masaryk Voiturette race at Brno in Czechoslovakia. That the ERA was a serious force to be reckoned with was no longer a matter for speculation and Hans von Stuck, number one driver for Auto Union, said of the British cars, '. . . I think that they are infinitely superior to their competitors. I have driven most of the others, especially Maserati, but I cannot see how the ERA predominance can be ended next year.'

Several more cars were sold to private owners before the start of the 1936 season (the price was a very modest £1050) and a good indication of the popularity and support that the team had gained was the formation of an ERA Club. In the 1935 Mountain Championship at Brooklands Mays had driven a car fitted experimentally with a Zoller vane-type supercharger and he continued to race a car fitted with this blower in 1936.

Now the competition was much stronger; Maserati introduced a new 6-cylinder Voiturette known as the Tipo 6CM and although it was not as powerful as the latest ERAs the model scored a large number of successes on the European mainland. Dick Seaman, acting on the advice of his chief mechanic, Giulio Ramponi, switched allegiance to the straight-eight Delage previously raced by Lord Howe. Although the Delage was ten years old (the model had dominated the 1500 cc Grands Prix of 1926-7), in rebuilt form it proved a match for the ERAs and, sad to relate, humiliated Bourne at many of the season's races. Some good came out of this, however, for Lord Howe acquired a new ERA, R8B, which he raced as a member of the works team.

ERA's first successes of the 1936 season were scored by Pat Fairfield. In January he took third place in the South African Grand Prix and, on his return to Europe, followed this up with a fine second place to Dick Seaman (on this occasion at the wheel of a 2.7-litre Maserati) in the handicap British Empire Trophy race at Brooklands. The first clash between the ERAs and the 1500 cc Maseratis came in the Prince Rainier Cup, a Voiturette race preceding the Monaco Grand Prix, but at this point in the season Bologna was still relying on its older 4-cylinder cars. At Monaco there was one of those very unfortunate mix-ups that have punctuated the history of this tortuous circuit; several of the ERAs were involved and Fairfield was subsequently disqualified for restarting his car without using the starting handle (in the mêlée it had been bent under the car and could not be turned). Lord Howe took the lead with his ERA from the Maseratis of Villoresi and Tenni, but all three ran into mechanical troubles and the ERAs of B Bira, Lehoux and Embiricos came through to take the first three places. This was the greatest success in ERA's so far very short history.

Perhaps the most exciting battle of the season was in the 262-mile JCC International Trophy race at Brooklands. Although B Bira was leading, his cousin and racing manager Prince Chula was firmly convinced that Mays was a lap ahead (in fact the works car had made a second refuelling stop that had cost it the lead) and it was not until Humphrey Cook, very sportingly, had visited the White Mouse Stable's pit to explain the true position that the Siamese driver was signalled to speed up to fight off the challenge. At the chequered flag B Bira's blue car pipped the green works car by the margin of only a second.

Dick Seaman and the Delage dominated the 194-mile RAC Light Car race held on the Douglas circuit in the Isle of Man and the ERAs of B Bira and Cyril Paul trailed home in second and third places. In this race Mays with the Zoller-blown car was eliminated by half-shaft failure. Another defeat followed in the Eifelrennen Voiturette race in which Mays was delayed by plug trouble and B Bira was beaten into third place by the Maseratis of Trossi and Tenni. At this race Count Trossi was at the wheel of the first of the new 6-cylinder Maseratis. Revenge for these defeats was gained in the 91-mile Picardy Grand Prix in which the ERAs of B Bira, Pat Fairfield and Lord Howe took the first three places. Another ERA 'grand slam' in 1936 was in the Nuffield Trophy race at Donington in which Charles Martin, Arthur Dobson and Peter Whitehead finished first, second and third. Two defeats in succession were inflicted by Seaman and the Delage at Pescara and Bremgarten. In the JCC 200 miles race at Donington, Seaman's Delage was able to run through the full distance without a refuelling stop. Lord Howe fought hard to build up a lead with his ERA sufficient to allow for a pit stop, but this proved impossible and Howe had to settle for second place despite refuelling in only 38 seconds. Seaman also shared the winning Alfa Romeo with Hans Ruesch in the Donington Grand Prix. In this last race an ERA shared by Peter Whitehead and Peter Walker finished third. An especially sad event in ERA history had been the death of works driver Marcel Lehoux, killed in a collison with Giuseppe Farina's Alfa Romeo at Deauville.

Total production of ERA cars by the end of 1936 amounted to seventeen, four A-type and thirteen B-type. In an effort to match the sheer speed of the Delage and the ever-present threat from Maserati, the team introduced the improved C-type car for 1937. There were three C-types, but all were in fact modified B-types. The most important change was the adoption of Porsche trailing link and torsion bar independent front suspension (as used on the German Auto Union Grand Prix cars) and the cost of manufacturing the suspension uprights and trailing links alone amounted to £500 per car. The C-type also had a stiffer, box-section chassis, Lockheed hydraulic brakes and a ZF limited slip differential. The sometimes unreliable Zoller vane-type supercharger was adopted as standard on these cars (the Zoller blower was mounted at the rear of the engine, poking into the cockpit, whereas the Murray-Jamieson blower was at the front of the engine) and new and much stronger connecting rods were now used on all cars (these had been the principal cause of the many engine failures suffered in 1936). With the Zoller blower the power output of the 1500 cc engine was 240 bhp at 7500 rpm and the top speed in this form was around 140 mph.

Both Pat Fairfield and Lord Howe competed in a series of handicap races held in South Africa at the beginning of 1937 and the opposition included a brace of works Auto Union cars for Rosemeyer and von Delius. The first race of the series was the 199-mile South African Grand Prix at East London which Fairfield won at 89.17 mph. In the Grosvenor Grand Prix at Cape Town the Auto Unions took the first two places, but the ERAs of Lord Howe and Fairfield were not disgraced and finished third and fourth. The final round in the series was the 169-mile Rand Grand Prix at Johannesburg and here the ERAs of Fairfield and Lord Howe took first and second places.

Soon the 1937 European season was under way and later Raymond Mays commented, 'Looking back on it, I can't imagine how we managed to pack into the 1937 season the enormous number of races we did cover.' (*Split Seconds,* published by G T Foulis & Co Ltd, 1951.) The team's season started with the class handicap British Empire Trophy race held over a distance of 204 miles at Donington Park; here Mays kicked off to a fine victory with a C-type car in 1100 cc form, Maclure's unsupercharged Riley finished second and third place went to the B-type ERA of Peter Walker.

Another victory followed on 18th April in the 73-mile Turin Voiturette race held on the Valentino circuit; here the winner was Norwegian driver Eugen Bjornstadt, a newcomer to the ranks of the ERA drivers, who had recently acquired the very first car, R1A. Second place went to René Dreyfus with a Maserati and Reggie Tongue was third for ERA. Six days later the opening meeting was held at the Crystal Palace. Mays won his 40-mile heat of the Coronation Trophy from Arthur Dobson with another ERA, but he retired with brake trouble in the 60-mile final and Fairfield and Dobson took the first two places for the Bourne team.

The 76-mile Naples Voiturette race witnessed a fierce struggle between the Maseratis and the private ERAs, but on this occasion Bologna came out on top and Count Trossi with his 6CM Maserati won the race from the ERAs of B Bira and Bjornstadt. Next came the Campbell Trophy, a 227-mile race over a new course at Brooklands, where all the ERA drivers were out of luck. Lord Howe crashed badly and the race was won by B Bira with a three-year-old 3-litre Maserati.

A Voiturette race of especial interest was the Avusrennen run over seven laps of the 12-mile Avus circuit in Berlin which for the first time incorporated the new steeply banked North curve. This race proved a straight fight between the ERAs of Charles Martin and Bjornstadt and five Maseratis. Early in the race Martin nosed in front of the strong Maserati opposition and gradually pulled away from the red cars to score a convincing victory at the impressively high average speed of 119.67 mph. After the race Martin was garlanded by Huhnlein (German Minister for Sport) with an enormous laurel wreath and subsequently he was presented with a gigantic trophy by *Reichsminister* Göbbels for the best performance at the meeting by a non-German driver.

The 195-mile RAC International Trophy at Douglas in the Isle of Man proved a complete ERA benefit and B Bira, Mays and Fairfield finished in the first three places. Two days later Mays with a 1500 cc ERA reduced his own record for Shelsley Walsh hill climb to 39.09 sec. More success was gained in the Nuffield Trophy race at Donington Park in which the ERAs of Fairfield, Dobson and Mays took the first three places. Only a week later poor Pat Fairfield was killed at the wheel of a Frazer Nash-BMW in a multi-car crash at Le Mans. The ERA works team now tackled two Continental races and won them both. At Picardy the Maseratis occupied five of the first six positions, but in first place was Mays's ERA and second place finisher René Dreyfus was a long way behind. Of this race Mays wrote, '. . . the margin by which my car beat Rene Dreyfus' 6-cylinder works Maserati left little doubt that for the time being anyway the ERA could be considered Europe's supreme racing Voiturette.'

ERA ran two cars in the Albi Grand Prix, the results of which were decided on the aggregate of two heats. In the first heat Mays led the field until a half-shaft broke on the last lap and Humphrey Cook with the second car finished third, some 90 seconds behind the winner. Mays took over Cook's car for the second heat and the outcome is best described in his own words (from *Split Seconds*): '. . . by taking every corner absolutely on the limit, and going well "into the red" on the gears, I managed not only to set up a lap record of 99.99 mph, but also finished sufficiently far ahead of the second-place man to more than offset the 1½ minutes deficit and give me a clear-cut victory overall. It was many years before that day's lap record fell.'

The ERA team returned home to compete in the London Grand Prix (despite its grandiose title a very short race) which was held at the Crystal Palace. In his heat Mays again suffered a broken half-shaft on the last lap, but crossed the line half a second ahead of Ian Connell with a similar car. In the final the ERAs of B Bira and Connell took the first two places. On August Bank Holiday Monday Mays drove a 2-litre ERA in the JCC International Trophy at Brooklands; as in 1936, there was a furious duel between Mays and B Bira, but on this occasion the Siamese driver was at the wheel of his 3-litre Maserati. B Bira led until his Maserati expired in a cloud of steam and Mays went on to win this 204-mile handicap race from Johnny Wakefield's 6CM Maserati.

Perhaps ERA's most important and successful race of the 1937 season was the Prix de Berne, the Voiturette race preceding the Swiss Grand Prix. Here a total of twelve Maseratis (including seven 6CMs and one of the new 4CM cars which combined the 6CM chassis with a 4-cylinder engine) were challenged by four ERAs. Emilio Villoresi with a 6CM Maserati won the first heat from Mays and Charles Martin and in the second heat the winner was new recruit to the ERA team Arthur Dobson. Heavy rain began to fall shortly before the start of the final and on the rain-soaked Bremgarten circuit the Maseratis handled atrociously, even sliding on the straights. As the track dried out the ERA domination became even more pronounced and at the end of this 95-mile race the Bourne cars of Dobson, Mays and B Bira were in the first three places. Except perhaps at Bologna, it was now felt that the question of the ERA's superiority over its Italian rival had been settled beyond doubt.

Six days later the ERAs were in action again in the JCC 200 Miles race at Donington Park. Mays was leading when yet again a half-shaft broke and Arthur Dobson went on to win from B Bira (Maserati). In the Phoenix Park races at Dublin Mays enjoyed mixed fortunes. He retired his 2-litre ERA in the unlimited capacity handicap race with a con-rod through the side of the block, but won the 1500 cc scratch race from Wakefield's Maserati. Shortly afterwards Charles Martin finished second with his private ERA to Luigi Villoresi's Maserati in the Circuit of Brno in Czechoslovakia and B Bira rounded off ERA's most successful season to date by winning the Imperial Trophy at the Crystal Palace in October.

Mays and Lord Howe travelled out to compete in the handicap races held in South Africa in December 1937 and January 1938. The handicap faced by the British drivers in the first of these races, the Rand Grand Prix, was so severe that they were completely out of the picture and, despite hard driving, had to settle for eighth and ninth places. Mays was in second place in the South African Grand Prix with time in hand to catch the slower car ahead of him when his car was slowed by fuel starvation and he dropped back to finish seventh. In the final race of the series, the Grosvenor Grand Prix at Cape Town, Lord Howe scored a fine victory from the Maseratis of Piero Taruffi and Luigi Villoresi.

Lord Howe and Mays continued to represent the works in 1938 Voiturette races. Howe's car, R8B, had been brought up to C-type specification and Mays raced a much-modified car known as R4D; the modifications to the latter included extensively drilled chassis side-members, extra Luvax shock absorbers, shortened trailing arms to the front suspension and external radius arms to the rear axle. This last feature, which prevented rear axle patter under braking, was adopted on Bob Gerard's cars in post-war days. R4D, incidentally, was the only ERA to have the steering box on the left-hand side of the chassis frame. For 1938 the ERA team reverted to its original light green racing colour. R12C, the car Mays raced in 1937, was sold to Prince Chula to enter for his cousin B Bira. Chula named the car 'Hanuman' after a miracle-working monkey in Hindu mythology.

The ERA works team had its first European outing in 1938 in the British Empire Trophy race at Donington Park, but Howe retired with engine failure and Mays had a lucky escape after suffering complete brake failure on the approach to the Melbourne hairpin (he succeeded in slowing the car on the gearbox and scraped his way round the bend). The race was won on handicap by Charles Dodson's diminutive Austin 750 cc single-seater. Next came the 202-mile JCC International Trophy race at Brooklands, a race marred by a horrible accident; Joseph Paul's Delage caught fire and ran into the spectators, killing Tom Murray-Jamieson who had been on the ERA design staff and a woman onlooker. Mays drove an ERA with the engine bored out to 1750 cc to fit into a new handicap class introduced that year. In the early laps of the race Mays pulled out a substantial lead, but he fell back behind Maclure's Riley during a first pit stop and lost more time when a rough-running engine necessitated a second stop for a change of plugs. At the finish Mays was beaten into second place by just over a second. A week later Mays, Tony Rolt and Ian Connell took first three places with their ERAs in the 100-mile Coronation Trophy race at Donington Park.

In June the ERAs and the Maseratis met up in the Picardy Grand Prix at Peronne and four representatives of each *marque* qualified for the 91-mile final. Mays lost the use of bottom gear early in the final, and as a result of this he overshot a slow corner and B Bira whistled into the lead with 'Hanuman'. Mays chased the Siamese driver as hard as possible and he was slip-streaming him at close to 130 mph when the leading ERA's engine disintegrated – one of the con-rods flew through the air and just missed Mays's head! The works driver went on to score his second successive victory and ERA's third from the Maseratis of Bianco and Soffietti. The Siamese driver was compensated for this rather expensive disappointment with wins shortly afterwards in the so-called London Grand Prix at the Crystal Palace (the final was over a distance of only 32 miles) and the Nuffield trophy at Donington Park.

Mays retired with supercharger failure at Albi (Luigi Villoresi won for Maserati) and he was eliminated by the same trouble in the Prix de Berne at Bremgarten where the winner was Armand Hug with a Maserati. Yet another retirement for Mays followed in the JCC 200 Miles race at Brooklands on 27th August, but the day was saved for ERA by Johnny Wakefield who led home B Bira with his 3-litre Maserati and Lord Howe's ERA. In September Mays drove his ERA in 2-litre form and now painted in a blue-grey finish, to a new record of 37.86 secs at Shelsley Walsh hill climb.

An event of especial interest in 1938 was the 192-mile BRDC Road Race held at Brooklands on 17th September. Mays drove his ERA in 2-litre form and B Bira was at the wheel of his older Murray-Jamieson-supercharged ERA which he considered to be more reliable. The race was run on a handicap basis and the class in which Mays ran had to complete 60 laps of the circuit to the 59 of Bira's class. Although Mays forged well away from the rest of the field on the road, B Bira continued to lead on handicap – until he made a rare mistake and spun. Mays was now unchallenged, despite Bira's efforts to make up lost ground, but only seven laps from the finish the works ERA began to misfire badly and on the last lap B Bira snatched victory from Mays's grasp. Raymond Mays did, however, have the consolation of setting the fastest race average at 84.40 mph.

That the run of successes scored by the familiar ERA models was not likely to last much longer had become evident with the appearance in 1938 of the new and impressively fast straight-eight Alfa Romeo 158 Voiturettes; these new Italian cars had scored runaway victories in the Coppa Ciano at Leghorn and in the Prix de Milan, but had failed at both Pescara and Modena. In 1939 Maserati introduced their new 4CL car with 4-cylinder 16-valve engine. ERA's answer was the completely redesigned E-type car which had originally been conceived as a Grand Prix car, a project abandoned for financial reasons. Day after day in the early months of 1939 the exhaust note of the E-type could be heard rending the air of the Derbyshire countryside as Mays tuned in test lap after test lap at the Donington Park circuit.

On paper at least the E-type was a vast improvement over its predecessors, although right from the outset it seemed doubtful whether its push-rod engine, still showing strong signs of its Riley ancestry, would prove powerful enough to match the bhp of the latest Italian designs. The cylinder dimensions had been changed to 63 × 80 mm, giving a capacity of 1487 cc, and with a Zoller vane-type supercharger and a special twin-choke SU carburettor, power output was 260 bhp at 7500 rpm, claimed to endow the E-type with a top speed of around 170 mph. Wet instead of dry sump lubrication was now used.

The chassis was a very much more sophisticated design, inspired by German Grand Prix design practice; there was a new tubular frame, suspension at the front was similar to the C-type cars, but at the rear were torsion bars parallel with the frame and a de Dion axle. The gearbox was in unit with the final drive which incorporated a ZF limited slip differential. The body was low and sleek with a long, shapely tail and, in original form, a divided air intake.

Since the inception of the *marque* Humphrey Cook had met all the costs personally and he estimated that his total expenditure on the ERA project amounted to around £90,000. He concluded that he could no longer finance the team on his own and a public subscription was opened; it was hoped to raise £8000 and Cook agreed to add to this £4000 of his own money. Works driver Arthur Dobson scored a victory in the BRDC Road Championship at Brooklands on Easter Monday and it was planned that Mays should drive the new E-type on its debut in the JCC International Trophy race at Brooklands in May. Although the E-type practised at Brooklands for this race, it was far from fully sorted and there was no alternative but to scratch the entry.

The public subscription had failed to raise the hoped-for money and Cook decided to close down the ERA project. It was then announced that the British Motor Racing Fund would take over ERA and Cook agreed to carry on with the team while the arrangements for the take-over were worked out. Some while previously Mays had decided that he and Cook should part company and it was very unfortunate that he should at this time, when the future of the project was so uncertain, announce his resignation from ERA Ltd. Mays failed to explain why he left the company, but it is likely that one of the principal reasons was his belief that ERA should be developing a Grand Prix car, a belief that he nurtured to reality in post-war days with the tragically unsuccessful V-16 BRM. Mays bought R4D from ERA and raced it in events both before and after the war. ERA had no alternative but to vacate the premises at Bourne and Cook arranged to transfer the team to new works at Coppice Farm at Donington Park.

Although the older ERAs were still performing well, the works team was still facing serious problems with the E-type. Arthur Dobson was entered with the new car in the Nuffield Trophy at Donington Park, a race which the *marque* had won in every year since it was first held in 1934 and which an older ERA driven by B Bira won again in 1939. In practice the E-type was plagued by oil pump problems and the lack of adequate lubrication resulted in serious engine damage. A replacement engine was fitted, but there was insufficient time to run it in and the car was withdrawn from the race.

Two cars were entered in the Coupe de la Commission Sportive, the Voiturette race preceding the French Grand Prix at Reims on 9th July. In fact only one E-type arrived at the circuit, but it went magnificently in practice, it was attaining 160 mph along the straights and Dobson had the satisfaction of setting joint fastest lap. It was discovered, however, that the car was overheating because the hot air was not escaping from under the bonnet. Louvres were hastily cut in the bonnet, but it was too late, the engine had been damaged and yet again the car was posted as a non-starter.

Humphrey Cook now announced that he would not race the E-type again in 1939, but would concentrate on development work with a view to undertaking a full season's racing in 1940. However, successful tests at the Montlhéry circuit near Paris encouraged Cook to reconsider his decision and he entered the car in the Albi Grand Prix. Dobson and the E-type went magnificently in practice and took pole position on the grid with a lap in 3 min 25 sec. It was much the same story in the early part of the race. Dobson went straight into the lead at the start and on his fourth lap turned in fastest time of the day in 3 min 22 sec (98.57 mph). Five laps later the E-type cut out on one cylinder and Dobson was signalled to come into the pits. For some inexplicable reason, immediately after seeing the signal Dobson slammed on the brakes and skidded into the straw-bales in the starting area. The fuel tank and rear suspension were damaged and there was no alternative but to withdraw the E-type. At the time most onlookers were convinced that the new car was well on the way to its first victory. Wakefield and Tongue took the first two places with their new 16-valve Maseratis and B Bira finished third for ERA.

Cook had now decided to carry on running the ERA concern on his own, but the outbreak of war precluded any further appearances by the E-type in 1939. In 1946 the original E-type was sold to Peter Whitehead and a second example, GP2, yet to be completed, was acquired by Leslie Brooke. Whitehead raced his car in 1946 and in early 1947 without any success and then sold it to Reg Parnell. On completion Brooke's car was shipped to the United States to compete in the 1947 Indianapolis race, but, as was almost inevitable with a completely untested and unproven car, it failed to qualify as a starter. It was then shipped back to Europe and both E-types were fitted with Murray-Jamieson blowers (it was hoped that with less stress the engines would prove more reliable), but they achieved only failure in race after race.

In November 1947 Humphrey Cook sold out his interest in ERA and Leslie Johnson became both Chairman and Managing Director. Johnson was determined to make the E-type into a race-winner, but his efforts, despite a great deal of expense and so much anxiety that his health deteriorated, proved utterly abortive. Johnson bought back GP2, replaced the original Zoller supercharger and fitted the car with a conventional straight-line transmission (originally a reduction gear behind the clutch housing lowered the line of the prop-shaft by three inches). Yet again in 1948, success (and, usually, even the ability to finish) eluded the E-types and the best performance in 1948 was a fifth place by Johnson in the British Empire Trophy race held in the Isle of Man.

For 1949 Johnson proposed building a new E-type car. GP2 was sold to TASO Mathieson and Peter Whitehead bought back GP1 for Peter Walker to drive. In fact the new car was never completed, Johnson continued to race GP2 and the unlucky E-type's career was almost at an end. GP2 ran at Goodwood in April, non-started in the Jersey Road Race because of engine failure and was not again raced in 1949. Peter Walker, despite overheating and gears jumping out, finished fifth in the *Daily Express* Trophy at Silverstone; he wound up the season with what was probably the best performance in the E-type's ill-starred career. At the autumn Goodwood meeting he battled furiously with Reg Parnell's 'San Remo' Maserati and was narrowly beaten into second place in two short races; and in a handicap race he came through from the scratch mark to finish third. Johnson's next and last appearance with GP2 was in the 1950 British Grand Prix in which he retired when the supercharger disintegrated; the following month GP1 was completely burnt out when it crashed in the Isle of Man as a result of drive-shaft failure.

Although the E-type as such was never raced again, the engine from GP1 enjoyed a long and successful career powering Rob Walker's 1500 cc Delage. That this angular, dark blue hybrid performed so well in the hands of Tony Rolt was proof enough that the many troubles suffered by the E-types emanated from chassis shortcomings and not from the engine. The chassis of GP1, together with the body from Johnson's GP2, reappeared in a new guise in 1955; with Jaguar engine and cycle wings they formed the basis of the none too successful ERA-Jaguar sports car raced by garage owner Ken Flint.

While the E-types were disgracing the honoured name of ERA, the older cars were still being raced with considerable success. Leslie Brooke won the 1946 Grand Prix des Frontières at Chimay in Belgium with R7B (raced in pre-war days by Arthur Dobson), Bob Gerard won the 1947 British Empire Trophy from Peter Whitehead (the latter was at the wheel of R10B, the car he had owned since it was built) and Geoffrey Ansell won the 1948 British Empire Trophy from other ERAs driven by David Hampshire and Leslie Brooke. Raymond Mays continued to campaign R4D and was RAC Hill Climb Champion in both 1947 and 1948.

Without doubt, however, the most successful post-war ERA driver was Bob Gerard whose almost amazing string of successes with R14B (raced by Johnny Wakefield in 1938 and one of three ERAs in the Gerard stable) included wins in the 1947, 1949 and 1950 British Empire Trophy races, the 1947 Ulster Trophy and the 1948 and 1949 Jersey Road Races. His finest performances were not victories, but high placings scored in the face of the strongest International opposition; Gerard finished third in the 1948 British Grand Prix behind the Maseratis of Villoresi and Ascari and second in the 1949 race to Emmanuel de Graffenried's Maserati.

Apart from R3B, Lehoux's car written off in his fatal crash at Deauville in 1936, every one of the early ERAs has survived to form the life-blood of the Historic Racing Car events organised by the Vintage Sports Car Club.

Two more designs were to emerge from the ERA works which Leslie Johnson had transferred to Dunstable in Bedfordshire. In 1949 ERA was entrusted with the design of the chassis of the Jowett Jupiter sports car and Professor Robert Eberan von Eberhorst, a pre-war Auto Union designer, came to Dunstable to take charge of the operation. After ERA had completed the construction of the prototype and the early development work, Jowett took over the project themselves.

For the 1952 season ERA built a Bristol-powered Formula Two car which was raced for the works by Stirling Moss. The Formula Two car, which was designated the G-type, was the work of David Hodkin (he had assisted von Eberhorst on the Jupiter project). The chassis of the G-type was based on two very large, but very light, oval-section magnesium-alloy tubes. The front suspension was by wishbones and coil springs and at the rear there was a de Dion axle and trailing links. The gearbox was in unit with the final drive, there were light alloy spoked wheels and at the rear the Lockheed hydraulic brakes were mounted inboard. An unusual feature of a car built purely as a single-seater was the offset steering, the purpose of which was to enable the driver's seat to be placed alongside the prop-shaft. The rather square body was a temporary expedient and it was intended that it should be replaced at a later date by a much more aerodynamic design.

The G-type did not appear until the European Grand Prix at Spa-Francorchamps in June 1952 and it achieved no success apart from a third place in a minor race at Boreham and a second place at Goodwood. At the end of the year ERA withdrew from racing and the G-type together with all the drawings was sold to the Bristol Aeroplane Company, manufacturers of Bristol cars and engines. Bristol redesigned the car with a steel chassis and in this form the G-type formed the basis of the 450 coupés and open 2-seaters that won their class at Le Mans in 1954-5 and at Reims in 1953-4.

Now, forty years after the first ERA turned a wheel, it is possible to look back on the *marque* with a sense of historical perspective. The early cars were consistently successful, partly because the opposition was not of the strongest, the later models hopeless failures. Throughout ERA history there was a persistent lack of sufficient money for the team to develop the cars as it would have liked; but the early ERA successes, the first substantial British racing car successes since the Sunbeam-Talbot-Darracq combine had undertaken a full racing programme in the 'twenties, formed the foundation stones of later and greater victories. From the inspiration given by ERA victories flowed the disastrous V-16 BRM project, the efforts of the impecunious Connaught team and the brilliant World Championship victories of Vanwall and Cooper.

4:

A Thousand Miles of Racing:

The Mille Miglia, 1927-57

Long-distance sports car racing over public roads was a unique Italian tradition, a tradition that died slowly. The Mille Miglia was last run in 1957, but survived as a rally for a couple of years longer; the Circuit of Mugello held over a 66-kilometre course near Florence was abandoned after 1970; and the Sicilian Targa Florio was transferred from the 44.7-mile 'Little Madonie' circuit to a short track at Enna in 1974. In an age when motor racing pundits and experts were becoming preoccupied with safety measures to protect both drivers and spectators, the road race was a glorious anachronism that tested a driver's skill to the limit and beyond, provided the spectator with the greatest excitement and a sense of participation and had an atmosphere unmatched by any other form of racing.

The Targa Florio was the longest-surviving of all the road races, its existence jealously protected by the Italian government and its history remarkably accident-free. However the bastions of Sicilian vested interest finally crumbled under outside pressures, although the Targa Florio was revived as a purely Italian National event in 1975. Both the Targa Florio and the Mugello race were held over comparatively short road circuits (although the Sicilian race was in fact run as a single 671-mile circuit of the island in 1948-50); but neither could be compared with the greatest of all road races, the Mille Miglia, a hard-fought thousand-mile race round the mainland of Italy from Brescia to Rome and back to Brescia that filled the whole nation with fervour and enthusiasm.

When the Mille Miglia was first announced, it was greeted with astonishment abroad. The comments of *Motor Sport,* a magazine then in its infancy but now one of the most respected motoring journals, makes interesting reading. 'Twenty-four years ago the Paris–Madrid race was stopped at Bordeaux by order of the French government, and the last of the town-to-town races seemed to have been run for all time. It remained for Mussolini's government in Italy, however, to revive what is certainly the most attractive form of motor sport. On 26th and 27th March a race was held for cars of the "tourer-racer" variety, over a course of no less than 1,000 miles to a lap, starting and finishing at Brescia. Starting from that town, the route led to Parma, Bologna and Florence to Rome; thence across the Apennines to Ancona on the Adriatic, and back to Bologna, Padua and Feltre to Brescia. The idea of being allowed to race on a circuit of this nature is so astonishing to us in England where we cannot close 10 miles of deserted roads for a motor race, that the Italian competition has been referred to in the English press as a "high-speed trial" while in reality it was a genuine race.'

The race was devised by Count Franco Mazzotti, President of the Brescia Automobile Club, and it is said that Mussolini supported him because he believed that the Mille Miglia would demonstrate the toughness and virility of the Italian nation. To enable the race to take place, hundreds of road-repairing schemes were brought forward and 40,000 members of the Fascist militia gave their services as marshalls to keep carters and jay-walkers off the roads while the race was in progress.

Although the Mille Miglia was destined to be inseparably linked with two great *marques,* Alfa Romeo in pre-war days and Ferrari thereafter, the Alfas were not to the fore in the first race of the series and Portello was represented by only two works drivers and three private owners, all with push-rod 22/90 cars. Both works drivers retired, Count Brilli-Peri near Spoleto while leading the race, and the results were dominated by the 2-litre side-valve OM cars, cars that were delightful fast touring machines in the best Vintage traditions, but far divorced from the concept of the out-and-out racer that consistently won the race in later years. The products of Officine Mecchaniche whose home town was Brescia took the first three places in the order Minoia/Morandi, T Danieli/Balestrero and M Danieli/Rosa; the winning car averaged 47.99 mph. Victory in the 8000 cc class went to Count Maggi and Alfieri Maserati (founder in 1926 of the company bearing his name) who averaged 45.74 mph.

In early 1928 Alfa Romeo introduced a 6-cylinder 1500 cc sports car designed by Vittorio Jano, and one of these cars driven by Giuseppe Campari and Giulio Ramponi won the 1928 1000-mile race at an average of 52.27 mph. Although the OMs had not succeeded in repeating their 1927 victory, the Brescia cars finished second (Mazzotti/Rosa) and took the first eight places in their class. Out of 83 starters there were only 42 finishers.

OM were determined to gain their revenge in 1929 and fielded two teams, each of three cars, three 2-litre models fitted with Cozette superchargers (OM had taken a leaf out of Alfa's book in this respect) and three unsupercharged cars with the engine capacity increased to 2.2 litres. But Alfa Romeo had progressed since 1928 by introducing a 1750 cc version of Jano's 6-cylinder design, and four of these cars were entered. Much to the disappointment of the residents of Brescia, the blown 1750 of Campari partnered by Ramponi brought this pair their second successive victory in the race; the Alfa was followed home by the OM of Morandi and Rosa with another Alfa driven by young Achille Varzi and Colombo in third place.

In 1930 W F Bradley, Continental Correspondent of *The Autocar,* rode in a Lancia Lambda running as an official entry and checked out from Brescia behind all the small capacity cars (which left the start first) and an hour ahead of the large sports cars that were vying for outright victory. Bradley wrote, 'The roads were not closed to ordinary traffic; no orders had been issued from headquarters forbidding citizens to drive or walk on the highway, and we saw no posters with instructions to the population. Instead, the newspapers had made an appeal to the sporting spirit and the discipline of the people, and the way in which that appeal had been met was most amazing . . .

'Running over level dusty roads, often with a stream of water on each side, the competitors made their way through village after village, with the natives safely ensconced in doorways, at windows, on ledges, in the trees or, occasionally in the more important centres, behind a rope or protected by a flimsy hoarding . . .

'The timekeepers at Bologna had their table on the footpath in front of a barber's shop, the clients of which could throw their heads back and through the mirror watch the proceedings outside while their chins were being scraped . . . A tramcar rumbled by ponderously from time to time, or was stopped by much waving of flags if a racing car was in sight. Occasionally, the tramway man preferred to stop until he was peremptorily ordered on.'

Bradley's car pulled off the course and returned to Brescia where he described the finish: 'Dawn broke as we waited for them. The early morning chatter of the birds was silenced, the electric lights were switched out, and a thousand faces were turned eastward in the hope of catching sight of one of the champions down the long straight road.' Tazio Nuvolari with a 1750 cc supercharged Alfa Romeo crossed the line to win at a record average of 62.42 mph and Achille Varzi was second with a similar car. Nuvolari's time for the 1005 miles was 16 hours 18 min 59.4 sec (compared with 21 hours 4 min 48.2 sec for the winning car in the first race of the series). Much comment was made of the fact that the leading drivers, who were not well known outside Italy at this stage in their careers, were also racing motor-cyclists, Nuvolari for the Bianchi team and Varzi for the British Sunbeam concern.

In the 1930 race German driver Rudolf Caracciola, partnered by Christian Werner, finished sixth with an enormous, brutish SSK 7-litre Mercedes. There was a lot of criticism of the poor place achieved by this powerful and swift car, but Caracciola, one of the finest drivers of the 'thirties, was primarily interested in gaining experience of the race for a much more serious effort the following year. The 1931 race developed into a straight fight between Stuttgart and Portello whose entry included two of the new Jano-designed straight-eight 8C-2300 cars driven by Nuvolari and Arcangeli. This year Varzi was at the wheel of a 4.9-litre Bugatti, but retired without making any serious impression.

The Alfas were very fast along the more tortuous sections of the course and much faster than the Mercedes which could gain only on the straights; but they were hastily prepared and suffered from a host of problems. Nevertheless, by Rome, Tazio Nuvolari and co-driver Battista Guidotti (later Alfa Corse team manager) had pulled out a lead of three minutes. But after this control point nothing seemed to go right for the Alfas; Nuvolari was forced to make a total of eighteen wheel changes because of persistent tyre failures and he also crashed, but managed to get the car back on the road and carry on. For Arcangeli there were ten wheel-changes before he lost control in the wet at Verona and crashed into a wall. The race was now led by Campari's 1750 cc Alfa, but the Mercedes of Caracciola who was partnered by Wilhelm Sebastian pulled ahead on the long straight into Brescia to win by a narrow margin. Second place went to Campari and in third spot came the 2.2-litre supercharged OM of Morandi and Rosa. Nuvolari with the new 2.3 Alfa struggled home in ninth place behind seven smaller capacity Alfas. An unexpected British success was a win in the 750 cc class by the Austin of Trevisan and Goodacre.

By 1932 Scuderia Ferrari, which entered the Alfa Romeos on behalf of the works, had the Mille Miglia thoroughly sewn up and the 2.3s of Baconin

Borzacchini and Count Felice Trossi took the first two places. With the exception of a Lancia in eighth position the first twelve places were filled by Alfa Romeos of one type or another. In the 1100 cc class Tuffanelli with a new 4-cylinder Maserati was the winner from Lord de Clifford (MG Magnette). British cars rarely competed in the Mille Miglia, but an interesting entry in the 1932 race was the Hon Brian Lewis's Talbot 105 which he drove single-handed to twenty-fifth place despite a crash.

The following year's race was almost a repetition of the 1932 event. Alfa Romeo took the first twelve places apart from a Lancia which disrupted this clean sweep by finishing tenth. The 1933 winner was Tazio Nuvolari with a typical 2-seater medium-chassis 8-cylinder Alfa Romeo who averaged 67.46 mph in a drive lasting just over fifteen hours. In second place came one of the more interesting Alfa Romeos in the race, a Monza (the racing version of the straight-eight model) fitted with road equipment. This car, driven by Carlo Castelbarco and Franco Cortese, almost failed to make the start; on the eve of the race it had caught fire in the Alfa Romeo works while being fuelled up, and it was repaired in time, only for a mechanic mistakenly to pour a can of water into the fuel tank an hour before the start. In the 1100 cc class the usual Maserati domination was upset by a team of supercharged MG Magnettes and George Eyston and Count 'Johnny' Lurani won the class with one of the British cars.

Alterations were made to the Mille Miglia course in 1934 and the rules were changed. The touring car class was abolished and only sports cars took part with the restrictions limited to the fitting of two or more seats, wings and electrical equipment. Scuderia Ferrari fielded a team of Alfa Romeo Monza cars in 2.6-litre form and running on racing fuel; these very potent cars were driven by Tadini, Chiron, Varzi, Bonetto and Ghersi. Tazio Nuvolari, who was running as a privateer in 1934, drove a 2.3-litre Monza entered by the Scuderia Siena. By Rome Tadini led by one minute from Varzi and Nuvolari who was another four minutes behind the leader. Rain falling throughout the race made it a thoroughly miserable event for all the drivers and many cars slid off the lethally greasy roads. In the words of Eddie Hall, driver of a British MG Magnette, the roads resembled 'soap on marble'. Tadini retired and at the Venice control Varzi led Nuvolari by eight minutes. Despite desperate driving by Nuvolari, whose car was handling atrociously, he was unable to close the gap and at the finish he was still eight minutes behind his deadly rival.

Two of the very latest front-line Grand Prix cars, with only minor modifications to comply with the very lax regulations, looked the most serious contenders in the 1935 race. Scuderia Ferrari entered one of their Tipo B Monoposto Grand Prix cars for Carlo Pintacuda who was partnered by the Marquis della Stufa. A second seat had been squashed into the narrow body and there was so little room that the co-driver was almost bulging out of the car; this out-and-out racing car with sketchy little hood and cycle-type mudguards was said to develop 250 bhp and to be capable of attaining 130 mph. From Maserati came one of the latest 3.7-litre 6-cylinder Grand Prix cars with very flimsy 2-seater body; this was driven by Achille Varzi. Initially the race was a three-cornered fight between Tadini with a 2.6-litre Alfa Romeo Monza, Pintacuda and Varzi. The very powerful Maserati was delayed by oil scavenge pump problems and finally retired when the body began to break up. Pintacuda had pulled clear of the opposition by Florence and went on to win from Tadini by the very comfortable margin of 42 minutes.

The car raced by Pintacuda in 1935 acted as the prototype for a new line of Alfa Romeo sports cars, a full team of which were entered in the 1936 race. The new model was the 8C-2900A with 2.9-litre straight-eight engine (exactly as used in the Monoposto), fully independent suspension and two-seater, much roomier, cycle-wing bodywork. Pintacuda's winning car, now with 3.2-litre engine, was privately entered for Clemente Biondetti and presented a serious threat to the Scuderia Ferrari cars. Biondetti was delayed by tyre problems and by a slow and inefficient refuelling stop at Perugia and as a result he fell back to third place behind the 8C-2900A cars of Antonio Brivio and Giuseppe Farina. At Verona, only twenty-five miles from the finish, Brivio switched on the headlamps to find that they were inoperative; a quick check revealed that the glass had been smashed, almost certainly by stones thrown up by cars that he had been overtaking, and the lamps themselves were filled with mud. There was no alternative but to carry on at reduced speed, running at between 50 and 60 mph. Farina had started fourteen minutes after Brivio and when the latter reached the finish, he had an anxious wait to see whether or not he had been caught on time in the closing miles of the race. Farina failed to beat the time-gap by 30 seconds and Brivio was the winner at the record average of 75.57 mph.

Because the Mille Miglia had become dominated during the last couple of years by Grand Prix cars thinly disguised with sketchy sports car equipment, the rules were stiffened for 1937 and only genuine sports cars were admitted to the race. Scuderia Ferrari fielded a team of the new 6-cylinder

Alfa Romeo 2.3-litre cars and once again, with one exception, Alfa Romeo dominated the leading positions at the finish. There was a close battle for the lead between Farina and Pintacuda, but the latter went ahead to win by a margin of 18 minutes and averaged 71.30 mph, almost identical to his winning speed in 1936 with a Grand Prix Alfa Romeo. The next car home was an unblown 3500 cc French Delahaye driven by Carrière (the first time that there had been a foreign interloper in the first three since 1931). In fourth place came another 6-cylinder Alfa driven by Boratto (who was Mussolini's chauffeur) and Guidotti; this car, fitted with coupé bodywork by Carrozzeria Touring, won the touring car category.

Changes to the route of the Mille Miglia were made again in 1938 and the course was now faster because it included more stretches of Autostrada. Scuderia Ferrari no longer entered the works Alfa Romeos and Portello now fielded its own entries under the name 'Alfa Corse'. For the 1000-mile race the Alfa works produced yet another new model, the 8C-2900B; like its predecessor which had won the 1936 race, this was based on the design of the Monoposto Grand Prix cars, but it had aerodynamic 2-seater bodywork built by the Carrozzeria Touring concern. These 130 mph supercharged cars were reliable as well as fast and the Alfa Corse entries of Biondetti and Pintacuda took the first two places, although Pintacuda had gone off the road while leading and had lost eight minutes struggling to get his car back on the road. A private 2.9B driven by Piero Dusio, who founded the Cisitalia company after the war, took third place.

The 1938 race was really the last of the pre-war series of Mille Miglia races. Over the years the spectators had become less and less 'self-disciplined' and during the last race there were a number of nasty accidents. Accordingly it was decided in 1939 to hold the race over a circuit of roughly the same length between Tobruk and Tripoli in the Italian colony of Libya. Alfa Romeo won yet again (for the eighth time in succession), but the 2.5-litre 6-cylinder cars entered by Alfa Corse faced a severe challenge from a team of German BMW 2-litre streamlined saloons. Giuseppe Farina's Alfa blew up its engine and the first three places went to the Alfas of Boratto/Sanesi, Biondetti/Monzani and Pintacuda/Mambelli with Briem's BMW trailing home in fourth place, six minutes behind the winner.

Italy did not enter the war until 1940 and in the early part of that year three important races were held on Italian soil: the Tripoli Grand Prix, the Targa Florio (both events were held as Voiturette races) and a race variously described as the Mille Miglia and the Brescia Grand Prix. This was a 'substitute' Mille Miglia held over nine laps of a 100-mile circuit linking Brescia, Cremona and Mantua. It is almost incredible that, with the Polish invasion not long over and at a time when Hitler was in the throes of his invasion of Norway and Denmark, Germany could spare the resources to send a full team of streamlined BMWs to compete in Italy. On this occasion the BMWs were more than a match for the Alfa opposition and the streamlined 2-litre '328' coupés of von Hanstein (Porsche PRO in post-war days) and Baumer led home the Alfa Romeo 6C-2500 of Farina/Mambelli with another open BMW driven by Brudes/Röse in third place. These BMWs were very advanced cars; as late as 1955 the British Bristol-built derivative of the 6-cylinder engine powered the winner of the 2-litre class at Le Mans and the streamlined open body was closely aped by Jaguar for their XK 120 series.

The Brescia Automobile Club was desperately anxious to get the Mille Miglia under way again as soon as possible after the cease of hostilities, probably because it suspected that if it was not restarted almost immediately, it would be banned on safety grounds. The first post-war race was held in 1947, but it was postponed twice and was finally run on 21st-22nd June after the Italian Minister of Commerce had been cajoled into making available 20,000 gallons of petrol for the use of competitors. Alfa Romeo were concentrating their limited post-war resources on running a team of Grand Prix cars and so all sixteen Portello cars running in the 3-litre category (that from which the winner was expected to come) were private entries. But this reckoning failed to take into account one competitor, the great Tazio Nuvolari, driving a little 1100 cc Fiat-based Cisitalia sports car. He failed to win, but added immeasurably to the legend surrounding his great racing career.

Admittedly the Alfa Romeos laboured under the handicap that superchargers were banned in this race and so all the sixes and eights from Portello were suffering from a severe power deficiency. Nevertheless the only Alfa to perform well was Clemente Biondetti's 2.9B fixed head coupé running on four Solex carburettors. Over the long 1130-mile course chosen for the 1947 race Nuvolari led for most of the way, while Biondetti was slowed by the loss of first and second gears and delayed by fuel-feed problems. Heavy rain began to fall during the closing stages of the race and at Asti, 145 miles from the finish, Nuvolari lost a lot of time because of waterlogged ignition. Biondetti took the lead on the fast run back to Brescia and crossed the finishing line with fifteen minutes in hand. Third place went to another Cisitalia driven by Bernabei/Pacini.

Biondetti was to score a 'hat-trick' in the Mille Miglia by winning in both 1948 and 1949, but his later victories were achieved at the wheel of Ferrari cars and Maranello won every race between 1948 and 1953. The new V-12 Ferraris had first appeared in 1947 in 1500 cc form at a race at Piacenza in northern Italy and by the following year their engine capacity had been increased to 2000 cc. In the 1948 Mille Miglia 2-litre Ferraris were driven by Biondetti, Cortese and Nuvolari. The 'Flying Mantuan' was leading the race with a car fitted with stark cycle-wing bodywork when he crashed into a wall near Leghorn, damaging the rear suspension and losing the engine cover; he carried on with his battered car, but later retired at Reggio because of rear axle failure resulting from the crash. Cortese lost the use of third gear and retired at Bologna on the run home to the finish. So Biondetti scored his second successful victory with a Ferrari fitted with a bulky box-like coupé body (the same car with which a month previously he had won another road race, the Tour of Sicily, but now fitted with a Berlinetta top).

As a result of this victory in the 1000-mile race the fastest version of the 2-litre Ferrari became known as the 'Mille Miglia' model and several of these cars were entered in the 1949 race. Biondetti was at the wheel of a 'Mille Miglia' fitted with a very handsome open body by Carrozzeria Touring known as the 'Barchetta' (little boat), a style that was widely adopted on 2-litre Ferraris and copied by a number of competition car builders in Britain. In accordance with his usual tactics Biondetti held back in thc opening stages of the race and he took the lead only after Taruffi's similar car retired at Ravenna. Biondetti averaged the very high speed of 81.53 mph, but this was not really comparable with previous races as a shorter and faster 991-mile course was used in 1949. Second place went to Felice Bonetto with another Ferrari 'Mille Miglia' and this driver spent a frantic twenty minutes at Pescara while desperate efforts were made to restore braking power. Third place in this race was taken by Franco Rol with a 2500 cc 6-cylinder Alfa Romeo.

All these early Ferrari successes were gained with cars designed by Giacchino Colombo who, in pre-war days, had been a member of the Alfa Romeo design staff. Mainly because of political in-fighting at Maranello, Colombo's star was falling fast by 1950; in that year's Mille Miglia Ferrari's hopes were largely pinned on new 3.3-litre V-12 cars which were the work of Aurelio Lampredi, originally Colombo's assistant, who had joined Ferrari from Piaggio, the aircraft and scooter manufacturers. Two of the new cars were driven by Ascari and Villoresi, but they were plagued by tyre and rear axle problems and both retired. Villoresi did, however, lead in the early stages of the race, averaging around 92 mph for the first three hundred miles. Then private owner Giannino Marzotto, one of three motor-racing sons of the founder of Italy's largest woollen concern, went ahead to win with a powerful 2-litre car with the usual Barchetta body. Second place went to Dorino Serafini with a works 2.3-litre Ferrari.

Alfa Romeo were still taking an interest in the Mille Miglia, albeit on a much reduced scale, and in the 1950 race fielded a team of four cars, three of the familiar 6-cylinder 2500 cc models driven by Fangio, Rol and Bonetto and an experimental car with a 3-litre engine driven by chief tester Consalvo Sanesi. Fangio brought his car through into third place, despite the fact that it was less powerful than the Ferrari opposition and had inferior handling. Sanesi suffered the fate of many drivers in the days of closed competition cars without seat belts; he hit his head on the roof when the car struck a bad bump, lost control and crashed. British cars performed well in this race; Leslie Johnson was fifth with a production Jaguar XK 120 and Franco Cortese brought a Frazer Nash Le Mans Replica across the line in sixth place.

Another new Ferrari model, the 4.1-litre 'America', made its debut in the 1951 race and Villoresi drove the new car to victory despite an off-course excursion which smashed the left-hand wing and despite the loss of all gears in the 5-speed 'box except fourth. A total of 34 Ferraris were entered in this race. Second place went to a Lancia Aurelia GT, a modified Grand Touring car designed by Vittorio Jano who had been responsible for the long line of pre-war competition Alfas. This car was driven by Giovanni Bracco.

Mercedes-Benz had made a 'trial return' to racing in 1951 by fielding a team of the 1939 3-litre supercharged Grand Prix cars in the Formule Libre races held in the Argentine in the January of that year and in 1952 Stuttgart made a serious come-back with a team of the dramatically styled 300SL sports/racing coupés. The Stuttgart team's first race was the Mille Miglia; it seemed impossible for them to break Ferrari's stranglehold on the Italian classic with new cars and with personnel having no recent experience of the race, but the impossible was almost achieved.

Some indication of just how impossible was the task is given by Gordon Wilkins' remarks on the Mille Miglia in *The Autocar* of 23rd May 1952: 'It covers every kind of road from the long, well-surfaced straights down the Adriatic coast to the winding, dusty mountain roads over the Apennines to Rome; then the endless variety of the northward run back to Brescia where high-speed main-road motoring alternates with the hazards of the Radicofani, Futa and Raticosa passes, with rain, mist and sometimes snow to add to the difficulties . . . This year there was a specially rough section near Ferrara where the recent flooding of the Po river had laid waste a desert of putrefaction and ruin ten miles wide across the face of Italy.

'Spectators constitute a hazard sufficient to unnerve most newcomers, for despite the efforts of the carabinieri and the local police, they frequently edge forward until they meet in the middle of the road, stepping back at only the last possible minute to let the cars through and then closing in again behind them. Add to this the fact that it is almost invariably raining, and that the Italian main roads have a peculiarly treacherous and slippery surface, and you begin to realise why it requires great courage to do well in the Mille Miglia.'

Mercedes-Benz took their entry very seriously and sent their crews to Italy to learn the course two months before the race. In contrast David Brown, *patron* of the British Aston Martin team, was summoned to the Bank of England to explain why he needed consent under the Exchange Control regulations for the money to finance the team's trip to Italy a mere two *weeks* before the race. Small wonder that a British car never won the Mille Miglia! Thirty personnel from Stuttgart were sent to look after the three Mercedes and Stuttgart had a string of service stations round the course.

The Mercedes went magnificently from the start of the race, while with one exception the Ferrari oppostion soon fell by the wayside. Surprisingly a British car was well up on the leader board for much of the race. The Ferrari exception was the wild, tousle-haired Giovanni Bracco, well fortified by brandy, who drove like a man on suicide bent and seemed destined to live up to his reputation that one year he would win the Mille Miglia or die in the attempt. The British driver was Stirling Moss at the wheel of a works C-type Jaguar fitted experimentally with disc brakes; despite a leaking fuel tank he rose to third place only to retire with mechanical trouble at Bologna, a mere 150 miles from the finish.

Bracco had pulled out a lead of nearly five and a half minutes by the time he had reached the Ravenna control, 188 miles from the start, averaging over 90 mph despite heavy rain; one Mercedes, driven by pre-war Grand Prix 'ace' Hermann Lang, was already out of the race because of a crash. Bracco's wild pace resulted in his Ferrari developing a voracious appetite for tyres and by Acquila, 455 miles from the start, he had dropped to fifth place, thirteen and a half minutes behind the leading Mercedes of Karl Kling.

Bracco fought back, reducing the lead slightly by the time he reached Rome where he was in third place; Taruffi's second-place Ferrari expired with transmission trouble at Poggibonsi. Bracco was in his element over the mist-enveloped mountainous roads between Florence and Bologna and he picked up minutes over the Futa and Raticosa passes; by the time his sleek, red coupé had reached Bologna, he had turned the deficit into a lead of 1 min 20 secs.

Kling had been kept fully informed of the position and fought hard to regain the advantage, but to no avail; and the tradition of the race that the leader at Rome was never the winner held true. Bracco crossed the finishing line with a lead of 4 min 32 secs, having averaged 79.90 mph for the 972 miles. Kling finished second ahead of the Lancia Aurelia GT of veteran Luigi Fagioli, the other surviving Mercedes of Rudolf Caracciola took fourth place and the highest-placed British car was Leslie Johnson's Nash-Healey in seventh spot. There were over six hundred entries in the 1952 race including four military jeeps, the fastest of which averaged 57.37 mph!

Later in 1952 Mercedes-Benz scored victories in the Le Mans 24 Hours and Carrera Panamericana Mexico races. The team withdrew from racing at the end of the season to concentrate on the development of their new Grand Prix cars to be raced in 1954, but, nevertheless, there was a conspicuously diverse entry in the 1953 1000-mile race. Alfa Romeo made a serious return to racing with a team of handsome, brutal-looking 3.5-litre coupés driven by a strong team consisting of Juan Fangio, Karl Kling and Consalvo Sanesi; Lancia, previously content merely to dip their toes into the water with the Aurelia GT cars, had now taken the plunge and entered a team of six 3-litre twin-cam coupés designed by Vittorio Jano for competition work. While Ferrari entered a very mixed bag of cars that included two handsome 4.1-litre *Spyders* with bodies by Carrozzeria Touring for Mike Hawthorn and Nino Farina, private 4.1s with bodywork by Vignale were driven by 1950 winner Giannino Marzotto and American driver Tom Cole. David Brown was still persevering in the Mille Miglia and entered three of his DB3 3-litre sports/racing cars, and from Coventry came three C-type Jaguars.

The race proved a straight fight between Maranello and Portello. The superb-looking Alfas, distinguished by the traditional Alfa symbol of the quadrifoglio (four-leafed clover) in a large white triangle on the sides of the sleek red bodies, soon proved themselves as fast as the Ferraris. By Ravenna, Sanesi led from Farina and he was still in the lead at Pescara having averaged a shattering 109.88 mph. Before Rome, however, he was out with engine trouble, Farina's Ferrari succumbed to mechanical problems, and Kling was in the lead. It was a short-lived advantage, however, for his Alfa was eliminated soon afterwards by rear axle failure. The fortunes of the team now rested on Fangio's broad shoulders. The Argentinian was leading as his savage-looking coupé thundered along the mountainous roads north of Florence, but he then discovered that only the right-hand front wheel was responding to the steering. A lesser driver would have thrown in the towel, but Fangio fought on, easing off to take the tighter bends at a crawl; by the time the leading cars had passed through Bologna, the 4.1 Ferrari of privateer Marzotto was well in the lead. Fangio took second place, nearly twelve minutes in arrears. In this race Marzotto wore a jacket and tie! Third place went to the Lancia of Felice Bonetto, Tom Cole brought his more sedately driven Ferrari across the line in fourth place, and Reg Parnell finished fifth with the first of the Astons.

The Alfa Romeos failed again at Le Mans and their only victory during the year was a win by Fangio in a minor race in September. At the end of the season Alfa Romeo withdrew from racing and in the next few years contented themselves with entering modified versions of production cars. Both Ferrari and Lancia had made substantial changes to their cars before the 1954 race which for the first time permitted only one driver to be carried in the car at the entrant's discretion. At scrutineering, however, it was necessary to show that the car could carry two people if required. Maranello had now increased the capacity of the V-12 engine to 4.9 litres and the 1954 Tipo 375 'Plus' was an unwieldy monster by any standards; two of these cars were driven in the 1000-mile race by Farina and Maglioli, but both crashed. This left the door wide open for a victory by Lancia who were now racing the much-improved D.24 3.3-litre *Spyder,* a car that combined an excellent power to weight ratio with superb handling characteristics.

Both Alberto Ascari and Luigi Villoresi had contracted to drive for Lancia in 1954, but Ascari, Formula One Champion in 1952-3, so hated the Mille Miglia that it had been specifically excluded from his contract with the team from Turin. However, when his great friend Luigi Villoresi was injured in a practice crash while his mechanic was at the wheel, Ascari agreed to step into the breach. Of the four Lancias entered, three retired, but Ascari driving steadily and intelligently came through to win at an average of 86.77 mph from a 2-litre Ferrari 'Mondial' driven by Vittorio Marzotto (younger brother of Giannino) and a 2-litre Maserati with Luigi Musso at the wheel. Both Aston Martins retired through accidents, although at one stage Parnell and Collins held sixth and eighth places. Aston Martin never achieved success in the Mille Miglia, although their efforts were always meritorious. As *Autocourse* said, 'There is little doubt that the Aston Martin represents the most likely non-Italian winner of the Coppa Franco Mazzotti [The Cup named after the founder of the race which was awarded to the winner] – provided its builders resist the temptation to find very high power output, and concentrate on roadholding, stability and manageability.' A very fine tribute to the qualities of the DB3S Aston which always performed well on courses where roadholding qualities were at a premium.

Autocourse, unable to predict the developments that would emanate from Stuttgart, was wrong in one major respect, and a very different non-Italian contender won the 1955 Mille Miglia. Having achieved four victories in six Grands Prix in 1954, Mercedes-Benz now tackled sports car racing as well with the straight-eight 300SLR cars which were capable, with the appropriate gearing, of speeds in excess of 180 mph. As in 1952 the Mille Miglia was Mercedes' first race and every care was taken to increase their chances of victory. Extensive pre-race practice from February onwards meant that the drivers of the German cars had an even more intimate knowledge of the circuit that the local Italians, and Karl Kling, who had driven in the race twice before, had alone covered more than 30,000 miles in training.

Although Piero Taruffi's 3.7-litre 6-cylinder Ferrari led until Pescara, the winning car was the Mercedes of Stirling Moss, partnered by Denis Jenkinson who supplemented the driver's knowledge of the course with hand signals from information contained in an elaborate roll of notes. Moss, the only British driver ever to win the race, averaged a record 97.96 mph and Fangio with another Mercedes finished second despite a delay while a broken fuel injection pipe was replaced. Herrmann retired his Mercedes and Kling broke three ribs when he crashed into a tree near Rome. Maglioli finished third with a Ferrari and in fifth place came yet another Mercedes, a 300SL (the production version of the car driven into second place in the 1952 race) with American John Fitch at the wheel. The Mercedes team won the Swedish Grand Prix, the Tourist Trophy and the Targa Florio before withdrawing from all forms of motor sport at the end of the year. The highest-placed British car in the 1955 race was the Austin-Healey 100S of George Abecassis which came home in eleventh spot.

A power in sports car racing that grew in strength during the early 'fifties was the Maserati team; with the 2-litre A6GCS cars the *marque* achieved sixth place and a class win by Giletti in the 1953 race, a third place and a class second by Musso in 1954 and a fourth and a class win by Giardini in 1955. Cesare Perdisa had driven the new 3-litre Maserati 300S in the 1955 race without success; but by the following year Officine Alfieri Maserati was all set to make a much more determined effort with a team of two very competitive cars, a new but untried 3500 cc model driven by Stirling Moss and one of the more familiar 3-litre cars entrusted to Mille Miglia veteran driver Piero Taruffi. Unfortunately for Modena both cars crashed and the race proved yet another Ferrari landslide. Eugenio Castellotti won with a new V-12 Ferrari, Peter Collins and Luigi Musso took second and third places with 4-cylinder 3.4-litre cars and Fangio, driving a sedate race compared with his team-mates, was fourth with a V-12.

Maserati were still striving to beat their national rivals in 1957 and entered two of the new and monstrous 4.5-litre V-8 cars for Stirling Moss and French driver Jean Behra. It was an ill-fated effort; after only thirteen miles of racing the brake pedal on Moss's car broke at 130 mph on the approach to an 80-90 mph bend. In the words of Denis Jenkinson who was again riding as passenger, ' . . . our approach speed was higher than reasonable even for Moss, and I realised that he was working overtime to regain control. Fortunately he did so, and our brakeless 90 mph machine eventually came to rest. Had his natural instincts not made him take the emergency line into the corner, and had he not been practised in the art of slowing a car by means of the front tyres, he would have tried to get round the corner on the normal line and we should have suffered the most almighty crash on the outside of the corner. This was a wonderful example of experience saving our lives and is just one of the reasons why I have so much faith in the top drivers that I am prepared to be their passenger at Grand Prix speeds' (*The Racing Driver,* B T Batsford Ltd, 1958). Behra failed to start the race after colliding with a lorry during testing.

The real tragedy of the race, however, struck the Ferrari team. Scuderia Ferrari had entered a team of 4.1-litre V-12 cars for Peter Collins, Piero Taruffi and the Marquis de Portago together with a 3.8-litre V-12 for young German driver Wolfgang von Trips. The Marquis de Portago was a wealthy but brilliant sportsman who had already earned a distinguished reputation as an amateur jockey, yachtsman and swordsman. For much of the race de Portago was well up with the leaders, at the Rome control he had leapt theatrically from his car to embrace Linda Christian, ex-wife of Tyrone Power, with whom he was said to be passionately in love, and by Bologna he was still in fifth place. On the final run home to Brescia his Ferrari burst a tyre, skidded into a ditch and rebounded into the ditch on the other side of the road; de Portago, his passenger Edmond Nelson and fourteen spectators were killed.

Peter Collins was leading the race at Bologna, but he retired with half-shaft failure and, for the last time, the tradition of the race that the leader at Rome never won held true. Veteran Piero Taruffi, the 'silver fox' of motor racing, scored a victory in the Mille Miglia after years of trying; von Trips took second place, and a Grand Touring Ferrari driven by Olivier Gendebien finished third. A very gallant effort in the 1957 race was Ron Flockhart's drive with an Ecurie Ecosse-entered Jaguar D-type, a car far better suited to the billiard-table smooth surfaces of Le Mans than the twists, turns and undulations of the Italian road race. Flockhart rose to seventh place before retiring at around half-distance when the body of the Jaguar started to part company with the chassis. One of the few American cars ever to compete in the Mille Miglia was Akton Miller's big Chrysler-entered special from California which ran well in 1957 until it was eliminated by mechanical trouble.

As a result of de Portago's accident, the Scuderia Ferrari cars were impounded by the Italian government pending an enquiry which dragged on through the summer months with Enzo Ferrari becoming angrier and angrier. Eventually it was held that the accident was in no way attributable to Scuderia Ferrari. But the harm had been done, conservative public opinion was strongly opposed to the Mille Miglia and it was decreed that the race should not be held again in its existing form. There was a Mille Miglia rally in 1958-9, but thereafter the event disappeared from the calendar of sporting events. So died one of the greatest races in the history of the sport.

Sadly, this race is very badly documented and there is no history of it in the English language. Indispensable reading to anyone interested in the race is Denis Jenkinson's account of his ride with Moss in the 1955 race, a unique and brilliant piece of journalism and history that was subsequently reprinted together with accounts of Jenkinson's other rides with Moss. The Mille Miglia had been featured in at least two films: *The Racers* (1955) based on Hans Ruesch's novel of the same name, traces the rise of a young racing driver (Kirk Douglas) including his winning drive in the Mille Miglia, and the footage includes some fascinating shots of real Mille Miglia races of the early 'fifties. In *The Green Helmet* (1961), based on Jon Cleary's novel of the same name, the story is concerned with a small British concern's efforts to win the race with a team of thinly disguised Lister-Jaguar cars. Authenticity is lacking and the fact that the young hero is named 'Tazio' kills any hope that the knowledgeable viewer might be impressed.

Results

Year	*Distance (miles)*	*Winner*	*Speed*
1927	1005	Minoia/Morandi (OM)	47.99 mph
1928	1005	Campari/Ramponi (Alfa Romeo)	52.27 mph
1929	1005	Campari/Ramponi (Alfa Romeo)	55.73 mph
1930	1018	Nuvolari/Guidotti (Alfa Romeo)	62.42 mph
1931	1016	Caracciola/Sebastian (Mercedes)	62.85 mph
1932	1018	Borzacchini/Bignami (Alfa Romeo)	68.28 mph
1933	1025	Nuvolari/Compagnoni (Alfa Romeo)	67.46 mph
1934	1004	Varzi/Bignami (Alfa Romeo)	71.03 mph
1935	1004	Pintacuda/della Stufa (Alfa Romeo)	71.30 mph
1936	992	Brivio/Ongaro (Alfa Romeo)	75.57 mph
1937	1020	Pintacuda/Mambelli (Alfa Romeo)	71.30 mph
1938	1007	Biondetti/Stefani (Alfa Romeo)	84.13 mph
1939	933	Boratto/Sanesi (Alfa Romeo)	87.86 mph
1940	923	Hanstein/Baumer (BMW)	103.60 mph
1947	1133	Biondetti/Romano (Alfa Romeo)	68.63 mph
1948	1133	Biondetti/Navone (Ferrari)	75.16 mph
1949	990	Biondetti/Salani (Ferrari)	81.53 mph
1950	1016	Marzotto/Crosara (Ferrari)	76.79 mph
1951	972	Villoresi/Cassani (Ferrari)	75.52 mph
1952	972	Bracco/Rolfo (Ferrari)	79.90 mph
1953	992	Marzotto/Crosara (Ferrari)	88.45 mph
1954	992	Ascari (Lancia)	86.77 mph
1955	992	Moss/Jenkinson (Mercedes-Benz)	97.96 mph
1956	992	Castellotti (Ferrari)	85.40 mph
1957	992	Taruffi (Ferrari)	94.84 mph

5

Twenty Years On:
The Maserati 250F

Twenty years have now elapsed since the first appearance of the Maserati 250F, the only design to run in the first and last races held to the very successful 2500 cc Grand Prix Formula of 1954-60. Certainly the 250F was not the most successful car of the Formula (that distinction lies with the rear-engined Cooper-Climax), but it did achieve a substantial number of victories; it was produced in greater numbers than any other Formula One car of the period and it was a comparatively simple, rugged design that withstood the hardest driving of the fastest Formula One *pilotes* and the worst abuses of the slowest.

Maserati relied on gradual technical development rather than the introduction of dramatic new designs, and the evolution of the 250F can be traced over a span of almost twenty years. In 1936 the Maserati brothers introduced the Tipo 6CM 1500 cc 6-cylinder Voiturette, an underpowered, disappointing car that proved no real match for the works ERAs. The 6CM was largely superseded just over a year later by the 4CM which combined a 4-cylinder engine with the same chassis.

In 1947 Maserati produced the A6, a 1500 cc 6-cylinder touring car with an engine derived from that of the 6CM. The A6 had a single overhead camshaft engine developing 65 bhp, but later in 1947 Modena produced a much more potent version, the 125 bhp 2-litre A6GCS sports/racing car. Early A6GCS cars had an iron-block engine, but the later versions, built in considerable numbers between 1953 and 1956 featured an aluminium cylinder block and twin overhead camshafts as on the team's Formula Two cars. The original A6GCS formed the basis of the first Formula Two Maserati, the rather square-rigged A6GCM, which Froilan Gonzalez drove into second place in the 1952 Italian Grand Prix.

Because of delays in the development of the A6GCM and driver problems (Fangio crashed badly on the model's European debut at Monza and put himself out of racing for the rest of the season), Maserati ran in only a few Formula Two races in 1952. The following year, however, the *marque* contested all the rounds in the World Championship with the improved A6SSG cars. Most of the improvements were the work of Giaocchino Colombo who had joined Maserati from Alfa Romeo. The engine had revised cylinder dimensions and greater power output, there was a strengthened chassis and smoother and lower bodywork.

Although the A6SSG with an output of 200 bhp was some 10 bhp more powerful than the rival Tipo 500 Ferrari that dominated racing in 1952-3, and was faster in a straight line, it was inferior in both braking power and roadholding – as far as the latter was concerned this was primarily because of the retention of a rigid rear axle. Maserati team-leader Juan Fangio was forced to settle for second places at Reims, Silverstone and the Nürburgring and his sole Championship race victory at Monza was gained only after Ascari's totally out of character spin on the last lap.

Colombo was well satisfied with the basic concept of the A6SSG, but an extensive redesign was carried out for 1954. Engine capacity was increased to 2493 cc to suit the new Formula and although it was claimed that this resulted in an increase in power output to 240 bhp at 6800 rpm, a more realistic figure would be 220 bhp. Maserati introduced a new multi-tubular chassis (not in fact a true space-frame) to replace the A6SSG's simple ladder-type frame, a very effective de Dion axle replaced the original rigid axle and there was a new 4-speed gearbox in unit with the final drive (on the A6SSG the gearbox was in unit with the engine). The new car was first tested at Monza in December 1953.

Maserati were primarily interested in selling the new 250F to private entrants and did not intend fielding a works team on a regular basis. Because of the company's strong trading connections with the Argentine, however, two 250Fs were went to compete at Buenos Aires at the beginning of 1954. Fangio drove one of these cars to victory in the Argentine Grand Prix, but it was something of a hollow victory. The Maseratis were slower than the Ferraris in the dry, Fangio took the lead during a rain-storm after stopping for rain tyres to be fitted and went on to win the race. The Ferrari team manager had entered a protest on the grounds that five instead of the permitted three mechanics had worked on Fangio's car during its pit stop, and on the assumption that this would be upheld had slowed off his cars.

The works team failed in the Buenos Aires City Grand Prix, but it was largely because of the Argentine win that Maserati decided to field a team in the European rounds of the Championship. Juan Fangio again drove a 250F to victory at Spa-Francorchamps; but after this Maserati lost his services, for the 1951 World Champion had contracted to drive the new Mercedes-Benz W196 which made its debut at Reims.

Maserati were desperately short of drivers for the rest of the season. The team's number one driver was Argentinian Onofre Marimon, originally a protégé of Fangio, but he was killed when he went off the road in practice for the German Grand Prix. The team also borrowed the services of Ascari and Villoresi from Scuderia Lancia (whose own cars were not yet ready to race). Alberto Ascari was a dismal failure at the wheel of the Modena cars, and blew up his 250F at Reims and both his own and Villoresi's at Silverstone. Maserati was therefore very dependent on the many private owners who had bought 250Fs at £5000 a time. Sergio Mantovani, Luigi Musso and Roberto Mieres all ran as works entries during the year, but they were driving cars that were their own property and had originally intended to race them as privateers.

The leading privateers were Roy Salvadori and Stirling Moss. Roy's British Racing Green car was entered by Gilby Engineering and it made its debut in inauspicious circumstances at Goodwood on Easter Monday, 1954. In the main race of the day, the 21-lap Glover Trophy, there was a tremendous battle between Ken Wharton with the V-16 BRM and Salvadori. The BRM, leading the race, was faster along the straights, but it was dragging its heels through the corners with the Maserati right up its exhausts. The battle was waged for eighteen laps, but on the nineteenth Salvadori nudged Wharton at Lavant, the BRM spun and the two cars collided. Wharton rejoined the race to win from McAlpine's Connaught, but Roy was out of the race with a stalled engine. A protest lodged by Gilby *patron* Sid Greene was rejected.

In the main the Gilby Maserati ran in short-distance British events and on its few appearances on the Continent it enjoyed little success. Roy Salvadori turned in some magnificent drives with this car and perhaps his finest was in the 1956 British Grand Prix in which he held second place for many laps ahead of a host of works cars from Ferrari, Maserati and Vanwall. Most experts felt that Salvadori deserved a regular drive in a works car, but it was not forthcoming until he was offered a place by BRM in 1957.

The Gilby Maserati, chassis number 2507, enjoyed a very checkered career. It was returned to the works for a rebuild after the throttles had jammed open in the 1954 Oulton Park Gold Cup and it had run into a tree. Later, at the end of 1955, it was returned for another, but routine, rebuild and had to return for yet another rebuild after Salvadori had rolled it in the 1956 *Daily Express* Trophy race. Salvadori left the Gilby organisation at the end of 1956 and after 2507 had been driven in a few races in 1957 by Ivor Bueb, Jim Russell and Keith Greene (the *patron*'s son), it turned up in 1959 in the stock of Performance Cars at Brentford with a price tag of £950.

Stirling Moss and his 250F, chassis number 2508, made a cautious start to the season with a fourth at Bordeaux, but followed this up with a win in the Aintree '200' race and a brilliant third place in the Belgian Grand Prix. Moss was holding second place in the British Grand Prix when the de Dion axle broke (this was the Achilles heel of early 250Fs) and it was at this point in the season that he was invited to join the works team. Moss still raced his own car, now painted red but retaining a green nose-band. No major successes came Moss's way during the remainder of 1954 because of mechanical failures, but he came very close to winning the Italian Grand Prix. Stirling worked his way into the lead and was in an unassailable position when his 250F lost its oil pressure because of a cracked pipe.

Moss left Maserati at the end of 1954 to drive for the Mercedes team, but he continued to race his own 250F in minor events and also loaned it to a number of other drivers. Guest drivers of the Moss car included Peter Walker, Lance Macklin, John Fitch, Bob Gerard and Mike Hawthorn. For 1955 the Moss 'Maser' was fitted with Dunlop magnesium-alloy wheels and disc brakes (these had been adopted in 1954 on the Owen car referred to below) and his mechanic Alf Francis also experimented with SU fuel injection. In 1956 Moss had his 250F converted back to wire wheels before selling it and he drove it to victory in this form at Aintree and the Crystal Palace.

The Owen Organisation bought 2509 and raced it while work progressed on the new 2500 cc BRM. Ken Wharton drove this car in 1954, but it was plagued by mechanical troubles and failed to achieve real success. In 1955 Peter Collins signed up with the Owen Organisation and drove 2509 to victory in the *Daily Express* Trophy at Silverstone. Mike Hawthorn drove it into third place in the 1956 Argentine Grand Prix and on its return to Europe it was sold to Jack Brabham. Jack reckoned that the car was in such poor shape that to put it right would cost more that he could possibly afford and he sold it very quickly. It was with this car that Chris Amon gained his early motor racing experience in New Zealand.

Mercedes-Benz still dominated Grand Prix racing in 1955 and won every one of the year's Championship races apart from Monaco where Trintignant's Ferrari was the winner. For Maserati, whose team was now led by Jean Behra, it was a dismal year that brought no real success. Technical developments were limited to the introduction of a 5-speed gearbox and a new streamlined car which Behra drove into fourth place in the Italian Grand Prix at Monza. Luigi Musso was the team's most successful driver and apart from a third place in the Dutch Grand Prix, he scored seconds at Bordeaux (where Behra was the winner), Naples and Siracusa. In fact the Siracusa performance represented humiliating defeat rather than success, for Musso and his team-mates were soundly trounced by the British Connaught driven by young dental student Tony Brooks.

At one race in 1955, the Oulton Park Gold Cup, Stirling Moss drove a works Maserati in place of Behra who had been badly injured in the Tourist Trophy. Moss scored a fine victory from Hawthorn's Ferrari-entered Lancia and this was an omen for the coming season. On Mercedes' retirement from racing Stirling returned to Modena; a previously happy relationship was quickly renewed, Jean Behra was content to give up the role of team leader but stayed with Maserati, and the team was invigorated with new energy and enthusiasm.

Behra started the season well with a good second place in the Argentine Grand Prix, and Moss scored the works team's first victory of the year at Goodwood where he won the Glover Trophy with a car fitted experimentally with Bosch/OM fuel injection. Although the fuel injection boosted power output, it also increased fuel consumption to the point that the car could not run through most Grands Prix without a pit stop and as a result it was not persevered with.

At Monaco Moss scored his second ever World Championship race win (the first was with a Mercedes at Aintree in 1955) and after his own car had shed a wheel at Spa he took over team-mate Cesare Perdisa's 250F to finish third. The 250F usually had a central accelerator, but Moss's works car was fitted with a right-hand accelerator, as was Perdisa's so that it could be taken over by the team-leader if necessary. Behra was third in the French race and third at Silverstone. In the British Grand Prix Moss had led until mechanical trouble ended his fast run and he and Behra were second and third to Fangio's Lancia-Ferrari at Nürburgring.

As the season progressed, it became increasingly obvious that the 250F lacked the sheer speed of the rival V-8 from Maranello, and Maserati, with the additional spur of a financial reward for any new Italian car to appear at the race, hastily built two new cars in time for the final round of the Championship at Monza. Although the basic layout was unchanged, the engine was now mounted at an angle of five degrees to the centre line of the car; this permitted the prop-shaft to run diagonally across the floor of the cockpit and the seating position to be lowered alongside the shaft. The body was lower and smoother, with a long nose, higher cockpit sides and a very shapely tail and fairing formed by the fuel tank.

The 1956 Italian Grand Prix was run on the combined road and banked track at Monza, the Lancia-Ferraris were plagued by tyre and steering arm failures and Moss won the race; but it was a near-run thing for he ran out of fuel on the circuit (the tank was leaking), was given a push by private Maserati driver Piotti that set him coasting back to the pits and he regained the lead after the steering broke on Musso's Lancia-Ferrari.

For 1957 Maserati built a team of three so-called 'lightweight' cars inspired by the Monza model. The chassis of the new cars were, however, constructed from tubing of much smaller diameter and the engines were mounted straight in the frames. The bodies had the same general lines, but air was directed to the three Weber twin-choke carburettors by a long intake on the right-hand side of the nose cowling. The 1957 cars, chassis numbers 2527, 2528, and 2529, are the most coveted of 250Fs, for they represent the model in its most competitive and successful form.

Moss had now left to drive for the Vanwall team and the three lightweight cars were driven by Fangio, Behra and Harry Schell. At most races, a fourth car, usually 2501 that had been rebuilt in 1956 with long-nose bodywork, was entered for Menditeguy or Scarlatti. In 1956 Maserati had marred their chances of success by trying to incorporate modifications in the team cars during the season. No experimental work was carried out on the team cars as such in 1957 and as a result they were better prepared and much more reliable.

The Ferrari team was unable to regain the fine form that it had displayed the previous year and during the early part of 1957 Maserati dominated Grand Prix racing. Fangio won both the Argentine and Buenos Aires City Grands Prix and Behra scored a victory at Pau. Another win for Fangio followed at Monaco where Moss's Vanwall crashed and the Lancia-Ferraris of Collins and Hawthorn ran into the debris. In the French Grand Prix held on the difficult and testing Rouen circuit Juan Fangio demonstrated that he was still at the peak of his form and, revelling in a virtuoso display of controlled power slides through Rouen's high-speed corners, he scored what was probably the most impressive victory in his long career. Musso scored Ferrari's only victory of the season in the non-Championship Reims race, but Behra took second place with a 1956 250F.

Then came the European Grand Prix at Aintree and a sharp reversal of Maserati fortunes. All three Maseratis retired with mechanical failures (Behra's engine blew up while he was leading the race) and Moss came through to score a magnificent victory with the Vanwall that he had taken over from team-mate Brooks. The Vanwalls were out of the picture at the Nürburgring because of suspension problems and the race devolved into a straight fight between Fangio and Ferrari drivers Hawthorn and Collins. The Argentinian had started the race with a half-full tank and, after stopping to refuel and for new rear tyres, he rejoined the race in third place. For the first three laps after his pit stop Fangio made no impression on the leading Lancia-Ferrari drivers who were lulled into a state of false security. Then he dramatically reduced his lap time, closed right up on the leaders and forged ahead to score his fourth Championship race victory of the season.

Vanwall superiority reasserted itself at Pescara, a race included in the Championship series in 1957 only, and Fangio was beaten into second place. It was much the same story at Monza where Jean Behra drove the new V-12 Maserati on only its second race outing. After a fierce struggle Moss won for Vanwall, Fangio was beaten into second place and Behra retired the V-12 car with internal engine damage caused by overheating. Despite Vanwall's successes in the latter part of the season, Fangio had clinched his fifth World Championship with 40 points to the 25 scored by Stirling Moss and at long last Maserati had achieved their ambition of thoroughly trouncing Ferrari. Jean Behra rounded off an exciting year with victories in the non-Championship Modena and Moroccan Grands Prix.

Because of financial difficulties Maserati withdrew from racing at the end of 1957 and the intended successor to the 250F, the V-12 car using the same chassis, was never raced on a regular basis. Development work did not cease altogether, however, and during 1958 Maserati produced a new 6-cylinder car with shorter wheelbase and lighter chassis known as the 'Piccolo'. The 'Piccolo', which was financed by American enthusiast Temple Buell, first appeared in practice at Spa in 1958 and was raced at Reims by Fangio on what was to prove his last race appearance; he took fourth place after a pit stop. Scuderia Buell fielded a 'Piccolo' car at Monza and Casablanca and then took two to race in New Zealand where they were subsequently sold.

The final expression of the 250F theme was the Tec-Mec, based on factory development work, but completed at Studio Tec-Mec by former Maserati designer Valerio Colotti. The Tec-Mec was driven by Fritz d'Orey in the 1959 United States Grand Prix, but by the standards of Cooper and Lotus it was completely outdated, it was uncompetitive at Sebring and retired early in the race. This car made no further International appearances and was later acquired by Tom Wheatcroft.

From 1958 onwards the now obsolescent 250Fs gradually faded from the racing scene, but never quite disappeared. As late as 1960 Gino Munaron drove a 250F into third place in the Buenos Aires City Grand Prix and Bob Drake rounded off the model's Formula One history by driving 2529 into thirteenth place in the United States Grand Prix, the last race of the Formula. Even after the 2500 cc Formula came to an end, cars were still raced in New Zealand. In 1965 the Vintage Sports Car Club admitted front-engined cars built between 1954 and 1960 into Historic Racing Car events. Initially the 250Fs dominated the class and in 1967 Charles Lucas lapped Silverstone in 1 min 44.2 sec (101.12 mph), a bare second slower than the best ever lap during the 2500 cc Formula by Moss in the 1956 British Grand Prix. The Maseratis could not, however, match the engine power of Neil Corner's 3-litre Aston Martin DBR4/250 or the cornering power of the Lotus 16s. But the 250F is the only car of the 2500 cc Formula to have raced without a break for over twenty years.

6

Calendar of Calamities:
The BRM Story

In the history of motor racing there have been few constructors who have enjoyed such a long career as BRM and none that has suffered so many misfortunes. The BRM team ran in its first race in 1950 and since then it has staggered from disaster to disaster, from failure to failure, for twenty-five years of misery, alleviated by only four seasons of consistent success during 1962-5, the years of the 1500 cc unsupercharged Grand Prix Formula. Yet BRM, now headed by Louis Stanley, still races on, and in 1974 it seemed that success might yet return to this ill-fated team, following Beltoise's fine drive in the South African race.

Type 15 (1500 cc supercharged and 4500 cc unsupercharged Grand Prix Formula, 1947-53)

It had long been the ambition of Raymond Mays, leading amateur British racing driver and co-founder of the ERA Voiturette team to build a serious British Grand Prix contender. In post-war days Mays and his long-time associate Peter Berthon embarked on the project which became known as the BRM. The technically advanced V-16 cars were raced from 1950 onwards and took part in their last race in 1955 by when they had been rendered completely obsolete by changes in the racing regulations.

The BRM in its original form featured a very complex V-16 engine with the cylinders at an angle of 135 degrees, a capacity of 1496 cc (49.53 × 47.8 mm), twin overhead camshafts per bank of cylinders, cast-iron wet liners, a two-piece ten-bearing crankshaft and a Rolls-Royce two-stage centrifugal supercharger. The claimed power output was 430 bhp at 11,000 rpm. The transmission incorporated a triple-plate clutch, a 5-speed gearbox mounted transversely at the rear and a ZF-type limited slip differential. In its original form the BRM was fitted with Girling hydraulic three-shoe brakes, but

Girling disc brakes were later substituted. The chassis featured a tubular frame with two main members on each side and four cross-members, and there was an aluminium body and fuel tanks. At the front suspension was by trailing arms and Lockheed pneumatic struts (basically similar to that of late pre-war ERAs) and at the rear by a de Dion axle, single radius rods and Lockheed pneumatic struts (similar, pneumatic struts apart, to that of the 1938-9 Grand Prix Mercedes-Benz). The maximum speed of the V-16 car was in the order of 190 mph.

The development of the V-16 car was protracted; it had basic technical defects and it non-started at many races. The engine suffered from poor breathing, water leaked into the cylinders because of difficulties in machining the cylinder liners and because of the centrifugal supercharger the power came in within a sudden rush that made controllability of such a potent car exceptionally difficult.

1945
March
Raymond Mays launched his appeal for financial support for the new British Grand Prix contender. Early and substantial support was offered by Oliver Lucas of Joseph Lucas Ltd and Alfred Owen of the Rubery Owen organisation. By the end of 1946 over one hundred companies were backing the project by financial contributions and by the offer to supply components and to make available development facilities. The BRM workshops were established close to Mays's home at Bourne in Lincolnshire.

1947
July
The British Motor Racing Research Trust was formed to act in an advisory capacity and to relieve Mays of some of the responsibility for the project. The company building the cars, originally known as Automobile Developments Ltd, was renamed British Racing Motors Ltd.

1949
December
The first car was completed and was shown to the public on 15th December.

1950
May
Raymond Mays demonstrated the V-16 at the European Grand Prix meeting at Silverstone.

August
Two cars were entered in the *Daily Express* Trophy race at Silverstone. The cars missed the first day's practice, during testing at Folkingham (near Bourne) both cars broke a cylinder liner and finally one car appeared at the start of the race without having run during official practice. At the start of his heat driver Raymond Sommer let in the clutch and a half-shaft broke.

September
Reg Parnell drove the V-16 to victory in two short races at Goodwood, BRM's first victory and the last for nearly two years.

October
Two cars driven by Parnell and Peter Walker ran in the Penya Rhin Grand Prix at Barcelona; they were faster along the straights than the Ferraris, but both retired.

1951
May
Two cars were entered in the Swiss Grand Prix, but the entries were scratched as, partly because of financial difficulties, the BRMs could not be made ready in time.

July
The BRM team scratched from the French Grand Prix, but two cars driven by Parnell and Walker ran in the British race at Silverstone. Because of the lack of adequate insulation in the bodywork both drivers were badly burned by the exhaust system, but, nevertheless, carried on to finish fifth and seventh.

September
Two cars were entered in the Italian Grand Prix and, almost incredibly, one was to be driven by Ken Richardson whose Grand Prix experience was limited to a few laps at Silverstone. The RAC telegrammed to prohibit Richardson from competing, but in any case the cars were withdrawn because of gearbox trouble only three hours before the start of the race.

1952
April
BRM entered the Turin Grand Prix and once again failed to start. Many

organisers had already decided to hold their 1952 race to Formula Two rules, but BRM's withdrawal from this race resulted in almost all Grands Prix (including World Championship races) being held to the lesser Formula.

June
Two cars were entered in the Albi Grand Prix; Fangio with a V-16 set fastest lap in practice, but both he and Gonzalez retired. Later in the month two cars for Fangio and Moss were entered in the Ulster Trophy race, but both again retired.

July
Both BRMs retired in the Formule Libre race at the British Grand Prix meeting at Silverstone.

August
Gonzalez and Wharton drove the cars at the International meeting at Boreham, but the Argentinian driver spun off the wet track and the British driver retired. At this race the cars appeared in a dark green colour finish in place of the original light green. This was BRM's sixth successive race failure. Later in the month Reg Parnell drove a BRM to a victory at a minor meeting at Turnberry in Scotland.

September
At an Extraordinary General Meeting of the BRM Trust on 4th September it was unanimously decided to sell BRM Ltd. A month was allowed for offers and if no satisfactory offer was received within that time, the company would be wound up. Plans to run the cars at Goodwood towards the end of the month remained unchanged and at this minor meeting three cars were entered. Gonzalez, Parnell and Wharton took the first three places in the Goodwood Trophy race, but there was no serious opposition.

October
At another Extraordinary General Meeting the offer of Alfred Owen to take over both BRM assets and liabilities was accepted. The existing set-up continued in largely unchanged form.

1953
April
British Formule Libre races devolved into a duel between the BRMs and

Tony Vandervell's Ferrari 'Thin Wall Special'. At Goodwood, in the Glover Trophy, Wharton won for BRM from Taruffi with the 'Thin Wall'.

May
BRM had the chance to redeem itself in International racing at Albi where the Grand Prix was held in two heats (for Formula One and Formula Two cars respectively) and a final. The opposition included several 4.5-litre Ferraris, among them a works car driven by Alberto Ascari. The BRMs of Fangio and Wharton took the first two places in their heat and Gonzalez was fifth after a pit stop for a wheel-change. Initially the BRM's held the first three places in the final, but they were attaining 180 mph on this high-speed road circuit and the strain of braking and acceleration proved too much for the tyres. Gonzalez' car twice threw tyre treads, but after two pit stops he fought on to finish second to the Ferrari of Louis Rosier. Fangio's car was withdrawn after a thrown tyre tread at 190 mph resulted in collision with a bank and a damaged hub. Wharton spun at 130 mph, shot backwards down the road at undiminished speed, hit a bank and turned over; the driver was thrown out uninjured, but the car wrote itself off against a brick wall. It was claimed that at this race the car driven by Fangio was developing 585 bhp at 11,800 rpm.

July
The battle in British races between the BRMs and Vandervell's Ferrari continued; in the Formule Libre race at the British Grand Prix meeting the 'Thin Wall' driven by Farina beat the BRMs of Fangio and Wharton into second and third places. BRM fought back at Snetterton where Wharton won two races in the absence of the 'Thin Wall' and at Charterhall in August where the 'Thin Wall' retired and Wharton won for BRM.

September
Work was now in hand on a contender for the new 2500 cc Grand Prix Formula of 1954 onwards, while the team continued to race the V-16 cars. At Goodwood Mike Hawthorn drove the 'Thin Wall' to victory in two races and BRM had to settle for second places by Fangio and Wharton.

October
Wharton drove a BRM to victory in a short Formule Libre race at Castle Combe in Wiltshire.

1954
January
Ken Wharton and one of the BRMs were sent out to compete in a couple of Formule Libre races in New Zealand. The first race was the New Zealand Grand Prix at Auckland; the track had been resurfaced just before the race and broke up badly, Wharton spun off and later suffered brake trouble. The timekeepers became muddled and did not know who was the winner until after much arguing Horace Gould (Cooper-Bristol) was credited with a victory and Wharton was classified second.

February
The second race in the New Zealand series was the Lady Wigram Trophy at Christchurch. Wharton led for most of the race, but as a result of fuel-line failure in the closing stages he pushed his car 300 yards to cross the line in third place.

April
For 1954 BRM built two lightweight MkII versions of the V-16 cars to develop components for the new 2500 cc car and to give the team something to race while the new car was being built. Thc MkII cars (one of which was a rebuild of the first V-16) had tubular space-frames, shorter wheelbase and smaller wheels. The new car with Wharton at the wheel won a 5-lap race at the Easter Goodwood meeting, but for the main race of the day Wharton switched to the older car. For many laps he duelled with Roy Salvadori at the wheel of a brand-new Maserati 250F, the BRM was faster along the straights and slower through the corners, and Salvadori was unable to get past. The BRM spun and the two cars collided; Wharton rejoined the race to take first place, but Salvadori was out with a stalled engine. Salvadori's entrant, Sid Greene, entered a protest which was rejected. This was the MkI BRM's last race. Shortly afterwards Flockhart won a Formule Libre race at Snetterton with the new car.

May
Flockhart won a Formule Libre race at Ibsley in Hampshire and was third in the Aintree '200'.

July
The Owen Organisation had acquired its own Maserati 250F so as to be able

to compete in Grand Prix Racing. Wharton drove the new car on its debut in the French Grand Prix, but retired, and he subsequently finished eighth in the British race at Silverstone.

August
Wharton took sixth place with the Maserati in the Swiss Grand Prix, but the MkII BRMs finished a poor third at Snetterton (beaten by Collins with the 'Thin Wall' and Nuckey's Cooper-Bristol) and second at Castle Combe (Gerard's Cooper-Bristol was the winner).

September
Flockhart with the V-16 retired at Charterhall in Scotland and Wharton was beaten into second place at Goodwood by Collins with the 'Thin Wall'.

October
Flockhart with the V-16 finished a poor third at Aintree and Wharton with the Maserati could do no better than eighth place in the Spanish Grand Prix.

1955
April
Tony Vandervell was no longer racing the 'Thin Wall' Ferrari and in its absence Collins, now driving for the Owen Organisation, won the short Chichester Cup at Goodwood with a V-16 car.

May
Peter Collins with the Maserati won the *Daily Express* Trophy race at Silverstone, an important victory, and also won the minor London Trophy at the Crystal Palace at the end of the month. Flockhart with the V-16 finished second to Salvadori's Maserati in a race at Snetterton.

September
Collins with a V-16 won a Formule Libre race at Aintree.

October
Flockhart, driving the V-16 on its last race outing, finished second to Schell's Vanwall in the *Empire News* Formule Libre race at Castle Combe.

Type 25 (2500 cc Grand Prix Formula, 1954-60)

For the 2500 cc Grand Prix Formula the Owen Organisation developed a completely new car with 4-cylinder 2497 cc (102.87 × 74.93 mm) engine developing in its original form 248 bhp at 9000 rpm. Transmission was by a 4-speed BRM-designed 'crash' gearbox in unit with the final drive. The chassis was a multi-tubular space-frame and there was a magnesium-alloy body skin. At the front the suspension was by unequal-length double wishbones used in conjunction with the familiar oleo-pneumatic struts. At the rear there was a de Dion axle located by a parallel-link motion running from the nearside hub to the chassis and twin radius arms on each side and oleo-pneumatic struts. Lockheed disc brakes were used, but with a single transmission disc brake operating on the gearbox output shaft at the rear.

1955

September

The new car was entered at the *Daily Telegraph* Trophy race at Aintree on 3rd September. In practice the oil scavenge pump failed, oil from the engine breather was sprayed over the rear tyres and driver Peter Collins lost control and collided with a concrete post. The car failed to start in the race. Later in the month Collins drove the new car in the Gold Cup race at Oulton Park. He was in second place behind Moss's Maserati when the oil pressure failed and the car was withdrawn. It was later ascertained that the car had a faulty gauge.

1956

April

Mike Hawthorn crashed at the Easter Goodwood meeting when the transmission locked up. He escaped with a shaking and a lacerated ankle. At Aintree the same month he ran off the road when the brakes failed because a pivot pin had fallen out.

May

The works cars were withdrawn from the Monaco Grand Prix because the inlet valves were distorting in practice (very large valves were fitted because of the markedly over-square engine dimensions).

July

At the British Grand Prix, BRM's first race since May, Hawthorn led until oil began to leak from the final drive. Team-mate Brooks stopped at the pits with throttle linkage trouble and rejoined the race only to have the throttles jam open at Abbey Curve; the car rolled over and burst into flames – Brooks escaped with a broken jaw. The cars were not raced again in 1956.

1957

The 1957 works cars had higher cockpit sides and a wrap-round perspex screen. BRM scrapped the oleo-pneumatic struts at the rear and replaced them with a transverse leaf spring. Early in 1957 Colin Chapman was brought in as a consultant and as a result of his advice coil spring suspension was fitted front and rear.

April

At the Easter Goodwood meeting the cars were plagued by locking brakes, Salvador spun out of the race, but Flockhart managed to finish third despite spinning three times.

May

The brakes were locking up so frequently and so unexpectedly that Salvadori began to imagine that it was happening when it wasn't. He had lost confidence in the cars, failed to qualify at Monaco and left the team. Flockhart started at Monaco, but retired.

July

Flockhart crashed badly in the French Grand Prix after hitting oil dropped by Salvadori's Vanwall. A week later the team's other driver Herbert Mackay Fraser was killed driving a Lotus at Reims. The first glimmer of hope came later that month. Jean Behra agreed to drive a BRM in the minor Caen Grand Prix. The opposition was negligible, but Behra scored an unexpected and encouraging victory.

September

Because of a lack of drivers BRM did not race again until the *Daily Express* Trophy race at Silverstone (postponed until September because of the fuel shortage following the Suez crisis). No other works teams were entered and the BRMs of Behra, Schell and Flockhart took the first three places. Later in September both cars driven by Bonnier and Flockhart retired in the Modena Grand Prix.

October
Trintignant drove a BRM into third place in the Moroccan Grand Prix.

1958
BRM developed a much revised version of the Type 25 with a new lighter and stronger space-frame chassis; the cockpit panels were now of the conventional detachable type to reduce costs. The transmission, brakes and rear suspension were unchanged, but the front suspension had been redesigned. The team drivers were now Jean Behra, Harry Schell and Joakim Bonnier.

April
Behra was leading the Glover Trophy at Goodwood when his brakes locked in the 'off' position at the chicane and the BRM demolished itself against the brickwork. In the same race Schell's car was withdrawn because the brakes were locking in the 'on' position.

May
Behra was leading the *Daily Express* Trophy at Silverstone when his goggles were shattered by a stone and glass entered one eye. After a pit stop he rejoined the race to finish fourth. Both cars retired at Monaco, but at Zandvoort Schell and Behra took second and third places behind Moss's winning Vanwall.

June
In practice for the Belgian Grand Prix at Spa Behra lost control at 150 mph because of oil from the breather blowing on to the rear tyres. The driver was uninjured, but both Behra and Schell lost their confidence in the cars and drove apathetically in the race.

July
In the British Grand Prix Behra's car ran into a hare and one of the animal's leg bones punctured a tyre! Schell finished fifth. Shortly afterwards BRM travelled to Caen in the hope of repeating their 1957 victory, but despite the absence of serious opposition both cars retired.

August
BRM ran in the German Grand Prix at the Nürburgring for the first time, but the cars were plagued by serious suspension problems and neither finished the race.

September
At the start of the Italian Grand Prix von Trips' Ferrari ran up the back of Schell's BRM and over the driver (leaving red paint on his helmet) and both cars were out of the race. Behra was in second place when his brakes weakened and he eventually retired with transmission trouble.

October
Bonnier finished fourth in the Moroccan Grand Prix, but Behra withdrew from the race out of pique because he could not match his team-mate's speed.

1959
April
Stirling Moss drove a new Cooper with BRM engine for Rob Walker in the Aintree '200' race. The gearbox failed when Moss was leading the race and this car was not raced again because of inherent defects in the design of the gear selectors (a reflection on Colotti and not on BRM).

May
Moss drove a works BRM in the *Daily Express* Trophy race at Silverstone, but spun out of the race when the brakes failed. In the Dutch Grand Prix at Zandvoort later in the month Joakim Bonnier scored BRM's only Championship race victory of the 2500 cc Grand Prix Formula.

July
Stirling Moss drove a BRM loaned to the British Racing Partnership and painted pale green in the European Grand Prix at Reims. He was in second place when he spun off on melted tar and was unable to restart because the clutch had failed. The same month Moss drove the BRP-entered BRM into second place in the British Grand Prix.

August
Hans Herrmann drove the British Racing Partnership BRM in the German Grand Prix held on the Avus banked track. The car was almost completely destroyed when the brakes failed at 160 mph. The driver was thrown out and escaped with abrasions.

1960
At the 1959 Italian Grand Prix the BRM team produced a rear-engined

prototype known as the Type 48 and although the front-engined cars were raced in the Argentine at the beginning of the season, the team relied on the Type 48 cars for the remainder of the season. Once again, as in 1959, the cars proved no match for the Cooper opposition and gained very little success.

January
Bonnier was leading the Argentine Grand Prix when his car developed valve spring trouble and he dropped back to finish fifth.

April
Bertie Bradnack, appointed racing manager for 1960, resigned and issued the following statement: 'After special practice early on Easter Monday morning I considered the matter very carefully and decided to resign my position as BRM racing manager, as the whole outfit has changed completely from when I had sole control in the Argentine.

'Since then there has been complete lack of co-operation by the organisation at Bourne, and although I made countless enquiries regarding tests of the 1960 rear-engined BRM, the first time I saw the cars was Saturday morning at Goodwood Circuit.

'I felt that my appointment by Mr A G B Owen was deeply resented by the organisation at Bourne and consequently the team spirit which is essential in an enterprise of this kind was completely absent. . . .'

The rear-engined BRMs were out of the picture at the Easter Goodwood meeting and in his autobiography *(Life At The Limit,* William Kimber, 1969) Graham Hill, at that time having his first season as a BRM works driver, wrote, 'We brought out the first rear-engined BRM . . . and what a pig it was. I remember testing it at Goodwood and it really was terrible . . . I found that every now and then the car would suddenly take a dive and dart straight into the infield out of control.'

June
Hill's engine failed when he was in second place on the last lap but one of the Belgian Grand Prix.

July
Graham Hill stalled at the start of the British Grand Prix and lost a third of a lap before he joined the race; he drove with fire and determination to fight his way through the field and took the lead from Brabham's Cooper on lap

55; only four laps from the finish he tried to pass two slower cars under braking for Copse corner, the brakes locked up and Hill spun out of the race.

1961

Contrary to the wishes of all the British constructors the very successful 2500 cc Grand Prix Formula was replaced at the end of 1960 by a new Formula for cars of between 1301 cc and 1500 cc unsupercharged. Hoping that they could persuade the Commission Sportive Internationale to prolong the existing Formula, none of the British teams had taken steps to develop new 1500 cc engines and for the first year of the Formula all, including BRM, were forced to use the elderly FPF 4-cylinder engine introduced by the Coventry-Climax concern back in 1957. Throughout 1961 BRM raced the MkII version of their Type 48 chassis which had been originally designed to take the 2500 cc engine and was much heavier than other British cars.

In 1961 the BRM drivers were Graham Hill and Tony Brooks and the *marque* failed to score a single victory. In World Championship races the team's best performancec were a sixth by Hill at Reims, a fifth by Brooks at Monza and a third by Brooks at Watkins Glen.

1962

In the words of Raymond Mays, BRM chose a V-8 engine for the new Formula 'on the basis of the maximum potential for minimum bulk'. This 1497.7 cc (68.5 × 50.8 mm) engine with twin overhead camshafts per bank of cylinders and Lucas low-pressure fuel injection initially developed 184 bhp at 10,000 rmp, but this output was soon increased by steady development work. There was a new multi-tubular space-frame chassis designed by Tony Rudd and this was typed the 56; the double wishbone and coil spring front suspension was similar to that of the Type 48 car, but at the rear there was a new suspension layout with double wishbones and low-level adjustable coil spring/damper units. The new car first appeared in practice at the 1961 Italian Grand Prix and by the start of the following season it was fully raceworthy and very competitive.

This year marked the start of a Golden era for BRM spread over four seasons, during which the *marque* enjoyed persistent success and disappointments and failures were few and far between. The initial success of the V-8 BRM can in part be attributed to the fact that Sir Alfred Owen had informed Raymond Mays that the team could only ensure its future existence if it was more successful in 1962 than in past years.

During that season the drivers were Graham Hill and Ritchie Ginther and the many successes can be summarised as follows:

1st, Hill, Richmond Trophy, Goodwood
1st, Hill, *Daily Express* Trophy, Silverstone
1st, Hill, Dutch Grand Prix
2nd, Hill, Belgian Grand Prix
2nd, Hill, Reims Grand Prix
3rd, Ginther, French Grand Prix
1st, Hill, German Grand Prix
1st, Hill, 2nd, Ginther, Italian Grand Prix
2nd, Hill, United States Grand Prix
1st, Hill, South African Grand Prix

Graham Hill won the Drivers' World Championship with 42 points to the 30 of Jim Clark, and BRM won the Manufacturers' Championship. Even so, BRM's season was not completely troublefree and a typical Bourne misadventure occurred at the Brussels Grand Prix, the team's first race in 1962. This race was run in three heats, the first of which Hill won. At the start of the second heat Hill was unable to fire his engine (later investigation revealed that the starter motor had suffered an electrical failure) and the BRM was push-started, only to be disqualified at the end of the first lap. The English version of the race regulations, which was a reprint of the previous year's regulations, permitted a push-start within one minute of the start of the race, but the wording of the French version of the regulations was, 'De toute facon le moteur devra toujours etre mis en marche par les moyens de bord'.

A strong cause for complaint in 1962 was the total failure of the V-8 cars sold to private entrants Jack Lewis and Tony Marsh; these cars disappeared from the racing scene in mid-season.

1963

Throughout the years of the 1500 cc Formula BRM's greatest rival was the new monocoque Lotus 25 (later versions were known as the 33) driven by Jim Clark. The Coventry-Climax-powered cars brought Clark his first victory in the Drivers' Championship in 1963, but even so, Hill and Ginther enjoyed substantial success and Hill took second place in the Drivers' Championship. BRM successes in 1963 were:

1st, Hill, Lombank Trophy, Snetterton

1st, Hill, Aintree '200'
1st, Hill, Monaco Grand Prix
3rd, Hill, French Grand Prix
3rd, Ginther, German Grand Prix
2nd, Ginther, Italian Grand Prix
1st, Hill, United States Grand Prix
3rd, Ginther, Mexican Grand Prix
3rd, Hill, South African Grand Prix

In the French Grand Prix Hill drove a new semi-monocoque BRM with a stressed skin monocoque structure of Duralumin sheeting forming the centre-section and tubular framework front and rear. Although Hill also drove this car in the German race, for the rest of the season the team relied on the 1962 cars and the semi-monocoque was abandoned. The team also ran the successful Rover–BRM gas-turbine prototype at Le Mans.

1964

For 1964 BRM adopted a full monocoque design powered by the familiar V-8 engine and during the season the team also revealed an experimental four-wheel-drive car. Once again Hill continued to notch up success after success and although he was beaten in the Drivers' Championship by John Surtees (Ferrari), the circumstances of Surtees's victory were unfortunate. Before the Mexican Grand Prix, the last race of the season, Hill led with 39 points to the 34 of Surtees and 30 of Clark. In the race Graham worked his way up to third place, a position which he was content to hold as it was good enough to ensure him victory in the Championship. As the race progressed, Bandini (Ferrari) began to harass the BRM driver, striving to overtake him at the hairpin bend where there was clearly no room to get by. Graham shook his fist warningly at the Italian, but Bandini took no notice and when he again tried to pass the BRM, the two cars collided and one of the Ferrari's wheels buckled the BRM's exhausts. As a result of this incident Surtees was able to move up into second place (winning the Championship) and poor Hill finished eleventh after two pit stops for repairs to the BRM's exhausts.

The BRM successes in 1964 were as follows:

2nd, Hill, Aintree '200'
2nd, Hill, *Daily Express* Trophy, Silverstone
1st, Hill, Monaco Grand Prix
2nd, Hill, French Grand Prix

2nd, Hill, British Grand Prix
2nd, Hill, German Grand Prix
2nd, Ginther, Austrian Grand Prix
1st, Hill, United States Grand Prix

1965

For 1965 Richie Ginther left BRM to drive for the Japanese Honda team and Graham Hill was now partnered by Jackie Stewart who proved the sensation of the season and on more than one occasion trounced his more senior team-mate. Clark and the Lotus 33 scored convincing victories in the Drivers' and Manufacturers' Championships, but, as in past seasons, the BRM team was hot on his heels at most races and scored a large number of successes:

3rd, Hill, South African Grand Prix
2nd, Stewart, Race of Champions, Brands Hatch
2nd, Hill, Richmond Trophy, Goodwood
1st, Stewart, *Daily Express* Trophy, Silverstone
1st, Hill, 3rd, Stewart, Monaco Grand Prix
2nd, Stewart, Belgian Grand Prix
2nd, Stewart, French Grand Prix
2nd, Hill, British Grand Prix
2nd, Stewart, Dutch Grand Prix
2nd, Hill, German Grand Prix
1st, Stewart, 2nd, Hill, Italian Grand Prix
1st, Hill, United States Grand Prix

1966

BRM were anxious to repeat their successes of the years 1962-5 by building a car for the new 3000 cc Grand Prix Formula of 1966 onwards that would have a long development life ahead of it. Unfortunately, the team chose an excessively complicated H-16 engine design which had a well-founded reputation for incurable vibrations and it was a layout that had previously been used only for aircraft engines. The H-16 engine had two horizontally opposed banks of eight cylinders, one above the other, with dimensions of 68.95 × 48.89 mm, giving a capacity of 2999 cc. The claimed power output was 400 bhp at 10,000 rpm. Transmission was by a 6-speed gearbox in unit with the final drive. The chassis was a direct derivative of that used for the 1965 cars; there was a riveted monocoque, front-suspension by upper rocking arms and lower wishbones and rear suspension by lower wishbones, single transverse struts and twin radius rods. Throughout its short racing career the Type 83 H-16 car was plagued by mechanical problems and at many races during 1966-7 the BRM team was forced to rely on the old V-8 cars with engines enlarged to 2 litres.

May
The H-16 car appeared at Monaco, but the BRM drivers raced the old V-8 cars and finished 1st (Stewart), 3rd (Hill) and 4th (Bondurant with Wilson's private car).

June
In the Belgian Grand Prix many cars, including all three BRMs, were eliminated when they skidded off the rain-soaked track on the first lap; Jackie Stewart was trapped in his car and suffered a broken collar-bone, cracked ribs and petrol burns.

July
Graham Hill drove a 2-litre BRM into third place in the British Grand Prix. Shortly afterwards he took second place in the Dutch race.

September
BRM were told by the organisers of the Italian Grand Prix to run the H-16 cars or not bother to come. Neither H-16 showed good form in practice, but remarkably enough, there was a 2-litre V-8 BRM on display in a Festival Museum which *happened* to be in racing trim. Hill used it in practice, but it suffered mechanical trouble and both drivers handled the H-16 cars on what was their race debut. Hill and Stewart were out of the race within six laps.

October
The H-16s finished at the tail of the field in the United States Grand Prix, but the race-winner proved to be Jim Clark with a Lotus powered by the H-16 BRM engine, a source of great encouragement to the Bourne team.

1967
April
The H-16 displayed a good turn of speed at long last. Stewart was fastest in

practice for the *Daily Express* Trophy at Silverstone and held second place in the race until he fell back with mechanical problems and subsequently retired because of sheared universal joint bolts.

May

It seemed that the H-16 was making real progress; it had made its debut at Monaco in 1966 and now a year later Spence drove one of these cars into sixth place, covering 96 of the 100 laps.

June

Stewart with the H-16 took the lead in the Belgian Grand Prix after Clark's new Lotus 49 stopped at the pits because of plug trouble; unfortunately the BRM developed gearbox problems, Stewart had to hold the car in gear and was passed by Dan Gurney's Eagle.

July

At the French Grand Prix held on the Bugatti circuit at Le Mans two H-16 cars were entered, but Stewart drove a V-8 2-litre borrowed from the Reg Parnell team. Stewart finished third, but Spence with the H-16 retired. A fortnight later both H-16s retired in the British Grand Prix.

August

In the first Canadian Grand Prix Bruce McLaren drove his new M5A car powered by a completely new BRM V-12 engine. It was suggested that this engine was primarily a sports car unit intended for sale to private owners rather than for use by the works team.

October

In the last race of the season, the Mexican Grand Prix, Mike Spence took fifth place with an H-16 car.

1968

By the middle of the 1967 season the BRM team had concluded that the vibration and transmission problems suffered by the H-16 unit were incurable and decided to race new cars in 1968 powered by the V-12 engine. To expedite development BRM 'contracted out' design and construction of the first chassis to Len Terry and these early cars were known as the P126. The later cars of identical specification, but built in the BRM works, were known as the P133. The V-12 engine had a capacity of 2999.5 cc (74.6 × 57.2 mm) with twin overhead camshafts per bank of cylinders, two valves per cylinder and, in the form raced in 1968, a power output of around 400 bhp. Transmission was by a Hewland 5-speed gearbox.

January
In the South African Grand Prix the V-12 BRM driven by Pedro Rodriguez made its race debut and the H-16 in the hands of Mike Spence made its farewell appearance; both cars retired. The same month the team ran a pair of V-12 cars with engines reduced in capacity to 2500 cc for McLaren and Rodriguez in the Tasman races.

May
BRM driver Mike Spence, team-leader following Stewart's departure, was killed at Indianapolis while practising with a Lotus 56 gas-turbine car. As a result only one car ran in the Spanish Grand Prix driven by Rodriguez, but by the Monaco race on 26th May Dickie Attwood had been brought into the team. Attwood took second place at Monaco, BRM's best performance for two years.

June
Rodriguez finished second for BRM in the Belgian Grand Prix, and followed this up with a third place in the Dutch race.

July
Rodriguez took the lead in the rain-soaked French Grand Prix, but was repassed by Ickx' Ferrari and eventually finished twelfth and last as a result of gearbox trouble.

September
The BRM team was heavily criticised because Dickie Attwood was dropped at the Italian Grand Prix without warning and replaced by American driver Bobby Unser who had no Grand Prix experience. However Unser flew to the USA to compete in the Hosier 100 race on the Saturday and was disqualified from taking part in the Grand Prix on the Sunday as International regulations forbid drivers to compete in two races within 24 hours. Only Rodriguez' car started the race and this retired.

October
Unser was again entered for the team at the United States race. He was slowest but one out of nineteen starters and retired with engine trouble when in tenth place.

1969
BRM persevered with the V-12 cars and in the early part of the season raced the improved P138 car with their own gearbox instead of the Hewland. BRM had now developed a more powerful version of the V-12 engine with four valves per cylinder and a claimed power output of 450 bhp (but it is likely that the true output was very much lower). In 1969 the team drivers were John Surtees and Jack Oliver.

May
Surtees took fifth place in the Spanish Grand Prix, but a BRM did not finish in the first six in a Championship race again until October. In the Monaco Grand Prix later in the month Surtees was weaving to hold off Jack Brabham when his gearbox broke, the BRM suddenly slowed and the two cars collided.

July
BRM missed the French Grand Prix to sort out their many problems and concentrated on the British race a fortnight later. Tony Rudd, BRM's chief engineer who had also been acting as team manager for several years, was asked to resign. At Silverstone Surtees drove the new P139 car, but retired on the first lap when the front suspension collapsed.

August
In practice for the German Grand Prix Surtees's P139 was plagued by an oil leak and was scratched. Only Oliver started the race and he retired with a cracked sump caused by bottoming on the Nürburgring's many bumps.

September
Tim Parnell, who had previously run the Reg Parnell Racing Team of private BRMs, now joined the BRM organisation as team manager, but still fortune failed to smile on the team. In the Italian race Oliver retired and Surtees trailed round at the tail of the field to finish eleventh and last.

October
Surtees achieved BRM's best performance of the season by finishing third in the United States race.

1970
An apparent transformation had taken place at Bourne by the start of the 1970 season. The team now raced the much improved P153 cars with 'bath-tub' monocoque designed by Tony Southgate and the engine was now claimed to develop the much more realistic power output of 425 bhp at 10,500 rpm. BRM chief Louis Stanley had arranged a major sponsorship deal with the Yardley company and for the next two seasons the cars were raced in Yardley's white, gold and brown colours. The principal drivers were Rodriguez and Oliver, while a third car was entered for Canadian George Eaton who paid for his drives.

March
For the last time the full BRM team ran in BRM's traditional dark green colour finish. In practice for the South African race the P153s were plagued by overheating cockpits and in the race the sole finisher was Rodriguez who took a miserable ninth place.

June
After dismal failures in the first three races of the season Pedro Rodriguez scored a fine victory for the team in the Belgian Grand Prix. This was BRM's first Grand Prix victory since 1966.

August
BRM had failed to finish in the first six at any Grand Prix since the Belgian race, but at the Austrian Grand Prix in August there was cause for hope as Rodriguez and Oliver took fourth and fifth places.

October
Rodriguez took the lead in the United States Grand Prix and seemed all set for victory when he ran out of fuel only seven laps from the finish; after a pit stop he rejoined the race to take second place behind Fittipaldi's Lotus.

1971
For 1971 Bourne introduced an inproved V-12 car known as the P160

with lower and wider monocoque, modified suspension geometry, more powerful engine and lighter gearbox. Jack Oliver had been dropped from the team and his place taken by Jo Siffert. Howden Ganley now drove BRMs with finance from his sponsor Barry Newman. In some respects the season was the most encouraging enjoyed by BRM for many years, but it was also among the most depressing in the team's history.

April
Rodriguez took an encouraging fourth place in the Spanish Grand Prix.

June
Rodriguez finished second with a P160 in the Dutch Grand Prix.

July
Rodriguez was killed at the wheel of a Ferrari sports car at Nuremberg in Germany.

August
Jo Siffert won the Austrian Grand Prix.

September
Peter Gethin, brought into the team to succeed Rodriguez, won the Italian Grand Prix.

October
Jo Siffert finished second in the United States Grand Prix, but later that month was killed at the wheel of a BRM in a minor Formula One race at Brands Hatch. At the American race at Watkins Glen the BRM team ran five cars, an omen of their misguided plans for the future.

1972
In December 1971 Louis Stanley held a press conference at the Paul Ricard circuit in France where he announced grandiose plans for 1972. To the more hardened journalists these appeared to verge on folly. BRM had already been criticised for running a team of five slow and uncompetitive cars in the 1971 American race, but now Stanley announced that the team would be racing with Marlboro sponsorship and would at most races field a grand total of six cars, three for the 'first-string' team

consisting of Jean-Pierre Beltoise, Peter Gethin and Howden Ganley and a 'second-string' consisting of Alex Soler-Roig (Marlboro-BRM-Espana), Helmut Marko (Marlboro-BRM-Austria) and Gijs van Lennep (Marlboro-BRM-Holland). In fact van Lennep's drive failed to materialise because of sponsorship problems, but throughout the season Stanley played 'musical chairs' with the BRM team cars and, in addition to the drivers named above, several others handled BRMs during the year: Reine Wisell (Argentine, Spanish, Monaco, German and Italian races only), Jack Oliver (British race only), Brian Redman (United States race only), Bill Brack (Canadian race only) and Vern Schuppan (two non-Championship races). During the early part of the season the more junior drivers raced the P153 cars in modified form, but the standard team car was the P160B which was a much-modified version of the 1971 car. The team also produced the new P180 designed by Tony Southgate, but although this made a number of appearances during the year and actually won a race, it was regarded as a failure and was abandoned at the end of the season.

January
Five BRMs ran in the Argentine Grand Prix. Two of them crashed and none finished in the first six.

April
Beltoise took second place in the *Daily Express* Trophy race at Silverstone.

May
Alex Soler-Roig had his second crash in only his second Formula One race of the season at Jarama and decided to retire from Grand Prix racing. Out of five starters not a single BRM finished the race. Later in the month Beltoise scored a freak victory in the Monaco Grand Prix which was run in torrential rain. This was BRM's only important victory of the season.

June
The more usual BRM pattern reasserted itself in the Belgian race at Nivelles where five cars were entered, one failed to start, two retired and the two survivors finished eight and tenth.

July
Helmut Marko was hit in the eye by a stone during the French Grand Prix

and suffered injuries which resulted in his retirement from racing. Out of five starters, the sole BRM finisher was Beltoise in fifteenth place. In the British race there were three starters and one finisher, Beltoise in eleventh place.

August
Ganley finished fourth in the German Grand Prix, one of BRM's best performances of the season.

October
Beltoise won the John Player Challenge Trophy at Brands Hatch with the BRM P180.

1973
Marlboro continued to sponsor BRM in 1973, but it was obvious that they were becoming dissatisfied with the team's lack of success. In 1973 BRM adopted a more restrained attitude to racing by entering only three cars for Beltoise, ex-Ferrari driver Clay Regazzoni and ex-March driver Niki Lauda. Tony Southgate had left the team and been replaced by Mike Pilbeam. There were no major developments for 1973 and the team continued to race the familiar V-12 cars in an even further modified form known as the P160E.

January
Of the three BRMs entered in the Argentine Grand Prix, two retired and the survivor driven by Clay Regazzoni finished a poor seventh.

February
BRM fortunes improved albeit marginally, in the Brazilian Grand Prix at Interlagos where Regazzoni finished sixth and Lauda eighth.

March
All three BRMs retired at Kyalami; Regazzoni collided with Hailwood's Surtees on the second lap and caught fire – he was rescued from the car unconscious, but with only minor burns, and Hailwood was later awarded the British Empire Medal for his efforts to rescue the Swiss driver.

April
Beltoise finished fifth in the Spanish Grand Prix at Barcelona.

May
Lauda finished fifth in the Belgian Grand Prix.

June
At Monaco Niki Lauda displayed the promise that was to lead to major victories for Ferrari the following year by holding third place until his gearbox broke on lap 21. Regazzoni retired and Beltoise crashed.

July
This unhappy saga continued at the French race where the three BRMs finished ninth, eleventh and twelfth. At Silverstone, scene of the British race, the highest-placed car was Regazzoni's in seventh position.

August
All three BRMs retired in the German Grand Prix.

September
By the Canadian Grand Prix the team had achieved no success and at this race Clay Regazzoni was dropped from the team because, in the words of team manager Tim Parnell: 'Mr Stanley has decided Regazzoni is to be rested – he hasn't been driving well recently.'

1974
So yet another season ended without BRM achieving any success. BRM had no major sponsorship in 1974, but Louis Stanley tried to argue that the team was better off without it. The cars were now painted green and silver, BRM signed up three French drivers, Beltoise, Henri Pescarolo and Francois Migault, and was in fact in receipt of some sponsorship from the Motul oil concern. There was also a new car, the much lighter P210, and it was hoped that Beltoise would find this less tiring to drive (he suffers from a severely weakened arm, the result of a bad accident early in his racing career).

March
Beltoise with the P201 took second place in the South African Grand Prix, an exceptionally encouraging performance.

April
Three cars ran in the Spanish Grand Prix, but the sole finisher was Pescarolo with an old P160 car who took twelfth place.

May
BRM fortunes looked up at Nivelles where Beltoise finished fifth with the P201. This should have been an omen of better times to come, but instead it was the Bourne team's last encouraging performance in 1974 and at Monaco later in the month all three BRM entries were eliminated.

June
The sad saga continued with all entries slow in practice, slow in the race and retiring at both Anderstorp in Sweden and Zandvoort in the Netherlands.

July
Nothing to boast of, but Francois Migault, an underrated French driver, battled on with his BRM to finish fourteenth in his National Grand Prix and this gave the team some measure of encouragement.

August
A spate of engine troubles in the German Grand Prix resulted in the appearance of only a single car for Beltoise in Austria. Despite this concentration of effort the P201 was yet again a victim of engine trouble early in the race.

September
By the Italian Grand Prix the team had built a total of four of the new and lighter P201 cars and at Monza fielded a full team of three. All three cars retired – two of them on the first lap of the race! Chris Amon was entered with a BRM in the Canadian Grand Prix, but both he and team-mate Beltoise were in and out of the pits with handling problems and after pitifully slow drives both were too far behind at the finish to be counted in the results. The following month Amon drove the sole BRM entered in the United States Grand Prix and finished ninth.

Post Script
In December 1974, at the end of BRM's twenty-fifth consecutive racing season, the Rubery Owen organisation finally lost patience with BRM's

persistent history of failure and wasted expenditure and the team was wound up. For BRM this was not quite the end of the road, for Louis Stanley announced that he was taking over the team; many of the staff at Bourne left the organisation, including team manager Tim Parnell and designer Mike Pilbeam and during 1975 one car was fielded as the 'Stanley-BRM'. At the Argentinian and Brazilian Grands Prix the driver of the sole P201 was Mike Wilds and although no success was gained, many critics were favourably impressed by Wild's performances. But his efforts were not good enough and for the South African race the wheel of the Stanley-BRM was taken by Bob Evans. Throughout the year the cars proved sadly deficient in power output and the team was forced to miss races to concentrate on engine development.

The chances of the Stanley-BRM team achieving success in the future appear slim indeed. Many enthusiasts would have preferred to see the name BRM disappear rather than watch the team struggle from failure to failure and there really seems little point in Stanley continuing such a hopeless, uphill struggle.

7

The Italian Grand Prix

Originally there was but one 'Grand Prix', the French Grand Prix which was first held at Le Mans in 1906, and it was not until after the first World War that other countries followed the French lead and organised their own national Grand Prix. The first to join the French race was the Spanish Grand Prix (held as a race for touring cars in 1913) and then came the Italian Grand Prix which was held at Brescia in September 1921 over a distance of 322 miles. This first race is also sometimes known as the Brescia Grand Prix.

Earlier in the year the European manufacturers had suffered a severe set-back at Le Mans where the French Grand Prix was won by Jimmy Murphy's American Duesenberg. By the Italian race the American team had returned to the New World, the Anglo-French Talbot team did not enter at Brescia and the 'Grand Prix' proved a dull little affair contested by only the Italian Fiat and French Ballot teams, both of which were racing straight-eight cars. With only six starters there was little to excite the spectators and the Fiats of Bordino and Wagner soon built up a good lead over the Ballots of Chassagne and Goux. The Fiats, however, were plagued by tyre troubles and Bordino was eliminated by mechanical problems on the fifteenth lap. Wagner was forced to stop at the pits for a wheel to be changed on five occasions and the Ballots, out of luck at races earlier in the year forged ahead.

One of the onlookers suggested that Wagner was stopping at the pits out of caution rather than dire necessity, thereby throwing away Fiat's chance of victory, and substantiated his argument by mysteriously producing three sound tyres which he claimed had been removed from the Frenchman's car. Hostility against Wagner was soon whipped up and one of the group of 'Italian patriots' mounted an oil drum and with sinister gestures demonstrated the fate that should befall any foreigner who threw away the chance of an Italian victory through cowardice. This pantomine was interrupted by the arrival in the pits of Wagner with yet another tyre shredded to ribbons and the crowd's hostility was rapidly replaced by a round of applause for the speed with which he and his mechanic effected the wheel-change. But all Wagner's efforts were to no avail and he was forced to settle for third place (there were only three finishers), some ten minutes behind the winning French car.

By 1922 a 2-litre capacity limit had replaced the 3-litre Grand Prix Formula adopted the previous year and the Italian Grand Prix had been transferred to what was to be its near-enough permanent home in Monza Park near Milan. The first race was held at Monza within six months of the start of excavations and the track itself had been constructed in the space of a mere 110 days. The course used was an exciting combination of road and banked track with a length of 6.214 miles and this same course was used for the next six races in the series.

A glittering entry had been received, but on race-day, 10th September, there were only eight starters, of which three were the works Fiat Tipo 804 6-cylinder cars which had made their debut in that year's French Grand Prix at Strasbourg. No other competitive works team entered and the Fiats of Bordino and Nazzaro dominated this 497-mile race which was run in a steady drizzle of rain. The third Fiat driven by Giaccone broke its clutch at the start. The small number of starters was a great disappointment for the organisers, especially so because the turn-out at the French Grand Prix in July had been much greater.

Fiat had abandoned their 6-cylinder cars in favour of a new straight-eight design by 1923, while the British Sunbeam concern was now racing 6-cylinder cars that were virtually identical to the 1922 Fiats. Sir Henry Segrave scored a brilliant victory for Sunbeam in the French Grand Prix, but, for reasons best known to themselves, the Anglo-French Sunbeam-Talbot-Darracq group declined to contest the Italian race. This was displeasing to Fiat, for although the Turin company was anxious to win at Monza, it also strongly desired a victory that was coupled with the defeat of its British rivals. Instead the opposition was limited to three American Millers of the type that had dominated the 1923 Indianapolis race, the very eccentric sleeve-valve French Voisins which at a casual glance resembled a rather primitive piece of farm machinery and the slightly less eccentric Rolland-Pilains from the same country (one was fitted with a so-called cuff-valve, ie single as opposed to double-sleeve-valve engine); the field was completed by one of the very advanced Benz rear-engined cars designed by Dr Rumpler. Alfa Romeo had entered a team of their new 6-cylinder P1 Grand Prix cars, but withdrew from the race after Sivocci's fatal crash in practice. This was ostensibly as a tribute to Sivocci, but in fact the P1s were very slow and uncompetitive. The Fiats gained their revenge, finishing one-two in the order Salamano-Nazzaro, but most of the other entries retired with mechanical trouble and Jimmy Murphy brought his Miller across the line in third place.

Nowadays Grand Prix teams run in every Championship race, unless there is some compelling reason why they should not (such as serious mechanical problems); it was rather different in the early 'twenties. Teams tended to run only if there was some inducement and there was at this time no Championship to lure them into chasing after points. The 1924 Monza race was scheduled to be run on 7th September and the only competitive entries had come from Alfa Romeo with four of their new straight-eight P2 cars (which had already won the French Grand Prix), three Fiats, and four new Mercedes cars designed by Dr Porsche. Bugatti, Delage and Sunbeam failed to enter, apparently concentrating their efforts on the San Sebastian Grand Prix later in the month because the pickings there would be easier (and Segrave duly won for Sunbeam). Any hopes of a good race at Monza were dashed when Fiat scratched just after the start of practice, alleging that two of their drivers were unfit because of arm injuries (ie they did not wish to be defeated by Alfa again), and, on the same day, Mercedes telegraphed to say that they would not be running because their new cars required more development work.

In the hope of whipping up some more entries in the meanwhile, the organisers postponed the race until 19th October. Their hopes were dashed again, for although the Mercedes team arrived, no Fiats turned up and no one else seemed interested in running in the race. The Alfa Romeos performed with perfection; they were much faster than the Mercedes and much more reliable. Antonio Ascari won this 497-mile race at an average speed of 98.79 mph (a speed not bettered until 1928) and he was followed across the line by the other Alfa drivers, Wagner, Campari and Minoia. Three-quarters of an hour elapsed before another driver took the chequered flag, one of the also-rans, Goux with his cuff-valve Schmid (a rebuild of the Rolland-Pilain referred to previously). The Mercedes were uncompetitive and the race was marred by the death of one of their drivers, Count Zborowski, who skidded off the track at the Lesmo curve on lap 48 and struck a tree. An enquiry was held after the race and, although the official verdict was that Zborowski had slid on oil dropped by one of the Alfas, it was common knowledge that all was not well with the roadholding of the Stuttgart cars.

In 1925, perhaps to persuade reluctant manufacturers to enter more races, a World Championship of Manufacturers was introduced with the results decided on the basis of points scored in the French, Belgian and Italian races and at Indianapolis. Alfa Romeo won at Spa (Delage was the only other team entered), but withdrew their cars from the French Grand Prix at Montlhéry following Ascari's fatal crash; the Delages of Benoist and Wagner took the first two places. Delage did not enter the Italian race held at Monza on 6th September and the principal opposition to the Alfas came from the Duesenbergs of Tommy Milton and Peter Kreis. Kreis with his straight-eight Duesenberg took the lead on the second lap, but his advantage was short-lived and next time round he crashed at the Lesmo curve. After five and a quarter hours' racing Brilli-Peri with a P2 Alfa Romeo took the chequered flag at an average of 94.76 mph, ahead of team-mate Campari and Constantini with a 1500 cc Bugatti. Alfa Romeo won the 1925 Manufacturers Championship.

A new 1500 cc Grand Prix Formula was introduced for the 1926 season and the Italian Grands Prix of the next three years were dull, poorly supported events that can be passed over quickly. In 1926 the race distance was reduced to 373 miles and Bugattis took the first two places and there were no other finishers. Neither Delage nor Talbot, the two leading contenders, entered the Monza race.

The French team did, however, contest the race the following year when Robert Benoist won with a Delage straight-eight in appallingly wet conditions. At this race the new straight-eight OM made its debut. The Brescia company had expended £25,000 on the construction of the new design which remarkably enough for a competition car had only a 3-speed gearbox. Morandi took second place for OM ahead of an American Miller and another OM was placed fourth. OM realised, however, that the cars were not truly competitive and made no attempt to develop them further.

By 1928 the 1500 cc Grand Prix Formula had been abandoned, the official Formula merely prescribed a minimum weight of 550 kg and a maximum of 750 kg, but racing, primarily because of economic conditions, was at a low ebb and most races were held as Formule Libre events. In the Italian race the Bugattis of Chiron and Nuvolari sandwiched the second-place Alfa Romeo P2 shared by its new owner, young Achille Varzi, with Giuseppe Campari.

There was no Italian Grand Prix in either 1929 or 1930, but Italy's national event was restored to the racing calendar in 1931, still on the Monza road and track circuit. Racing had undergone a transformation since the last Italian Grand Prix; race distances had been considerably lengthened (now to a minimum of ten hours which necessitated the use of two drivers) and although still run on a Formule Libre basis, Grand Prix racing was much better supported than in recent years. The principal contenders were Alfa Romeo, whose cars were entered on their behalf by Scuderia Ferrari formed in December 1929, and Maserati; the Maserati team did not often field works cars, and very many of their successes in the early 'thirties were gained by private owners.

In 1931 Alfa Romeo had introduced an exciting new straight-eight 2.3-litre car designed by Vittorio Jano. The sports version had run without success in the Mille Miglia race and at the Italian Grand Prix, held on 24th May, the racing version, which subsequently became known as the Monza, made its debut. Another Alfa innovation at this race was the Tipo A car powered by two 1750 cc engines, an immensely powerful unwieldy brute that aped an earlier Maserati design.

Luigi Arcangeli was killed when he crashed the Tipo A in practice at Monza; the damage to the car was slight and it was driven in the race by Tazio Nuvolari. After two laps of racing, when Nuvolari was in third place, Jano ordered the Tipo A to be withdrawn from the race. Why the car was withdrawn remains a mystery; it can hardly have been on the grounds of safety, for if Jano was concerned about this he would not have allowed the car to start the race. The principal opposition to the Monzas came from a brace of works Bugattis, but the French cars could not match the speed of the Alfas and the Monzas of Campari (partnered by Nuvolari after his Tipo A had been withdrawn) and Minoia/Borzacchini took the first two places; the surviving works Bugatti of Chiron/Varzi finished third.

In 1932 Scuderia Ferrari unveiled yet another new Alfa model at the Italian Grand Prix. The Monza was in reality a modified sports car, but the new Monoposto was an out-and-out single-seater racing car with a 2.6-litre straight-eight engine and was conspicuously faster than most of its rivals. The race distance was reduced to five hours and Nuvolari and veteran driver Campari were entered to drive Monopostos single-handed. Nuvolari went ahead at the start and was fighting off a challenge from Louis Chiron's

4.9-litre Bugatti when Fagioli with the twin-engined Maserati passed them both. Fagioli made a long pit stop. Chiron retired and Nuvolari went on to win the race at an average of 104.13 mph from the Maserati and Borzacchini's Alfa Romeo. For Alfa Romeo it was a remarkable feat to have won a Grande Epreuve with a new model two years in succession.

There was a change of roles in 1933, for Tazio Nuvolari left Scuderia Ferrari to drive a private Maserati, while Luigi Fagioli, previously the scourge of Alfa Romeo, was now driving the Milan cars for Scuderia Ferrari. The 1933 race was held on 10th September and devolved into a duel between Nuvolari with his 3-litre Maserati and the Monopostos driven by Fagioli and Chiron. Louis Chiron was leading the race when he retired with valve trouble and the famous combination of yellow jersey and red Maserati now had a 30-second lead over Fagioli's Alfa which was painted a more sombre shade of red. With only two laps to go to the finish the 'Flying Mantuan' was forced to stop for a wheel-change and Fagioli roared into the lead to win by a margin of 30 seconds. Fourteen years were to elapse before Alfa Romeo again won the Italian Grand Prix.

After the excitements of the Italian Grand Prix, the day at Monza turned to one of death and tragedy. The Monza Grand Prix was run in the afternoon on the 2.8-mile banked track only in three heats and a final. In the second heat Campari (Alfa Monoposto) and Borzacchini (Maserati) were battling for the lead when they both skidded on a pool of oil dropped in the first heat by Trossi's Scuderia Ferrari-entered Duesenberg. Campari, whose great ambition was to be an opera singer, was killed instantly, and Borzacchini died shortly afterwards. Yet another tragedy occurred in the final when Count Czaykowski crashed his Bugatti and was killed.

It was as a direct result of these fatalities that the organisers decided to use a slower course for the 1934 race. This 2.485-mile course, known as the Short Florio circuit, ran anti-clockwise and incorporated the slightly banked South Curve of the track circuit with chicanes to slow the cars, a section running diagonally to link up with the road circuit, the South Curve of the road circuit (this part taken in a clockwise direction), the pits road and an acute hairpin bend which led back on to the outer track and South Curve again. Since 1933 there had been another change of Formula and there was now a strictly observed maximum weight limit of 750 kg (1473 lb) without fuel, oil, water or tyres.

Two new and very serious contenders had taken Grand Prix racing by storm, the technically very advanced and very aerodynamic Mercedes-

Benz W25 and rear-engined Auto Union A-type cars; initially the German cars suffered from teething troubles, but they had achieved domination by the latter part of the 1934 season and trounced the Italian cars at Monza. The new course proved very tiring and drivers who had already retired were roped in to relieve their flagging team-mates. Victory went to the Mercedes-Benz of Rudolf Caracciola, partnered later in the race by Luigi Fagioli, and Auto Union took second place with a car shared by Hans von Stuck and the Prinz zu Leinigen. Varzi's Alfa Romeo held second place for a while, but retired with gearbox trouble, and the best that Scuderia Ferrari could manage was third and fourth places by Trossi/Comotti and Chiron (who drove solo) ahead of Tazio Nuvolari with a new 6-cylinder Maserati.

In 1935-6 yet another permutation of the Monza circuit was used, the 4.281-mile Florio road circuit which ran clockwise round the South Curve, took a diagonal turn inwards to join the road circuit and followed this through the road circuit; a total of five chicanes were incorporated to slow the cars. Four Mercedes and four Auto Unions were entered, and Tazio Nuvolari appeared with a new Alfa, the 8C-35 with independent suspension front and rear, a bulbous streamlined body and the Monoposto straight-eight engine in 3.8-litre form. A rare contender in this year's race was the streamlined V-8 Maserati, a car that was frequcntly entered but rarely appeared, in the hands of Philippe Etancelin. Caracciola led away for Mercedes at the start of the race, but one by one the Stuttgart cars retired, Etancelin wrecked the Maserati when the throttles jammed open at one of the chicanes and by lap 41 (there were 73 laps in all) von Stuck led for Auto Union with Nuvolari in hot, but futile pursuit. Nuvolari's Alfa expired in a cloud of blue smoke, and now, with only five cars left in the race, Tazio continued the chase with Dreyfus's 3.8-litre Monoposto. A valve broke on Nuvolari's new mount and he finished second on seven cylinders, 1 min 41 sec behind von Stuck's Auto Union. It was typical of Nuvolari's generosity that he should insist that all the prize money for second place should go to Dreyfus.

Mercedes-Benz were plagued with mechanical troubles with a new car in 1936 and did not enter the Italian Grand Prix. As usual Auto Union and Alfa Romeo were out in force and the Scuderia Ferrari entries included two new 12-cylinder 4.1-litre cars using the same chassis as the 8C-35. Young Bernd Rosemeyer was reaching the peak of his ability and driving superbly, but none of the other Auto Union *pilotes* could hold a candle to Nuvolari who, at long last, was at the wheel of a car that was near-enough competitive. Rosemeyer won at 84.10 mph and set the fastest lap, the great Nuvolari finished second (and, appropriately, was second fastest round Monza) and another Auto Union driven by Ernst von Delius finished third.

In 1936 Nuvolari had defeated the Auto Unions in the Coppa Ciano race on the Montenero circuit near Livorno (Leghorn) and the following year this course was chosen for the Italian Grand Prix. The reason was clear and no mere coincidence. Unfortunately Tazio was unable to repeat his 1936 performance, the Mercedes were in fine form, the Auto Unions only a fraction slower; this was one of the very few occasions on which Nuvolari lost interest in fighting a losing battle of catching the leaders, he pulled into the pits and handed his 12-cylinder Alfa over to Farina whose own car had already retired. The Mercedes W125 cars of Caracciola and Lang took the first two places, Rosemeyer (Auto Union) was third, Seaman (Mercedes) fourth and the Alfa of Nuvolari and Farina crossed the line in a rather hopeless seventh place.

For 1938 onwards the existing 750 kg Grand Prix Formula was scrapped in favour of a new and rather complicated Formula with a weight/capacity sliding scale having upper limits of 3000 cc supercharged and 4500 cc unsupercharged. Mercedes and Auto Union continued to dominate racing with 3-litre supercharged cars, Alfa Romeo's contribution to Grand Prix racing was now little more than a token effort and even Nuvolari deserted the Italian ranks to drive for Auto Union (to replace Rosemeyer who had been killed during a record-breaking attempt early in 1938). The Italian Grand Prix returned to Monza and was held on 11th September over a version of the Florio circuit with chicanes having a length of 4.345 miles.

It had taken the 'Flying Mantuan' some while to familiarise himself with the handling peculiarities of the rear-engined Auto Union, and the Mercedes had dominated earlier races in the season, but at Monza Nuvolari came into his own; four of the five Mercedes retired, as did the Auto Unions of von Stuck and Müller, and Nuvolari came through to win the last pre-war Italian Grand Prix at 96.76 mph; second place went to Giuseppe Farina who, perforce, drove a sluggish race with the slow but nicely handling 3-litre V-16 Alfa. In third place was the surviving Mercedes of Caracciola and von Brauchitsch; this car started the race with von Brauchitsch at the wheel, but the engine was running very hot and burning the driver's feet, and he was forced to take a break.

Following Hitler's invasion of Poland the 1939 Italian Grand Prix was cancelled and although Mussolini decided that everything would be all right and allowed motor racing to continue in 1940, he had changed his mind and gone chasing after what he thought would be an easy victory by September 1940. During the war years Monza was ravaged by use as a military depot, and park and circuit were shredded by caterpillar tracks. When the race was resumed in 1947, the damage had not yet been repaired and the first post-war Italian Grand Prix was staged on a 1.75-mile circuit round the site of the Milan fair (a similar but more tortuous circuit had already been used in 1946 for the Circuit of Milan).

The pre-war Grand Prix Formula had remained in force in 1946, but for the 1947 season it was replaced by a new Formula with capacity limits of 1500 cc supercharged and 4500 cc unsupercharged. The category for blown cars was identical to that for pre-war Voiturettes, a class in which both Alfa Romeo, with the Tipo 158 straight-eight cars introduced in 1938, and Maserati, with the 4-cylinder 4CL, were strong contenders. The big difference between the two *marques* was that Alfa Corse (the Alfa Romeo works team) was superbly organised, the cars were beautifully prepared and the team had a policy of constant development and improvement. In contrast Maserati left their representation to two private teams, Scuderia Milano and Scuderia Ambrosiana; the former's organisation was chaotic and their preparation work hasty and inadequate, and the Maserati design, which was in any case inferior to that of the Alfa, had been allowed to stagnate.

Alfa Romeo entered four cars in the 1947 race and took the first four places. There was, however, considerable dissension within the team because team-manager Battista Guidotti, apparently acting on instructions from the Alfa directors, usually dictated which of his drivers was to win. Farina was sacked from the team in 1946 for failing to obey orders, Jean-Pierre Wimille was suspended for defeating team-mate Varzi in the 1947 Belgian Grand Prix, and there were more ructions at Milan. It had been ordained that the winner should be Count Felice Trossi. Trossi disliked the system as much as his colleagues and, by way of silent protest, he merely toured round on the last lap, crossing the line just ahead of Varzi with his hands off the wheel and his goggles pushed up on his forehead to make it quite clear that he did not pretend to have beaten the great Achille Varzi fair and square. Consalvo Sanesi and Alessandro Gaboardi, the latter an Alfa mechanic included in the team for this one race, took third and fourth places ahead of one of the only two surviving Maseratis driven by Alberto Ascari.

In 1948 the Grand Prix was switched to a sinuous circuit in Valentino

Park, Turin; now the entry was very much more interesting and Alfa Romeo won, but rather less easily. Maserati had produced an improved, more powerful version of their 4-cylinder car which was known as the 'San Remo', but it was still no real match for the Alfas. The real sensation of the race was the V-12 Ferrari which was making its Grand Prix debut. This race was run in torrential rain and although Jean-Pierre Wimille with the latest and more powerful Alfa Romeo 158 led throughout to win at 70.38 mph, all went far from well for the other Alfa drivers; Sanesi crashed and buckled the front suspension of his 158 and Trossi retired with supercharger trouble. Second place was fought for in a furious duel between Villoresi (Maserati) and Raymond Sommer (Ferrari) and although the Maserati finally crossed the line $2\frac{1}{2}$ minutes ahead of its Maranello rival, its engine was very rough indeed and it is doubtful whether the car would have lasted another lap.

Monza was reopened on 17th October 1948 with the Monza Grand Prix held over the newly rebuilt road circuit which had a length of 3.915 miles. The winner was again Jean-Pierre Wimille with the Alfa Romeo 158. This same circuit was used for the 1949 Italian Grand Prix, but there were no Alfas entered as the Milan company had temporarily withdrawn from racing. The most successful contender was now Ferrari and the Maranello cars raced at Monza were much-improved versions of the V-12 cars with twin-stage supercharger, twin overhead camshafts per bank of cylinders and a much greater turn of speed. Ascari won the race with ease for Ferrari, team-mate Villoresi retired and Giuseppe Farina threw away what was a certain third place (second place after Villoresi's retirement) by withdrawing in a huff because he could not catch the V-12s with his much-modified Maserati-Milano. Second place in this 313-mile race went to 'Fi-fi' Etancelin, that great Maserati and Alfa Romeo driver of pre-war days, who was now at the wheel of a 4-5-litre unsupercharged Lago-Talbot.

Alfa Romeo returned to racing in 1950. During that season Ferrari switched to new 4500 cc unsupercharged V-12 cars that were as fast as their predecessors, but much more economical, thereby eliminating time-wasting refuelling stops; and racing witnessed the beginnings of a great Italian duel that persisted until the end of the 1951 season. In the opening laps of the 1950 race the Alfas of Farina and Fangio and the Ferrari of Ascari battled for the lead, but Ascari retired his Ferrari because of broken rocker gear and Fangio was eliminated by a seized gearbox. Ascari had led the race on two laps and if (there are always plenty of 'ifs' in motor racing) his Ferrari had held together he would have won the race on time saved over refuelling stops. Farina went on to win the race at 109.63 mph and clinched his victory in the first-ever Drivers' World Championship, while Ascari took over team-mate Serafini's unblown Ferrari and fought his way past veteran Luigi Fagioli's Alfa to finish second, a little over a minute in arrears.

Since Alfa Romeo had re-entered racing in 1946 the Grand Prix team had suffered but one defeat, in their first race in 1946 which was the St Cloud Grand Prix. But the thirsty, supercharged Alfa Romeos were now at the limit of their development, in 1951 auxiliary fuel tanks were installed here, there and everywhere in the team's efforts to cut out unnecessary refuelling stops and all the extra weight had adversely affected the handling. In contrast the unblown Ferrari which consumed fuel at the rate of 7–8 mpg compared with the Alfa's 1½ mpg was still a young design with plenty of scope for further development. While the grizzled stalwarts of the Alfa team clung grimly to their waning power, the young Ferrari team was hungry for victory and it was a matter of inevitability that Maranello would soon defeat the might of Milan. Alfa Romeo won the Swiss, Belgian and French races, but at Silverstone the ponderous Froilan Gonzalez, at the wheel of a less powerful 1950 Ferrari, trounced the Alfa team and scored a brilliant victory. At the Nürburgring, scene of the German Grand Prix, Ascari rubbed the lesson home with another Maranello win. Ferrari had now won on a medium-speed circuit and a slow, tortuous circuit and the question was whether the Ferraris could defeat the Alfas at Monza, a high-speed course, on which the ageing straight-eights were in their element.

At the start of the race Ascari and Fangio battled furiously for the lead, two of the Alfas were early victims of mechanical trouble and when Fangio's Alfa threw a tread and stopped at the pits for a wheel-change, it seemed that Ascari had an unassailable lead. Fangio rejoined the race and rose to third place before retiring with mechanical trouble. Nino Farina had taken over Bonetto's Alfa when the latter stopped to refuel; he rejoined the race in fourth place and began a feverish chase of the leaders, putting himself back on the same lap as Ascari's leading Ferrari, passing Villoresi to take third place and gaining as much as five seconds a lap on Gonzalez's second-place Ferrari. He had closed within thirty seconds of Gonzalez when he was forced to stop at the pits for a second refuel and a change of tyres.

Once again Nino embarked on his pursuit of the leaders, but on lap 70, ten laps from the finish, his engine coughed and spluttered and another refuelling stop was necessary. In fact the Alfa's main tank had split and as Farina accelerated away from the pits, the fuel could be seen spilling from the tail of the 158. Despite the fire hazard and because it was an Italian driver putting up a magnificent performance with an Italian car, Nino was not black-flagged and he finished a gallant third with the consolation of fastest lap at 120.97 mph. The final round in the World Championship was the Spanish Grand Prix in October; in this race the Ferraris were plagued by tyre failures and Fangio won for Alfa Romeo and secured the Drivers' Championship with 31 points to the 25 of Alberto Ascari.

On this final victory Alfa Romeo withdrew from Grand Prix racing. If Formula One had continued in its existing form there would have been a complete Ferrari landslide, for there was no other worthwhile opponent to the cars from Maranello. Although the existing Formula One still had two years to run, it was decided to hold all World Championship races to Formula Two rules, ie for cars of up to 2000 cc unsupercharged. In fact Ferrari remained dominant with his 4-cylinder cars and Ascari won the Drivers' Championship in both 1952 and 1953. In 1952 the Ferraris were almost completely unopposed before the Italian Grand Prix in which Froilan Gonzalez drove a new 6-cylinder twin-plug Maserati. Ascari won, but the Maserati was as fast as his Ferrari, shared fastest lap and lost the race only because its fuel tank had insufficient capacity for Gonzalez to run through the race without a pit stop.

The following season Maserati put up a very stiff fight at all the Championship races with a team of much-improved cars and drivers who included Juan Fangio. The Argentinian had missed most of the important 1952 races following a bad accident at Monza in June. Throughout the 1953 season the Ferraris succeeded in retaining the upper hand, often by only a very narrow margin, and it was not until the Italian Grand Prix that Officine Alfieri Maserati succeeded in beating them. Throughout the 1953 race there was a three-cornered fight for the lead between Ascari and Farina with Ferraris and Fangio at the wheel of a Maserati; for most of the race Marimon, the young Argentinian Maserati driver, tagged along with them to give his team-leader moral support even though he was several laps in arrear after a pit stop. As the race drew to a close Ascari and Farina seemed more and more firmly entrenched in first and second places and Fangio's prospects of passing them were slim. At the very last corner of the last lap, however, Ascari made a rare mistake and spun his Ferrari; Marimon's Maserati slammed into the stricken Maranello car, Farina spun on to the grass to avoid a collision and the wily Fangio sneaked through on the inside to score Maserati's only Championship race victory of the season.

For 1954 both the existing Formula One and Formula Two were abolished and replaced by a new Grand Prix Formula for cars of up to 2500 cc unsupercharged. Both Ferrari and Maserati raced cars that were developments of their Formula Two models, but the German Mercedes-Benz team re-entered racing with completely new, very complex, very fast and superbly prepared straight-eight cars. The first of the new Mercedes had streamlined bodywork and they scored a devastating victory on their debut at the French Grand Prix. Ferrari fought back and won the British race where the streamlined bodies of the German cars proved a severe disadvantage. At the German Grand Prix the Mercedes team produced a version of their straight-eight with conventional unstreamlined body and Fangio drove this to victory at both the Nürburgring and in the Swiss Grand Prix. By the Italian race the Italian team were still struggling to regain their supremacy, but much of the spirit had gone and they were now almost reconciled to defeat.

At Monza, Mercedes-Benz reverted to the streamlined cars and the opposition included Ferraris driven by Alberto Ascari and Froilan Gonzalez, and Maseratis for Stirling Moss and Luigi Villoresi, that grizzled veteran of the racing circuits. All four drivers battled with Fangio's Mercedes for the lead, three of them retired with mechanical trouble, but young Stirling Moss forged an advantage that Fangio could not challenge; he seemed all set for scoring his first-ever World Championship race victory when his Maserati ran its bearings, not through over-driving, but through a cracked pipe that allowed air to enter the lubrication system. It was only too typical of Stirling's sheer guts and determination that while Fangio cruised to an unexpected victory, a victory that he freely conceded belonged morally to Moss, the Maserati driver pushed his car across the line into tenth place.

For the 1955 Italian race the newly rebuilt banked track was used for the first time (the original had been demolished in 1939) and the use of this extended the circuit length to 6.214 miles. The Stuttgart domination of racing persisted in 1955 and at that year's Monza race the Mercedes *Stromlinienwagen* of Juan Fangio won from an unstreamlined Mercedes driven by Piero Taruffi. In 1955 Stirling Moss was a member of the Mercedes team, but he retired with gearbox trouble in the Italian race.

Mercedes-Benz withdrew from racing at the end of the 1955 season and Formula One reverted to the more familiar situation of an all-Italian duel between Ferrari and Maserati. Ferrari was now racing V-8 cars designed by

Vittorio Jano for the Lancia concern. Lancia had withdrawn from racing in June 1955 because of the combination of the death of their leading driver Alberto Ascari and their rapidly deteriorating financial situation. The Lancia D50 cars had been handed over to Ferrari who had modified them, doing his best to conceal their original identity, and raced them throughout 1956-7 with a strong team of drivers that included (in 1956 only) Juan Fangio. For the 1956 Italian race the Maserati team produced a new and lower-built version of their familiar 6-cylinder cars, two of which were driven by Stirling Moss and French ace Jean Behra.

The tyres of the Ferrari entries proved incapable of withstanding the stresses and strains set up by the new banking, and its bumpy concrete surfaces caused steering-arm failures on three of the V-8 cars and suspension failure on many other cars. Both Castellotti and Musso brought their Lancia-Ferraris into the pits with tyre failures early in the race, de Portago and Castellotti retired and Juan Fangio's car stood for a long time in the pits while a broken steering arm was replaced. By half-distance Moss led for Maserati from the Lancia-Ferraris of Luigi Musso and Peter Collins. The Lancia-Ferraris had been called into the pits for a precautionary tyre check and Peter Collins handed his car and his chances of winning the World Championship to Juan Fangio with the comment, 'I've got plenty of opportunity in the future.'

There was more drama when Moss's Maserati ran out of fuel on the course and only managed to get back to the pits after private 'Maser' driver Piotti had given it a nudge that set it rolling. While Moss was in the pits, Musso flashed by into the lead, but the young Italian's hopes of victory were shattered three laps from the finish when a steering arm broke and the Lancia-Ferrari slithered helplessly off the track. Moss went on to win the race from Juan Fangio whose second place, shared with Collins, gave him enough points to ensure his fourth World Championship. On the morning after the race Moss's Maserati was taken back to Monza for testing. It was discovered that only a couple of pints of fuel remained in the tank and when more was poured in, it poured straight out again through a crack in the alloy!

Juan Fangio joined the Maserati team for 1957 and won the first three Championship races of the season. The scales were tipped against the Italian team in the British race at Aintree where Stirling Moss took over team-mate Brooks's Vanwall to score the *marque*'s first Championship race victory. At the Nürburgring, Fangio won again and on this circuit the Vanwalls were plagued by suspension problems. An addition to this Championship series that year was the Pescara Grand Prix and here Moss scored his second victory for Vanwall. The battle continued, with Ferrari now very much an also-ran, at the Monza race which was run on the road circuit only. Here Moss and Fangio waged a titanic battle which was eventually settled in favour of the British driver for the second year in succession. The Argentinian had to settle for second place, but had nevertheless accumulated sufficient points to win his fifth World Championship.

Maserati withdrew from Grand Prix racing at the end of the 1957 season and in 1958 Ferrari raced his new Dino V-6 cars which were largely the work of the great Vittorio Jano. Apart from the first two Championship races of the season, in which rear-engined Cooper-Climax cars scored unexpected victories, the year's racing was fought out between Vanwall and Ferrari; the British cars retained their ascendency in the early part of the season, but the Italian V-6s improved in both speed and reliability as the season progressed. Vanwall won the Dutch, Belgian, German and Portuguese races, the Ferraris were victorious at Reims and Silverstone and Moss and Hawthorn were neck and neck in the World Championship. A keen battle was expected and was witnessed in the Italian Grand Prix at Monza. The fight was furious, Moss was eliminated by mechanical trouble, but Tony Brooks with his Vanwall came through to win the race despite a pit stop, from the Ferraris of Hawthorn and Phil Hill. Moss won the final round of the Championship at Casablanca, but Hawthorn finished second and took the Drivers' Championship by a margin of but one point.

In 1959 the rear-engined Cooper-Climax was the dominant *marque,* Vanwall had now withdrawn from racing and the front-engined Ferraris were overshadowed by their British rivals. Jack Brabham with a works Cooper was leading the Drivers' Championship and Stirling Moss was driving a private Cooper for Rob Walker. At Monza it was thought that the race would be run at such a furious pace that both the Ferraris and the Coopers would have to stop at the pits for wheel-changes. If this were necessary, the Coopers, which were fitted with bolt-on wheels, would be at a severe disadvantage, while the Ferraris would save valuable seconds because of the speed with which their wheels with knock-off hubs could be changed. In fact the Cooper drivers were planning to conserve their tyres and drive through the race non-stop. Nevertheless they assiduously practised wheel-changes and succeeded in deluding the Ferrari team into a state of false security. Moss was content to sit on the tail of Phil Hill's Ferrari in the race, cornering and accelerating gently and leaving the Maranello driver to set the pace.

Inevitably, one by one, the Ferrari drivers stopped at the pits for their wheel-changes and Moss and Brabham moved up into the first two places. Phil Hill fought back and although he passed Brabham before the finish, Moss won the race at 124.38 mph, a speed that indicated that the modern Monza road circuit was a fast course by any standard.

Nevertheless the organisers decided to revert to the combined road and track circuit in 1960, a move that thoroughly displeased the British entrants. None of the British teams were prepared to enter the race and used the feeble excuse that their cars had not been designed for track racing, a silly proposition that Cooper debunked themselves when they ran a slightly modified 1960 car for Brabham at Indianapolis the following year. The real motives behind the failure are far from clear, but one thing was sure, that they had nothing to lose by not entering, for Brabham and Cooper had their respective Championships in the bag on the strength of wins earlier in the season. In the absence of the British contingent the Ferraris were completely unopposed and the front-engine and outdated Dinos of Phil Hill, Richie Ginther and Willy Mairesse cruised into the first three places.

Part of the British teams' attitude over the 1960 Monza race may have stemmed from the fact that the Italians supported the new 1500 cc Grand Prix Formula that came into force in 1961, while the British teams opposed it (and had left their efforts to build new engines too late for them to be ready before 1962). Grand Prix racing in 1961 was Ferrari-dominated and the only races Maranello lost were the Monaco and German Grands Prix which Stirling Moss with an outdated Lotus won on sheer driving ability. The Monza race was again held on the combined road and banked track circuit and this year the British teams entered without complaint. It was a sad race for Ferrari, for although Phil Hill won with one of the Commendatore's rear-engined V-6 cars, the other four Maranello entries were eliminated and one of these in very tragic circumstances. On the second lap there was a collision between Jim Clark's Lotus and 'Taffy' von Trips' Ferrari at the Parabolica curve; the Ferrari was hurled up the grass bank, ejecting the driver, and smashed against the wire-mesh fence on which many of the spectators were leaning. Von Trips and eleven onlookers were killed and many others were badly injured.

By 1962 all the British teams were racing cars powered by new V-8 engines; BRM used their own unit and Cooper, Brabham, Lola and Lotus all relied on the Coventry-Climax. The new British cars were more than a match for the Italian opposition and Graham Hill drove BRMs to his first

World Championship. The Monza race was once more run on the road circuit only and provided a remarkable display of BRM speed and reliability; Hill and Ritchie Ginther with the Bourne cars led throughout and took the first two places ahead of Bruce McLaren's Cooper.

It had been the intention to hold the 1963 race on the combined road and banked track circuits, but this was abandoned after Bob Anderson's Lola suffered an accident on the banking in practice. Existing practice times were cancelled and the 1963 race and all subsequent events have been held on the road circuit only. The British domination continued that year with a victory by Jim Clark at the wheel of a monocoque Lotus from Ginther's BRM and McLaren's Cooper.

After 1961 Ferrari had a miserable time in 1500 cc Grand Prix racing and 1964 was the only season in which the team's fortunes looked up. At Monza, Ferrari driver John Surtees was in terrific form and scored an impressive victory over Bruce McLaren (Cooper), a consistent finisher in the first three at Monza, and team-mate Bandini. Surtees was the winner of that year's Drivers' Championship. By 1965 the Ferrari team had sunk back into mediocrity and the year's racing was largely dominated by Jim Clark and the latest version of the monocoque Lotus which was known as the 33. The BRM was still a force to be reckoned with, however, and at Monza the Bourne V-8s took the first two places ahead of Gurney's Brabham. Graham Hill was all set to win the race, but on the last lap but one he got 'crossed up' at one of the corners and his young team-mate Jackie Stewart went ahead to score his first Championship race victory.

The year 1965 was the last year of the 1500 cc Formula and it was replaced by a new Grand Prix Formula with a capacity limit of 3000 cc; this Formula has proved successful in terms of both spectator appeal and technical innovation and remains in force. During 1966 Jack Brabham at the wheel of his own Repco-powered cars proved almost unbeatable, but Monza was one circuit on which he failed to score a victory. The V-12 Ferraris were undoubtedly the fastest cars and although Maranello lacked the drivers with ability to exploit the car's potential on tortuous circuits, Monza was one circuit on which the less able *pilote* could put his foot down and take full advantage of the power at his disposal. In 1966 the race was won by Lodovico Scarfiotti at the wheel of a V-12 Ferrari and the similar car of Mike Parkes took second place. Nevertheless the name Brabham still featured in the results and Denny Hulme drove one of his boss's cars into third place.

Colin Chapman unveiled his tremendously potent and technically very advanced Ford-powered Lotus 49 cars in 1967, but in their first season they were plagued by teething troubles and often failed to make it to the finish. In the 1967 Monza race the failure of the 49s opened the door for John Surtees who scored his only race victory with the Japanese Honda, a bulky, ponderous car with indifferent handling and a poor finishing record at most circuits. The 1968 race was the first to be won by a Ford-powered car, but the first of four in the space of six seasons. Monza was now little more than a high-speed flat-out bash with the drivers constantly slip-streaming each other and jockeying for position. Tactics, speed and reliability were now the dominant factors and in 1968 the survivor of the fittest was Denny Hulme, now at the wheel of one of Bruce McLaren's own cars.

Jackie Stewart won the 1969 race with a Matra-Ford after a close fight that was settled at only the last corner when the canny Scotsman succeeded in pulling out a narrow advantage over Jochen Rindt and Matra team-mate Beltoise. Poor Rindt was killed in practice for the following year's race and Stewart, mentally shattered by the death of his close friend, drove a race of determination, but lacking in spirit, to finish a sweat-soaked second with his rather uncompetitive March-Ford. The winner was Clay Regazzoni with the new flat-12 Ferrari and this new Maranello car scored a run of four victories in 1970; unfortunately these proved a mere flash in the pan and by the beginning of the 1971 season the Ford-powered cars had regained the upper hand.

In 1971 Jackie Stewart drove Tyrrell's new car to his second World Championship, but he was out of luck at Monza where the winner was the improbable combination of Peter Gethin and a V-12 BRM. It had seemed that after five years of dismal failure the BRM star was in the ascendent in 1971, and Jo Siffert also scored a victory for the *marque* at the Österreichring. Unfortunately both of BRM's leading drivers, Rodrigüez and Siffert, were killed in 1971 and the *marque*'s promise of consistent success faded completely the following year. The all-conquering car/driver combination in 1972 was the distinctive black and gold John Player Special (née Lotus 72) with Emerson Fittipaldi at the wheel. Because of legal complications following Rindt's fatal accident in 1970, John Player Team Lotus was fearful of the arrest of Colin Chapman and the impounding of the cars and as a result only a single JPS was entered in the 1972 race under the name of World-Wide

Racing; the driver was Emerson Fittipaldi who was hungrily seeking points to clinch his first Drivers' Championship.

The organisers of the Monza were fearful that the close slip-streaming of recent races would result in a serious accident and in order to prevent such a tragedy there were long-term plans for major modifications to the circuit. As a temporary measure two chicanes to slow the cars were introduced in 1972; these were situated at the ends of the pits on the start/finish straight and just before the apex of the Ascari curve on the back leg of the circuit. Stewart's Tyrrell failed at the start, the early Ferrari domination soon evaporated and Fittipaldi went ahead to win the race from Mike Hailwood (Surtees-Ford) and Denny Hulme (McLaren-Ford).

For 1973 similar 'temporary' modifications were incorporated in the circuit and the race provided one of the finest displays of driving by Jackie Stewart in his long and distinguished career. Jackie did not win the race, but after a pit stop to replace a punctured tyre fought his way back to finish fourth behind the JPS entries of Peterson and Fittipaldi and Pete Revson's McLaren. It was perhaps indicative of the conflicts within the Lotus camp that Peterson was not instructed to ease off and let his Brazilian team-mate through into the lead and thereby preserve Fittipaldi's chances of winning the Drivers' Championship. Stewart now had the Championship in the bag with a total of 69 points and Fittipaldi, in second place with 48 points, could amass only a total of 66 if he won the season's two remaining races. In 1974 Niki Lauda delighted the very patriotic Italian crowd by leading for the first twenty-nine laps with his flat-12 Ferrari, but the Maranello entry's engine failed and Ronnie Peterson went ahead to win for the John Player Lotus team.

The Monza road circuit, overshadowed by the crumbling, cracking, spider-infested, bleached white remains of the now-derelict banked track, and enveloped in a riot of ragged trees and sprawling uncut grass, is one of the most important centres of European motor racing; it is a circuit at which the spectators, fenced away from the track by wire netting, have only the briefest view of the cars as they flash by, yet at every race Italian patriotism and devotion to the *marque* Ferrari run riot. The authorities responsible for the Monza Municipal Park are reluctant to sanction extensive modifications to the circuit as this would involve extensive tree-felling, but in the passage of time they will no doubt relent, Monza will be modified to take account of the changing face of racing and the circuit will be the home of the Italian Grand Prix for many years to come.

Results

Year	*Distance and Circuit*	*Winner*	*Speed*
1921	322 miles (Brescia)	J Goux (Ballot)	89.94 mph
1922	497 miles (Monza)	P Bordino (Fiat)	86.90 mph
1923	497 miles (Monza)	C Salamano (Fiat)	91.03 mph
1924	497 miles (Monza)	A Ascari (Alfa Romeo)	98.79 mph
1925	497 miles (Monza)	G Brilli-Peri (Alfa Romeo)	94.82 mph
1926	373 miles (Monza)	'Sabipa' (Bugatti)	85.88 mph
1927	311 miles (Monza)	R Benoist (Delage)	90.05 mph
1928	373 miles (Monza)	L Chiron (Bugatti)	99.36 mph
1931	10 hours (Monza)	G Campari / T Nuvolari (Alfa-Romeo)	96.79 mph
1932	5 hours (Monza)	T Nuvolari / G Campari (Alfa Romeo)	104.09 mph
1933	311 miles (Monza)	L Fagioli (Alfa Romeo)	108.58 mph
1934	311 miles (Monza)	R Caracciola / L Fagioli (Mercedes-Benz)	108.58 mph
1935	313 miles (Monza)	H von Stuck (Auto Union)	85.18 mph
1936	313 miles (Monza)	B Rosemeyer (Auto Union)	84.10 mph
1937	224 miles (Livorno)	R Caracciola (Mercedes-Benz)	81.59 mph
1938	261 miles (Monza)	T Nuvolari (Auto Union)	96.76 mph
1947	214 miles (Milan)	C F Trossi (Alfa Romeo)	70.34 mph
1948	224 miles (Turin)	J-P Wimille (Alfa Romeo)	70.38 mph
1949	313 miles (Monza)	A Ascari (Ferrari)	105.09 mph
1950	313 miles (Monza)	G Farina (Alfa Romeo)	109.63 mph
1951	313 miles (Monza)	A Ascari (Ferrari)	115.45 mph
1952	313 miles (Monza)	A Ascari (Ferrari)	109.80 mph
1953	313 miles (Monza)	J M Fangio (Maserati)	110.62 mph
1954	313 miles (Monza)	J M Fangio (Mercedes-Benz)	111.91 mph
1955	311 miles (Monza)	J M Fangio (Mercedes-Benz)	128.42 mph
1956	311 miles (Monza)	S Moss (Maserati)	129.73 mph
1957	313 miles (Monza)	S Moss (Vanwall)	120.27 mph
1958	250 miles (Monza)	C A S Brooks (Vanwall)	121.21 mph
1959	257 miles (Monza)	S Moss (Cooper-Climax)	124.38 mph
1960	311 miles (Monza)	P Hill (Ferrari)	132.06 mph
1961	267 miles (Monza)	P Hill (Ferrari)	130.08 mph
1962	307 miles (Monza)	G Hill (BRM)	123.62 mph
1963	307 miles (Monza)	J Clark (Lotus-Climax)	127.24 mph
1964	279 miles (Monza)	J Surtees (Ferrari)	127.77 mph
1965	272 miles (Monza)	J Stewart (BRM)	130.46 mph
1966	243 miles (Monza)	L Scarfiotti (Ferrari)	135.93 mph
1967	243 miles (Monza)	J Surtees (Honda)	140.50 mph

The Italian Grand Prix

Year	*Distance and Circuit*	*Winner*	*Speed*
1968	243 miles (Monza)	D Hulme (McLaren-Ford)	145.41 mph
1969	243 miles (Monza)	J Stewart (Matra-Ford)	146.96 mph
1970	243 miles (Monza)	C Regazzoni (Ferrari)	147.07 mph
1971	196 miles (Monza)	P Gethin (BRM)	150.76 mph
1972	197 miles (Monza)	E Fittipaldi (JPS-Ford)	131.61 mph
1973	197 miles (Monza)	R Peterson (JPS-Ford)	132.63 mph
1974	187 miles (Monza)	R Peterson (JPS-Ford)	135.10 mph

The All-American Eagle

American contenders in Grand Prix racing have, unfortunately, been few and far between. As has been mentioned in an earlier chapter, an American Duesenberg won the 1921 French Grand Prix and Miller cars made occasional appearances in European Grands Prix during the 'twenties and early 'thirties, but it was not until post-war days that there was a serious American Grand Prix contender.

In 1960 Lance Reventlow, son of Woolworth millionairess Barbara Hutton, appeared on the European racing scene with his team of Scarab Grand Prix cars. The Scarabs were front-engined at a time when racing was dominated by the rear-engined Cooper and Lotus cars, they were far too heavy and were very slow, and the team was completely lacking in Grand Prix experience. After a few very unsuccessful appearances Reventlow decided to cut his losses and returned to the United States. The Scarabs reappeared in 3-litre form for the Inter-Continental Formula introduced the following season, and also built a rear-engined Inter-Continental Formula car before finally withdrawing from all forms of racing in 1962.

The Scarabs were American-designed and built, whereas the next single-seater team in Grand Prix racing to run under the American colours used what were basically British cars. In 1962 American enthusiast Hugh Powell acquired the assets of the Emeryson company, a small constructor that had built a number of Formula One cars powered by Coventry-Climax and Maserati 4-cylinder engines. The Emeryson, fitted with the much more powerful V-8 Climax engine, became the Scirocco and was raced in 1963 in American white and blue colours with Tony Settember and Ian Burgess as drivers. Little success came the team's way and the best performance before

Scirocco withdrew from racing at the end of the 1963 season was a second place by September in the non-Championship Austrian Grand Prix.

The first American team to make a really serious impact on Grand Prix racing was Dan Gurney's All-American Racers organisation which entered Formula One in 1966, the first year of the current Formula for unsupercharged cars of up to 3000 cc. Dan Gurney had a long and distinguished career as a driver before combining this role with that of entrant. He had driven for the works Ferrari team in 1959, finishing second in the German Grand Prix at Avus and third in the Portuguese race, and for 1960 had switched to BRM. His year with Bourne was hopelessly unsuccessful, and for 1961 the lanky Californian changed horses once more and for the next two seasons was seen at the wheel of Porsche single-seaters. With the air-cooled silver cars he finished a joint third in the 1961 Drivers' World Championship and he won the French and Solitude Grands Prix in 1962.

Porsche withdrew from Grand Prix racing at the end of that year and Dan then signed up to handle Jack Brabham's new Climax-powered turquoise single-seaters. Although Gurney was a very hard driver with little sympathy for the mechanics of his car and the Brabhams were neither the fastest nor the most reliable of Formula One machinery, he won the French and Mexican Grands Prix in 1964 and he took three thirds and two second places the following year.

The plan to race a team of American-inspired Grand Prix cars was originally concocted jointly by Gurney and fellow-American driver and Cobra constructor Carroll Shelby. Shelby, however, withdrew from the project during its early days and the dark blue and silver Eagle became Gurney's responsibility alone. Although American-financed and inspired, the All-American team was based at Ashford in Kent where it had almost palatial workshop facilities. The V-12 engine was designed and developed by Harry Weslake (responsible for Jaguar and Vanwall cylinder head designs and the recent Ford V-12 engine derived from the Eagle unit) and the Eagle chassis was the work of former Lotus designer Len Terry. The team also competed in United States Automobile Club races with a car of basically similar design from premises at Santa Ana in California.

Terry closely followed Lotus practice in the design of the Eagle chassis which was a riveted light alloy monocoque with front suspension by lower wishbones, upper rocking arms and coil springs and rear suspension by upper links, reversed lower wishbones, long tubular radius arms and coil springs. Outboard disc brakes were fitted front and rear and there were

15-inch alloy wheels. Transmission was by a Hewland 5-speed and reverse gearbox in unit with the final drive. A conspicuous and unusual feature of the design was that the upper rocking arms of the front suspension were inclined rearwards (they were at right-angles to the chassis on the Lotus and other designs), an arrangement which permitted the front bulkhead of the monocoque to be further towards the front of the car, thereby providing extra cockpit room for the very tall Gurney without increasing the length of the wheelbase. Almost equally conspicuous was the very high standard of workmanship in the chassis construction.

The V-12 engine was a unit of exceptional promise and although it was much more difficult and expensive to manufacture than the rival Cosworth, if the team had persisted with the design it could well have proved a match for the Ford-financed unit. Keith Duckworth of Cosworth has himself said, '. . . the Gurney-Weslake engine . . . was a well-designed motor. I liked the design of that engine and I thought that it could well have worked. However from what I've heard that unit was a notable example of a good basic design which was probably rather difficult to manufacture. In fact it was manufactured in such a way as to make maintenance extremely difficult.'

This 60-degree V-12 unit had a capacity of 2997 cc (72.8 × 60.3 mm); the specification included twin overhead camshafts per bank of cylinders driven by a train of gears from the front of the engine, four valves per cylinder and single-plug ignition with the inlet ports in the vee of the engine and the exhausts ports outside. The engine was of very compact construction with a single cast cam cover for each pair of camshafts and small, light valves and valve gear. Lucas fuel injection was fitted with the metering unit driven by a toothed belt from the rear of the right-hand inlet camshaft. There were two exhausts per bank of cylinders with megaphone ends. The claimed power output for this engine was 420 bhp at 10,000 rpm, but it was undoubtedly much lower when the engine was first raced.

There was considerable surprise, however, when it was learned early in 1966 that Dan Gurney was hustling round trying to buy up as many of the old Coventry-Climax 2.7-litre FPF 4-cylinder engines as he could lay his hands on. These engines were completely obsolete and had not been used seriously since 1960 when they had dominated the last year of the old 2500 cc Grand Prix Formula. Subsequently many of these units were enlarged to 2.7-litres for Inter-Continental Formula racing and they had also been used in a number of sports cars. Gurney's interest in the FPF stemmed from the fact that there had been delays in the development of the V-12 engine at

Weslake's workshops at Rye in Sussex and for most of the 1966 season the team was forced to rely on the outdated 4-cylinder units.

The Eagle made its debut with Gurney at the wheel in the Dutch Grand Prix on 12th June, but it was certainly not an impressive first outing. In practice the car was plagued by damper problems which necessitated all-night work by the mechanics on the eve of the race, Gurney was slowest of the fifteen starters and in the race he motored so slowly that he completed only 24 of the 28 laps, too few to be classified as a finisher. At the French Grand Prix held on the high-speed Reims circuit the Eagle displayed somewhat better form; although still well to the back of the grid after slow practice laps and never up with the leaders in the race, Gurney kept going steadily to finish fifth.

The steady improvement in the Eagle's performance continued in practice for the British race which was held at Brands Hatch and here Gurney lapped fast enough to take a place on the front row of the grid. He was lying second at the end of the first lap of the race and third on the second lap, but then slowed off in a cloud of blue smoke and pulled into the pits to retire with a broken piston on lap 9. Only a week later the Grand Prix circus was at Zandvoort for the Dutch race and here Dan Gurney maintained form by lapping in 1 min 28.8 sec (fifth fastest and faster than Jim Clark's circuit record). In the race Gurney was able to mix it with the leaders until lap 19 when he pulled out of fifth place and into the pits with a boiling engine. He rejoined the race, but his Climax engine was now sounding very rough and throwing out ominous clouds of blue smoke and he retired at the Tarzan hairpin on lap 24. By this stage in the car's development most of the 'bugs' had been eliminated from the chassis design, the car handled well and, engine apart, was proving the epitome of reliability. It was only too obvious, however, that the old Climax engines were not up to the job and no success would come the Eagle's way until the V-12 engine was raceworthy. At the Nürburgring the story was the same; the Eagle went well in practice and the race and Gurney seemed all set for fourth place when the condenser came adrift and resulted in complete electrical failure. Dan managed to sort the trouble out and rejoined the race to finish seventh.

At the Italian Grand Prix the Eagle team ran a car fitted with the new V-12 engine for the first time. This was in fact the very first of the V-12s to be completed, it had been run in testing very little and, rather as expected, was plagued by teething troubles in practice. Although Gurney qualified as a starter, he was on the back row of the grid with a time of 1 min 39.1 sec compared with the 1 min 31.3 sec of pole-position man Mike Parkes (Ferrari). No sooner had the flag fallen for the start of the race than Gurney pulled into the pits with engine trouble. He later rejoined the race and completed 24 laps before retiring because of very high oil temperature. At this race a 4-cylinder Eagle was entered for Phil Hill, but it failed to qualify as a starter.

There remained only the two Transatlantic rounds of the Championship and at the United States Grand Prix at Watkins Glen All-American Racers fielded two cars, a V-12 for Gurney and a 2.7 Climax-powered car for Bob Bondurant (Hill was in hospital for an operation). Since Monza the team had not track-tested the cars, so, perhaps not surprisingly, neither went well in practice. Bondurant dropped out early in the race with suspension problems and Gurney was eliminated by distributor-drive failure. Even so Dan won $3,100 in prize money and Bondurant $2,900! There was, however, no starting money paid at this race. At Mexico City the two Eagle drivers swapped cars in practice because the V-12 was pumping out its oil and Dan succeeded in bringing the 'four' across the line in fifth place. Poor Bondurant was plagued by an engine power loss, the fuel was vapourising badly and after trailing round at the tail of the field he retired on lap 24.

It had been a dismal first season for All-American Racers – and an expensive one – but at this stage of the 3000 cc Formula several other constructors were in exactly the same position; the new Lotus was not yet ready, the H-16 BRM was hopelessly unreliable and the only difference between AAR and these teams was that the American concern had no obsolescent model to fall back on when the latest cars gave trouble in practice!

Despite intensive development work on the V-12 engine at Rye, the unit still could not be relied on at the beginning of the 1967 season and at the South African race held at Kyalami on 2nd January Gurney drove a car fitted with the old Climax engine. As the faster cars fell by the wayside, Gurney rose to fifth place, but the American was out of luck and he retired on lap 44 when the left-hand rear inner wishbone mounting broke away from the chassis.

By the Race of Champions at Brands Hatch on 12th March most of the Eagle's problems had been resolved and, in the words of *Motor Sport*: 'The Eagle team were in fine form, confident of their cars, engines and drivers . . .' At this race two V-12s were entered for Gurney and Richie Ginther who had previously driven for the Honda team. In practice the Eagles went superbly, Gurney was fastest in 1 min 32.2 sec and he and Ginther sandwiched Surtees' Honda on the front row of the grid. This race was run in two 10-lap heats and a 40-lap final and Gurney won both heats and the final and set a new lap record of 1 min 32.6 sec (103.02 mph). Ginther took third place in the first heat and second place in the second heat, but retired in the final with engine trouble. On the strength of this performance it seemed that the Eagle was destined to enjoy a season of outstanding success.

Unfortunately, although the Eagle scored one major success in 1967, its promise was to remain largely unfulfilled. At Monaco Richie Ginther was unable to qualify as one of the sixteen starters, simply because he was too slow, and in the race Gurney's car survived only four laps before the toothed belt driving the fuel pump on the V-12 engine broke. All-American Racers took three cars to the Dutch Grand Prix at Zandvoort and on one car more extensive use of titanium had reduced the weight by 100 lb compared with the beginning of the season. Only one car ran in the race with Gurney at the wheel as usual, and he retired on only the seventh lap when the fuel metering unit disintegrated.

The big success of the season came in the Belgian Grand Prix at Spa-Francorchamps where, once again, only a single car for Dan Gurney was entered. Dan and the Eagle were in magnificent form on this very fast, very difficult 8.716-mile circuit and were second fastest in practice, sandwiched on the front row of the grid by the new Lotus 49 cars of Jim Clark and Graham Hill. Certainly the Lotus was the fastest car in the race and Jim Clark soon pulled out a good lead over Jackie Stewart (H-16 BRM) and Gurney. At the end of lap 12 there were dramas in the pits as Clark pulled in because of a disintegrated spark plug and Gurney stopped to complain about fluctuating fuel pressure. The Eagle was now in second place and AAR team manager Bill Dunne was not interested in hearing Dan's complaints, but with one word ('Git') and a pointing finger the Californian was hustled back into the race, still in second place and having lost only a few seconds on Stewart's BRM. As the race progressed, Gurney slowly closed in on the leading BRM, mainly because Stewart had gearbox problems and was having to hold the gear-lever with one hand to stop it from jumping out of engagement and steer with the other hand.

On lap 18 Gurney set a new outright circuit record of 3 min 32.8 sec, and three laps later he passed the ailing BRM to take the lead and yet again reduced the lap record to 3 min 31.9 sec (148.85 mph). By lap 25 Dan's lead had extended to 18.3 seconds and he finished this 28-lap race over a minute clear of the Bourne car. Apart from the fact that this was the first European

Grand Prix win by an American car since 1921, it was the fastest race ever run on a European road circuit.

With this brilliant victory behind them, and one gained in the face of the stiffest opposition, the AAR team travelled to the next round of the Championship with high hopes. This next race was the French Grand Prix which in 1967 was run on a silly little circuit at Le Mans that combined the pits straight with a tortuous course running through the land normally used for car-parking. For the first time AAR entered two V-12 cars in a Championship race, the lighter model for Dan Gurney and an older car for Bruce McLaren whose own BRM-powered car had proved a dismal failure in 1967. Gurney held third place during the race, but his engine developed a bad misfire and he was forced to retire because of a broken union in the fuel system. McLaren's car sounded flatter and flatter as the race progressed; it seems that the trouble was caused by a mechanical fault that caused retarded ignition and this Eagle also retired.

During the remainder of the 1967 season very little seemed to go right for the Eagle team and both Eagle drivers again retired at Silverstone, McLaren with engine failure and Gurney because his clutch was slipping. At the Nürburgring Gurney took a place on the front row of the grid with a lap in 8 min 17.7 sec (11.6 sec slower than pole-position man Jim Clark) and McLaren returned exactly the same time as the *patron*. Both drivers were out of luck in the race. McLaren retired because of a broken oil pipe on lap 4, while poor Gurney had an almost certain victory snatched from his grasp. Dan took the lead from Hulme's Brabham on lap 4 and by the end of lap 10 he had increased his advantage to 42 seconds; on lap 13, only two laps from the finish, a universal joint on one of the drive-shafts broke, the broken shaft cut through an oil pipe and the Eagle coasted to the side of the track and retirement. The Brabhams of Hulme and 'Black Jack' took the first two places ahead of Chris Amon's Ferrari.

An addition to the racing calendar in 1967 was the first Formula One Canadian Grand Prix which was held at Mosport on 27th August. Bruce McLaren appeared with a new car bearing his own name and powered by a BRM V-12 engine and at this race only the one works Eagle was entered for Dan Gurney. As a result of the misfortune suffered by the AAR team-leader at the Nürburgring, the Anglo-American car was now fitted with stronger drive-shafts. A second Eagle in this race was one of the 4-cylinder cars which had been sold to local driver Al Pease. The Canadian race was won on a rain-soaked, slippery track and in these miserable conditions many of the cars were plagued by water-soaked electrics. Gurney and the Eagle plugged on steadily, making two pit stops late in the race for clean goggles, and the blue and silver car finished third, a lap behind the winning Brabhams of Jack himself and Denis Hulme.

At the Italian Grand Prix at Monza a second V-12 Eagle was entered for Lodovico Scarfiotti who had won the 1966 race at the wheel of a V-12 Ferrari. Just as at Mosport, Gurney turned in a fast practice time (he was fourth fastest in 1 min 29.38 sec) and there was no doubt that the Eagle had the performance of a consistent race-winner, if not the reliability. In the race both Eagle drivers retired with engine trouble, but Gurney had led the race for the first two laps. The works Lotus 49s ran into mechanical problems and the 1967 Monza race was won by Surtees' Honda.

Because of the damage sustained to the two engines at Monza the AAR team had to scratch one of their entries in the United States Grand Prix at Watkins Glen. Gurney was fourth fastest in practice, held second place in the race until lap 8, but gradually fell back because of suspension problems and retired on lap 24. At Mexico City Gurney was third fastest in practice, but he was out of contention before the Eagle left the grid. When the starter lowered the flag, Gurney ran forward into the exhausts of Clark's Lotus and punctured the Eagle's radiator. Dan decided to carry on, but the radiator was streaming water and he retired after only three laps.

Throughout 1967 the Eagle had displayed impressive promise, promise that on two occasions, at Brands Hatch and Spa, had been fulfilled. It was one of the fastest cars racing, even if not as fast as either the new Lotus 49s or the Ferrari V-12 when Maranello was having a good day, but it was also one of the unluckiest, constantly plagued by minor faults. Nevertheless, Gurney still had a great deal of confidence in the car and was enthusiastic about his prospects for 1968. It had now been decided to transfer production of the engine from Rye to Ashford so that Weslake was left to concentrate on development work. Unfortunately the transition went far from smoothly and engine problems and shortages plagued the team throughout the year.

At the South African Grand Prix at the start of the 1968 season, however, it seemed that the Eagle had lost much of its speed. Gurney could secure only a place on the middle of the grid and in the race he held a steady seventh place, battling with Hulme's McLaren-BRM, until the American entry developed an oil leak. Dan made a brief pit stop to report the trouble on lap 33 and rejoined the race having lost only one place, but the leak worsened. On lap 59 the Californian pulled into the pits again to ask his team manager whether he should continue, for the oil level was now critically low and the Formula One regulations no longer allowed oil to be added during a race. Dan was advised to 'see how it goes', but he completed only two more laps before retiring.

Although he had won the race in 1967, Gurney missed the Race of Champions and the newly inaugurated Spanish Grand Prix, and next appeared at Monaco at the end of May. At this race Gurney's car was fitted with the first of the Eagle team's own engines with 'Eagle Mark 1A' instead of 'Gurney-Weslake' on the cam-box covers. Gurney had barely started practice when his brand-new V-12 engine disintegrated and he missed the second practice session while a spare unit was flown over from England. Dan's best practice time, 1 min 32.9 sec, was hopelessly uncompetitive, but luckily he had been guaranteed a place on the grid and he started from the back row despite the fact that two privateers who had lapped faster were eliminated. In this race the V-12 engine was popping and banging for no apparent reason, so Dan had to content himself with collecting his starting money and calling it a day after nine uncompetitive laps.

Poor Gurney was forced to miss yet another race, the Belgian Grand Prix, because of unserviceable engines, and for the same reason he drove the spare works Brabham in the Dutch Grand Prix held on 23rd June. The Zandvoort race was run in torrential rain, Dan had a thoroughly miserable race at the tail of the field and at two-thirds race-distance he decided to call it a day, although there was nothing wrong other than steamed-up goggles. There was no Eagle and no Gurney at the French Grand Prix, but the American duo reappeared at Brands Hatch where the Eagle was fitted with a flimsy rear aerofoil (aerofoils were all the rage at this time and had assumed enormous proportions on the works Lotus 49Bs). Certainly not the fastest car on the track, the Eagle was nevertheless running very well and Gurney obtained a slot on the third row with a time of 1 min 30.0 sec (compared with pole-position man Graham Hill's 1 min 28.9 sec). At the start the Eagle's engine cut out, Gurney pulled off the track and although he later joined the race, the V-12 was plagued by fuel-pump problems and he retired after only eight laps.

The AAR team travelled to the German Grand Prix at the Nürburgring with high hopes, for not only was Dan the lap record holder (he had set the record during his unlucky 1967 drive at the circuit), but it now seemed that all was well with the V-12 engine. Rain and mist marred both practice and the race, but although Dan was still unable to regain the form that he had shown the previous season, he took a place on the fourth row of the eight-row grid and seemed to have a good chance of finishing high up the field if the Eagle held together. But it was not to be. Gurney was in fifth place at the end of the first rain-soaked lap, battling with Ickx's Ferrari, a duel that ended two laps later when the Californian took to the grass at the Karussell and punctured a front tyre on a sharp rock. After a pit stop for a wheel-change Gurney was at the tail of the field which was led by Jackie Stewart's Matra and for the remaining eleven laps of this 199-mile race he was merely struggling to make up lost ground. At the finish Gurney was in ninth place, over eight minutes behind the winner.

At Monza the Eagle was still suffering from engine troubles and the car was very much down on power in practice. So depressed was Gurney by the performance of his car that he arranged to borrow the spare McLaren for the race, but the organisers would not accept a change of car at this late stage. He eventually managed a lap in 1 min 27.61 sec with the Eagle during Saturday's practice, good enough for the fifth row of the grid, but he retired with engine trouble on lap 20 of the race. For the last three races of the season Gurney bought the spare works McLaren and he campaigned this in place of his ill-starred V-12.

It came as no real surprise when the AAR team withdrew from Grand Prix racing at the end of the 1968 season, for the year had been one of complete failure and despair. It seemed that the engine problems were the cause of the team's withdrawal, but, equally compelling, there were personal reasons why Gurney decided to restrict his racing activities to the Western side of the Atlantic. In USAC racing the Eagles had performed well and continued to do so. At Indianapolis in 1968 Bobbie Unser and Dan Gurney drove Eagles into the first two places and Dan himself scored victories in the events at Mosport and Riverside Raceway. For 1969 Tony Southgate (later of BRM and Shadow) designed a new Eagle for USAC racing and Gurney drove one of these cars fitted with a stock-block Ford engine into second place at the Hosier Bowl. The team used the traditional Meyer-Drake-Offenhauser engine the following year and on this occasion Gurney finished third.

Following Bruce McLaren's death in a testing accident at Goodwood, Dan Gurney made a brief return to Grand Prix racing in 1970 as a member of the McLaren team. His first race for McLaren was at Zandvoort where his supporters painted 'Welcome back Dan Gurney' on the track on the eve of the race. Unfortunately it was a sad return to European racing, for Dan was unable to display any of his old fire; after retiring with engine failure in the Dutch race, he finished a poor sixth at Clermont-Ferrand and retired again at Brands Hatch. He also drove for the McLaren team in the first three races in the Can-Am series. After these races Dan's place in the McLaren team was taken by Peter Gethin and the Californian retired from all forms of racing at the end of 1970. Nevertheless, he maintained a keen interest in European racing and in 1973 he offered a challenge to European drivers and teams to match the lap times of the USAC Eagle at the Nürburgring. Nobody took up the gauntlet, partly because of the lack of any financial arrangements, but it did seem that this challenge was the prelude to a return to Grand Prix racing by the Eagle team. Dan Gurney's protégé, young Swede Savage, succumbed to terrible injuries suffered when his Eagle crashed at Indianapolis in 1973 and undoubtedly Savage would have played a leading role in the revival of an Eagle Formula One team. It now seems unlikely that Dan's cheerful grin will again be seen at the circuits of Europe. Gurney has however continued to play a very active role in American racing. Eagle cars took second, third and fourth places in Indianapolis in 1974 and this year Dan fulfilled his greatest ambition by seeing one of his cars driven by Bobby Unser win the classic 500 miles race.

9

Autodelta and the Alfa Romeo Tipo 33

For a period of over forty years the Alfa Romeo company enjoyed a competition record of distinction; sometimes they dominated racing as they had with the P2 2-litre cars in 1924-5 and the Tipo 158 'Alfettas' in 1946-50, sometimes they were soundly trounced by the opposition as they had been during the years of the 750 Kilogramme Formula, 1934-7, when the German *marques* reigned supreme. In 1951 the blown 159 Grand Prix cars were finally defeated by their unsupercharged rivals from Maranello. The directors at Portello planned a much-revised Grand Prix car which they hoped would regain Alfa Romeo supremacy, but the anticipated government financial support was not forthcoming. Instead Alfa Romeo developed the 6-cylinder 'Disco Volante' sports cars and ran these in a number of races during 1953. Victory eluded the team until September when Juan Fangio drove an open 3-litre car to victory in the rather parochial Supercortemaggiore Grand Prix at Merano. After this season of disappointment Alfa Romeo withdrew from serious racing activities and contented themselves with entering modified production cars in a few events. Over ten years elapsed before an Alfa Romeo built purely for competition work was again seen on the circuits of Europe.

By 1964 the Alfa Romeo directors had decided that something should be done to restore the company's image in the field of high-performance motoring and in December of that year a new concern known as Autodelta was formed with a capital of five million lira. Former Ferrari engineer Carlo Chiti was appointed General Manager of Autodelta and he was assisted as sports manager by racing driver Roberto Bussinello. Chiti had been responsible for the overall design of the Ferrari V-6 cars that had dominated Grand Prix racing in 1961 and for the V-8 Prototypes raced in 1962. He had left Maranello at the end of 1961 and he became chief engineer of the ATS concern which had raced a brace of very unsuccessful V-8 Grand Prix cars in 1963. However Alfa Romeo's faith in Chiti largely arose from his activities as a director of Udine, a very small concern formed in 1962 for the purposes of developing and building higher-performance versions of the Alfa Romeo range of production cars.

Autodelta was located in new and spacious premises in the small village of Settimo Milanese in the open countryside well out of the centre of Milan. This site was chosen so that the works would be close to testing facilities and yet well away from the main Alfa Romeo headquarters at Arese where the staff would have been bound by strict union timekeeping and unable to put in the long hours necessary in a racing establishment.

During their first year Autodelta raced the TZ1 (Tubolare Zagato) version of the 1570 cc Giulia, a much-revised model with independent rear suspension and very stylish Zagato-styled body that had been built in the Udine works from 1964; with one of these cars Pinto and Todaro took fourth place in the 1965 Targa Florio. The team also developed the TZ2 car based on the same production model and with a specification that included a dry-sump engine and twin-plug cylinder head. This model made its debut in the Monza 1000 Km race in April of that year and finished eleventh overall in the hands of de Adamich and Zeccoli. At the same race Autodelta introduced the GTA, a high-performance version of the production saloon and this was homologated as a Touring car in June 1965. Autodelta have continued to race the Touring cars with great success and to manufacture a range of high-performance equipment for the production cars.

The great milestone in Autodelta history was the appearance of the Tipo 33, a 2-litre Prototype that back in 1967 looked all set to provide a direct challenge in its class to the then all-conquering Porsche 907 and 910 models. The engine was a conventional but very potent 90-degree V-8 with a capacity of 1995 cc (78 × 52.2 mm). Light alloy construction was used throughout, there were twin overhead camshafts per bank of cylinders, Lucas fuel injection and a claimed power output of 260 bhp at 9000 rpm. This engine was in fact designed by Alfa Romeo, as opposed to Autodelta, and was the work of engineering chief Orazio Satta (who died early in 1974) and Giuseppe Busso.

Perhaps the most unusual feature of the Tipo 33 was the chassis which was formed by two large-diameter light alloy side-members which also formed the fuel tanks; to the rear of the cockpit there was a similar tubular cross-member and at the front a magnesium-alloy bulkhead located the steering and front suspension. From the rear cross-member there extended two magnesium-alloy castings bridged by a sheet metal fabricated structure which carried the rear suspension. The V-8 engine was mounted between these castings ahead of the axle-line. Transmission was by a 6-speed twin-shaft gearbox mounted behind the engine.

Front suspension was by wishbones and coil springs, while at the rear there were links, radius arms and coils springs. There were ventilated disc brakes (those at the rear were mounted inboard) and 13-inch magnesium-alloy wheels. The body was a stark, open glass-fibre design of very aggressive lines with an enormous curved windscreen and, rearing above the engine compartment, a large duct for the fuel injection. Left-hand drive was fitted. On paper at least the Tipo 33 seemed a worthy successor to the long line of successful competition cars to wear the *quadrifoglio* and it seemed destined to enjoy a long and successful competition career.

During the early months of 1967 Chiti took the Tipo 33 to Monza and the Little Madonie circuit in Sicily for an intensive development programme. The car performed satisfactorily and it was now decided to give it an inconspicuous competition debut. In March 1967 Teodoro Zeccoli drove the new car in the Fléron hill climb in Belgium and set fastest time of the day. Later that month the Tipo 33 made its competition debut proper in the Sebring 12 Hours race in which two cars were driven by Adamich/Zeccoli and Bussinello/Engric. De Adamich actually led the race on the first lap, but then the 7-litre Ford GT40s thundered ahead, and both Autodelta entries eventually succumbed to ignition overheating.

It was much the same story at the Targa Florio in Sicily where four Tipo 33s were entered. In practice they displayed a distressing tendency to shed a front wheel as a result of the suspension breaking. There was too little time available in which to cure the trouble, so Chiti adopted a make-shift wire-cable device that prevented the hub from detaching itself completely. Despite the fact that there was little likelihood of the cars lasting the distance, the Autodelta drivers put up a tremendous fight and Andrea de Adamich/Jean Rolland were in second place and harassing the leading Porsche when their Alfa broke its front suspension top link on lap 8. Of the other Autodelta entries, another broke its suspension, the 'Geki'/Todaro entry went off the road and the car driven by Galli and Giunti struggled on to finish well down the field despite a badly misfiring engine.

Three cars were entered at the Nürburgring 1000 Km race, but two of the

Tipo 33s retired and the survivor, entered for Bussinello and Zeccoli and later driven by de Adamich and Galli, finished fifth. The following day, however, Autodelta scored a fine victory at Oulton Park in Cheshire where de Adamich won the Tourist Trophy with a GTA saloon. On existing form there was no prospect of the Tipo 33s lasting the distance at Le Mans and so the Autodelta entry was scratched. The team's next outing was in the Circuit of Mugello, a difficult road race held in late July over a 66.2-kilometre circuit incorporating parts of the old Mille Miglia course. Unfortunately the three Tipo 33s turned up looking ill-prepared and scruffy; the rear intakes had now been removed and the holes left in the bodywork roughly patched over. All three succumbed to mechanical trouble before half-distance and the race was won by the Porsche of Mitter and Schütz.

A total of eight Tipo 33s had been built in 1967 and although they were faster than the Porsche 2-litre opposition, they were sadly lacking in reliability and the season had been one of complete failure. The Tipo 33's only victory had been in the very minor Bettojia Trophy race run on the Vallelunga circuit at Rome and during the year two drivers, Jean Rolland and Leo Cella, had been killed in testing accidents.

The team's racing experience in 1967 had established that there was nothing wrong with the engine and transmission design, and the chassis layout had proved satisfactory. These basic components remained unchanged for 1968, but the rest of the car was completely redesigned. There was new and much stronger front suspension and instead of a water radiator in the conventional position in the nose of the car there were now twin radiators on either side, just ahead of the rear wheels. The wheelbase remained unchanged at 7 ft 4.6 in, but both front and rear track were slightly increased, to 4 ft 4.6 in and 4 ft 8.9 in respectively. The existing open body was scrapped and replaced by a conventionally styled coupé body with twin headlights each side, sleek profile and the choice of long or short tails depending on the nature of the circuit on which the cars were raced. The roof was detachable so that the cars could be raced in either open or closed forms.

This new model, which was designated the Tipo 33/2, was eventually homologated as a Competition Sports Car (minimum production of twenty five cars) in 1969 as the '33 Spider', but at the works it was known as the 'Daytona' (the circuit at which it was first raced). During 1968 a total of 28 of these cars were constructed; ten were retained by the works and the remainder sold to private owners. The leading private contenders were the Belgium VDS Racing Team which ran a brace of well-prepared 33/2s at most of the important races in 1968-9. Autodelta also produced a 2500 cc (78 × 64.4 mm) version of the Tipo 33 engine developing 315 bhp at 8800 rpm. Production of this larger engine was much delayed and the VDS Team did not receive theirs until just before the Norisring race in Germany in late June.

Throughout 1968 the 33/2s performed with speed and reliability and they usually had the legs of the Porsche 910 opposition. The team's first outing of the year was in February in the Daytona 24 Hours race in which they took fifth, sixth and seventh places overall and the first three places in their class. The team gave Sebring a miss and next ran at Brands Hatch in the BOAC '500' race; no success was gained by Autodelta at the Kent circuit, and of the three cars entered, the sole finisher driven by 'Nanni' Galli and Giancarlo Baghetti was classified a poor fourteenth.

It was on two of Europe's most difficult circuits that the Tipo 33/2s showed their true mettle. In the Targa Florio the Autodelta team came very close to defeating Porsche. The 2500 cc Alfa was crashed by German driver Udo Schütz, but the 2-litre cars of 'Nanni' Galli/Ignazio Giunti and Mario Casoni/Lucien Bianchi took second and third places and the VDS-entered 33/2 of Pilette/Slotemaker finished fifth. For one short but glorious spell the Alfa of Galli/Giunti had actually led the race.

On faster courses than the Little Madonie, the 2-litre Alfas were no real match for the latest 3-litre Porsche opposition. Stuttgart dominated the Nürburgring 1000 Km race, finishing first, second and fourth, but Galli and Giunti drove a fine race to finish fifth overall, a lap behind the winners and first in the class for 2-litre Prototypes. At this race a 2500 cc works Alfa was driven by Schütz and Lucien Bianchi; it challenged strongly in the opening laps of the race, but was delayed by battery trouble and eventually finished seventh. The third Autodelta entry in this race was another 2-litre car driven by Schültze and Vaccarella and this finished tenth after a pit stop to repair damaged bodywork.

At the end of July the Tipo 33/2 scored its first victory in the 328-mile Circuit of Mugello, but it would have been a disgrace if Autodelta had failed to win this event. The team had spent a full month in training and preparation work, four cars were entered and no other works team contested the race. It was almost as if Autodelta were determined to win something, however unimportant – and they almost failed! Three of the Tipo 33/2s retired and the survivor shared by Lucien Bianchi, Nino Vaccarella and Ignazio Giunti took the lead only because of a mix-up in the Hart-Ski

Porsche pit which cost drivers Siffert and Steinemann the race.

Another but easier victory was scored in the Shell 500 Km race at Imola in September and here the 2-litre Autodelta entries of Vaccarella/Zeccoli, Giunti/Galli and Casoni/Dini took the first three places. This was another race in which no other works team was entered.

The final race in 1968 for the Autodelta was the Le Mans 24 Hours event which had been postponed until the end of September by strikes in France. The John Wyer-entered Ford GT40 of Rodriguez/Bianchi scored a convincing victory ahead of a brace of flat-eight Porsche cars, but the performance of the Autodelta entries was very impressive and at one stage in the race it seemed that they might score an outright victory. Giunti/Galli, Facetti/Dini and Casoni/Biscaldi with 2-litre 33/2s took fourth, fifth and sixth places and first three places in the 2-litre class.

Towards the latter part of 1967 Autodelta had produced a road-going version of the Tipo 33 which was called the 'Coupé' to distinguish it from its competition counterpart. This was intended as a prestige model and only about twenty of these very handsome and very potent cars were built. The chassis was constructed in steel, the wheelbase was four inches longer than that of the competition cars and both front and rear track were wider. The V-8 engine, fitted with Spica fuel injection, was detuned to develop 230 bhp (DIN) at 8800 rpm and the claimed maximum speed was a little over 160 mph. Although the majority of these cars had superbly styled bodies by Scaglione (in light alloy instead of the glass-fibre of the competition cars), there were a couple of special exhibition cars. Few enthusiasts could forget Bertone's 'Carabo' coupé with 'layered' tail, frameless windscreens and doors that opened like beetle's wings, which was the star of the 1968 Paris and London Motor Shows. Pininfarina's 'Roadster GS' on the same chassis and with a combined roll-over bar and aerofoil was not so aesthetically pleasing. Even at this date Alfa Romeo was planning to build a series production car using the Tipo 33 engine.

Autodelta could look back on a successful 1968 season and now turned their attention to the development of a 3-litre Prototype that would be a serious contender for outright victory, a car that had very little in common with its predecessors. A 3-litre engine had been extensively tested in 1968 and at one stage it was hoped that it would be used in one of the works Cooper Formula One cars. It seems that Autodelta were disappointed with the power output in early testing and this unit was not raced until 1969. This extensively redesigned version of the V-8 engine had a capacity of 2993 cc

(86 × 64.4 mm) and a specification that included four valves per cylinder, Lucas fuel injection and Marelli 'Dinoplex' transistorised ignition. The 3-litre unit which weighed 350 lb, was claimed to develop 400 bhp at 9000 rpm.

For the 33/3 the big-tube chassis was abandoned and instead there was a conventional sheet-metal monocoque with large side-boxes containing foam-filled fuel bags. The suspension was basically similar to that of the 1968 cars, but Autodelta took full advantage of their own extensive welding facilities to use titanium suspension components, and there was open glass-fibre bodywork. Initially a 6-speed gearbox was used, but a 5-speed unit was substituted later in the season. The complete weight of the 3-litre car was just under 14 cwt. Six of these cars were built during 1969.

Although Porsche introduced their 4.5-litre 917 car in 1969, this model was not developed into a race-winner before the end of the year and most of the season's racing was fought between the 3-litre representatives of Ferrari, Porsche, Mirage and Matra. Unfortunately, hopes that the Alfa 33/3s would be battling it out for the lead in Sports Car Championship races were soon shattered and Autodelta ran the new cars in very few races during the year.

Autodelta sent three 3-litre cars to the Sebring race, but the entry was somewhat premature, for the team had only tested one of these cars before arrival in Florida and in any case was desperately short of spare engines. All three cars retired early in the 12 Hours race because of failure of the glue-assembled radiators. Initially the problem was tackled by increasing the size of the radiators and using a more satisfactory adhesive. The 3-litre next appeared at the Le Mans Test Weekend and it was here that tragedy struck when Lucien Bianchi driving a new car having a longer and more aerodynamically efficient tail crashed with fatal results. The cause of the accident was never satisfactorily resolved, but it appears that Bianchi may have crashed while trying to avoid a slower-moving GT Porsche that crossed his line.

Throughout 1969 competition appearances of the 3-litre cars were very few because the cars were neither fast enough nor sufficiently reliable. At the Targa Florio, Autodelta fielded a team of the familiar 33/2 2-litre cars, but none made it to the finish; 'Nanni' Galli was in second place when he was pushed off the road by Vic Elford with a works Porsche. Although a testing session with the 3-litre cars at the Nürburgring had proved satisfactory, the team decided to play safe and entered 33/2s in the 1000 Km race in the name of Alfa Romeo Deutschland; the car driven by Facetti and Schültze finished seventh overall and won the 2-litre Competition Sports Car class.

It was not until the Norisring race at Nuremberg at the end of June that the 3-litre 33/3 was seen in action again and here the single car entered for Giunti retired with engine trouble. A month later Autodelta ran two 3-litre cars in a minor race at Hockenheim in Germany; here Nino Vaccarella, at the wheel of a new fixed-head coupé version of the 33/3, and Ignazio Giunti took third and sixth places. At the opening meeting at the Österreichring in Austria on 27th July Autodelta scored its first, if somewhat dishonourable, victory with the 33/3. Masten Gregory crossed the line with his Porsche 908 ahead of de Adamich with the Alfa, but the Italian entry was awarded first place after Chiti had entered a protest on the grounds that the Porsche had not crossed the line under its own power (Gregory had been shunted across the line by Brostrom with another Porsche after his engine had blown up on the last lap).

A fortnight later at the same circuit the team did not fare so well. Autodelta entered three Tipo 33/3s in the Austrian Grand Prix, a 1000-km race that counted as a round in the Sports Car Championship, but two of the Alfas crashed and the third retired with engine failure. Another minor success for this unlucky team followed in the Enna Cup race held on a very fast circuit round the perimeter of Lake Pergusa. In Sicily, Vaccarella drove the 3-litre coupé and built up a good lead in the early laps of the race; when the Alfa's only serious opponent, the 3-litre Serenissima driven by Jonathan Williams, began to boil furiously, Vaccarella had the race in the bag and finished two clear laps ahead of the second-place Porsche. Autodelta's final outing of the season was in the rain-soaked Imola 500 Km race in which Giunti brought his 33/3 across the line in second place behind Jacky Ickx's winning Mirage; this was another hollow success, for Giunti was three laps behind the winner and assumed second place only after three Porsche 908s in front of him had spun off the streaming wet track.

By 1970 the 2-litre Alfa 33/2 was outdated and Autodelta was forced to rely on the 3-litre cars. A winter of feverish development work was spent on the V-8s and Chiti succeeded in signing up a strong team of drivers that included Grand Prix *pilote* Piers Courage and former Porsche driver Rolf Stommelen. At the beginning of the year the team dispatched two 33/3s to compete in the Buenos Aires 1000 Km race. In this event the best the team could manage was a poor sixth by de Adamich and Courage, but a week later the same pair won the Buenos Aires 200 Miles race.

1. One of two Sunbeams built in 1922 with a 5-litre engine dating back to 1919. H O D Segrave is seen at the wheel at Brooklands.

2. Henry Segrave at the wheel of the 4-litre V-12 Sunbeam with which he broke the Land Speed Record at Southport in 1926.

1 & 2

3

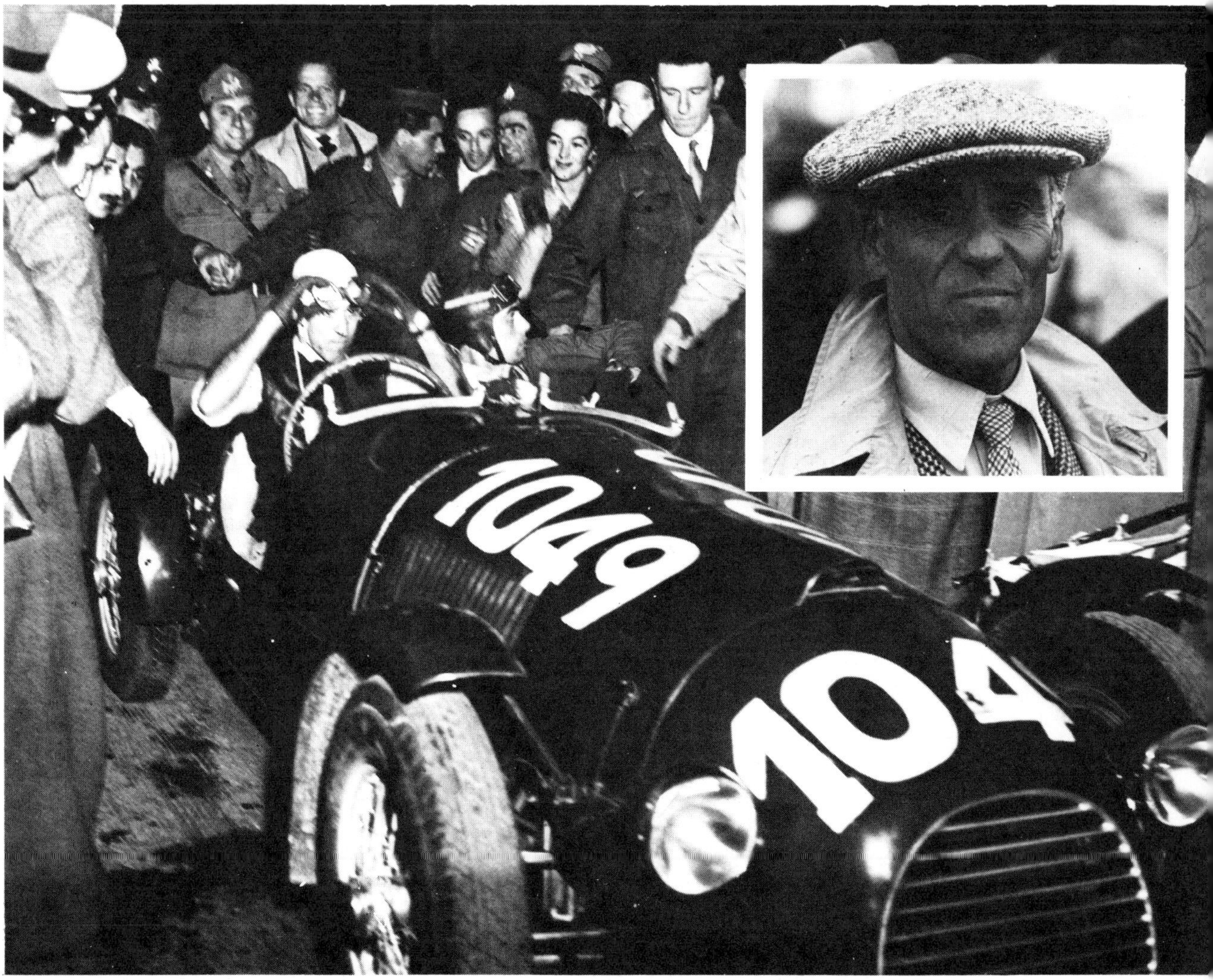

4

3. The great Tazio Nuvolari raced this private Maserati in 1934. He is seen in the 1934 Coppa Acerbo at Pescara in which he was beaten into second place by Fagioli's Mercedes-Benz.

4. The 'Flying Mantuan' at the wheel of a 2-litre Ferrari in the 1948 Mille Miglia.

5. Elder Statesman: Nuvolari at Silverstone in 1950.

6

8

6. Raymond Mays, co-founder of the ERA concern and the team's leading driver, on his way to second place in the 1938 BRDC Road Race at Brooklands. The race was won by 'B Bira's' private ERA.

7. Raymond Mays at Shelsley Walsh Hill climb in 1947. The car is R4D, the most highly developed of the original ERAs.

8. The car that never won a race: the E-type ERA seen here with Leslie Johnson at the wheel.

9

11

10

9. The straight-eight 2.3-litre Alfa Romeo made its debut in the 1931 Mille Miglia; this car was driven by Arcangeli and Bonini.

10. Dorino Serafini drove this 2.3-litre Ferrari into second place in the 1950 1000-mile race.

11. Yet another all-Italian victory. Eugenio Castellotti at the start of the 1956 Mille Miglia with the 3.5-litre V-12 Ferrari.

12

13

14

12. Ken Wharton, one of the few men who could really master the V-12 BRM, drove this modified car into third place in the Formule Libre race at Silverstone in 1953.

13. Mike Hawthorn led the opening laps of the 1956 British Grand Prix with the new 4-cylinder BRM, but, almost inevitably, retired because of mechanical trouble.

14. Joakim Bonnier in the 1960 *Daily Express* Trophy at Silverstone with one of the rear-engined cars raced by BRM that year.

15

17

15. The BRM team enjoyed consistent success during the years of the 1500 cc Grand Prix Formula. Here Graham Hill is seen on his way to second place in the 1964 British Grand Prix at Brands Hatch.

16. Although the BRM team brought these new H-16 cars along to the 1966 Belgian Grand Prix, they relied on the older V-8s for the race.

17. Jean-Pierre Beltoise scored a completely unexpected victory with the V-12 BRM in the rain-soaked 1972 Monaco Grand Prix. Here he leads team-mate Helmut Marko out of the Station Hairpin.

18. In 1954 Moss was leading the Italian Grand Prix when his Maserati 250F lost its oil pressure. He pushed his car across the line into tenth place.

19. Two years later at Monza, Moss was in luck and he won the Italian Grand Prix with his Maserati – despite a leaking fuel tank.

18 & 19

20

20. There was a furious battle for the lead in the 1957 Italian Grand Prix and here Fangio (Maserati) holds a narrow lead over the Vanwalls of Brooks and Lewis-Evans. Number 6 is Jean Behra with the V-12 Maserati and Moss, the eventual winner, is at the tail of this group.

21

22

23

21. In the 1966 British Grand Prix, Gurney with the original Climax-powered Eagle leads Bob Anderson's Brabham.

22. Dan Gurney and the All-American Eagle on their way to victory on the very fast, very beautiful Spa circuit in 1967.

23. Gurney at the mist-enveloped Nürburgring in 1968. He took ninth place in this race after stopping for a wheel-change.

24

25

26

24. Autodelta was out of luck in the 1968 BOAC '500' race; this 33/2 coupé driven by Vaccarella and Attwood retired because of camshaft failure.

25. The 3-litre Alfa Romeo 33/3 cars were superbly turned out at Le Mans in 1970, but all four were eliminated. This car was driven by Gregory and Hezemans.

26. De Adamich and Hezemans drove this Tipo 33/TT car into third place in the 1972 Targa Florio.

27

28

29

27. The first of the breed: the Lea-Francis-engined sports Connaughts of McAlpine and Clark at the Blandford circuit in Dorset in 1949.

28. At Goodwood in September 1952, Dennis Poore (A-series Connaught) leads Stirling Moss (G-type ERA).

29. Archie Scott-Brown drove this B-series 'Syracuse' Connaught into second place in the 1956 *Daily Express* Trophy race at Silverstone.

30

31

32

30. Colin Chapman in 1950 with the Ford-engined Lotus Mark 2.

31. Jim Clark and the monocoque Lotus 25-Climax on their way to victory in the 1963 British Grand Prix at Silverstone.

32. Almost as revolutionary a design was the Ford-engined Lotus 49, seen here at La Source hairpin in the 1967 Belgian Grand Prix with Clark at the wheel.

33

34

35

33. Colin Chapman with Jochen Rindt, posthumous World Champion in 1970 following his death in practice at Monza.

34. The experimental gas-turbine Lotus 56B Grand Prix car driven by Emerson Fittipaldi in the 1971 Race of Champions at Brands Hatch.

35. Fittipaldi with the Lotus 72D in the 1971 French Grand Prix; the Brazilian finished third.

36

37

38

36. Alberto Ascari at the wheel of a Tipo 625 4-cylinder Ferrari in the 1954 Italian Grand Prix. He worked his way into the lead, but retired with engine trouble.

37. Ferrari dominated Grand Prix racing in 1961 with the V-6 rear-engined cars, but the following year these proved uncompetitive. Here Phil Hill is seen in the 1962 British Grand Prix at Aintree.

38. Jacky Ickx with the 1970 flat-12 Ferrari 312B, derivatives of which are still being raced. Ickx is seen in the Monaco Grand Prix in which he retired with drive-shaft failure.

39

41

40

39. 1957 was Ecurie Ecosse's last year of great racing success. One of their braver but less successful efforts was the entry of this D-type Jaguar in the Mille Miglia. Ron Flockhart rose to seventh place, but retired because of chassis problems.

40. At Le Mans in 1957 Ecurie Ecosse scored their second successive victory with this ex-works 'long-nose' D-type driven by Flockhart and Ivor Bueb.

41. John Wyer devoted thirteen years to the development of Aston Martin cars and the most successful was the Sports Car Championship-winning DBR1. Here Carroll Shelby is seen at the wheel of the DBR1 he co-drove to victory in the 1959 Tourist Trophy.

43

44

42. Jacky Ickx at the wheel of John Wyer's BRM-engined Mirage on its debut in the 1969 BOAC race at Brands Hatch.

43. Le Mans in 1969 witnessed its most exciting finish since the 'thirties. Eventual winner Jacky Ickx with the Wyer-entered Ford narrowly leads Herrmann's Porsche as they lap a Ferrari 250 LM.

44. In 1970-71John Wyer was running the team of works Porsche 917s. This 5-litre 917 was driven to victory at Spa in 1970 by Jo Siffert and Brian Redman.

That the Tipo 33/3 was now much more reliable was confirmed at Sebring where a trio of cars was entered. All three suffered minor mechanical problems, but none retired and the car driven by Masten Gregory and Toine Hezemans finished third overall. The single entry in the BOAC 1000 Km race was retired after being crashed by both de Adamich and Piers Courage! Four cars ran in the Monza 1000 Km race, but they were outclassed by the 5-litre Ferraris and Porsche 917s on this high-speed course and the best the team could manage was a none-too-satisfactory seventh by Galli and Stommelen. All three 3-litre Alfas were crashed in the Targa Florio and at the Nürburgring the improved, lighter car entered for Stommelen and Courage retired with collapsed rear suspension. Another failure followed at Le Mans where all four beautifully prepared long-tail cars were eliminated, two by engine failure, one by a crash and one was disqualified for receiving outside assistance after Galli had stopped out on the course with a broken oil pipe.

Although Autodelta were achieving little success, the cars were much more competitive than in 1969, they were far better-prepared and the team was tackling its racing programme with greater enthusiasm and purpose. In the Austrian 1000 Km race on 11th October victory only just eluded the team. In the closing laps of the race the surviving Alfa of de Adamich and Pescarolo was being driven right on the limit to catch the race-leader, the ailing Porsche 917 of Siffert and Redman, when the engine blew up; although the Autodelta entry finished the race in the pits, it was classified second.

Throughout 1970-1 racing was largely dominated by the 5-litre Porsche 917s and Chiti realised that little success would come Autodelta's way in 1971 unless the German cars suffered mechanical failures. Throughout the next season Autodelta tactics were to keep the cars lapping as steadily as possible, within their rev limits, leading the Prototype category and waiting for their German rivals to break. It was a policy that paid dividends at several races and Autodelta enjoyed their most successful season to date.

Porsche 917s took the first two places in the Buenos Aires 1000 Km race, but the Alfas of Stommelen/Galli and de Adamich/Pescarolo were hot on their heels in third and fourth positions. Autodelta missed the Daytona race and next ran at Sebring where a Porsche was the winner yet again; but, just as at Buenos Aires, the now very reliable Alfas were well to the fore and the 33/3s took the next two places in general classification. The break for which Autodelta had waited so long finally came in the BOAC race at Brands

Hatch. The leading Porsche 917s entered by the Wyer team ran into trouble and the Alfas of Stommelen/Hezemans and de Adamich/Pescarolo moved up into the first two places. A con-rod through the side of the engine eliminated the race-leader in a cloud of white smoke (not a flicker of emotion crossed Chiti's inscrutable, long-suffering face), but the survivor cantered on to win by three laps from the new and experimental 3-litre flat-12 Ferrari of Ickx and Regazzoni.

At Monza the Alfas finished third, fourth and fifth and at the Spa 1000 Km race the only Autodelta entry driven by Pescarolo and de Adamich crossed the line in third place. Another Autodelta victory followed in the Targa Florio, the race which the team wanted to win more than any other (an Alfa had last won the Targa Florio in 1950). Two of the three Porsche 908/03 cars retired and the third was eliminated by broken suspension after hitting a kerb. The Alfas of Vaccarella/Hezemans and de Adamich/van Lennep achieved an easy domination of the race and finished in the first two places ahead of the Lola of Bonnier/Attwood. The Porsche team gained their revenge at the Nürburgring, however, and the 908/03s took the first three places ahead of the Alfas of de Adamich/Pescarolo and Hezemans/Vaccarella.

There were no Autodelta entries at Le Mans and the team next appeared at the Austrian 1000 Km race at the end of June. The Porsche 917 of Rodriguez and Attwood won the race, but Alfa 33/3s took the next two places. Autodelta's third major victory of the 1971 season followed at the Watkins Glen Six Hours race where the winning car was driven by Ronnie Peterson and Andrea de Adamich. An interesting Alfa Romeo development seen at Watkins Glen was a 4-litre version of the Tipo 33 engine and this was known, unofficially at least, as the 33/4. It had been intended to use this engine in the Can-Am race was held on the day after the Sports Car Championship event, but this proved impossible after one of the team cars crashed in practice. The 4-litre engine was whipped out and replaced by the more usual 3-litre and there was insufficient time to replace it before the following day's race.

In practice for the Targa Florio, Autodelta had revealed a new experimental car which was designated the Tipo 33/TT. This new car was clearly inspired by the lightweight Porsche 908/03 which had won the Targa Florio in 1970 and it was shorter, lower, narrower and lighter than the standard Tipo 33. The chassis featured a central monocoque box-section with a light alloy tubular framework. As on the Porsche, the gearbox (which was lighter than the standard 'box) was mounted ahead of the rear axle to improve weight distribution. This car reappeared in practice at the Österreichring and was entered to run in the Watkins Glen race. During practice at the American circuit Galli collided with a slower Porsche 911 and the 33/TT was too badly damaged to run in the race. Autodelta's plans to race the 33/TT in 1971 were frustrated yet again in October. Two cars were sent for testing at the Dijon circuit and then on to compete in the Paris 1000 Km race at Montlhéry. One car was badly damaged during testing and the other was crashed by Pescarolo on the warming-up lap before the French race!

In 1971 Autodelta had competed in nine of the eleven races in the Sports Car Championship; three the team had won outright and in eight it had won the Prototype category. From 1972 onwards the big 5-litre Porsche 917s were banned from Championship racing and despite the prospect of strong opposition from the flat-12 Ferraris and the V-12 Matras, Chiti was optimistic about the team's prospects. In 1972 Autodelta raced an improved version of the 33/TT cars. These featured a heavier steel tubular space-frame (which was considered to be safer in the event of an accident) and had front and rear sub-frames, suspension, engine con-rods and steering column all constructed from titanium. Autodelta was working hard on the development of its own flat-12 engine and this was expected to be raceworthy before the end of the season.

An interesting innovation was Chiti's own special fireproof fuel tanks which were based on a series of thin hollow layers intermeshing to provide alternate horizontal chambers, one series containing petrol and the other an extinguishing fluid. In the event of an impact the layers broke so that the extinguishing fluid mixed with the petrol and, hopefully, prevented a fire. Each of the two tanks fitted to the 33/TT cars weighed 52 lb more than a conventional tank, a terrible penalty to pay when reduction of weight was all-important.

From the first of the season's races the Ferraris dominated; Autodelta's hopes of success soon evaporated and it was only too clear that the V-8 cars were sadly underpowered and overweight compared with their Maranello rivals. As the season progressed Chiti struggled to make the cars faster and lighter and the fireproof tanks were abandoned in the team's weight-saving efforts; but success continued to elude the Autodelta team.

At the first of the season's races at Buenos Aires the team fielded three of the new cars, together with an older Tipo 33/3 model. The Ferraris dominated the race and took the first two places, the private 33/3 of Alberti/

Facetti finished third and the best of the 33/TTs driven by Elford/Marko finished a poor fourth. This pattern repeated itself in the next three rounds of the Championship; at each of these races Ferraris finished in the first two places and a 33/TT came home third. In the Daytona Six Hours race Elford/Marko were third with a 33/TT, at Sebring in the 12 Hours race it was Hezemans and Vaccarella, and at Brands Hatch in the BOAC 1000 Km event third place went to Stommelen/Peter Revson with a 33/TT.

Chiti could not foresee the strong possibility that the Alfas would be trounced in the Targa Florio, the most important race in the team's programme. In an effort to spend as much time as possible on development work and preparation for this race Autodelta scratched its entries at Monza and Spa. Autodelta fielded four cars in the Sicilian race for Vaccarella/Stommelen, Elford/van Lennep, de Adamich/Hezemans and Galli/Marko, but they faced a situation in which they could not possibly score a moral victory. With six victories already notched up in 1972, Ferrari decided to send only a single car for Arturo Merzario and Sandro Munari (a rally driver) to the Targa Florio; if the Ferrari won, Alfa would be a laughing stock; but if Alfa won, then everyone would say 'so they should have done'. Nor was luck on Autodelta's side; Elford retired on the first lap with engine failure, Stommelen retired three laps later because of valve spring failure and the Ferrari won by the narrow margin of seventeen seconds.

This unhappy saga continued at the Nürburgring where Ferrari again took the first two places and Marko/de Adamich brought their Alfa across the line in third place. Ferrari scratched from Le Mans, but Autodelta faced a very strong Matra team. The Matras were faster than the Alfas, the French cars took the first two places and the surviving Alfa of Vaccarella and de Adamich was a poor fourth. Chiti was now reconciled to the fact that the team would score no further success until the flat-12 engine was raceworthy and Autodelta missed the last two rounds of the Championship at the Österreichring and Watkins Glen.

At long last the flat-12 made its debut at the 1973 Spa 1000 Km race. The chassis was very similar to that of the 1972 Tipo 33/TT cars, but there was very distinctive bodywork sloping downwards from the top of the roll-over bar and with large tail fins; the new car soon earned the nickname of 'Batmobile'. A single car was entered at Spa for Stommelen and de Adamich, but, unfortunately, in practice a rear tyre threw a tread and de Adamich spun off into a barrier; the car was too badly damaged to run in the race.

Autodelta appeared with two cars at the Targa Florio, but it was another unlucky outing for the team. Regazzoni crashed one car in practice and Stommelen had set fastest lap and was leading the race when he collided with a slower car that he was lapping. Both cars retired because of a broken oil feed pipe in the Nürburgring 1000 Km race. The team's last appearance of the season was at the Österreichring where the flat-12s were plagued by the same trouble; breakage of this pipe which runs through the gearbox casing resulted in the failure of two engines in practice for the Austrian event and in the race itself the sole Alfa starter was plagued by fuel vapourisation problems and at the finish it had covered too few laps to qualify as a finisher. Two of the 33/TT cars were entered in the non-Championship Imola race in September, a flat-12 for Stommelen and a V-8 for Facetti. Stommelen was beaten into second place by Derek Bell with a Ford-engined Mirage and Facetti finished fourth.

Apart from one season, 1971, when Autodelta enjoyed a run of consistent success, the Alfa Romeo directors have seen very little return for the vast sums expended on the Tipo 33 racing programme. Over the years Alfa confidence in Chiti had slowly but surely lessened, although, for the time being at least he received Alfa's full financial support and the team tried once again in 1974 to attain major honours with the promising flat-12 car.

In 1974 the Autodelta team once again persevered with the unlucky flat-12 Tipo 33TT/12 cars, but they were to prove no match for the all-conquering French Matras that dominated the year's racing; the Autodelta cars were too heavy, they were insufficiently reliable and the team effort lacked that dedication that is so important if success is to be achieved.

After a surprising but convincing victory by Alfa Romeo drivers Arturo Merzario and Mario Andretti in the first of the season's Championship races at Monza, the Autodelta effort gradually disintegrated. Autodelta missed the Spa race held ten days later, claiming that they had insufficient time in which to prepare their cars, but turned out in force at the Nürburgring 1000 Km event. Matra scored a convincing victory, while of the Alfas, the Merzario/Redman car retired near the finish with a broken gearbox and the second- and third-place cars of Stommelen/Reutemann and Facetti/de Adamich were a full 14.19-mile lap behind the winner – even though the length of the race was shortened to 750 kilometres. Second and third places behind the winning Matra were repeated in the new round of the Championship at Imola in Italy, the team missed Le Mans (claiming that they had done insufficient endurance testing) and had to be satisfied with yet another second place in the Austrian 1000 Km race; at the Österreichring the team was able to display that in the right circumstances the flat-12 cars were very fast indeed, for Jacky Ickx with a Tipo 33TT/12 lapped at 138.01 mph, a new outright circuit record that even the Formula One cars were unable to match in the Austrian Grand Prix in August. After yet another failure at Watkins Glen in July, Autodelta withdrew from racing, missing the final rounds of the Championship at Paul Ricard in France, Brands Hatch and Kyalami.

There seemed to be little prospect of Autodelta re-appearing in Sports Car racing in 1975, for the Alfa Romeo factory was now tired of spending so much money for such poor results. But then a fairy godmother appeared to sustain the team for yet another season with sponsorship from several companies. Porsche entrant Willi Kauhsen fielded two cars with a formidable team of drivers that included Jacky Ickx, Arturo Merzario, Henri Pescarolo and Derek Bell. Matra had now withdrawn from racing, but there was a new and powerful opponent in the shape of the turbocharged 2-litre V-6 Alpine. The French Alpine won the first race in the Championship series at Mugello in Italy, but the Alfa Romeos won the Dijon, Monza, Spa and Enna races and subsequently clinched the Sports Car Championship. It must be remembered, however, that Sports Car racing had now lost much of its former greatness and really competitive cars were few and far between.

It had always been Alfa Romeo's ambition to build a production car that bore a direct technical relationship with the Tipo 33 competition cars. As long ago as 1967 a car with a chassis based on that of the production Giulia model cloaked in a very handsome Bertone coupé body was exhibited at the Montreal World Fair, Expo 67. This first prototype retained the production 4-cylinder engine, but there looked to be enough space under the bonnet for something rather more exciting. Three years later the prototype Montreal model with Tipo 33 engine appeared at the Geneva Salon. Unlike the competition car, however, the Montreal has a front-mounted engine in a coil-sprung chassis with rigid rear axle. In the form adopted for series production the V-8 four-cam engine has a capacity of 2953 cc (80 × 64.5 mm) and is fitted with Spica port fuel injection; the power output is 230 bhp at 6500 rpm and the Montreal is capable attaining 140 mph.

Although £5000 is a lot of money to pay for any car, this price tag makes the Montreal the least expensive of all 'Exotica' and it is now a fairly common sight on the European mainland.

10

Faster, Ever Faster:
The World's Land Speed Record

In every sphere of human endeavour the most ambitious and determined men have tried to fulfil their own objectives more efficiently than their rivals have done and these efforts are perhaps more conspicuous in the field of transport than in any other. Men tried and still try to run faster than their rivals, and to beat their rivals on horse, cycle, or motor-cycle, in car or aircraft. Speed for speed's sake consists of two separate categories: the race, in which to arrive first is paramount; and the record, in which man races against the clock and the knowledge of previous performances. In the upper reaches of achievement in the field of record-breaking, a vital factor in the reckoning is the penetration of the unknown, the battle with scientific forces the effects of which can only be estimated. Record attempts can be traced back to the dawn of motoring history and have continued until the present day.

There is, however, a significant difference between the latest record-breakers and their predecessors. Until 1965 all record-breaking cars were required to have at least two driven wheels, but in that year the Federation Internationale de l'Automobile, the governing body of motor sport, introduced a new category for so-called 'Specials' which dispensed with this requirement. The result was a generation of direct turbojet and rocket-powered cars which have proved faster than the more conventional record-breakers by more than 200 mph.

The Record-Breakers
1898: Following a successful timed hill climb held in November at Chanteloup (some 20 miles from Paris) and won by Camille Jenatzy's electric car, the magazine *La France Automobile* organised a speed trial on 18th December

over two kilometres of level, smooth road near St Germain. The first kilometre was timed as a standing start and the second as a flying start. The winner was the Comte de Chasseloup-Laubat at the wheel of an electric car known as the *Jeantaud* and over the flying-kilometre he was timed at 39.245 mph. This was the first official world's land speed record, but it was hardly an impressive performance, as it was slower by one second than the cycling record!

1899: Jenatzy had been unable to attend the speed trial, but challenged Chasseloup-Laubat to meet him under similar conditions. The meeting was arranged at the same place for 17th January. Jenatzy achieved a speed of 41.42 mph, but Chasseloup-Laubat succeeded in recording 43.69 mph. Ten days later Jenatzy returned to St Germain and recorded 49.92 mph. As the year progressed, so the battle increased in intensity. In March Chasseloup-Laubat recorded a speed of 57.6 mph, but Jenatzy had been hard at work building a new car with primitive but striking aerodynamics and two enormous electric motors. With this car, called *La Jamais Contente,* Jenatzy recorded a speed of 65.79 mph in April.

1902: During this year both the Hon C S Rolls with a French Mors car and American William K Vanderbilt with a Mors and a Mercedes made attempts on the record over the same course. Neither succeeded in beating Jenatzy's record, but with the Mercedes Vanderbilt equalled it. In April Léon Serpollet with a steam car of his own manufacture made an attempt on the record on the Promenade des Anglais at Nice during the annual speed trials held at this resort. Serpollet smashed the record with a speed of 75.06 mph. The record was broken three times more in 1902 and on all three occasions by Mors petrol-engined cars. In July the Baron Pierre de Caters matched Serpollet's speed with a Mors in a speed trial at Bruges and the following month Vanderbilt broke it with a speed of 76.08 mph. This was the first occasion on which the record was held by a petrol-engined car. In November Henri Fournier, winner of the 1901 Paris-Bordeaux and Paris-Berlin races, drove a Mors to a new record of 76.60 mph. Only a fortnight later a wealthy Paris merchant by the name of Auglères hired the record-breaking Mors from the factory and boosted the record speed to 77.13 mph.

1903: A new and very serious contender appeared in the form of the Gobron-Brillié, a *marque* manufactured in Paris and, in record-breaking form, having a 13-litre engine of the opposed piston type. At a speed trial near Ostend in July the Belgian driver Arthur Duray drove the Gobron-Brillié to a new record of 83.47 mph, an improvement of over 6 mph. Both Rolls and the Baron de Forest strove to improve on this speed with their Mors, but although they achieved marginally faster times, these were disallowed because of the timing methods used. Subsequently Duray and the Gobron-Brillié matched Rolls' unofficial speed of 84.73 mph and this was of course recognised as a new record.

1904: The first American manufacturer to take a serious interest in the Land Speed Record was Henry Ford and his successful attempt, over a mile and not a kilometre, was unique in that it was made on the frozen Lake St Clair near Detroit. The car was the *Arrow,* a monstrous, stark 16.7-litre device that had been built in 1902 and subsequently rebuilt after a fatal crash in 1903. Ford's attempt was a bumpy, skidding, bouncing windswept ordeal, but he succeeded in averaging a speed of 91.37 mph. Unfortunately the Automobile Club de France, the body that was responsible for ratifying record attempts, would not accept the speed as a new record as it did not recognise the American Automobile Association (which had timed the event). A fortnight later at the Florida Speed Week, held at the later very famous record-breaking venue on Daytona beach, William K Vanderbilt with a Mercedes '90' 12-litre car raised the record to 92.30 mph. The pendulum swung once more to Europe and during the Nice Speed Week in March Louis Rigolly with a Gobron-Brillié covered the now very bumpy course along the Promenade des Anglais at a speed of 94.78 mph. In May Baron Pierre de Caters regained the record for Mercedes with a speed of 97.25 mph on the Ostend-Nieuport road. This road was the scene of a speed trial in July and a meeting of the giants, for Rigolly with the Gobron-Brillié and Paul Baras with an 11.3-litre Darracq both competed. Rigolly was the resounding winner with a speed of 103.55 mph and this record survived until November when Baras and the Darracq recorded 104.52 mph over the same course. In July the Darracq had been unable to exceed 100 mph and there were suggestions that the November record had been achieved by dint of removing one of the kilometre stones a few yards down the road!

1905: The first attempt on the record in this year came from the British Napier company who dispatched Arthur E Macdonald and a 15-litre 90 hp car to compete at the Florida Speed Week. Macdonald narrowly bettered the Darracq's performance with a speed of 104.65 mph, but within an hour one Herbert Bowden with a special Mercedes called the *Flying Dutchman* and powered by two engines mounted one behind the other achieved a speed of 109.75 mph. The Automobile Club de France recognised neither record and the American Automobile Association refused to recognise Bowden's performance because his car weighed well over the limit permitted by the Speed Week regulations. The almost frenzied activity of 1904 had diminished and there was only one more successful attempt on the record in 1905. The need for specially built, more powerful and better streamlined cars was apparent (most previous record-breakers had been cars built for road-racing) and Alexandre Darracq built a V-8 22.5-litre car which was ready by the end of December 1905. On the road between Arles and Salon near Marseilles Victor Heméry achieved a speed of 109.65 mph, not quite as fast as Bowden's performance, but nevertheless an official record.

1906: In America work had been progressing on one of the most exciting and revolutionary of all record-breaking cars. Francis and Freeland Stanley of Stanley steam car fame built a record car with a steam engine mounted at the extreme rear of the chassis and with a very aerodynamic streamlined body. At the Florida Speed Week the new car was driven by Fred Marriott who set a total of five records, including the flying kilometre at 121.57 mph and the flying mile at 127.6 mph. In making the speed attempts the driver held the car on the brake until boiler pressure had built up to its maximum, released the brake, shot off like a rocket (which name the car was appropriately given) and built up speed for some five miles before crossing the start of the timed kilometre. The French authorities ratified the flying kilometre achieved by Marriott, but not that over a mile. The *Rocket* reappeared at the 1907 Speed Week in modified and much faster form; the sands were in terrible condition, Marriott lost control at a speed that has been estimated at almost all points between 130 mph and 200 mph and the car was completely wrecked. Almost miraculously the driver survived and made a complete recovery from his injuries.

1909: Three years elapsed before there was another successful attempt on the record and in 1909 the petrol-engine reasserted itself once and for all. The German Benz company produced a vast 4-cylinder 21.5-litre car which was called the *Blitzen* (Lightning). For somewhat obscure reasons the *Blitzen* was brought to the Brooklands banked circuit for its record attempt. Victor Heméry was at the wheel and, lapping in a reverse direction (clockwise) he covered a flying kilometre at 125.95 mph.

1910: After the successful Brooklands attempt the *Blitzen* was shipped to New York and after being displayed in the Benz company's New York show-rooms it was sold to Barney Oldfield. Oldfield, who toured with a circus of cars, competed with the *Blitzen* in the 1910 Florida Speed Week and achieved a speed of 131.275 mph for the flying mile. Almost needless to say this record was not recognised in Europe where the official body was the Association Internationale des Automiles Clubs Reconnus (AIACR).

1911: Oldfield raced the Benz on dirt and grass tracks in the United States until 1911 when he sold it to Ed Moross. Moross entered Bob Burman with the car in grass track events and in April at Daytona Burman set a new record of 141.37 mph. There were grave doubts that this was a genuine performance and the AIACR was now insisting that a record should be decided on the mean speed of two runs in opposite directions; in Europe at least Heméry's 1909 attempt was still regarded as the World's Land Speed Record.

1914: At Brooklands the British driver L G Hornsted with a Benz powered by a *Blitzen*-type engine achieved a speed of 128.16 mph in one direction and 120.23 mph in the other; the mean speed of 124.10 mph was recognised as a new record even though it was slower than Heméry's 1909 one-way record.

1919: Ralph de Palma with a streamlined V-12 Packard achieved a speed of 149.875 mph at Daytona, but this was not recognised as it had been set in one direction only. The same ruling applied to the 156.03 mph record by Tommy Milton with a twin-engined Duesenberg in 1920.

1922: In 1920 the Sunbeam works at Wolverhampton had built an awe-inspiring track car powered by a 350 hp 18.3-litre Manitou 60-degree V-12 aero engine. The car was the work of Sunbeam design wizard Louis Coatalen and it was only too obviously a very cheap job built to take full advantage of available components. Kenelm Lee Guinness and the Sunbeam attacked the Land Speed Record at Brooklands in May 1922 and achieved a mean speed of 133.75 mph. This was the last Land Speed Record set at Brooklands. Malcolm Campbell was greatly impressed by the performance of the V-12 Sunbeam and in 1923 purchased it from the works at a very high price. At a speed trial at Fanöe in Denmark Campbell recorded a mean speed of 136.31 mph, but the AIACR would not ratify the record, as they did not approve the electrical timing equipment (even though they confirmed its accuracy). After this meeting Campbell incorporated aerodynamic improvements suggested by the Boulton and Paul aircraft company, but two more years elapsed before Campbell succeeded in gaining the record.

1924: A year previously Delage, a leading French manufacturer, had built a Land Speed Record contender powered by a V-12 engine of 10.6 litres and developing 280 bhp. In 1924 the big Delage with René Thomas at the wheel appeared at a records meeting on 6th July at Arpajon and here his principal opponent was Ernest Eldridge with a Fiat; but it was a very special Fiat with a lengthened 1907 Grand Prix-type chassis and a 300 hp 21.7-litre 12-cylinder aero engine, a fearsome combination which he had built himself. Thomas averaged a mean 143.26 mph for the kilometre and 143.31 mph for the mile, an improvement on the existing record by a margin of 10 mph. Then Eldridge with his stark, chain-driven monster came to the line and roared away to achieve 146.8 mph for the kilometre and 145.2 mph for the mile. This seemed yet another record, but, very unsportingly, Thomas entered a protest on the grounds that the Fiat was not fitted with a reverse gear (a requirement imposed in the hope that record cars would bear some relation to their road-going counterparts). The organisers had no alternative but to disqualify Eldridge. The Englishman rushed to Paris, worked flat out to fit the car with reverse gear and returned to Arpajon for an attack on Thomas's new record on 12th July. After a run when his engine was misfiring badly, Eldrige snatched the record with a mean speed of 146.01 mph for the kilometre and 145.89 mph for the mile. Malcolm Campbell was as determined as ever to regain the record with *Bluebird,* the 350 hp Sunbeam, and travelled out to the Fanöe speed trials in Denmark in August 1924. It was estimated that Campbell was travelling at around 150 mph when the Sunbeam shed its offside front tyre; the tyre struck a boy spectator (who died from his injuries) and the car ran into the sea. Despite this tragedy Campbell persevered and in September took the Sunbeam to the 7-mile long Pendine sands in Carmarthenshire. Despite a strong cross-wind Campbell achieved an average of 146.16 mph, sufficient to give him the record by the narrow margin of an eighth of an mph.

1925: Campbell had tried, albeit unsuccessfully, to sell the 350 hp Sunbeam at the end of 1924, but he returned with it to Pendine in July 1925 and vindicated his earlier efforts with a worthwhile improvement on the record – 150.869 mph for the kilometre and 150.766 mph for the mile.

1926: While Campbell was campaigning the old Sunbeam and bringing both himself and its makers a great deal of prestige, at Wolverhampton, under the guiding hand of Louis Coatalen they were building a new contender that was beautifully engineered and was the last holder of the Land Speed Record that was a true racing car suitable for circuit events. This Sunbeam had a V-12 4-litre engine based on two of the team's Grand Prix cylinder blocks developing 306 bhp at 5300 rpm. After tests at Brooklands the V-12 Sunbeam was taken to Southport sands in March 1925 for Major Henry Segrave, winner of the 1923 French Grand Prix, to make an attack on the record. Segrave's efforts were plagued by the distortion and breaking of the casing of the very large supercharger and eventually one supercharger was modified at a local workshop in the hope that it would hold together for the three minutes needed to take the record. Segrave made another attempt on the record and during this he struck a stream of water flowing off the beach, the car took off and jumped a distance of nearly fifty feet, the revs soared and the supercharger failed; nevertheless Segrave gained the record with a speed for the kilometre of 152.33 mph. This Sunbeam also enjoyed a successful racing career and its present owner Neil Corner, still races it from time to time in events organised by the Vintage Sports Car Club. Segrave's record survived only a month before it was beaten by Parry Thomas. This superb Welsh engineer had bought a car known as the *Higham Special* from the executors of Count Louis Zborowski following his death at Monza in 1924. For the paltry sum of £125 Parry Thomas had acquired a typical Brooklands aero-engined special, in this case a chassis built by Rubery Owen with a 27-litre 400 hp V-12 American Liberty engine and transmission by an elderly Benz 4-speed gearbox and side chains. Thomas rebuilt the engine, replaced the body with a neat, aerodynamic single-seater and renamed the car *Babs.* He then took it to Pendine Sands and on 27th April, despite a bad engine misfire, smashed Segrave's record with a speed over the kilometre of 169.30 mph. But Parry Thomas was far from satisfied and on the following day broke his own record with 171.02 mph for the kilometre and 170.624 mph for the mile.

1927: Campbell in the meanwhile had devoted two years to the development of his latest Land Speed Record contender which he again named *Bluebird.* The heart of *Bluebird* was one of the latest 22.3-litre 450 bhp Napier Lion W-12 engines (ie the cylinders were in three banks of four) loaned by Napier with the special permission of the Air Ministry. The chassis was designed by Amherst Villiers and constructed by Vickers and there was a very handsome aerodynamic body with a long tail. This car was estimated to have cost around £10,000, ten times the amount expended by Parry Thomas on *Babs.* Campbell took *Bluebird* to Pendine in January, but the sand was too wet for a serious attempt and he returned to the sands in early February. Conditions were still far from ideal, but on his first run he covered the flying kilometre at 179.158 mph; on the return run he hit a bad bump, lost speed while he struggled to retain his goggles and averaged only 170.608 mph. Nevertheless his mean speed of 174.883 mph constituted a new record. Now Parry Thomas and *Babs* (much-modified since 1926) returned to the fray on 1st March and two days later the Welshman made a serious attempt on the record. After several abortive runs Thomas covered the mile at over 170 mph. Just as he completed the mile on the return run the car went out of control, rolled and then righted itself before spinning round on the sand. Thomas was dead, his neck almost severed by, it was believed, the offside driving chain which had come off its sprocket, but there is still some doubt as to the real cause of the accident. The skidding car had broken the timing apparatus and its speed on that last tragic run was never known. Parry Thomas was the first driver to be killed in pursuit of the Land Speed Record and *Babs* was buried in the Pendine sands from which it was exhumed by Owen Wyn Owen in 1969. Owen is now well advanced with the restoration of *Babs.* In March Segrave and the latest Sunbeam contender appeared at Daytona. This fantastic car, known as the '1000 HP CAR' (although its output was rather less) was powered by two World War One Sunbeam Matabele V-12 22.5-litre 435 bhp aero engines and it featured a sleek, full-width aerodynamic body enclosing the wheels. On 29th March Segrave made his great effort, clearly moving at tremendous speed and having to run into the shallow water lapping up on to the beach because the brakes were inadequate. The second run was less dramatic, but just as fast and Segrave had taken the record with a mean 202.988 mph for the kilometre, 203.792 mph for the mile and 202.675 mph for five kilometres. The existing record had been beaten by a staggering margin of 28 mph and it was the first time that 200 mph on land had been exceeded.

1928: Although Campbell had been among the first to congratulate Segrave on his success, he was working flat-out to rebuild *Bluebird* in a more competitive form. The engine was replaced by a more powerful version of the Napier Lion developing 875 bhp and a new body was fitted. Campbell and *Bluebird* arrived at Daytona in February 1928 and after an abortive run on the 12th when the car hit a bump and jumped into the air so fiercely that is was badly damaged on landing, he made his big effort on 19th February. On the first run he again hit a bad bump, was half thrown out of his seat, lost speed while he regained control, but still covered the kilometre at 214.7 mph. So strong was the wind on his return run that he could manage 'only' 199.9 mph, a mean speed of 206.956 mph and a new record. Two American contenders now challenged British supremacy in the record-breaking field. On the day after Campbell's successful run Frank Lockhart appeared with his very special Stutz Black Hawk, a beautifully engineered and streamlined car with a supercharged 16-cylinder 3-litre engine developing 385 bhp. Twenty-five-year-old Lockhart had largely built the car himself and raised the sponsorship, and badly needed to take the record if only for financial reasons. Because of supercharger problems, much of the time reserved for his runs was lost and when he did manage to start, rain was falling and visibility was bad. The Stutz was far from stable, Lockhart could barely see the course markers and he lost control; the car somersaulted twice and splashed into the sea. Apart from shock and a cut wrist Lockhart escaped unscathed. A day later, Philadelphia wire manufacturer Ray Keech was in action with his White Triplex Special. Although its construction was later to be justified, the Triplex was a real 'lash-up', based on a lorry chassis, powered by three Liberty aero engines (giving a total capacity of 81 litres) and with sketchy pointed bodywork that left the suspension and two rear-mounted engines exposed. On his first run a water hose burst and sprayed him with boiling water with the result that the record attempt had to be abandoned. Both Keech and Lockhart returned to Daytona in April. On his first run Keech achieved a speed of 203.97 mph against the wind, but the timing apparatus failed on his return run. By the time that this had been repaired, more than the permitted time (30 minutes) had elapsed and the fuming driver was forced to make both runs again. His mean speed for the mile was 207.552 mph, enough to give him the record by the narrowest of margins. Three days later Lockhart went into action. On his first run he achieved a speed of 203.45 mph against the wind and he was travelling at around 220 mph on the return run when a tyre burst. The Stutz Black Hawk somersaulted and

Lockhart was thrown out and killed instantly. This was a particularly tragic accident, for Lockhart was both a very talented engineer and a highly skilled driver (he had won the Indianapolis 500 Miles race in 1926).

1929: Segrave had now left Sunbeam, but he had a new and exciting privately sponsored project designed by J S Irving well under way. The aim was 240 mph and Irving designed a car with a Napier aero engine (as used in the Schneider Trophy Supermarine seaplanes) developing 925 bhp and a very interesting body design with exposed front wheels, fairings between the wheels and a long tail surmounted by an enormous fin; the car, known as the *Irving-Napier Golden Arrow,* was painted gold and unadorned apart from union jacks on the tail-fin. When Segrave made his record attempt in March 1929, the Daytona beach was bumpy and rippled as the result of heavy seas, but the car – and the runs – were almost troublefree and he achieved a mean speed for the mile of 231.446 mph, an improvement of 24 mph over the record set by the Triplex Special. Segrave received a knighthood for this performance. On the very next day the Triplex Special, now driven by one Lee Bible, made its effort to regain the record for America. Bible completed a first run of 183 mph and clocked 202 mph on the return leg, but then made a terrible mistake; he lifted off the accelerator much too quickly, the braking effect of the three Liberty engines were so savage that the Triplex was hurled into an enormous loop, rolling and smashing itself in a trail of wreckage, and the unlucky driver was thrown out and killed. Campbell was still striving to regain the record and in 1929 made an attempt at a dried-out lake known as Verneuk Pan around 450 miles from Cape Town. Nothing went right for Campbell during this attempt. The high altitude resulted in substantial engine power loss and the best that the Englishman and his beautiful blue car could manage was 217.6 mph for the kilometre; his only consolation was records for the five kilometres and five miles at 217 and 212 mph respectively.

1930: The earlier exploits of Sunbeam had been over-shadowed by the later successes of *Bluebird* and the *Golden Arrow,* but, despite its worsening financial situation, the Wolverhampton company strove to regain prestige with a new car, the *Silver Bullet,* which was dispatched to Daytona early in 1930. The *Silver Bullet* was a competely new design by Louis Coatalen featuring two V-12 24-litre engines developed from the company's aeronautical experience and blithely spoken of as developing 4000 hp (but the true output must have been substantially less). The 3-speed gearbox, in theory at least, gave speeds of 125, 166 and 248 mph and it had a very long, very handsome body with twin stabilising fins at the rear and a very novel horizontal air brake. Kaye Don was the driver, but he was completely out of luck and the project failed miserably. The engines had not been tested before the team left England and gave persistent trouble, and Daytona was in its only too usual poor condition; the highest speed achieved by the car was only a little over 186 mph, and the team returned to England in acrimony and disharmony. Promises to return to Daytona when the car had been fully sorted were never fulfilled.

1931: Bluebird had been completely rebuilt and although the existing chassis, steering and suspension were retained, the power unit was a 1929 supercharged Napier Lion developing 1450 bhp, there was new offset transmission alongside which the driver sat (thereby lowering the car) and a completely new body with long tail and tail-fin built by the Gurney Nutting company. Campbell made his attempt at Daytona in February 1931 and everything went perfectly; he achieved a mean 246.09 mph for the mile and returned to England to be knighted.

1932: Campbell was a man of restless ambition and now he was determined to achieve the magic 250 mph which was so close. *Bluebird* was fitted with a new nose and at Daytona in February 1932 Campbell raised the record to 253.97 mph.

1933: Still not content, Campbell had *Bluebird* rebuilt for 1933 with a 36.5-litre 2300 bhp Rolls-Royce V-12 engine (as used to win the 1931 Schneider Trophy) and at Daytona in February 1933 clocked a new record for the mile of 272.46 mph and for the kilometre 271.636 mph.

1935: Reid Railton had devoted 1934 to rebuilding *Bluebird* yet again with a full-width body incorporating air brakes and twin rear wheels. At Daytona in March 1935 Campbell achieved a mean speed of 276.816 mph, a small improvement on his existing record, but he was completely dissatisfied and frustrated. Daytona posed too many problems at the speeds that record cars were now achieving and weather conditions were too fickle. Campbell commenced the search for a more suitable venue and settled on the desolate, vast Bonneville salt flats in the north of Utah, used for long-distance record breaking by Ab Jenkins in 1932 and John Cobb in 1935. A 12-mile course was smoothed out and marked by a trail of oil and early in the morning of 3rd September Campbell made his attempt. On the first run the cockpit filled with fumes, Campbell was partially overcome, he swerved off the course and back on again and then a front tyre burst. Despite these so nearly lethal dramas Campbell had covered the course at 304.311 mph. The maximum interval between runs had now been increased to an hour, but because of the problems with the car and because of a broken timing wire Campbell made his return run only five minutes before the hour expired. His mean speed was given by the time-keepers as 299.87 mph and he resolved to make another attempt on the next day. Two hours later the time-keepers adjusted their timing to 301.129 mph, a complete anticlimax for Campbell who had striven so hard to achieve the 300 mph figure. Sir Malcolm Campbell now retired from the arena to allow others to carry the mantle of British prestige.

1937: Captain George Eyston, who had already broken many long-distance class records, now took up the gauntlet with a veritable monster of a car, the largest ever petrol-driven car, which he called *Thunderbolt.* The power came from two Rolls-Royce Schneider Trophy-type aero engines developing around 4700 bhp mounted side-by-side, there were eight wheels (four steering wheels at the front), there was a very aerodynamic body built in aluminium by a firm of boat builders and the complete car weighed seven tons. When Eyston and *Thunderbolt* arrived at Bonneville in October 1937 the car was completely untested, he recorded a one-way speed of 310.68 mph before clutch trouble intervened and it was not until November that the car was fully sorted. On 19th November Eyston achieved a mean speed of 312.00 mph for the kilometre and 311.42 mph for the mile. Heavy rain began to fall the same afternoon, heralding the start of the Utah winter, and Eyston departed in the knowledge that a much higher speed was well within the capabilities of the car.

1938: Eyston returned to Bonneville in August 1938, but he now faced another British contender in the person of John Cobb and his Railton. *Thunderbolt* had been slightly modified and on 24th August Eyston achieved a one-way run of 347.155 mph, only to find that the electric timing apparatus had failed to record his passage over the line. Three days later Eyston tried again and achieved 345.21 mph for the kilometre and 345.49 mph for the mile, an improvement of 33 mph on his own record. During this time Reid Railton had been ironing out teething problems with his radical new car which featured two World War One-designed Napier Lion aero engines each of 1250 bhp in a compact, light chassis with drive to all four wheels, proper suspension and an exquisitely smooth and compact all-enveloping body that could be lifted off in one piece to give complete access to the mechanics. On 12th September John Cobb snatched the record from Eyston by recording a mean 350.20 mph for the mile. On only the following morning Eyston replied with a speed of 357.50 mph.

1939: Cobb was in fact aiming for 400 mph, a target that was within the scope of the Railton, but clearly far beyond the limits of *Thunderbolt.* He returned to Bonneville in August 1939 and on 23rd August, just before the outbreak of war in Europe, achieved a mean 369.74 mph for the kilometre. At this time there was another contender lurking in the wings, but because of the outbreak of war he never had a crack at the record. Dr Ferdinand Porsche had designed a car powered by a Daimler-Benz DB 603 V-12 aero engine of 44.5-litres. Daimler-Benz built the car and Hans von Stuck was to drive it, but time ran out on the project. . . .

1947: John Cobb returned to Bonneville, only to find the sands in a terrible, bumpy, holed condition. The course was rolled as smooth as possible and with the Railton, now known as the Railton-Mobil Special, he made a one-way run of 375.32 mph on 14th September. The course was still so bumpy, however, that a split had developed in the bodywork and a return run was out of the question. Cobb still persevered and finally on 16th September achieved a mean speed of 394.196 mph. On his return run he had been timed at 403.135 mph, had crossed the line at around 415 mph and clearly under more favourable conditions would have achieved a mean speed of well over the elusive 400 mph mark.

1960: It was not until 1963 that Cobb's long-standing record was at last broken, but 1960 witnessed a confrontation of several powerful challengers, all of whom failed to achieve substantial success. From England came Donald Campbell, son of Sir Malcolm, with the latest *Bluebird,* built at a cost of one million pounds (and with another million needed to fund the record attempts), largely provided by British industry. The power unit was a Bristol-Siddeley Proteus gas turbine (as used in the Britannia airliner) developing about 4100 shaft hp and driving all four wheels through David Brown single-speed gearboxes (no clutches or gears were needed). The body was a beautifully smooth design with enormous bulges to accommodate the huge wheels. Facing *Bluebird* were four American contenders: Athol Graham's *City of Salt Lake* with a 3000 hp Allison piston aero engine; Art Arfons' *Green Monster* with a similar engine, but developing some 3800 hp; Dr Nathan Ostich's *Flying Caduceus,* a pure jet machine with an engine from a Boeing B36 bomber of around 7000 hp and, under the then rules, ineligible for the record as it had no driven wheels; and Mickey Thompson's *Challenger I* powered by four supercharged Pontiac engines giving a total output of around 2800 hp. The first runner was Graham who was travelling at over 300 mph when his car suddenly went sideways, reared into the air, came down upside down and rolled over and over. The driver was killed. Dr Ostich never succeeded in turning in a fast run because of a myriad of problems and finally withdrew because of steering failure. The most successful of the American cars was Mickey Thompson's *Challenger* which achieved 406.60 mph in one direction (the fastest ever reached), but the attempt had to be abandoned because of a broken supercharger chain. After a trial run at 249.57 mph and a return run on which a final drive bearing failed, Arfons concluded that his car was no potential record-breaker and withdrew from the struggle. Now it was Campbell's turn; after a number of trial runs during which he progressively built up his speed, he was travelling at about 345 mph when Bluebird ran off the course, slid sideways and rolled and bounced along the salt until it came to rest a shattered wreck. Campbell was held in by safety harness and escaped with a fractured skull, a pierced ear-drum and numerous cuts and bruises. So impressed was Sir Alfred Owen by the courage displayed by Campbell that he undertook to build a new *Bluebird* at his own expense.

1963: While a new *Bluebird* was being built, Craig Breedlove, an experienced Californian dragster exponent, was working on what his idea of a Land Speed Record contender should look like. Breedlove, like Ostich, favoured the direct propulsion of a gas-turbine engine and was totally disinterested in whether or not his record (should he gain it) be recognised. *Spirit of America,* as Breedlove named his project, was started in the garage in his back yard; it was powered by a General Electric turbojet engine and was a very streamlined three-wheeler (with a limited amount of steering movement on the single front wheel). Breedlove made his attempt at Bonneville on 5th

August 1963 and, after a run at 388.47 mph, went out for another go and achieved a mean 407.45 mph. Even if Breedlove's record was not recognised by the Federation Internationale de l'Automobile, it was treated as such by both the Federation Internationale Motocycliste and the United States Automobile Club.

1964: Donald Campbell and *Bluebird* returned to Lake Eyre in July 1964 and in conditions that were far from ideal succeeded at long last in beating John Cobb's record for wheel-driven cars; the speed was 403.10 mph exactly for each of the two runs. By the end of the year this performance, which was inferior to Breedlove's record with *Spirit of America,* was completely overshadowed by the ever-rising speeds of the pure jet cars that battled it out at Bonneville later in the year. On 2nd October Walt Arfons with his *Wingfoot Express* powered by a Westinghouse triple-jet engine covered the mile at a mean 413.2 mph. Three days later Art Arfons (brother of Walt, though the two rarely spoke to each other) made his attempt with a new car still called *Green Monster,* painted despite its name, red, white and blue and powered by a General General Electric 17,500 hp turbojet. On its run out *Green Monster* clocked only 396.3 mph, but the return run saw a remarkable 479 mph and a new record at a mean average of 434.02 mph. Now it was the turn of Craig Breedlove to try to recover the crown that he had so recently lost. On 13th October Breedlove turned in an almost nonchalant 468.72 mph and two days later raised his own record to a staggering 526.28 mph. The last run ended in near-disaster; *Spirit of America* was slowed in two stages, by a drag parachute and by Goodyear disc brakes. The parachute broke away from its mounting, the disc brakes were incapable of stopping the car from 500 mph and burnt out, and *Spirit of America* careered on for five miles, mowing down a telephone pole, launching itself into the air and stopping, partly submerged, in a brine lake. Breedlove eased himself out of the cockpit and swam for the shore! Art Arfons was not prepared to let the matter rest there and on 27th October made yet another attempt. His first run was not good enough, 515.98 mph, but on the return run he stepped up the speed to record 559.18 mph, a new record at a mean speed of 536.71 mph. The dangers of travelling at these very high speeds were only too obvious and the drivers restricted themselves to the absolute minimum number of 'squirts'. During that month the Federation Internationale de l'Automobile announced that it was prepared to recognise vehicles propelled by jet engines other than through the wheels and the category became known as International Records for Special Vehicles. The first record to be recognised was Art Arfons' 536.71 mph set on 27th October.

1965: Although the FIA had been prepared to recognise cars with direct jet propulsion, this august body would still not approve three-wheelers and Craig Breedlove returned to Bonneville in October with a new four-wheeler powered by a General Electric turbojet with a 15,000 lb thrust and known as *Spirit of America, Sonic I.* This car, designed to achieve eventual speeds of over 800 mph, was very long and very narrow and had all four wheels enclosed within the aluminium panels of the bodywork. On 2nd November Breedlove achieved 555.482 mph for the kilometre and 555.127 mph for the mile. Breedlove retained his record for only five days before Art Arfons with *Green Monster* responded with 576.553 mph for the mile and 572.545 mph for the kilometre. Just past the mile-mark on the return run the offside rear tyre burst, the rubber tore away one of the braking parachutes and its electrical firing mechanism, the cockpit was filled with smoke and Arfons ran off the course before smashing the cockpit glass, steering back on to the course and firing the second braking parachute manually. Now another contender came to the line, but this time it was a contender for the traditional class of vehicles driven through the wheels. The car was *Goldenrod,* a beautifully slim, long narrow device powered by four 6.9-litre Chrysler engines, much modified and mounted in-line. The builders were Bill and Bob Summers, very experienced 'hot-rodders', and on 13th November Bob Summers was at the wheel. Despite never getting out of third gear (there were two 4-speed gearboxes) Summers recorded 409.277 mph, thereby depriving Campbell of his record with *Bluebird.* Two days later Breedlove was in action again and recorded a mean 600.601 mph.

1966: Art Arfons and *Green Monster* returned to Bonneville in November and on the 17th of that month made his bid to top Breedlove's 600 mph. On his first turn, when *Green Monster* was travelling at close to 610 mph, a bearing in the right-hand front wheel broke up, the car veered out of control, rolled end over end and then rolled sideways for a mile, destroying itself with every impact and leaving a trail of debris. Miraculously Arfons escaped the fastest ever motoring accident with injuries no greater than a badly cut face.

1970: Back in 1964 Walt Arfons and his colleagues had been experimenting with a rocket-propelled car using jet-assisted take-off solid fuel rockets and in 1965 their latest car *Wingfoot Express II* had achieved a speed of 580 mph before the rockets ran out of thrust at about half-way along the measured mile. Elsewhere other rocket-propulsion experiments were under way. Richard A Keller and Ray Dausman had been working on a project for a liquid-fuel rocket-propelled car at the Illinois Research Institute at Chicago. Together with Peter Farnsworth, a specialist in dragster chassis construction, they formed a concern known as Reaction Dynamics Inc. During 1967-8 they ran successful rocket-powered dragsters and then put work in hand on their Land Speed Record contender. A rocket motor was built with a maximum thrust of 22,000 lb, but capable of running for only twenty seconds before the fuel ran out, and this was mounted in a 'fuselage' 38 ft 2.5 in in length (it was the longest of all land speed record cars) with wide-spread unsprung rear wheels trailing on out-riggers and the sprung front wheels, mounted only nine inches apart, buried in the fuselage. This device was known as the *Blue Flame* and it appeared at Bonneville in September 1970 with Gary Gabelich at the helm. During trial runs the speed gradually rose and finally, on 23rd October, Gabelich achieved a new record with speeds of 630.388 mph for the kilometre and 622.407 mph for the mile.

Seventy-seven years have now elapsed since the first Land Speed Record was officially recorded and serious contenders for the record are now travelling ten times faster than their illustrious pioneering forebears. As speeds rise, the dangers of penetrating the barriers of the unknown remain and it is remarkable that so few men have lost their lives in pursuit of the Land Speed Record. In record-breaking there is always the next goal to achieve and now the speed merchants of Bonneville Salt Flats are probing towards breaking the sound barrier on land, for which at Utah a speed of around 750 mph is required.

11

Connaught, The First of the Grand Prix Winners

23rd October 1955 was one of the most significant dates in British motor racing history. On a warm, sunny autumn day at Siracusa in Sicily a stubby, dark green racing car, its highly polished paintwork and young driver enveloped in dust, took the chequered flag to score Britain's first important Grand Prix victory since Segrave's win at San Sebastian in 1924. The car was the Connaught B-series, the driver was dental student Tony Brooks and the victory marked the turning point in Britain's Grand Prix fortunes. In 1956 Vanwall took up the gauntlet with determination, two years later Tony Vandervell's team from Park Royal won the Manufacturers' World Championship and this wave of success, crested at different times by Cooper, Lotus, BRM, Brabham and Tyrrell, has yet to ebb. For Connaught personnel and British racing enthusiasts it was a tragic blow that only two years after that magnificent performance at Siracusa, the Connaught works Grand Prix cars, together with all the team's equipment, came under the auctioneer's hammer because of financial difficulties.

One-time RAF flying officer, later hotelier and cinema manager Rodney Clarke was the brains behind the Connaught project. Clarke loved cars in general and thoroughbred Bugatti sports cars in particular. In 1943 he founded a business called Continental Cars at Chobham in Surrey (it was moved to Send in Surrey in 1946). He specialised in Bugattis and he ran his own Type 59 Grand Prix car fitted with sports equipment in early post-war British Club events. It was Clarke's ambition to obtain an agency for the make, but his hopes were dashed when Bugatti failed to restart regular production after the war and he decided to build his own sports cars.

These cars, which were given the name Connaught, were rather bizarre-looking streamlined two-seaters based on the Lea-Francis 14 hp chassis, but both this and the Lea-Francis push-rod engine with twin camshafts mounted high on the cylinder block in accordance with Riley practice were extensively modified. Engine development was the responsibility of Mike Oliver, another ex-RAF character, who had originally come to Continental Cars as a customer, but joined them to become service manager. When he was developing the Lea-Francis engine, Oliver worked in close collaboration with John Wyer who at this time was works manager at Monaco Engineering, the famous sports car garage at Watford in Hertfordshire. By using new camshafts and fitting four Amal motor-cycle carburettors, Oliver boosted power output of the Lea-Francis engine to 102 bhp at 5500 rpm, compared with the 70 bhp of the standard production unit.

The first Connaught sports car, bearing the registration number MPH 329, was acquired by Maserati driver Kenneth McAlpine and he first raced it in June 1949 at the Bugatti Owners' Club at Silverstone meeting where he took a fourth place. MPH 329 and MPH 996 with Clarke at the wheel were raced throughout 1949-50 in British Club and National races and achieved a fair amount of success. The cars were built for sale in small numbers and by the end of 1953 a total of twenty-seven had been built, mainly of the streamlined L3 type, but there were also a few L3/SR cars with stark cycle-wing bodywork.

The success of the sports cars encouraged Kenneth McAlpine to sponsor a Formula Two Connaught which was designated the A-series. Formula Two, which had been introduced for the 1948 season, was a subsidiary racing category for cars of up to 2000 cc unsupercharged or 500 cc supercharged (though in fact no one built a supercharged car). By 1950 Formula Two was supported by several Continental constructors, including Ferrari, and in England by the HWM team.

It had been hoped to have the A-series Connaught ready to race by the summer of 1950, but the prototype was badly damaged in a testing accident at Silverstone and it did not appear in its first race until the Castle Combe meeting in the October of that year. Although what was basically the Lea-Francis engine was retained, there was a new light alloy cylinder block (still at this stage with a capacity of only 1767 cc) and power output on alcohol fuel was around 130 bhp at 6000 rpm.

Clarke designed a new chassis based on two longitudinal large-diameter tubular members tapering towards the rear, with tubular cross-members and the 4-gallon oil tank for the dry sump system contained in the main front box-section cross-member. Although some of the Connaught's Continental rivals (including Maserati and Gordini) were still using a rigid rear axle three years later, Clarke had evolved a fully independent system by double wishbones and torsion bars front and rear. Transmission was by a preselector 4-speed gearbox (used primarily because the ratios were ideal) and a 'quick-change' final drive developed from a unit built in pre-war days by Peter Monkhouse of Monaco Engineering for use on an MG Magnette. A notable feature of the A-series was the absence of a body frame and the alloy body was supported by its own skin strength. This was not really satisfactory because it made the body very expensive to manufacture and repair, and alloy that was strong enough to support itself was very difficult to work. The fuel tanks were fitted on each side of the car so that the weight distribution did not change as the fuel was used up and the car was fitted with very handsome Elektron bolt-on wheels.

On the debut of the A-series at Castle Combe it was driven by Kenneth McAlpine who took a second place to Stirling Moss's HWM in an 18-mile race for cars of up to 2500 cc, and a fifth in the Formule Libre race.

The team was well satisfied with the progress so far made and with the car's performance at the Wiltshire circuit, but a large number of modifications were made over the winter of 1950-1. The most obvious change was the adoption of the very distinctive 'balance-box', a housing for the Amal carburettors on the right-hand side of the bonnet, and experiments had revealed that mounting the carburettors in this fashion gave better power in the middle range. The independent rear suspension had been scrapped and its place taken by a de Dion axle with the tube running above and behind the final drive. Lateral movement of the tube was restricted by a compound linkage running from the nearside hub to the chassis frame, and fore and aft movement was controlled by tubular radius arms on each side of the car. To take brake torque there was a short radius arm and rubber blocks mounted on the differential casing.

It was intended that the 1951 season should be a year of testing and development and the car's appearances were restricted to British events. At the Easter Goodwood meeting the car was driven by both McAlpine and Brian Shawe-Taylor who was usually seen at the wheel of an ERA. The Connaught's new rear suspension was still far from fully sorted and Shawe-Taylor's reports of the Connaught's bad handling and lack of stability gave it a reputation that it ill-deserved. For, as true as were the driver's comments at the time, by the car's next race, at Boreham in Essex, the handling problems had been resolved and the Connaught's roadholding matched that of any of its rivals. At this meeting McAlpine would have won the Formula Two race had he not by mistake selected neutral at the very last corner!

Later in the year the Connaught appeared at Gamston, Ibsley, again at Boreham and finally at Goodwood, all airfield circuits that are no longer used for racing. At Goodwood, where the car failed to start because of crankshaft damage caused by big-end failure, it appeared with new, larger fuel tanks which boosted the range from 150 miles to over 200. A few good places had been achieved during the season, development was well advanced and at Send construction was progressing steadily on a batch of six A-series cars intended for sale to private owners.

The withdrawal from Grand Prix racing by Alfa Romeo at the end of the 1951 season, coupled with the lack of a serious challenger to the all-conquering Ferraris, resulted in all World Championship races in 1952-3 being held to 2-litre Formula Two rules and so the Connaught, which had been built to a lesser Formula, became a Grand Prix contender. Mike Oliver had now developed full 1960 cc engines with a bore of 79 mm. In this form close to 150 bhp was developed and the 1952 A-series cars had a maximum speed of around 140 mph. The production cars had a one-inch longer wheelbase (7 ft 1 in) to facilitate removal of the engine. McAlpine continued to race the prototype car, and production cars were delivered to Ken Downing (who had previously raced a sports Connaught) and Philip Fotheringham-Parker.

Despite a power deficiency of some 30 bhp compared with the latest 4-cylinder Ferrari and the new 6-cylinder Maserati, the Connaughts handled as well as their Continental rivals (better than some) and put up some good performances during the 1952 season. The cars failed to start at the Easter Goodwood meeting because of oil starvation of the new lead-bronze bearings that were now used and they were out of the picture at the *Daily Express* Trophy race at Silverstone the following month; of three Connaught drivers to start the race the highest placed was McAlpine in tenth position. On 1st June Ken Downing drove his private Connaught in the Grand Prix des Frontières at Chimay, a race that was usually a private owner's benefit, and he led the race until the last lap when he eased up to much and was pipped at the post by Paul Frère's HWM.

The following month a grand total of four Connaughts ran in the British Grand Prix at Silverstone and these were driven by McAlpine, Downing,

Dennis Poore (with Fotheringham-Parker's car) and Eric Thompson (with a new works car). For this race the cars were fitted with new pistons which increased the compression ratio from 10:1 to 12.5:1 and, perhaps rather more important, had crowns of much improved shape. The result was a substantial increase in power output and the engine fitted to Thompson's car was found in testing to develop 155 bhp, the maximum recorded by an A-series using normal alcohol fuel. The increased power output also exposed a crankshaft weakness and, during practise for the Grand Prix, the crankshaft of Thompson's car broke. By dint of all-night work the engine was rebuilt in time for the car to run in the race and shortly afterwards the team introduced a crankshaft of improved design.

In the race the Connaught drivers performed magnificently. For many laps Dennis Poore, driving in his first Grand Prix, held third place ahead of one of the works Ferraris driven by Piero Taruffi; Poore fell back behind the Ferrari after a spin, but continued to harass the Maranello entry and moved up a place when Farina's Ferrari, which had been in second place, stopped at the pits because of ignition trouble. Unfortunately the Connaught's fuel tanks had insufficient capacity to enable it to run through a full-length Grand Prix without a pit stop and Poore lost his third place to Mike Hawthorn (Cooper-Bristol) as the result of a thoroughly disorganised refuelling stop. At the chequered flag Poore was in fourth place, Eric Thompson (also driving in his first Grand Prix) was fifth and the other Connaughts driven by Downing and McAlpine took ninth and sixteenth places.

In August Ken Downing, who was perhaps the most adventurous of the Connaught drivers, ran in the Dutch Grand Prix, but it was not a successful outing and he retired his A-series car with loss of oil pressure. Largely as a result of the success achieved in the British race, an entry of three cars managed by Dennis Poore and under the banner of 'Connaught Racing Syndicate' ran in the Italian Grand Prix held in September. At Monza the cars were driven by McAlpine, Poore and Stirling Moss. On this high-speed circuit the Connaughts were outclassed by the Ferraris and Maseratis and Moss, the fastest driver in the team, never rose above ninth place. Both Stirling and McAlpine retired and Poore, whose engine refused to fire after a refuelling stop in the closing stages of the race, pushed his car across the finishing line into twelfth place.

During 1952 Rodney Clarke had almost despaired at the problems involved in tuning four motor-cycle carburettors which, in any case, were never intended for use on a racing car, and the following year the American

Hilborn-Travers fuel injection system was adopted on the works Connaughts. In some races in 1953 the Connaught team also used nitromethane, a foul-smelling, oxygen-bearing fuel additive that cost around £10 per gallon, but boosted power output to 165 bhp, almost enough to be competitive. Two new cars were completed in 1953 and these featured a longer 7 ft 6 in wheelbase which slightly increased the polar moment of inertia and provided more room in the cockpit. Both cars had reprofiled body lines, and the final car, chassis number AL10, which was completed late in the 1953 season, had a number of other modifications including a lever on the dash that could be used to adjust the rear suspension and thereby alter the handling characteristics to suit the circuit or the driver's tastes. For 1953 Rob Walker, still today a very successful private-entrant, acquired Downing's car; it was painted in his usual dark blue colour scheme and driven by Tony Rolt. Fotheringham-Parker's car was sold to band-leader Johnny Claes who raced it in a Belgian yellow colour finish. The car raced at Silverstone by Eric Thompson was sold to Ecurie Ecosse and another Connaught privateer was Leslie Marr who had acquired his car late in the 1952 season.

Connaught's first outing of the 1953 season was at Goodwood on Easter Monday and here new recruit to the works team Roy Salvadori drove superbly; he led throughout the Formula Two Lavant Cup only to have his engine cut out on the last lap. He was passed by Baron Emmanuel de Graffenried's new Maserati and coasted across the line to take second place. It was much the same result at the *Daily Express* Trophy race at Silverstone, where the winner was Mike Hawthorn with a works Ferrari, but Salvadori again took second place, followed across the line by Tony Rolt with the dark blue Walker car. In its report of this race the *Daily Mirror,* with its customary accuracy, referred to the success of the *American* Connaught!

In 1953 Connaught's racing programme was much more ambitious, but, although the team contested several Continental races, no success was gained. In the Dutch Grand Prix at Zandvoort, works drivers Salvadori and McAlpine were joined by Stirling Moss who was temporarily without a regular mount because his own special Cooper-Alta car had proved a dismal failure. Salvadori and McAlpine both retired with engine trouble and Moss finished ninth and last after a pit stop to reconnect a fuel lead. Two Connaughts, for Salvadori and 'B Bira' (Siamese Prince Birabongse), were entered in the French Grand Prix at Reims, but this was another high-speed circuit on which the cars were completely outclassed and both retired with engine failure.

Connaught had hopes of repeating their 1952 performance in the British Grand Prix, but this time they were out of luck; the Continental opposition was stronger than ever and the sole Connaught driver to finish was B Bira in seventh place. The team next appeared at the German Grand Prix at the Nürburgring, perhaps the most demanding and arduous of European circuits. Salvadori retired at the end of the first 14.19-mile lap because his car had lost all its water, B Bira was eliminated by engine trouble and the sole finisher was McAlpine who gamely plugged on to finish thirteenth, despite a loose radius arm which caused a monumental rear-end oversteer.

The results of the German Grand Prix were only too typical of Connaught performances in major International races. In comparison with the Ferraris and Maseratis, the Connaughts were under-powered and unreliable, and retirements frequently resulted from drivers over-stressing their cars in their efforts to stay with the Continental opposition.

In September Connaught competed in two races on Italian soil. Three cars were entered in the Italian Grand Prix for Salvadori, McAlpine and Jack Fairman. Minor mechanical problems resulted in the British cars making a succession of pit stops, on occasions all three cars were in the pits at once (which was more than the pit staff could cope with), Salvadori retired and although Fairman and McAlpine struggled on to the finish, they had covered insufficient laps to be classified. While the team was in Italy, it competed in the Modena Grand Prix, but the sole finisher was McAlpine who took eighth place after a long pit stop. Some consolation for an unsuccessful season was gained by Salvadori's victory in the Formula Two race at the Autumn Goodwood meeting.

Rodney Clarke was well advanced with the design of the Connaught contender for the new 2500 cc Grand Prix Formula that came into force in 1954, a car that incorporated all the lessons learned the hard way with the A-series 2-litre cars. In the meanwhile McAlpine continued to race an A-series car during the early part of 1954 and Rob Walker entered an ex-works fuel injection car for Tony Rolt. There was a large collection of parts for the A-series cars at the works at Send; partly to put these to good use and partly to provide a stop-gap car for the team to race until the new 2500 cc car was ready, a couple of sports cars were built up for the 1954 season using these components. These cars, designated the ALSR, had a chassis almost identical to that of the A-series, the engine reduced in capacity to 1484 cc (in which form it developed 115 bhp) and bodywork reminiscent of the Aston Martin DB3S. One car was raced by McAlpine and the other was sold to John Coombs. Coombs considered that the Connaught chassis was too heavy and in mid-season transferred the engine and gearbox to a Lotus Mk VIII chassis which was both very light and very aerodynamic. For 1955 the works two-seater was rebuilt with more aerodynamic bodywork similar to that of the new Grand Prix car but with twin tail-fins. This car was raced at Le Mans in 1955, where it was timed at 135 mph before it retired with valve failure, but it was burnt out in a multi-car crash in the Tourist Trophy that cost the life of its young driver, Bill Smith.

Connaught's contender for the new Grand Prix Formula was first demonstrated to the press in August 1954 at Goodwood, where Clarke, showing off its paces, was almost asphyxiated by fumes from the SU fuel injection. The new car, designated the B-series, was an impressive and advanced design, but, in retrospect, it can be criticised because it incorporated too many new features for a team whose financial resources were very limited.

The most distinctive feature of the new car was the streamlined bodywork and it was coincidental, but nevertheless very interesting, that both Connaught and Mercedes-Benz should have introduced stream-lined Grand Prix cars at about the same time. On the Mercedes, access to the mechanics was poor and the driver's vision from the cockpit was restricted. Neither of these criticisms could be levelled at the Connaught. The body of the B-series was divided along the waist-line so that the upper section could be lifted off in one piece to give complete access to the mechanical components. The driver's range of vision was excellent because of a high seating position, but, admittedly, this resulted in a large frontal area and aerodynamics that were inferior to those of the Mercedes-Benz. Dominating the rear of the Connaught was a single large tail-fin.

Simplicity with efficiency was the key-note of the chassis design which was very similar to that of the A-series car, with a tubular ladder-type frame, double wishbone and coil spring front suspension and a de Dion rear axle. Although torsion bars were no longer used at the front, longitudinal torsion bars were retained at the rear. The body was now supported by a welded structure of small-diameter steel tubes and a total fuel capacity of 50 gallons, sufficient for a non-stop run through a full 300-mile Grand Prix, was provided by tanks in the tail and in the body sides just forward of the driver.

The biggest problem facing any Grand Prix constructor in Great Britain was the lack of a suitable engine. Several teams had been planning to use the new Coventry-Climax 'Godiva' V-8 which is was hoped would be ready by the latter part of the 1954 season. Rodney Clarke had designed a rear-engined car, designated the J3 Series C, to be powered by the 'Godiva' unit, but Coventry-Climax abandoned development of their engine and what would have been a revolutionary Connaught design was never completed.

Clarke and McAlpine had, however, made arrangements for the exclusive use of another proprietary engine, Geoffrey Taylor's Alta, a much developed and improved version of that used to power HWM Formula Two cars, but nevertheless a design of pre-war ancestry. This 2470 cc (93.5 × 90 mm) 4-cylinder unit featured twin overhead camshafts driven by a single, long, roller Duplex chain from the rear of the crankshaft, a one-piece light alloy cylinder block and crankcase with a single casting inserted in the block to form four wet cylinder liners (as on the 1954 Maserati 250F) and a one-piece nitralloy forged crankshaft running in three main bearings. There were two valves and two plugs per cylinder. Connaught's Mike Oliver carried out a lot of development work on this engine himself and it was claimed, rather optimistically, to have a power output of 240 bhp at 6400 rpm. As on the A-series, there was an Armstrong-Siddeley preselector gearbox, which was mounted close to the rear axle, and Connaught's own 'quick-change' final drive unit with magnesium-alloy casing.

Originally the B-series was fitted with Borrani wire wheels with knock-on hubs and Girling hydraulic brakes, but by the time the car was first raced these had been replaced by Dunlop disc brakes and magnesium-alloy wheels. The Dunlop discs were a constant source of trouble; they tended to lock up at the most embarrasing moments and were the cause of both Oliver's crash at Silverstone in 1956 and Reg Parnell's crash at the Crystal Palace later the same year. After extensive tests Clarke decided to abandon the SU fuel injection and the team's own fuel injection was adopted in 1955 (this was based on the Hilborn-Travers system); but later the same year Connaught switched to using two Weber twin-choke carburettors.

Design and development of the B-series cost around £15,000 and it was estimated that £50,000 per year would be required to field a full team in major International events. Finance of this order was just not available and the team had to content itself with running in just a few major events each year, always hoping that a 'fairy godmother' would appear to sponsor them. Orders for B-series cars at £5000 a time were received from Leslie Marr, Rob Walker and Peter Whitehead. Both

Walker and Whitehead ordered cars with exposed-wheel bodywork, but the latter cancelled his order.

The new car was not raced until 1955 and it made its debut at the Easter Goodwood meeting where it was driven by Tony Rolt. Rolt, co-driver of the winning Jaguar in the 1953 Le Mans race, was an excellent choice to handle the B-series on its first outing. He was a fast, safe, precise driver, but at the same time he knew when to exercise caution and had a great deal of mechanical sympathy for the cars which he drove. Rolt took fourth place in the Chichester Cup, a Formule Libre race, but he retired the Connaught with broken throttle linkage in the Glover Trophy, the main race of the day. Even though the Connaught had achieved no success, it impressed with the neatness of its design and the high quality of its construction and finish.

By the *Daily Express* Trophy race at Silverstone the following month two works cars were ready and these were driven by McAlpine and Jack Fairman. They went well in the opening laps of the race, holding third and fourth places, but both retired. By the end of May Leslie Marr had taken delivery of his B-series car and he drove it to the model's first victory in a minor race at the Davidstow circuit in Cornwall on Whit Monday. In 1955 the British Grand Prix was held at Aintree and by this race Rob Walker had taken delivery of his car which was shared at the northern circuit by Tony Rolt and Peter Walker; Marr entered his car and a single works entry was driven by McAlpine. The works Mercedes-Benz completely dominated this race, the Connaughts were outclassed and they tagged along at the tail of the field. Both the works and Walker entries retired with loss of oil pressure; Marr indulged in a violent spin at Anchor Crossing and, after flailing through the grass, reversed smartly up the escape road and then rejoined the race. During the off-course excursion one of the Connaught's brake pipes was torn away and this resulted in its retirement.

The team's next race of any importance was the *Daily Telegraph* Trophy at Aintree in September. Here Reg Parnell drove a works car and he led the Maserati oppostion until the Alta engine ran a bearing and he retreated to the pits in a cloud of blue smoke. As the 1955 season progressed, Rodney Clarke had become increasingly concerned at the very high cost of repairing the streamlined bodywork after minor accidents both on the track and in the paddock and he had decided that all the cars should be rebuilt with conventional, exposed-wheel bodywork. The first of the rebuilt cars (the prototype, B1) was driven by Reg Parnell in the Oulton Park Gold Cup race later in September; opposition came from works Maseratis and Ferrari-entered

Lancias and Parnell did well to finish fourth despite one of the twin magnetos fitted to the Connaught cutting out completely.

Once already, at the end of 1953, Kenneth McAlpine had considered withdrawing his support for the Connaught team because of the very heavy expenditure and he was in the throes of doing so two years later when Connaught received an invitation to run in the Syracuse Grand Prix in October. The starting money seemed out of this world – about £1000 per car – and the team decided to have one last fling. The decision to enter was made at the last moment and finding drivers at such short notice was a serious problem. Eventually Clarke chose Tony Brooks, a young Mancunian dental student who had driven the works sports cars in a couple of races, and Les Leston, who drove the ex-Coombs sports car for Peter Bell. After a testing session at Goodwood the cars were bundled into the ex-Green Line coaches used by the team as transporters and these set off on the long trek across Europe.

The Connaught transporters arrived late and the team missed the first practice session. On the eve of the race, however, Brooks, who had been given a choice of cars and selected the exposed-wheel model, found the bumpy, 3.4-mile circuit with its gentle curves, two slow corners and a difficult, very slow hairpin much to his liking and he put himself on the front row of the grid with third fastest practice time. Fastest were the works Maseratis of Luigi Musso and Luigi Villoresi.

While Musso and Villoresi shot away into the lead at the fall of the flag, Brooks made a slow start and he was in fourth place on the first lap. Three laps later the Connaught roared past Schell's streamlined Maserati and two laps later it overtook Villoresi's Modena car. On lap 11 Brooks, looking completely relaxed and driving well within his permitted rev limit, passed the leading Maserati of Musso; the Italian went ahead again a lap later and then Brooks eased his way in front once more and stayed there. As Brooks fought to retain the lead, he broke the lap record, and Musso, in his efforts to regain it, broke the record twice. Then Musso, troubled by weakening brakes and gear-selector problems, began to lose ground, and by the chequered flag Brooks had pulled out a lead of 51 seconds. The Connaught driver had averaged 99.05 mph for this 241-mile race and set a new lap record of 102.30 mph. The Syracuse victory – in the face of a strong and well-prepared Maserati team, albeit without their number one driver Jean Behra – represented a humiliating defeat for Italy and provided a magnificent fillip for British motor racing in general and Connaught in particular.

McAlpine retracted his decision to withdraw from racing and instead plans were laid to field two or three cars in as many events as possible in 1956. And the victory sufficiently impressed Sicilian Piero Scotti, a mineral water manufacturer and previously a driver of sports Ferraris, to buy a B-series car for 1956. The team set about converting all the cars to unstreamlined bodywork and in this form they were known as the 'Syracuse' in recognition of the Sicilian victory.

Over the winter months Leslie Marr competed in New Zealand and for the Formule Libre races in the Southern hemisphere his car was fitted with a Jaguar D-type 3.4-litre engine. Marr's best performances were a fourth in the New Zealand Grand Prix and a third place in the Lady Wigram Trophy race at Christchurch. On his return to England Marr sold his car back to the works.

There was an impressive turn-out of Connaughts at the Easter Goodwood meeting, but fast newcomer to the team Scott-Brown retired, and the other drivers were unable to match the speed of the Maseratis of Moss and Salvadori and trailed home in third, fourth and fifth places. Shortly afterwards Scotti and Desmond Titterington with a works car ran at Siracusa, but neither was able to match the lap times achieved by Brooks the previous autumn and both retired. As far as Connaught were concerned, the sensational driver of the 1956 season was Archie Scott-Brown, who suffered the unfortunate deformity of an unformed right hand and whose previous experience was limited to fairly low-powered sports cars. Scott-Brown was a natural fast driver, precise and courageous; he had led at Goodwood before retiring with a broken crankshaft, he fought for the lead in the Aintree '200' and finished second to Moss's winning Vanwall in the *Daily Express* Trophy race at Silverstone. A driver of the skill and enthusiasm of Brooks or Scott-Brown was the ideal tonic for the team and his performances did much to encourage McAlpine to continue the unequal struggle.

Scotti had driven his red-painted 'Syracuse' into seventh place at Silverstone and he next contested the Belgian Grand Prix at Spa where he retired with mechanical trouble. By now Scotti was thoroughly weary of what he regarded as the shortcomings of a car for which he was paying so dearly (indifferent drivers, like poor workmen, blame their tools); as he was buying the car on hire-purchase, he simply stopped the payments and left the car to languish at the Connaught works.

At the British Grand Prix the intrepid Scott-Brown was in sixth place when his car shed a wheel. He was 'tigering' furiously with the Italian

Lancia-Ferraris and, had his car not broken, he would have undoubtedly finished in the first three. Jack Fairman brought the team some consolation with a steady drive into fourth place. The team's financial problems meant that the only other World Championship race which Connaught could afford to enter in 1956 was the European Grand Prix at Monza in September. Because of his disability Scott-Brown was not allowed to compete and at the last moment his place was taken by Ron Flockhart, usually seen at the wheel of BRM cars. This race was run on the combined road and banked track and the bumpy surface of the banking resulted in a high rate of mechanical attrition and tyre failures. As a result of unspectacular, but consistent driving Flockhart brought his B-series across the line in third place behind the winning Maserati of Stirling Moss and a Lancia-Ferrari shared by Fangio and Collins. Fairman crossed the line in fifth place, with the front wheels leaning inwards and the sump scraping on the track as the result of a collapsed front cross-member. Despite the small number of races entered Connaught's 1956 season cost McAlpine £20,000

By the 1957 season the Alta engine was no longer really competitive and the B-series chassis was rapidly becoming outdated. There was no alternative engine available and Connaught made the best of the situation by introducing stronger connecting rods and modifying the valve gear. Clarke was working on two new chassis designs (neither of which was raced) and introduced a new and very aerodynamic body style. The new body, built on the chassis of Marr's old car, was dart-shaped, with a long-tapering, squarish nose and high tail, and was soon dubbed the 'toothpaste-tube'. The new designs were the C-series car, with a new and much more modern chassis of space-frame design, strut and coil spring front suspension and inboard rear brakes, and the D-series, a new rear-engined project which was never completed.

Connaught's first race in 1957 was the Syracuse Grand Prix, but it proved an even less successful outing than in 1956. In practice the 1955 winner, the prototype car (chassis B1), was burnt out; driver Les Leston had just accelerated away from the hairpin bend when the right-hand drive-shaft broke and flailed through the almost-full fuel tank, the fuel ignited, Leston steered the car off the road and jumped clear. In the race the sole finisher for Connaught was Ivor Bueb who took fifth place on his first Formula One drive.

Fortune, however, smiled on the team from Send at the Easter Goodwood meeting and, after the retirement of the faster Vanwalls, Stuart Lewis-Evans won the Glover Trophy with the 'toothpaste-tube'. The same day

Connaught fielded two cars in the Pau Grand Prix, a slow race over a difficult street circuit, and Ivor Bueb did well to finish third behind a brace of works Maseratis. One of the Pau cars was then transported to Naples where it was driven by Lewis-Evans, a determined, but inexperienced driver cast very much in the same mould as Brooks and Scott-Brown. The little Welshman worked his way up to second place, sandwiched between the Lancia-Ferraris of Collins and Hawthorn, only to be eliminated by the fracture of a front hub. No one was more impressed by this performance than the Ferrari mechanics who previously enjoyed a low opinion of what they called the 'Connoft'. At Monaco Lewis-Evans drove the 'dart', fitted for this race with a special short nose to prevent damaged bodywork from blocking off the airflow to the radiator, and he took a satisfactory fourth place. Poor Lewis-Evans' motor racing career was a short one, for he died of bad burns sustained when his Vanwall crashed in the 1958 Moroccan Grand Prix.

It was after the Monaco race that McAlpine and Clarke, who had always hoped in vain that some support from the motor industry would be forthcoming, announced that they could no longer afford to run the Connaught team and no more works entries were made. The cars were auctioned in September, from time to time they were entered in Formula One races, but without works support or any sort of development programme, these one-time bearers of British Grand Prix hopes soon faded into obscurity. At the auction one B-series car, B6 raced by Piero Scotti, remained unsold and this was later loaned to the Science Museum in London where it still languishes, a scruffy, neglected reminder of a gallant team that so nearly achieved greatness.

12

Colin Chapman and the Lotus:

The Birth of a Legend

Throughout its 80-year history motor racing has been dominated by the influence and success of a very small number of outstanding *marques;* Panhard-Levassor at the dawn of motor racing; Bugatti in the 'twenties; Alfa Romeo in the 'twenties and 'thirties; Mercedes-Benz in the 'thirties; and in post-war days the names to conjure with have been Ferrari and Lotus.

Both the Italian company and the British firm have achieved their outstanding success through the ambition and ability of a single leader. Both Ferrari and Chapman have gathered fine teams of engineering, production and racing staff, but the policy and direction of the company have emanated purely from themselves. Ferrari was brilliant and vastly experienced, but he was also fortunate. After the severance of his relationship with Alfa Romeo, he set up a small machine-tool factory, a business that flourished during the second World War. When hostilities were over, Ferrari had adequate financial means to embark on his ambitious motoring and racing projects. In contrast Colin Chapman had no money and very little experience, and all his success derived directly from his ability and his enthusiasm. His first Lotus cars were home-built specials; the Austin Seven-based Mark 1 trials car appeared in 1948 (the year in which Chapman graduated as a BSc from London University), the Mark 2 of 1950 was an Austin Seven-based trials car with a Ford engine that was also used for circuit racing and the Mk 3 750 Formula car (a Formula for Austin Seven-based competition cars) dominated its class in 1951.

The Mk 3 was the first Lotus that gave any real hint of Chapman's potential. Chapman devised a conversion of the standard Austin two-port 'siamesed' inlet arrangement to a four-port layout, a modification that resulted in a vast improvement in performance and was so successful that this arrangement was subsequently banned by the 750 Motor Club.

It was at this point that the story of the Lotus really took off. Colin Chapman's new developments followed each other in quick succession: first outstandingly successful competition sports cars, then the first single-seaters and the forerunners of a long, immensely popular and greatly admired line of production cars.

The Sports Cars

Early Lotus competition sports cars were always technical leaders, almost unbeatable in their class and built in substantial numbers for sale to private owners. As the Chapman empire grew, as Lotus efforts were concentrated more and more on the team's Grand Prix programme and production cars, so Chapman gradually lost interest in sports cars (especially after a very bitter experience at Le Mans) and six years have now passed since the last competition sports car was built. Despite the comparative brevity of the company's participation in International sports car racing, Lotus scored achievements that will rank as major milestones in the history of motor racing. These early models also represent milestones in the emergence of Lotus as a major force in the automobile world.

The Mk 6

This production sports car was one of the last of the true sports cars and whatever the adherents of the *marque* Morgan may claim for today's 'Plus 8' model from Malvern, often described as the last of the true sports cars, the Mk 6 and its successor the 'Seven' offered the relatively impecunious enthusiast a car that he could assemble himself at low cost, drive everyday to work and race at weekends. The 'Plus 8' combines a traditional (and one might add very outdated) chassis and body with a modern, large-capacity power unit; it is little more than an over-powered, but charming anachronism. The space-frame Mk 6 first appeared a a 'Club' racer in 1952, but its greatest year was 1954 when one of these cars, powered by a bored-out MG engine, performed so brilliantly in the hands of Peter Gammon. During 1954 Gammon, who had previously raced a modified MG ran in seventeen races, scoring fourteen firsts, two seconds and a third. His finest hour was at the British Grand Prix meeting at Silverstone on 17th July when he finished second in the 1500 cc sports car race, behind *le patron* with the new Lotus Mk 8, but ahead of a very strong field that included Hans Herrmann with a works 1500 cc Porsche.

The Mk 7

More familiarly known as the 'Seven', this model was introduced as a successor to the Mk 6 at the 1957 Earls Court Show. It carried on the image of a light, cheap, stark, superbly handling *true* sports car that would wipe the floor with anything costing three or four times as much, provided that the driver was an enthusiast who did not object to a waterlogged cockpit because of the ill-fitting hood and leaky floor. The demand for the 'Seven' was never exactly overwhelming, but it was persistent, so persistent that the Series 4 car remains in production today. The 'Seven' is no longer made by Lotus, but the rights to its manufacture were sold to Caterham Car Sales when Lotus was endeavouring to revamp its image as a serious, quality manufacturer. Surely, if any car can be claimed to be the last of the true sports cars, it is the 'Seven' and not the 'Plus 8'.

The Mk 8

It was with this 125 mph model that Colin Chapman forged his reputation as a serious and able racing driver at International level, and it was this revolutionary car that was first raced under the banner of Team Lotus. Under the skin there was a new space-frame incorporating all the lessons that Chapman had learned with the earlier Mk 6 and a modified MG 1500 cc engine and gearbox. The most revolutionary feature was the body, the work of Frank Costin, an aerodynamist with the de Havilland company, combining sleek lines evolved on aircraft principles with neat twin tail-fins that set a fashion imitated by many other racing car constructors.

Certainly the Mk 8 was not without its problems, but it enjoyed a successful season and apart, from the victory at Silverstone referred to above, Chapman broke the sports car record at both Brands Hatch and Crystal Palace. At this time Chapman was still working at a full-time job and these added to the complications when he was racing abroad. When Team Lotus competed at the 1954 Eifelerennen race at the Nürburgring, Colin drove the Lotus to the office, left it outside in the road all day (parking restrictions were less severe in those days!), changed in the lavatory in St James's Square after work and departed for Germany. At the Nürburgring the Lotus was driven by German driver Erwin Bauer (Chapman was not allowed to compete because of his lack of experience) and finished fourth. During the August Bank Holiday weekend Team Lotus again competed at the Nürburgring, but Colin was also competing at both Brands Hatch and Crystal Palace on the Bank Holiday Monday! Unfortunately the German trip at the Nürburgring on the Sunday morning was unsuccessful. Chapman retired with a broken de Dion tube which was hastily welded up, and the team rushed to the coast to catch an overnight boat across the Channel. At Brands Hatch Colin finished fourth in his heat; he then drove to the Crystal Palace where he retired on the second lap with carburation trouble and rushed back to the Kent circuit to borrow Nigel Allen's similar car (which had also competed in Germany) to run in the final of his race there. Once again he retired with carburation problems – the source of the trouble was that the carburettors had been adjusted for conditions at the Nürburgring. This weekend of frantic activity represents a very good example of a young man biting off more than he could chew, but it also vividly illustrates the great energy which Chapman applied to his motor racing activities!

The Mk 9

This was the improved car evolved for the 1955 season when Chapman had given up his job and was running Lotus Engineering as a full-time business from modest premises at Tottenham Lane, Hornsey. The Mk 9 was built with MG, 1100 cc Coventry-Climax and Ford engines and a works car ran, albeit unsuccessfully, at Le Mans. In 1955 Lotus made its first appearance at the Motor Show, ostensibly as an accessories manufacturer, but displaying a Mk 9 complete apart from body panels. At the end of the year Chapman allowed a number of leading magazines to test the two works cars; the 1100 cc Climax-powered version in the hands of John Bolster of *Autosport* attained 127.7 mph (and covered the standing quarter-mile in 15.8 secs), while the 1500 cc MG version achieved 128.6 mph. Lotus also built the Mk 10 with a Bristol 2-litre engine. The Mk 10 was no real match for the rival Lister-Bristol driven by Archie Scott-Brown, but despite the failure of this model the *marque* Lotus had well and truly made its mark on the motor sporting scene.

Eleven

For 1956 Chapman, aided by Mike and Frank Costin, produced what could be described as the 'definitive' front-engined Lotus sports car. The Eleven (Chapman had dropped the system of prefixing the design number by 'Mk') was compact, sleek and handled superbly. Throughout 1956 Chapman himself raced an Eleven powered by a 1500 cc Coventry-Climax engine and his battles with Mike Hawthorn, who owned his own private Eleven, were many and close. At Le Mans in 1956 an Eleven driven by Peter Jopp and Reg Bicknell won the 1100 cc class, but the model's finest hour was in the following year's 24 Hours race. A total of five entries appeared at the Sarthe circuit, three of them works cars. A 1500 cc car failed to make the start because of engine problems, but the other four cars all made it to the finish with the following results:

9th: Mackay Fraser/J Chamberlain (works 1100 cc car) – first in the 1100 cc class and second in the Index of Performance.
13th: R Walshaw/J Dalton (1100 cc car entered by John Green) – second in the 1100 cc class.
14th: C Allison/K Hall (works car with experimental 744 cc Climax engine) – winner of the Index of Performance and the 750 cc class.
16th: Hechard/Masson (1100 cc car privately entered) – fourth in the 1100 cc class.

Apart from anything else, Team Lotus had committed the unforgiveable sin (as far as the French were concerned) of defeating the French DB cars in the 750 cc class and the Index of Performance. This was a success that was to have repercussions several years afterwards.

Later Front-Engined Sports Cars

By 1957 Team Lotus was racing its first single-seaters and, partly because of the team's concentration on these, the later sports cars were comparative failures. Neither the Fifteen which appeared in 1957 and was designed to take Coventry-Climax engines of 1500 to 2200 cc nor the lightweight Seventeen (even lighter and more compact successor to the Eleven) fulfilled Chapman's expectations for a variety of technical reasons. These were the last front-engined Lotus competition sports cars.

Rear-Engined Sports Cars

In 1960 Lotus built six rear-engined sports based on that year's Grand Prix chassis typed the 19 and known familiarly as the 'Monte Carlo' (a reference to the rival Cooper concern's rear-engined Monaco sports car). These cars were immensely successful in British events, particularly those owned by the UDT-Laystall team and driven by Stirling Moss, Innes Ireland and others. The 19 was not, however, a serious International challenger, as it did not comply with the detailed Appendix 'C' regulations of the Commission Sportive Internationale and was not eligible for World Championship events.

Two years later Lotus produced another rear-engined sports car which was to prove in every way a direct successor to the Eleven. The new car, typed the 23, featured a widened version of the team's rear-engined Formula Junior chassis with neat aerodynamic bodywork and a choice of twin overhead camshaft Ford engines ranging from 997 cc upwards. The first car, powered by a 1498 cc engine (a prototype of the Harry Mundy-designed engine that was later to power the production Elan) was driven in the 1962 Nüburgring 1000 Km race by Jim Clark who led the race on a damp track for the first eleven laps, despite a strong entry of works Ferraris. Mairesse with the second-place Ferrari was rapidly closing the gap on the Lotus when Clark, partially overcome by fumes from an exhaust leak, failed to correct a slide and went off the road and into a ditch.

The sheer speed of the new Lotus had startled the opposition and there is little doubt that when a works 997 cc car and a UDT-Laystall-entered 750 cc car appeared at Le Mans, the French René Bonnet (successor to DB) and Panhard teams were convinced that their stranglehold on the Index of Performance and in the 750 cc class was about to be broken. When the Lotus 23s were presented for scrutineering, they were rejected. The front wheels had four-stud fixings and the rear wheels had six studs; therefore, said the scrutineers, the spare could only be used either at the front or the back. Chapman took the cars away and modified them so that four-stud fixing was standard front and rear. The scrutineers refused even to look at the cars, blithely commenting that as the rear wheels had been designed for six studs, they must be unsafe with only four. French vested interests were protected, Colin Chapman was livid and threatened to sue the Automobile Club de l'Ouest (the race organisers); but he calmed down and vowed never to enter Le Mans again. Chapman is a man of his word and no works Lotus has ever again run in the 24 Hours race.

The 23 enjoyed a large number of wins and two years elapsed before another sports-racer emerged from the Lotus works. Interest, largely stemming from Roger Penske's Zerex-Climax (a Formula One Cooper rebuilt as a sports car) had been growing in small, light, immensely powerful sports cars. Bruce McLaren bought the Zerex in 1964, fitted an Oldsmobile engine and developed it as the first of the long line of McLaren Can-Am cars: Roy Salvadori was racing a Cooper powered by a 4500 cc Maserati engine; and Eric Broadley was working on the first of the Chevrolet-powered Lola T70s. Colin Chapman's contribution to this class of racing was the Lotus 30 powered by a 4.7-litre Ford engine with a backbone-type chassis basically similar to that of the Elan and a neat, close-fitting body. For no obvious reason the 30 was an unmitigated failure. Certainly the 30 was an unlucky car (the prototype was supplied to Ian Walker Racing and written off during the year at Brands Hatch), but much of the trouble was caused by Lotus attempts simultaneously to compete in Formula One, Formula Two and at Indianapolis.

In 1965 Lotus endeavoured to overcome the weaknesses of the 30 design with the improved Series 2 model which featured a more powerful engine, modified chassis, improved brakes and a new body. Still the car was plagued by misfortune, the iron-block Ford engine was to heavy, the transmission was unreliable and the handling was unsatisfactory. By the Austrian Grand Prix in August 1965 Lotus had evolved the 40 with stronger chassis, 5.3-litre engine as standard and stronger transmission. After an unsuccessful appearance at Riverside Raceway in California the 'big-banger' sports project was abandoned and the works Lotus 40s were sold off.

Since 1965 the only competition sports cars built by Lotus have been the 47 (a competition version of the production Europa) and the 62 which had a chassis based on the 47 and was powered by the prototype of the production engine fitted to the Jensen-Healey and the new Lotus Elite. Driven by John Miles and Brian Muir one of these cars won its class in the 1969 BOAC '500' race at Brands Hatch.

Lotus Single-Seaters

Colin Chapman evolved his first single-seater in 1956 and entered his first Grand Prix two years later, but he had already played an active role in the development of two other Grand Prix contenders. In 1954 Tony Vandervell's 'Vanwall Special' had made its racing debut and by 1955 he was fielding two of these all-British cars, now known simply as 'Vanwalls', in most of the year's Formula One races. Vandervell was determined to produce a car that would break the Italian stranglehold on Grand Prix racing, but it was only too obvious that the Vanwall in its existing form would never achieve this ambition. The performance of the Lotus sports cars during the 1955 season had greatly impressed Vandervell, particularly as far as their roadholding was concerned, and he invited Chapman to act as consultant on the development of a revised Formula One contender. The Lotus chief designed a new lighter and stiffer multi-tubular space-frame chassis and redesigned the suspension, while Frank Costin evolved a completely original body style. The Vanwall achieved little success in 1956, but made its break-through the following season when Stirling Moss won three of the year's Championship races.

As a token of Vandervell's thanks for achieving such vast improvements to the Vanwall design, Chapman was offered a works drive at the 1956 French Grand Prix. In practice team-mate Hawthorn was doing a warming-up lap, followed by Chapman who was travelling rather faster; unfortunately Chapman's brakes locked, he rammed the tail of the leading Vanwall which was pushed up the escape road, and Chapman's car hit a concrete pylon. The Lotus *patron's* car was too badly damaged to run in the race, so it was never discovered whether the tremendous potential which he displayed at the wheel of his sports cars could be sustained at the wheel of a much more potent Formula One contender. Colin had realised that he needed all his energies to promote the development of Lotus Engineering and retired from racing at the end of the season.

When BRM approached Chapman in 1957, it was an act of desperation as much as a compliment to the young designer's ability. The new 4-cylinder BRM had proved hopelessly, almost fatally, unreliable and its handling left much to be desired. Chapman was consulted with regard to the handling only and after trying one of the Bourne cars at Goodwood advised changes in the suspension design which BRM adopted.

Few of Chapman's own single-seaters have lacked technical ingenuity, few have failed to live up to their maker's expectations and although Lotus at one time built racing cars to comply with many different Formulae, it is proposed to discuss only the team's Grand Prix models:

1958

The prototype Lotus single-seater had first appeared at the 1956 Earls Court Motor Show and had been built to comply with the 1500 cc Formula Two of 1957 onwards. This model, designated the 12, was a slim light car with a front-mounted Coventry-Climax engine (as used in the team's sports cars) and Chapman's ingenious 'strut' rear suspension. A works team of Lotus 12s competed regularly in 1957 Formula Two races, but in the early part of the season they were plagued by transmission problems and in any case they were no match for the rival rear-engined Coopers. An enlarged 2-litre version of the Climax engine became available for 1958 and Chapman decided to contest Formula One events with the same cars. Cliff Allison drove a Lotus into fourth place in the Belgian Grand Prix but, generally, the 12s were out of the picture and certainly no match for the Ferrari Dinos and Vanwalls that were struggling for supremacy. An improved car, the 16, appeared at the French Grand Prix; this model had a delightful streamlined body designed by Frank Costin and so closely resembling Tony Vandervell's race-winning cars that it was dubbed the 'Mini-Vanwall'. The 16 was rather too clever, featuring an engine canted almost to an horizontal position (this caused carburation problems and transmission power losses) and exhaust system running inside the body (causing chronic overheating). In contrast the Coopers were the ultimate in simplicity and in 1959, when Coventry-Climax offered a full 2500 cc engine, the rear-engined cars were driven by Jack Brabham to victory in the World Championship and the Lotus entries staggered from retirement to retirement.

1960

It was now obvious that it was impossible to beat the Coopers with the front-engined cars and that the only answer was to join them. Chapman was quick to learn and his answer to the Cooper supremacy was the 18, an exceptionally squat, compact car with entirely new rear suspension by transverse links. The 18 handled better than the Coopers and was faster on most circuits, but, throughout the year, the cars were plagued by misfortune. In their third year in Grand Prix racing Team Lotus failed yet again to win a World Championship race, but Stirling Moss, driving a private dark blue Lotus for Rob Walker, won the Monaco and United States Grands Prix.

1961

As mentioned elsewhere, British constructors had opposed the introduction of the new 1500 cc Grand Prix Formula of 1961 onwards and because they had delayed the development of new engines had to make do with the old 4-cylinder Climax engine throughout the year. Chapman produced the 21 for 1961 Grand Prix races, a sleeker, lighter, more compact car. Jim Clark and Innes Ireland drove the works cars, but Chapman declined to sell Rob Walker a 21 and so Moss drove the 1960 18 which was modified as the season progressed. Although Ferrari dominated most of the season's races, Stirling

Moss won at both Monaco and the Nürburgring through sheer driving skill and despite, rather than because of, his car. As for the works team, both Clark and Ireland turned in some good lap times during the year, but it was not until the United States Grand Prix in October that Team Lotus won its first World Championship race; the driver was Innes Ireland and, significantly, the works Ferraris were not entered.

1962

By 1962 Lotus had taken delivery of their V-8 Coventry-Climax engines and Chapman had evolved two new cars; the 24 was a conventional multi-tubular space-frame design for sale to customers, but the 25 (raced in modified form throughout the years of the 1500 cc Formula) was a revolutionary monocoque design, light and exceptionally rigid. Throughout 1962 racing was fought out between Graham Hill with the new V-8 BRM and Jim Clark with the Lotus 25. There was absolutely nothing to choose between the two cars for performance; but Hill was the more experienced driver and the BRM was more reliable. At the end of the season Hill had won four races and the World Championship and Clarke had scored three wins. This was the first year in which Team Lotus enjoyed a run of substantial success.

1963

The two rival British *marques* continued to dominate racing in 1963 and Clark now attained the upper hand, winning seven races and the World Championship.

1964

Early in the 1964 season Chapman introduced the improved 33 Grand Prix car, with modified suspension geometry and other chassis changes. Jim Clark enjoyed another successful season, winning three Championship races, but Champion driver was John Surtees at the wheel of a Ferrari.

1965

Jim Clark's command of the 1965 season was complete; he won six races in succession (but not Monaco which he missed because of Indianapolis), including the Belgian and British Grands Prix for the fourth year in succession.

1966

Although Lotus was not prepared for the 3000 cc Grand Prix Formula which came into force for 1966, it was not for want of trying and work was in hand on a car that was to dominate racing. During 1966 Lotus relied on the old 33s powered by either 2-litre Climax or BRM engines, and the new 43 which had a very complex H-16 BRM engine. For much of the season Team Lotus was outclassed by Brabham and Ferrari, but remarkably enough the H-16 engine held together for Clark to score his twentieth Championship race victory at Watkins Glen.

1967

The new Lotus 49 which made its debut at Zandvoort in June was revolutionary in more than one respect. Like the Lancia D.50 of 1954-5 it used the engine as a structural member to stiffen the chassis (Jano, designer of the Lancia, was a great pioneer, but Chapman made the idea really work) and it was the first successful Grand Prix car powered by a Ford engine. Chapman had persuaded Ford to put up £100,000 for the Cosworth concern to develop the V-8 Grand Prix engine and a Formula Two unit, and for this year Team Lotus had exclusive use of the new unit. Clark drove the 49 to victory on its debut (an historic happening in itself, as in the past only Alfa Romeo and Mercedes-Benz had won on the debut of a new Grand Prix car) and although the 49s were plagued by minor engine and chassis teething problems, later in the year Clark scored other victories at Silverstone, Monza, Watkins Glen and Mexico City.

1968

Lotus made history once more by being the first Grand Prix team to be in receipt of direct sponsorship; the cars were painted in Players Gold Leaf red, white and gold colours and entered under the banner of 'Gold Leaf Team Lotus'. At the first Championship race of the year, the South African Grand Prix, the 49s were still painted in the now-traditional Lotus shade of green and Jim Clark scored his last World Championship race victory. Three months later Clark was dead, killed in a Formula Two race at the Hockenheim circuit in Germany. This was a terrible blow to Chapman, for not only was Clark a very close friend, but, apart from Ireland's win in 1961, every works Lotus Championship race victory since the *marque*'s inception had been scored by Clark. Graham Hill had been signed up as a joint number one driver for 1967 and after Clark's death he achieved all that could possibly be hoped for; Hill scored victories in the Spanish, Monaco and Mexican races and won his third World Championship. Another significant Lotus win in 1968 was Jo Siffert's victory with a Rob Walker-entered 49 in the British Grand Prix. The last previous Championship race win by a privateer had been Moss's victory with a Walker Lotus at the Nürburgring in 1961 and since then no private entry has won a Grand Prix.

1969

Former Cooper and Brabham driver Jochen Rindt was signed up as joint number one for 1969, but for most of the season he and Hill behaved like deadly rivals and, through their fierce personal duels, weakened the team's chances of success. Hill scored his fifth victory at Monaco, but crashed badly at Watkins Glen in the United States Grand Prix, a race in which Rindt scored his first-ever Grand Prix win. During 1969 Lotus also raced the four-wheel-drive 63 cars, but they were not competitive and were abandoned at the end of the year.

1970

By 1970 the Lotus 49 was regarded as outdated and Chapman and designer Maurice Phillippe had produced a successor in the form of the 72, a car that was as revolutionary as its predecessors; the specification included a 'shovel' nose, inboard-front brakes, mid-mounted radiators and torsion bar suspension. In the early part of the year the 72 was plagued by teething troubles and Rindt drove a 49 to victory at Monaco. With the 72 he subsequently scored wins at Spa, Zandvoort, Clermont-Ferrand, Brands Hatch and Hockenheim (scene of that year's German Grand Prix). Then tragedy struck; Rindt was killed in practice for the Italian Grand Prix and became the first, and hopefully the only, posthumous World Champion. Lotus missed the Canadian Grand Prix and next appeared at Watkins Glen where young Brazilian driver Emerson Fittipaldi drove the 72 to yet another victory.

1971

Lotus continued to race the 72s in 1971, but the team consisted of two very inexperienced drivers, Fittipaldi who had driven in four Formula One races prior to 1971 and Swedish driver Reine Wisell whose first Formula One race had been at Watkins Glen in 1970 when he had finished third. It took most of the season for the Lotus drivers to 'find their feet' in Formula One and the team suffered staff problems. For the first time since 1959 Team Lotus failed to win a Championship race and the best performances were a second by Fittipaldi in Austria and third places in the French and British races. Chapman was still making history, however, and the most significant Lotus event of the year was the appearance of the 56B, the first ever gas-turbine Grand Prix car. The 56B was based on the four-wheel-drive 1968 Indianapolis chassis and was powered by a Canadian-built Pratt & Whitney engine. The car appeared in a number of non-Championship Formula One races and was crashed by Dave Walker in the Austrian race. Its most significant outing, however, was at Monza. Because of the possible repercussions following Rindt's fatal crash in 1970, Team Lotus as such did not enter the 1971 Italian Grand Prix. Instead, under the banner of 'World Wide Racing', the 56B painted in smart black and gold colours was entered for Fittipaldi who drove it into eighth place. The 56B was regarded as purely experimental and was not raced after the end of the 1971 season.

1972

The black and gold colours seen at Monza were adopted for all the team 72s the following year; the cars were now known as 'John Player Specials' and were entered in the name of John Player Team Lotus. Now Fittipaldi realised the potential which Chapman had believed him to possess and with victories in the Spanish, Belgian, British, Austrian and Italian races the Brazilian won the World Championship with 61 points to the 45 of Jackie Stewart.

1973

Chapman signed up Swedish driver Ronnie Peterson as joint number one and, although Jackie Stewart was to win his third and final World Championship, the Lotus drivers were more successful overall. Lotus or, rather, John Player Special won the Manufacturers' Championship with 92 points to the 82 of Tyrrell, and Fittipaldi and Peterson were second and third in the Drivers' Championship. Fittipaldi won the Argentine, Brazilian and Spanish races and Ronnie Peterson won the French, Austrian, Italian and United States Grands Prix.

1974

By 1974 Lotus had been racing the 72 for four consecutive seasons, and it was felt that the model was now reaching the limit of its competitive life.

Chapman was planning its replacement by a new John Player Special (the Lotus 76) designed by Ralph Bellamy under Chapman's direction. The new car was 100 lb lighter than its predecessor and incorporated an automatic clutch. Unfortunately the new model fell far short of expectations and, throughout the year, the team relied on the ageing 72s. Peterson was now partnered by Jacky Ickx, but the Swedish driver was far more successful than the former Ferrari man and upheld Lotus reputation by scoring wins in the Monaco and French races.

The Score-Sheet

In post-war Grand Prix racing two *marques,* Ferrari and Lotus, have been significantly more successful than any of their rivals. Lotus heads the statistics with 55 victories, all since 1960, while Ferrari's victories are spread over a longer period and some pre-date the introduction of the Drivers' Championship in 1950. For the purpose of the table set out below, the only Ferrari victories prior to 1950 included are those races which later formed rounds in the Championship. Ferrari did of course score a number of other Formula One wins, but these have been disregarded.

	Lotus	*Ferrari*
1949		2
1950		–
1951		3
1952		7
1953		7
1954		2
1955		1
1956		5
1957		–
1958	–	2
1959	–	2
1960	2	1
1961	3	5
1962	3	–
1963	7	1
1964	3	3
1965	6	–
1966	1	2

1967	3	–
1968	5	1
1969	2	–
1970	6	4
1971	–	2
1972	5	1
1973	7	–
1974	2	2
	—	—
	55	54

During the early part of 1975 the Ferrari team increased its score of 57 with victories by Niki Lauda at Monaco, Zolder and Paul Ricart, while Lotus have been handicapped by the failure of the 76 and their dependence on the old 72 model dating back to 1970.

Lotus Drivers

During 1957, Lotus's first season of single-seater racing in Formula Two, the team fielded cars for Cliff Allison, Herbert Mackay Fraser and Keith Hall. Mackay Fraser was killed at Reims at the wheel of a sports Lotus and later in the season Graham Hill joined the team. Both Allison and Hill remained with the team in 1958 and at the British Grand Prix they were joined by Alan Stacey who had performed well at the wheel of sports Lotus Elevens. In Italian circles Allison was regarded as a driver of great potential and for 1959 he received an invitation to join Scuderia Ferrari. His career with Maranello was cut short following a bad crash in practice for the 1960 Monaco Grand Prix. By the end of 1959 Graham Hill was tired of battling with Lotus unreliability and joined BRM.

For 1960, the year of the first of the rear-engined cars, the works drivers at the beginning of the season were Alan Stacey and Innes Ireland. In addition John Surtees also appeared for the team when his motor-cycle racing commitments permitted. Poor Stacey was killed in the Belgian Grand Prix – he was struck in the face by a bird and was stunned and lost control – and his place in the team was taken by Jim Clark.

Clark remained faithful to Chapman and Team Lotus throughout his Formula One career. While the World Champion went from success to success until his death in 1968, other members of the Lotus Formula One team enjoyed mixed fortunes. Innes Ireland remained in the Lotus team in

1961, but despite his win in the United States race had blotted his copybook rather badly with a serious crash in the tunnel in practice for the Monaco race; he was having difficulty in familiarising himself with the new ZF transmission fitted to the Lotus 21 and inadvertently changed down instead of up! At the end of the season Ireland was told that his services were no longer required and he signed up to drive for the UDT-Laystall team.

Trevor Taylor joined Team Lotus for 1962-3, but 1963 proved unsuccessful and he left the team at the end of the year. For 1964 the Lotus number two was Peter Arundell who had a serious crash in a Formula Two race at Reims in 1964; Mike Spence took over the number two seat and stayed with Team Lotus until 1967 when he signed up with the BRM team. It was not until 1966 that Arundell was considered fit to race again, but, as he still had a bad limp, his driving lacked the sparkle and flair that he had displayed in Formula One during the early part of 1964 and he retired from racing at the end of the year. There are few more perceptive team managers than Colin Chapman and few enjoy a reputation for being more ruthless; Chapman must have been quite sure in his own mind that Arundell would never make the grade again after his accident, yet he was prepared to give him a fair chance to find his old form.

1967 was the first year in which Chapman adopted the 'two number one drivers' approach, by bringing in Graham Hill, who had been with BRM since 1960, as joint number one with Jim Clark. Team Lotus introduced the 49 at the Dutch Grand Prix and for the rest of the season Chapman was fully occupied with sorting out teething troubles on the new model. Although it is quite clear that both Lotus drivers were given equally well prepared cars, Clark was certainly luckier than Hill and enjoyed far more finishes during the year. Jim Clark's terrible death in a Formula Two race at Hockenheim in April 1968 left Hill as sole number one driver and by the Monaco Grand Prix in May Chapman had signed up promising Formula Two recruit Jack Oliver as number two in the team. Oliver's spell with the team was short and not so sweet. He suffered a most unpleasant accident in practice for the French Grand Prix at Rouen when his car shot off the road at around 120 mph, hit a stone gate-post and broke in two (the cause was almost certainly turbulence affecting the very tall aerofoil fitted to the Lotus); he led the British Grand Prix at one stage, but retired; and his only successes were a fifth at Spa and a third place in the Mexican race. At the end of the year poor Oliver was dropped from the team, but succeeded in getting a drive with the BRM organisation.

It was back to the joint number one arrangement again in 1969 with Graham Hill partnered by Jochen Rindt. Despite the strained relations between Hill and Rindt, despite Hill's bad crash in the United States Grand Prix and despite the great disappointment of the failure of the four-wheel-drive cars, it was not a totally unsuccessful season for Lotus; in addition to Hill's fifth win at Monaco, Rindt proved himself by winning the race at Watkins Glen. Several other drivers handled works Lotus entries during the year. Italo-American Mario Andretti had driven for Team Lotus in two races in 1968 and in 1969 he appeared at several races with the 63 four-wheel-drive car. While Rindt was recovering from an accident suffered in the Spanish Grand Prix, his place at Monaco was taken by Dickie Attwood, a very unlucky and underrated driver, who took a fine fourth place. Later in the year John Miles, son of actor-manager Bernard Miles, drove the 63 on a regular basis, primarily because Chapman wanted the car handled by a driver without any preconceived notions as to how a Grand Prix car should behave.

John Miles was given a regular place in the works team in 1970 but, following Rindt's fatal accident at Monza, he quietly disappeared from the Grand Prix scene. By the United States race, Team Lotus's first outing after the Monza disaster, Chapman had chosen young Brazilian Emerson Fittipaldi as team-leader (he had driven a Lotus at three races earlier in the season) and brought in Swedish driver Reine Wisell. Neither enjoyed much success in 1971 but, at the end of the year, Wisell, a fine driver by any standard, was dropped and replaced by Dave Walker, a young Australian who had performed well in Formula Three. It is now a matter of history that Fittipaldi won the World Championship and Walker suffered the only too familiar lot of a Lotus number two driver, race after race accompanied by failure after failure; he left the team at the end of the year.

For the 1973 season former March driver Ronnie Peterson joined what was now known as John Player Team Lotus as joint number one with World Champion Fittipaldi. As the season progressed, so Peterson improved in skill and speed and in the latter part of 1973 it was evident that it was Peterson rather than Fittipaldi who was in receipt of Chapman's fullest support and confidence. This was particularly evident at the Italian Grand Prix where Peterson and Fittipaldi were holding first and second places in the closing stages of the race. If Fittipaldi won, he still stood a chance, albeit slight, of catching Jackie Stewart in the World Championship, but, significantly, Peterson was not signalled to ease his pace to allow the Brazilian to take the lead.

Emerson Fittipaldi moved on to drive for the Marlboro-McLaren team in 1974 and Peterson was joined by one-time stalwart Ferrari man Jacky Ickx. Although Lotus was plagued by development problems with the new 76 car, Peterson continued to enjoy a fair measure of success with the old, proven 72 model. Ickx, who had in the past demonstrated that he was one of the world's finest and fastest drivers, gradually faded from the forefront of racing as the season progressed. It seems very unlikely that Ickx will stay with John Player Team Lotus after 1975 and guesswork suggests that he may now be so disillusioned that he will retire from racing altogether.

Lotus At Indianapolis

One of the most significant aspects of Lotus racing history has been the team's performances in the Indianapolis 500 Miles race. The inspiration of later British successes in the Memorial Day Classic was Jack Brabham's drive into ninth place with a slightly modified Grand Prix Cooper at 'Indy' in 1961. Dan Gurney was convinced that the Lotus 25 monocoque car that appeared in 1962 Grands Prix was a potential Indianapolis winner, and the result of his discussions with Chapman was a proposal to the American Ford company that they should supply their very potent 4.2-litre V-8 unsupercharged engines. After Jim Clark had demonstrated the United States Grand Prix-winning Lotus 25 at Indianapolis, the Ford engineers were convinced of the merits of the scheme. The car built for the 500 Miles race was typed the 29 and on Lotus's first effort at winning the race Jim Clark finished second, just over nineteen seconds behind the winner; Dan Gurney with the second Lotus entry finished seventh, mainly as the result of a very slow pit stop.

The 1964 Indianapolis car was the 34 with sleeker bodywork and a new Ford engine with twin overhead camshafts per bank of cylinders. Jim Clark started from pole position and led on the first lap, but the race was stopped because of a multi-car accident and restarted after an hour and three-quarters. Jim was leading the race after 40 of the 200 laps when his Lotus developed a rear-end tremor; as he slowed, the left-hand rear suspension collapsed (the result of tyre trouble) and he was forced to abandon it on the infield. Dan Gurney's car was subsequently withdrawn as a safety precaution.

For Lotus it was third-time lucky at Indianapolis in 1965 and for Jim

Clark it was one of innumerable triumphs scored during the year. Clark and the improved Lotus 38 won the race at an impressive 150.69 mph (a race record) and the team earned a total of $150,000! By 1966 Chapman's three-year contract with Ford had come to an end and the Dearborn company had decided to back Dan Gurney's All-American Racers team. Chapman was, however, determined to have another crack at winning the 500 Miles race and Jim Clark was entered with one of the 1965 cars. The car handled atrociously but, despite spinning twice, Clark finished second to Graham Hill with a Lola.

By 1967 Chapman had arranged a deal with Andy Granatelli's STP concern and at Indianapolis Lotus fielded two cars with Ford engines for Clark and Hill. These cars, typed the 42F, had originally been built for the 1966 race when it was intended they should be powered by 4.2-litre versions of BRM's H-16 engine. It was an unhappy race for the team, as both cars retired with engine trouble.

A gas-turbine car, the STP-Paxton had run in the 1967 event, and for 1968 Andy Granatelli commissioned Colin Chapman to build a team of four four-wheel-drive gas-turbine cars for the 500 Miles race; these were designated the 56 and were powered by modified Pratt & Whitney engines. Jim Clark had tested one of these cars prior to his death at Hockenheim and after this tragedy it was agreed that his place in the team should be taken by number one BRM driver Mike Spence. After lapping at 169.56 mph (the second fastest ever achieved at the circuit) Spence was doing some test laps with one of the 56 cars when he hit the wall at Turn One, the right-hand front wheel was torn off, it rebounded off the nose and struck Spence on the head with tremendous force. Poor Mike Spence was gravely injured and died without recovering consciousness. Chapman was distraught at the death of yet another driver whom he knew intimately, a bare month to the day after the death of Jim Clark. Even though a metallurgist had confirmed that there had been no structural failure on the Lotus. Chapman decided to scratch the cars from the race and he has never again competed at Indianapolis. The 1968 Indianapolis car formed the basis of the 56B gas-turbine model that ran in a few Grands Prix in 1971.

Lotus And The Future

Whether Chapman's future and that of Lotus are inextricably entwined is doubtful and it is more than likely that at some stage he will divert his very considerable talents to another equally challenging field of technical activity. Although Lotus Cars is a public company, Chapman has kept Team Lotus quite separate and entirely under his personal control. Since Chapman first secured John Player sponsorship for the Lotus team in 1968, many other constructors have also obtained heavy sponsorship and the finances of Grand Prix racing and advertising promotion are now indivisibly linked. Only Ferrari, thanks to Fiat's financial interest, can race without a major sponsor. Lotus's racing future must inevitably be dependent on the retention of John Player as a sponsor or Chapman's ability to find another company with a heavy advertising budget.

The fortunes of Lotus cars are linked to the commercial success of the company's new Elite model. Over the years Lotus have built several different high-performance models, the original Climax-powered Elite, the Elan and the mid-engined Europa, all with superlative handling, a mixed reputation for quality and reliability, and all selling at very reasonable prices. The Elite is a very much more luxurious car, selling at a price of over £6000 ready to run on the road. When similar performance and equivalent quality, but admittedly inferior handling under hard cornering, can be purchased for little more than half the price, and when cars of established and proven quality such as BMW and Porsche can be bought for the same price, it is difficult to see that the Elite will prove the commercial success which Lotus so obviously seek.

13

Ferrari In Focus, 1947-75

No other manufacturer in the history of Grand Prix racing has competed for so long or with so much consistency as Ferrari; no other manufacturer has achieved so many post-war Grand Prix victories (Bugatti probably won more racing car events during the inter-war period and Lotus has won more World Championship races); no other manufacturer has enjoyed such a long and successful history in sports car racing. Enzo Ferrari's achievements are many and varied. He has never been a technical innovator, but has always followed proven, well-established lines of development and usually only adopted technical improvements when they have been successfully tested by other contenders. He has proved himself (through his engineers) the master of modern engine designers, lavishing great care on the development of a whole range of engines of different configurations and sizes. Other constructors have produced equally successful engines (for example the Jaguar XK 120 unit that in developed form consistently beat Ferrari at Le Mans, and the modern Ford V-8 unit that has dominated Grand Prix racing in recent years), but for versatility and consistency on road and track Ferrari has remained supreme.

Ferrari stamped his own personality on International motor racing and for many years, by setting the pace in performance standards, moulded the whole pattern of Grand Prix racing to his tastes. Of all the Grand Prix constructors Ferrari and the hopelessly unsuccessful BRM team alone manufacture not only the chassis but the engines and gearboxes of their cars. Ferrari won seven of the nine Sports Car Championships held between 1953 and 1961 and four of the six Prototype Championships held between 1962 and 1967, and although he was pushed out of the picture in Sports Car racing between 1968 and 1971, he bounced back to win the newly inaugurated World Championship for Makes with his flat-12 3-litre cars in 1972.

Since 1950 Ferrari has been building very high performance road cars, his V-12 chassis has appeared with a myriad of body styles by the leading Italian coachbuilders and their ready availability did much to assist and encourage the Italian coachbuilding tradition. Ferrari still manufactures some of the fastest cars in the world – the V-8 'Dino' and the flat-20 'Berlinetta Boxer' – and, even if for exotic styling and theoretical flat-out performance these are now surpassed by certain of the products of Lamborghini, the Ferraris remain among the fastest, practical road cars available.

Enzo Ferrari was born in February 1898, the son of a railway engineer, and he became a fervent motor racing enthusiast at a very early age. With the CMN concern he gained experience as a mechanic, a racing motorcyclist and, finally, as a racing driver. He was invited to drive for Alfa Romeo for 1920 and, despite recurrent ill-health, soon proved his worth as a racing driver. Ferrari became more and more involved with the administrative and organisational side of Alfa Romeo racing activities and in 1929 he left Alfa Romeo (although still retaining close links) to form Scuderia Ferrari which was entrusted with the entry of the official Alfa Romeos on behalf of the works. Alfa Romeo had raced Grand Prix cars in 1924-5 (and revamped these cars for the 1930 season) and sports cars throughout the 'twenties, but the Milan factory started a really serious onslaught on racing with the introduction of the Vittorio Jano-designed straight-eight 'Mille Miglia' and 'Le Mans' sports cars and 'Monza' racing car in 1931. The following year there appeared the even faster Monoposto Grand Prix car and, apart from a short spell when Alfa withdrew for financial reasons in 1932, this model bearing the famous Scuderia Ferrari prancing horse badge dominated Grand Prix racing until German supremacy began to assert itself during the 1934 season. The German Auto Union and Mercedes-Benz teams expended far more money on their Grand Prix teams than Alfa Romeo could ever afford and the Italians constantly lagged behind in terms of both technical development and team organisation. Scuderia Ferrari struggled on and occasionally succeeded in defeating the Germans.

In 1938 Alfa Romeo decided to resume racing on their own behalf under the name Alfa Corse, but Enzo Ferrari remained with the Milan factory until 1939 and was closely involved in the construction and development of the 1500 cc 'Alfetta' Voiturette on which Alfa Romeo was pinning its hopes for the future. In 1940 Ferrari built his first cars, using Fiat 508C Balilla components and with straight-eight 1500 cc engines. Because of his severance agreement with Alfa Romeo when Scuderia Ferrari had been wound up at the end of 1937, he was unable to call the new cars 'Ferraris' and they were known simply as the Vettura 815. The two cars entered in the 1940 Brescia Grand Prix (the Mille Miglia 'substitute' race), but both retired. During the war years Ferrari concentrated on the manufacture of machine tools at his small works at Modena, but after these were bombed he transferred his works to Maranello ten miles south of Modena. It was here that the long line of post-war Ferrari cars was built.

1947

Ferrari's first V-12 cars appeared in 1500 cc sports car form at a minor race at Piacenza in May. One car crashed in practice and failed to start in the race, and the other retired. Later in the year the new cars won a total of five races. There was nothing very significant or dramatic about the performance of these first Ferraris, but what was significant was that despite early post-war material shortages Ferrari and his chief engineer Giaocchino Colombo had succeeded in the space of less than two years in building a complex competition model using both his own gearbox and engine designs.

1948

By 1948 Ferrari had enlarged the capacity of the V-12 engine to 2 litres; a small number of production cars were built and during the year Ferraris won three important long-distance sports car events and three Formula Two races. The most important Ferrari event of the year was the appearance of the new V-12 Grand Prix cars in the Italian race at Turin in September. Whereas the other contenders, Alfa Romeo, Maserati and Talbot all relied on pre-war designs, Ferrari had built a complete team of cars from scratch, cars that were fully competitive and well-sorted on their first appearance. The best Ferrari could manage at Turin was third place, but he gave both Alfa Romeo and Maserati a good run for their money and convinced the former that it should withdraw from racing as the opposition would be too strong in 1949!

1949

Largely as a result of the absence of opposition from the Alfa Romeo team, Ferrari won five Formula One races during the year, but suffered unexpected defeats at the hands of the lumbering French Lago-Talbot in the Belgian race (the unsupercharged French car ran through the race without a refuelling stop) and Maserati in the rather less important Lausanne race. The Grand Prix Ferraris were inadequate in terms of both roadholding and power output, a situation that Colombo endeavoured to rectify by the introduction at the Italian race of a new variant with a longer chassis and much-modified engine having twin overhead camshafts per bank of cylinders (instead of a single cam per bank) and twin-stage supercharging. In sports car racing the *marque* continued to reign supreme, largely because other constructors had not made such a rapid recovery from the ravages of war and there was little competitive opposition. Ferrari completely dominated the 2000 cc Formula Two category with new cars that combined the 2-litre sports car engine with the Grand Prix chassis and won all nine races entered.

1950

Alfa Romeo returned to racing in 1950 and Ferrari immediately lost his grip on this class of racing. He had, however, realised that the development of the 1500 cc supercharged cars was a blind alley and had switched his attention to the alternative class for cars of 4500 cc unsupercharged. The first full 4500 cc Ferrari did not appear until the Italian race in September and Alberto Ascari took over team-mate Serafini's car to finish second after his own had retired with engine failure. Ferrari's speedy appreciation of the situation meant that there would be a titanic struggle in 1951 between the new unblown Ferraris and the all-conquering Alfa Romeo 158s which had suffered only one defeat since the war (in their first post-war race at St Cloud near Paris in 1946). During this year Ferrari raced new 2.3-litre sports cars in addition to the familiar 2-litre model (but scored rather less success than anticipated) and built his first road-going cars. For Formula Two there was yet another Ferrari variant – early evidence of Ferrari's fantastic ability to evolve new models with lightning rapidity – and this compact, very fast, well-balanced V-12 car featured a 4-speed gearbox in unit with the final drive; the new car was entered in twelve races in 1950 and won eight of them.

1951

The 1951 Grand Prix scene witnessed the predicted battle between the ever-improving, unsupercharged 4500 cc Ferrari and the ageing, overdeveloped, voraciously thirsty 1500 cc supercharged Alfa Romeo. After a string of second places at Bremgarten, Spa-Francorchamps and Reims, the *marque* defeated the Alfas for the first time in the British Grand Prix at Silverstone. This in itself made motor racing history and was the result of careful design and intensive development work, but what was so remarkable about this victory was that it was scored by Froilan Gonzalez, the swarthy, bull-like Argentinian who had only driven a works Grand Prix Ferrari in one previous race; and he was at the wheel of a less powerful 1950 car. Later in the season Alberto Ascari, the 'star' of Scuderia Ferrari, trounced the Alfas at the Nürburgring and Monza. Ferrari's domination of Formula Two racing continued that year and the *marque* won a total of seven races for 2000 cc unsupercharged cars. In addition Ferrari produced yet another 2000 cc car, the 4-cylinder Tipo 500 which was the work of young designer Aurelio Lampredi and this car, owing almost nothing of its ancestry to previous Ferrari design practice, was to prove one of the most successful and significant models in the history of the *marque.* At the Brussels Show in late 1950 Ferrari had unveiled a 4.1-litre sports car with an engine similar to that of the team's unblown Grand Prix cars and Luigi Villoresi drove a 4.1 Ferrari to victory in the 1951 Mille Miglia. It was, however, a generally unsuccessful year for the team in sports car racing and Ferrari was defeated by Jaguar at Le Mans and by a privately owned Frazer Nash in the Targa Florio.

1952

Alfa Romeo withdrew from Grand Prix racing at the end of the 1951 season, the British V-16 BRMs were still far from raceworthy and if Formula One had continued in its existing form it would have proved a pure Ferrari benefit. The Federation Internationale de l'Automobile and the various World Championship race organisers put their heads together and decided that all Championship races in 1952-3 would be held to Formula Two rules. Despite strong opposition from the French Gordini team, the appearance of a new Formula Two car from Maserati, and the gallant but impoverished efforts of the several British teams, Ferrari remained the dominant *marque* and the tough, torquey and fast 4-cylinder cars were beaten in only one race during the year. That race was the Reims Grand Prix where the winner was Jean Behra's Gordini and the Ferrari 'Fours' notched up a total of twenty victories during 1952. In addition Ferrari drivers took the first three places in the World Championship. As far as sports car racing was concerned, the most significant Ferrari development of the year was the appearance of the

Tipo 250 *Sport* V-12 3-litre car in the Mille Miglia; this model formed the basis of the long line of Grand Touring Ferraris that scored so many successes in the late'fifties and early 'sixties, even today's Daytona can trace its ancestry back to this model. Giovanni Bracco drove the 250 *Sport* to victory in the 1000-mile race, despite opposition from a very strong team of Mercedes-Benz 300SL cars and it was driven by Ascari and Villoresi at Le Mans where it set a new lap record. Few other sports car successes came Ferrari's way in 1952, primarily because the Scuderia was preoccupied with its intensive Formula Two racing programme.

1953

In 1953 Scuderia Ferrari continued to race the now familiar 4-cylinder Formula Two cars and dominated racing almost as easily as the previous year, despite a much-strengthened challenge from the Maserati team. The 4-cylinder cars won fourteen races during the year and Ascari won the World Championship for the second year in succession, but the team did suffer two unexpected defeats. At Siracusa at the beginning of the European season all four works entries retired, three of them because of faulty valve springs. As the season progressed, the Maseratis had improved in terms of both speed and reliability; Fangio was second at Reims (where he was defeated by young Ferrari driver Hawthorn by less than a car's length), Silverstone and the Nürburgring and finally won at Monza after a race-long battle with Ascari who, unaccountably, spun off at the very last corner. For sports car racing Ferrari relied on a revised 4.1-litre car and, from Le Mans onwards, the 4.5-litre Tipo 375 '*Mille Miglia*' model. In a sentence, Jaguar of Coventry dominated the Le Mans race and Ferrari won almost every other event entered in 1953. Maranello's victories encompassed the Mille Miglia, the Belgian 24 Hours race at Spa, the Pescara 12 Hours race and the Nürburgring 1000 Kilometres event and the *marque* won the newly inaugurated World Sports Car Championship. An interesting Ferrari development was a 4-cylinder sports car derived from the Formula Two model; a 2.5-litre model ran in the Inter-Europa Cup at Monza in June and later in the year Ferrari introduced the production *Mondial* 2-litre model.

1954

By the end of 1953 Ferrari was at the peak of his motor racing power but the following year saw a sad reversal of his fortunes through a combination of complacency in the face of innovations elsewhere and bad planning. The new 2500 cc Grand Prix Formula had come into force for the 1954 season and, despite the knowledge that Lancia and Mercedes-Benz were planning new Grand Prix contenders, Ferrari was content to race improved versions of his now three year-old 4-cylinder design. Although the 4-cylinder Ferraris won a large number of minor races during the year, their only World Championship successes were at Silverstone and Barcelona. Maserati won two World Championship races and Mercedes-Benz were victorious in four out of six races entered. For sports car racing Ferrari had developed a monstrous 4.9-litre V-12 car, the Tipo 375 '*Plus*', an ill-handling brute of a car that was suitable only for the very fastest courses. With the 375 '*Plus*' Ferrari won at Le Mans and in the Panamericana Mexico road race and took the Sports Car World Championship, but suffered a humiliating defeat at the hands of Ascari and his Lancia in the Mille Miglia. At Monza in June Ferrari revealed a full 3-litre version of the 4-cylinder sports car and this formed the basis of the production '*Monza*', another ill-handling brute, but one that sold well to private entrants and achieved a fair amount of success in the hands of the braver private drivers.

1955

Despite the lack of success of the Grand Prix cars in 1955, Ferrari had no immediate remedy. His chief engineer Aurelio Lampredi was working on a new 6-cylinder Grand Prix design, but this would not be ready until 1956, and so there was no alternative but to carry on racing the existing cars. Ferrari's only Grand Prix win was at Monaco where one of his 4-cylinder cars was driven to victory by Frenchman Maurice Trintignant, but only after the retirement of the entire Mercedes-Benz team. There were only six races in the 1955 World Championship and five were won by Mercedes-Benz. Lampredi's new 6-cylinder sports car was ready for the 1955 season but, although it was probably the fastest car racing, it proved sadly lacking in reliability. The model's only win was in the non-Championship Tour of Sicily, and the 1955 Sports Car Championship was another Mercedes-Benz benefit.

1956

Despite Ferrari's failure in 1955, he had come out at the end of the year with one very big bonus, the complete team of Lancia Formula One cars and the Lancia technical racing staff. Potentially the V-8 Lancia D.50 designed by Vittorio Jano was the fastest of all contemporary Grand Prix cars, but ever since its first appearance at Barcelona in October 1954 it had been plagued by teething troubles. Scuderia Lancia fortunes had improved little in the early part of 1955, the team had spent far too much money on its racing programme and was finding itself in financial difficulties and the final straw was the death of the team's number one driver Alberto Ascari in a practice crash with a Ferrari sports car at Monza in June. Lancia withdrew from racing, in July the Lancia D.50s were handed over to Ferrari and he was given a financial subsidy from Fiat to assist his racing programme. Ferrari raced the Lancias throughout 1956, calling them simply 'Ferraris', with a strong team of drivers that included Juan Fangio and young Englishman Peter Collins. Although Ferrari enjoyed a very successful 1956 season, his loss of independence seemed to be accompanied by a loss in the team's character and from that point just a little of the magic seemed to be missing. The team won five out of the seven World Championship races and Fangio took the World Championship for the fourth time. Aurelio Lampredi had left the team, Ferrari abandoned the disastrously unsuccessful 6-cylinder sports cars and throughout 1956 raced the familiar 4-cylinder models and a range of new V-12 cars from the drawing board of Vittorio Jano. At the beginning of the year Ferrari 'cobbled together' a couple of new 4.9-litre V-12 cars to run in the first Championship Sports Car race of the season, the Buenos Aires 1000 Kilometres event, but these failed miserably and the race was won by Maserati. Jaguar dominated the Le Mans 24 Hours race and otherwise it was much the same story as in 1953; Ferrari won the Mille Miglia and the Swedish Grand Prix and gained the Sports Car World Championship for the third time.

1957

Maranello continued to race the Lancia V-8 cars in 1957, but they were now much-modified and known as the Ferrari Tipo 801s. Despite a strong team of drivers that included Mike Hawthorn, Peter Collins and Luigi Musso, Scuderia Ferrari proved no match for the latest products from the rival Italian Maserati team and for the British Vanwalls which had improved immeasurably since their first appearance in 1954. Maserati and Vanwall shared the honours (Fangio won four races for Maserati together with his fifth and final World Championship and Moss scored three victories for Vanwall). Ferrari's only win was in the non-Championship Reims race. In 1957 the Federation Internationale de l'Automobile introduced a new 1500 cc Formula Two category to which Ferrari responded with a new V-6 car, designed by a team under the leadership of Vittorio Jano and clearly inspired by Lancia racing practice. Maurice Trintignant drove the new car to victory at Reims in July. The Ferrari team raced 3.8 and 4.1-litre V-12 cars in 1957 Sports Car races but, although Piero Taruffi won the last-ever Mille Miglia and Ferrari took his fourth Sports Car World Championship, most of the year's sports car honours went to other teams; Maserati won at Sebring and in the Swedish race, Aston Martin was victorious at the Nürburgring and Jaguar scored its fifth and final win at Le Mans.

1958

An important change in the Formula One regulations for 1958 was the requirement that cars used 140-octane aviation fuel or 'Avgas' in place of the previous alcohol-based brews. The V-8 Lancia-Ferraris were not suitable for modification to run on 'Avgas' and so Ferrari relied on an enlarged 2416 cc version of the V-6 Formula Two car known as the '*Dino*' in memory of Ferrari's son who had died in 1956. Maserati had now withdrawn from racing and so the team's main opposition came from Vanwall and Cooper (whose 2-litre Climax-powered cars won at Buenos Aires and Monaco). In the early part of the season the V-6 Ferraris handled badly and were down on engine power, but Ferrari persevered with their development and by the end of the year they were a match for the very fast Vanwalls. Hawthorn finished second in the Belgian race and won the French, and Collins won the British Grand Prix. Mike took second place in the Portuguese, Italian and Moroccan Grands Prix to win the Drivers' World Championship by the margin of only one point. It was, however, a tragic Grand Prix season for Ferrari, for Musso was killed in the French race and Collins lost his life at the Nürburgring. The Formula Two Dino made only two appearances during the year and was defeated on both occasions. In World Championship Sports Car events there was now a 3000 cc capacity limit; Ferrari relied on the V-12 '*Testa Rossa*' model which had appeared in experimental form in 1957 and was also sold in substantial numbers as a production car. The '*Testa Rossas*' were defeated by Aston Martin at the Nürburgring and did not contest the Tourist Trophy, but still clinched the Sports Car Championship with victories at Buenos Aires, in the Targa Florio and at Le Mans. It was only in 1958 that Ferrari production cars began to be built in substantial numbers and in June Maranello introduced one of the first of the really successful production cars, the 250 GT coupé with Pininfarina bodywork; the 250 GT had first appeared for 1955 and was powered by a detuned version of the engine used in the '*Testa Rossa*'.

1959

The team continued to rely on the *Dino* V-6 Grand Prix car in improved form in 1959, but racing had changed dramatically and, except on very fast circuits, the front-engined cars from Maranello were no longer competitive. Vanwall had retired from serious racing and the leading wearer of the British Racing Green was the rear-engined Cooper, now powered by a full 2500 cc version of the Coventry-Climax engine. The Coopers were adequately powerful, were light and compact and handled admirably; and with Jack Brabham and Stirling Moss at the wheel they dominated the year's Formula One racing. Ferrari had to settle for wins by Tony Brooks in the French Grand Prix at Reims and in the German Grand Prix held on the very fast, but very dangerous, Avus track in Berlin. Appearances by the Formula Two cars were still few and far between and the smaller V-6 achieved no success. Sports Car racing proved another straight fight between Ferrari and Aston Martin, but in 1959 the British *marque* came out on top, winning at the Nürburgring, at Le Mans and in the Tourist Trophy (and gaining the Sports Car Championship); the '*Testa Rossa's*' only victory was at Sebring. An important Grand Touring development was the appearance of the short-wheelbase 'Berlinetta', a production car destined to win many races, which was first exhibited at the Paris Salon in the autumn of 1959.

1960

By 1960 Ferrari was only too well aware of the shortcomings of the *Dino* Grand Prix car, but the 2500 cc Formula came to an end that year and all Maranello development work was aimed at producing a competitive contender for the 1500 cc Grand Prix Formula of 1961 onwards. Ferrari's only Formula One win in 1960 was at Monza (a race boycotted by the other constructors because it was run on the combined road and track circuit), but in the hands of young Wolfgang von Trips the Formula Two model won at Siracusa. As part of the development programme for 1961, Ferrari built a rear-engined Grand Prix *Dino* which ran in the 1960 Monaco Grand Prix and a rear-engined Formula Two car that appeared later in the year, won at the Solitude circuit in Germany, won the Formula Two class of the Italian Grand Prix and finished second in a Formula Two race at Modena. Aston Martin had now withdrawn from sports car racing and so this category proved largely a Maranello benefit. Ferrari continued to race the '*Testa Rossas*', but was also now fielding the *Dino 246S*, a model which combined the *Dino* Grand Prix engine with the '*Testa Rossa*' chassis. Ferrari was also achieving a great deal of success in 1960 Grand Touring car events with the beautiful 3-litre 'Berlinetta'; one such race was the Tourist Trophy at Goodwood where Stirling Moss, enjoying one of his very few Ferrari drives, was at the wheel of the winning Ferrari.

1961

The British teams which had dominated Grand Prix racing during the years 1959-60 had opposed the introduction of the new 1500 cc Grand Prix Formula, had delayed development of new engines in the hope that they could get the new Formula quashed and, during 1961, were forced to rely on the outdated 4-cylinder Coventry Climax engine which had been used in Formula Two cars since 1957. The German Porsche team had been working on a new flat-eight Formula One car, but this was delayed by technical problems. The result was that in 1961 Grand Prix racing was dominated by Ferrari and the rear-engined V-6 Maranello cars scored victories in every race except the Monaco and German Grand Prix which Stirling Moss, at the wheel of an elderly Lotus, won through sheer driving skill and brilliant tactics. Ferrari's season was, however, marred by the death of Wolfgang von Trips at Monza when he had been leading the World Championship. Phil Hill won for Maranello at Monza and became the first and only American World Champion. In Sports Car racing Ferrari continued to rely on the faithful old '*Testa Rossa*' model, but also raced the new exciting Tipo 246 SP which was a rear-engined car powered by the old V-6 Grand Prix engine. Ferrari won every round of the Sports Car Championship except the Nürburgring 1000 Km event (in which the winner, as in 1960, was a Maserati) and in Grand Touring car events the *marque*'s successes included another win by Stirling Moss in the Tourist Trophy at Goodwood. This was one of the few years in which Ferrari had virtually every category of International racing 'sewn up' and it was one of the most successful in the history of the *marque.*

1962

Despite the sweeping successes scored by the team in 1961, the Ferrari staff were in a state of dissension and many of them – including chief engineer Carlo Chiti – quit Maranello at the end of the year. More problems followed when it became only too obvious that the new V-8 BRMs and Lotus-Coventry-Climax cars were more than a match for the V-6 Ferraris which had only been slightly modified since the previous year. At some circuits the cars were slower than in 1961 and the team failed to win a single Championship race during the year (though Hill was second at Monaco and third at Spa and Zandvoort); the only victories scored were in the rather parochial races held at Brussels, Naples and Pergusa in Sicily. The Sports Car Championship had been scrapped and its place taken by a new Championship for so-called Grand Touring Prototypes. Ferrari continued to race the 246 SP rear-engined V-6 cars, but also fielded new rear-engined V-8 models (which were unsuccessful and were abandoned at the end of the year) and at Le Mans entered an interesting variant that combined the '*Testa Rossa*' chassis with a 4-litre V-12 engine. There was very litttle opposition to Maranello in this class of racing in 1962 and Ferrari won at Sebring (with a North American Racing Team-entered '*Testa Rossa*'), in the Targa Florio and Nürburgring 1000 Km events (with 246 SP cars) and at Le Mans (with the 4-litre '*Testa Rossa*'). The Ferrari drivers at Le Mans were Olivier Gendebien and Phil Hill, enjoying, respectively, their fourth and third victories with Ferraris at the Sarthe circuit. For the Grand Touring class Ferrari had produced the 250 GTO (meaning Grand Turismo Omolgato or homologated), a direct development of the earlier 250 GT cars but with lower, sleeker lines and a 3-litre engine in full '*Testa Rossa*' tune with six twin-choke carburettors. The 250 GTOs scored many class wins in 1962 and Innes Ireland drove one of these cars to victory in the Tourist Trophy. They were to prove themselves one of the most successful and sought-after Ferrari models.

1963

Although work was progressing on new engine designs, the first of which was raced in 1964, Ferrari continued to race V-6 powered Grand Prix cars in 1963; these were, however, much lighter cars with improved handling and were far more competitive than their 1962 predecessors. Phil Hill had been dropped from the Ferrari team and Maranello's Formula One *pilotes* were young John Surtees, Belgian driver Willy Mairesse and Lodovico Scarfiotti. After a mediocre start to the season Surtees finished second in the British Grand Prix at Silverstone and went on to score a victory in the German race at Nürburgring; later he won non-Championship races at Pergusa and Kyalami in South Africa. This year was marked by the appearance of a

Grand Touring Prototype that represented both a very logical development of earlier Ferrari design practice and the first of a long line of brilliantly successful Prototypes; the new car was the 250 P which combined the '*Testa Rossa*' engine with the 246 SP rear-engined chassis; during the year, 250 Ps won at Sebring, the Nürburgring and Le Mans, but were defeated by Porsche in the Targa Florio.

1964

Surtees was joined by Lorenzo Bandini in the 1964 Ferrari Formula One team and the team's new V-8 car made its debut in the non-Championship Siracusa race in April. Surtees was the victor in Sicily and later in the year finished second at Zandvoort, third at Brands Hatch and won at the Nürburgring and Monza, while Bandini with a V-6 was the winner in the Austrian Grand Prix. 'Big John' went on to win the Drivers' Championship by a margin of one point, but only after Bandini, accidentally or otherwise, had put Surtees's closest rival, Graham Hill, out of contention by ramming him at one of the bends in the final race of the season at Mexico City. Ferrari raced rear-engined V-12 Prototypes in both 3.3 and 4-litre forms in 1964; the team missed the Targa Florio, but scored victories at Sebring, the Nürburgring and Le Mans (Ferrari's fifth successive victory at the Sarthe circuit). Maranello was still building the 250 GTO in improved form in 1964, but at the 1963 Paris Salon had revealed the model intended as its successor. This was the 250 LM, to all intents and purposes a closed version of the 250 P. It had been hoped that the 250 LM would be homologated as a Grand Touring car, but the Federation Internationale de l'Automobile refused because insufficient examples had been built; this was a bitter blow to Ferrari, for both Maranello (with the 250 GTO) and Jaguar (with the lightweight E-type) had previously persuaded the FIA to homologate cars even though far less than the required number had been built. Enzo Ferrari made a great fuss about this set-back, complained bitterly to the Italian Automobile Club that it had not supported him adequately and handed in his competitions licence, vowing that he would never again race under Italian colours. At the United States and Mexican Grands Prix in 1964 the works Ferraris were entered by the North American Racing Team in the white and blue colours of the United States. Almost needless to say, by the start of the 1965 season, Ferrari had forgotten all about his row with the Italian national club and the works Maranello cars appeared once more in their familiar red colour finish. Ferrari's improved 250 GTO, was defeated in the Grand Touring Championship by Carroll Shelby's team of Ford-powered Cobras.

1965

Ferrari's new flat-12 car had appeared at the 1964 Italian Grand Prix and had run in both the United States and Mexican races. In 1965 Maranello fielded both the new model and the familiar V-8 – but with very little success. Racing was dominated by Jim Clark and Lotus, hotly pursued by the BRMs of Graham Hill and Jackie Stewart, and the Ferrari team was little more than a mediocre also-ran. In Championship racing the team's best performances were seconds by Surtees (V-8) in South Africa and Bandini (flat-12) at Monaco and in fact the team's fortunes deteriorated rather than improved as the season progressed. A terrible blow struck the team in October. John Surtees crashed badly when a hub broke on his Lola in practice for the sports car Canadian Grand Prix, and for a while his life hung by a slender thread and it seemed that he would never race again. In sports car racing Ferrari faced the financial might of the American Ford team for the second year in succession. During 1964 the Fords were too new, too fragile to perform well, but now they provided really serious opposition for the latest Ferrari 3.3-litre 275 P2 and 4-litre 330 P2 Prototypes. Ferrari lost to Ford at Daytona, was beaten at Sebring by an American Chaparral (a sports car as opposed to a Prototype) – though only private Ferraris contested this race – and scored victories at Monza, in the Targa Florio and at the Nürburgring. At Le Mans all the works Fords and all the works Ferraris retired, but Maranello still won the day thanks to the efforts of private teams. First place was gained by Jochen Rindt and Masten Gregory at the wheel of a 250 LM entered by the North American Racing Team and a similar Belgian-entered car finished second. An exciting Ferrari development in 1965 was the appearance of a 'baby' Prototype, the 1600 cc *Dino* 166 P coupé; this model first appeared at Monza (where it retired on lap one), but subsequently took a brilliant fourth place overall in the Nürburgring 1000 Kilometres race. Although Maranello had lost interest in Grand Touring events after the end of 1964, the factory did produce a very interesting lightweight version of the new 275 GTB production 3.3-litre coupé and at Le Mans this finished third overall, winning its class.

1966

After the dismal failure of the Maranello cars in 1965, Ferrari must have viewed the ending of the 1500 cc Grand Prix Formula with some relief. The present 3000 cc Grand Prix Formula came into force for 1966 and Ferrari, as so often in the past, was well advanced with development work and had displayed his new car before the 1965 season was over. For the new Formula Ferrari reverted to his traditional V-12 engine layout (last used in a Ferrari Grand Prix car in 1951) and with a team consisting of John Surtees, who had made an almost miraculous recovery from his accident, and Lorenzo Bandini, seemed destined to enjoy a very successful season. Surtees won the non-Championship Syracuse Grand Prix at the beginning of the season, was second in the *Daily Express* Trophy at Silverstone, Bandini was second (with a 2.4-litre V-6 car) at Moncao and Surtees was the victor in the rain-soaked Belgian Grand Prix. Then, less than a week later, one of the more unfortunate episodes in Ferrari history took place at Le Mans. Ferrari team manager Eugenio Dragoni (poor Dragoni, a most unpopular figurc, dicd in 1974) did not consider that Surtees was sufficiently fit as a result of his accident to withstand the rigours of the 24-hour race and nominated Scarfiotti as the spare driver for the car to be shared by Surtees and Parkes. Surtees was to start the race, but thereafter Scarfiotti would share the driving with Parkes. This was a sordid insult to a man who had fought so hard to recover his health and Surtees walked out of the Ferrari team. Maranello had lost their only top driver, and during the remainder of the Formula One season the team's successes were limited to a second place by Parkes at Reims and a 1-2 finish by Scarfiotti and Parkes at Monza. Significantly both of these successes were scored on high-speed circuits where cockpit skill was rather less important than brake horsepower. In 1966 Prototype races Ferrari fielded the much-improved 4-litre Tipo 330 P3 cars, but it was an unlucky year for Maranello and the team's successes were restricted to wins at Monza and Spa; Porsche won the Targa Florio, Chaparral was the winner at the Nürburgring and Ford was victorious at Daytona, Sebring and Le Mans!

1967

For 1967 Formula One races Ferrari signed up young New Zealander Chris Amon and cars were also driven by Bandini, Parkes and Scarfiotti. It was an unhappy year for Ferrari. Poor Lorenzo Bandini crashed at Monaco and succumbed to terrible burns, and Mike Parkes was badly injured in a crash at Spa. As a result of these accidents Lodovico Scarfiotti decided to withdraw from Grand Prix racing (he returned at the wheel of a Cooper-BRM in

1968, but was killed driving a Porsche in a hill climb that year). So Chris Amon was the sole Ferrari representative at most 1967 Grands Prix, but racing was becoming increasingly more competitive and the best that he could manage were thirds at Monaco, Spa, Silverstone and the Nürburg-ring. The 1967 Ferrari Prototype was known as the P4 and it was one of the most beautifully balanced, superbly engineered and glamorously styled of all Ferrari models. As Le Mans was to reveal, the P4's only shortcoming was that it lacked the sheer speed of the 7-litre Fords. This was a good year for Ferrari in Prototype racing, even if Ford won at Le Mans, and the P4s scored victories at Daytona and Monza, were second and third at Le Mans and second in the BOAC '500' race at Brands Hatch. By way of comparison, at Le Mans all the 7-litre Fords were timed at over 200 mph (one at 213 mph) and the Ferraris at 193 mph. Ferrari had last competed in Formula Two in 1953, but an interesting new development in 1968 was a 1600 cc Formula Two car powered by the Ferrari-designed V-6 engine that powered the Fiat Dino sports tourer. The new car made but one appearance at Rouen, although it was to be extensively raced the following year.

1968

Between the years 1966 and 1969 Ferrari progressively improved the V-12 Grand Prix cars, but they were no match for the Ford-powered Lotus 49 which had made its debut at Zandvoort in 1967. From 1968 onwards the Ford engine was freely available to other constructors and between the French Grand Prix in 1968 (the last Ferrari victory for two years) and the Belgian Grand Prix in 1970 every Championship race was won by a Ford-powered car. The 1968 French Grand Prix, run on a rain-soaked track, was won for Ferrari by young Belgian driver Jacky Ickx. Otherwise it was a poor year for the team and the only other performances worthy of a mention were a third by Ickx at Spa and second and third by Amon and Ickx at Brands Hatch. For 1968 the Commission Sportive Internationale had imposed a 3-litre capacity limit for Sports Prototypes (a decision not announced until June 1967) and Ferrari found it impossible to get new cars ready in time. Ferrari built a 6.2-litre Can-Am sports car in 1968, but development was delayed and it arrived in the United States in time only for the last race of the series at Las Vegas. This car, driven by Chris Amon, retired on the first lap with the throttles jammed by dirt. At the beginning of the year Amon dominated the Tasman races in New Zealand and Australia with a Formula Two car powered by a 2.4-litre V-6 engine. In European Formula Two races the cars, now almost completely redesigned, competed regularly without much success, but at the end of the season the team won three out of four races held in the Argentine.

1969

Ferrari soldiered on with the V-12 Grand Prix cars in 1969, but no success was achieved apart from a third place at Zandvoort and the team's hopes were pinned on a new flat-12 car which was scheduled to appear at Monza in September. Unfortunately the flat-12, typed the 312B (the 'B' stands for 'Boxer', the Continental term for a horizontally opposed engine) suffered engine trouble in unofficial practice before the Italian race and its debut was postponed until 1970. The team returned to sports car racing with the exciting 312P based on the V-12 Grand Prix cars and throughout the year this presented a strong challenge to the all-conquering Porsche 908s. The Ferrari effort was undermined by the team's reluctance to field more than one 312P in most races and, although it failed to win a race, the V-12 Prototype finished second at Sebring and Spa. Another exciting Ferrari sports car to appear in 1969 was the Tipo 212 '*Montagna*', a 2-litre flat-12 car derived from the 1964-5 Formula One design and itself the inspiration of the 1970 Grand Prix cars. The '*Montagna*' was built specifically to compete in the European Hill Climb Championship, a series which it dominated, with Peter Shetty driving the model to victory in seven of the eight events. For Can-Am racing Ferrari took the dust covers off the car that had competed in 1968 and Amon took several good places behind the works McLarens. Amon and Derek Bell dominated the Tasman series with modified versions of the car raced by Amon the previous year and the Formula Two cars appeared in a number of European races, although they were eclipsed by the Lotus and Matra opposition. Perhaps the most striking aspect of Ferrari's 1969 season was the sheer multiplicity of events in which the team competed!

1970

After such a mixed and largely unsuccessful year in 1969, Ferrari restricted his efforts the following season to Formula One racing and the Sports Car World Championship. The flat-12 Formula One car was plagued by teething troubles in the early part of the season, but gradually improved in speed and reliability. The break-through came in Austria where Ickx and the Ferrari defeated the Ford-powered opposition and this success was followed by wins by Clay Regazzoni (sensational newcomer to Formula One) at Monza and by Ickx in the Canadian and Mexican races. To appreciate Ferrari's efforts in sports car racing in 1970, it is necessary to look back to Porsche's achievement in 1969. Stuttgart had dominated that year's racing with the 908 3-litre cars, but had also introduced the monstrous 917 4.5-litre model. This 4.5-litre car was eligible for Championship racing really only as a result of what amounted to a loop-hole in the regulations. When the 3-litre capacity limit was introduced for 1968, the Commission Sportive Internationale had allowed 5-litre Competition Sports Cars to compete on even terms with the Prototypes provided that at least fifty had been built. This was to protect owners and manufacturers of larger-capacity cars of which there were many being raced. For 1969 the homologation figure was reduced to twenty-five, primarily to assist the smaller specialist manufacturers. Porsche decided to build twenty-five new 4.5-litre cars from scratch and after a few unsuccessful appearances (and one victory) in 1969 these were handed over to John Wyer to race on behalf of the works. For 1970 Ferrari responded by building a batch of twenty-five 5-litre Tipo 512S cars and during that year the blue and orange of Gulf-Porsche and the red of Maranello waged a titanic duel. Unfortunately for Maranello the 512S was not quite as fast as the Porsche 917, the Porsche factory had also produced a small, lithe 3-litre Prototype for use on the more tortuous circuits and Ferrari team management and standards of race preparation failed to match that of the Wyer organisation. Of the ten rounds in the Championship, Porsche won nine; Ferrari's sole victory was at Sebring, but works 512S cars finished second at Monza and Spa.

1971

During this year Ferrari introduced an improved flat-12 Formula One car known as the 312B/2 and possessed a very strong team of drivers consisting of Ickx, Regazzoni and Italo-American Mario Andretti. Throughout the year the Ferraris were unexpectedly plagued by engine problems, the latest versions of the Ford engine were more powerful and more reliable and Ferrari's Championship victories were limited to the South African race (which Andretti won only after the front suspension of Hulme's leading McLaren had collapsed) and the Dutch race (dominated by Ickx on a rain-soaked track). Although Ferrari produced an improved version of the 5-litre car for private owners to race, the works team concentrated its efforts in Sports Car racing on a new 3-litre Prototype derived from the latest Grand Prix cars. From 1972 onwards the 5-litre cars were banned and once again Ferrari was making sure that he was well prepared! The first of the new 312Ps (the model was given the same designation as the 1969 cars) was written off in tragic circumstances in the first round of the Championship at Buenos Aires. French driver Jean-Pierre Beltoise was pushing his car back to the pits after it had run out of petrol and was foolish enough to push it *across* the road at one of the corners. Ignazio Giunti, leading the race, was lapping another car and failed to see the Matra which he struck at high speed. The Ferrari ricocheted some two hundred yards down the road, burst into flames and the driver was killed instantly. Later in the year the 312P finished second in the BOAC 1000 Km race and, although it failed to achieve success elsewhere, Ferrari's season of testing and development were to produce brilliant results in 1972.

1972

Ferrari continued to race the 312B/2 flat-12 Formula One cars in 1972, but substantial success still eluded the team and the Ford V-8 reigned supreme for yet another year. Early in the season Ickx took a third place in the Argentine race and was second in the waterlogged Monaco event, a slow, wet, miserable race throughout which he trailed Beltoise's leading BRM. With one very notable exception the rest of the season was barren of victories for Maranello. Ickx completely dominated the German Grand Prix; he took the lead on the first lap, stayed in front for the remaining thirteen and slashed the lap record over and over again. To rub the point in – that when the Ferraris went well, they were more than a match for anything – Regazzoni brought his Ferrari across the line in second place. It was only too obvious that Ferrari shortcomings lay in their standards of preparation and organisation and the flat-12 design was potentially the fastest in the world. In one class of racing, the Sports Car Championship, the flat-12 reigned supreme and the Ferrari 312Ps won ten of the eleven rounds in the Championship. The eleventh race, Le Mans, the team did not enter.

1973

The 1973 season proved one of the most dismal and unsatisfactory in Maranello racing history. An improved Formula One model, the 312B/3, appeared at the Spanish Grand Prix, but success still eluded the team. Neither Ickx not team-mate Arturo Merzario achieved any respectable performances and Ickx withdrew from the team after the British Grand Prix in July. Ferrari missed the German Grand Prix, reappeared with a single much-modified car for Merzario in Austria and entered cars for both Ickx and Merzario at Monza – still without success. Only Merzario appeared in the final two races of the season and before the end of the year Ickx had signed up to drive for John Player Team Lotus. In Sports Car racing Ferrari efforts were much less determined; Maranello missed the Daytona race at the beginning of the season and was defeated by the French Matra team at Vallelunga, Dijon, Le Mans, the Österreichring and Watkins Glen. Another defeat was suffered at Spa where the winner was the British Gulf-Mirage and Ferrari's only victories were in the races at Monza and the Nürburgring. Some consolation for the failure of the Prototypes was the continuing success of the production 4.4-litre 'Daytona' model in the Grand Touring class and at Le Mans one of these cars driven by Elford and Ballot-Lena finished sixth overall and won the class.

1974

By 1974 Ferrari prestige was at an all-time low and Maranello realised that only a drastic overhaul of its racing department – and its racing philosophy – could bring the team the success that it yearned for so much. Although an improved Prototype had been developed, this was not raced and Ferrari efforts were concentrated solely on Formula One. Mauro Forghieri, who had engineered Ferrari racing efforts in 1969-70, gave up a senior position within the company to take direct control of the racing programme and Clay Regazzoni (returning after a miserable year with BRM) and Niki Lauda (another ex-BRM man) signed up to drive the improved 312B/3 cars. Second and third places in the Argentine (in the order Lauda-Regazzoni) were followed by a second in Brazil (Regazzoni), first and second in Spain (Lauda-Regazzoni), second in Belgium (Lauda), and first and second at Zandvoort (Lauda and Regazzoni). Even though Ferrari reliability has been suspect on occasions, the cars have always displayed outstanding speed. Second and third places followed in the French race at Dijon and at Brands Hatch Niki Lauda lost a certain victory when his car developed a slow puncture in the closing laps; he stopped at the pits, but officials prevented him from rejoining the race and after an appeal to the FIA he was awarded fifth place. Clay Regazzoni led throughout the German Grand Prix and he was second in Canada. Despite so much promise the World Championship had again eluded the team, Fittipaldi was again Championship driver with 55 points with Regazzoni second (52 points) and Lauda fourth (38 points).

1975

Ferrari had now developed a very promising version of the flat-12 car, the 312T, with slimmer revised chassis and transversely mounted gearbox. The 312T made its debut at the South African race and early in the season Niki Lauda won the Monaco Grand Prix and the Belgian race at Zolder. Further successes followed and by the middle of the season there seemed little doubt that Lauda would become the 1975 World Champion.

Postscript.

Enzo Ferrari is now 77; over the years the company which he founded has gradually evolved from a small, specialist racing team, building only a very limited number of production cars – and these highly-tuned, fickle, temperamental beasts – to a highly sophisticated factory manufacturing ultra-fast, refined production cars in substantial numbers and with the racing side of the business a very small part of the whole. Fiat now owns a 50% interest in Ferrari and is greatly concerned with the commercial future of the production cars. The autocratic founder of the company retains full control of Ferrari racing activities and will brook no interference from Fiat or anyone else. The future of Ferrari racing activities must be surrounded with uncertainty. Ferrari had no son to take over the running of the business (after a long illness Dino Ferrari died in 1956) and although the company has many talented engineers, Ferrari, largely as a result of his stormy temperament, has never groomed a successor. It is unlikely that the Ferrari prancing horse will survive as a major force in motor racing for more than a few years.

14:

The Jaguars That Were Dressed In Blue

The evolution of the Jaguar as a serious competition car, and its decline in the late 'fifties, was paralleled by the rise and fall of the now almost legendary Ecurie Ecosse team. While the works Jaguar team restricted its activities to major races, Ecurie Ecosse, first with production cars and later with ex-works machinery, raced in major and minor races and scored a whole string of successes in both. Ecurie Ecosse continued to race long after the works Jaguar team had disappeared from the International scene, but its victories became fewer and fewer and the last cars, built specially for the team's use, proved dismal failures.

In early post-war days Scottish businessman David Murray had been a successful driver of Maserati 4CLT/48 'San Remo' cars. Although his racing activities were organised in a thoroughly professional manner, Murray was above all a lover of racing as a sport. After Murray had given up racing himself, he decided to run his own team and in 1952 formed Ecurie Ecosse which was based on his garage known as Merchiston Motors in Merchiston Mews, Edinburgh.

The team's first cars were a trio of standard Jaguar XK 120 open two-seaters, but later in the 1952 season these were joined by one of the first production C-type Jaguar cars which were built purely for competition purposes. This car was delivered on 3rd July 1952 and was registered JWS 353. All these cars, distinguished by a Scottish blue colour finish and wearing the shield of St Andrew, were cared for by the team's mechanical wizard W E Wilkinson who had previously been Reg Parnell's chief mechanic. 'Wilkie' carried out no drastic modifications to the Jaguar twin overhead camshaft 6-cylinder 3442 cc engines, but concentrated on detail improvements; the engines were stripped down, the connecting rods were crack-tested, weighed, balanced and realigned and the pistons were balanced. The team incorporated its own special 'tweaks' and passed the lessons learned from their racing experience to the Coventry manufacturer; but as Murray later pointed out, although Jaguar was able to take advantage of some of the suggestions made by the Scottish team, these were greatly outnumbered by the improvements that emanated from Coventry.

Ecurie Ecosse's first appearance as a team was, appropriately enough, at the Scottish Charterhall meeting on 6th April 1952 and here the trio of XK 120s was entered in a three-hour relay race; the new team was very harshly handicapped and failed to feature in the results. Later in the day, however, twenty-year-old Ian Stewart at the wheel of one of the blue XK 120s led for eight of the ten laps of the Formule Libre race, but was then passed by Bill Dobson with a racing Ferrari; Stewart crossed the finishing line thirty yards behind the winner. Another success followed at Ibsley on 19th April and here Stewart finished third in the 10-lap race for unsupercharged sports cars of over 2500 cc.

The team's first major race was the Production Sports Car event at Silverstone on 10th May. This race was dominated by the works C-type Jaguars and DB3 Aston Martins and the best that Edinburgh could manage was a ninth place by Stewart who was proving the team's most successful driver. An unexpected defeat for Ecurie Ecosse followed at Crimond in Scotland on 24th May and in the unlimited capacity sports car race at this circuit the winner was Jack Walton's Frazer Nash (an out-and-out competition car) and Stewart and Dobson were beaten into second and third places. In the Formule Libre race held the same day Stewart retired with clutch trouble and Sir James Scott-Douglas, at the helm of the second Ecurie Ecosse entry in this race, in the words of *Autosport,* 'took the Jaguar into the heather amidst a certain amount of clangor . . .'.

An exciting event in the British calendar at this time was the British Empire Trophy, run as a sports car race over what would now be considered a quite unacceptably dangerous 3.8-mile street circuit in the Isle of Man. The full distance was 52 laps, but cars of up to 1500 cc were allowed four credit laps and those of up to 3000 cc one credit lap. The strong entry included Duncan Hamilton (with the first privately owned C-type Jaguar), Geoff Duke (works Aston Martin DB3), Stirling Moss and Mike Hawthorn with 2-litre Frazer Nash cars and from Ecurie Ecosse a full team of XK 120 Jaguars driven by Ian Stewart, Sir James Scott-Douglas and David Murray himself (*le patron* had raced over this circuit many times previously).

Hamilton and Duke retired, the handicapping system favoured the smaller cars which were almost as fast as the larger-capacity models over this difficult course and the Lester-MGs of Griffith and Ruddock took the first two places ahead of the Frazer Nash entries driven by Hawthorn, Salvadori and Mitchell. Despite the fact that it was only too obviously a road-going as opposed to a racing car and with definite roadholding limitations, the XK 120 fared well and Scott-Douglas drove a magnificent race to finish sixth overall and win the over 3-litre class. David Murray ran out of brakes and hit a shop window frame at Onchan with the tail of his XK 120, and on Stewart's car a fuel pipe broke.

The Manx race was held on Thursday 29th May and only two days later the team was competing on home ground at Charterhall. Here the only car entered was driven by Scott-Douglas, but he was out of the picture in the unlimited sports car race and finished seventh behind Tyrer's streamlined BMW and a string of Frazer Nash entries. Ian Stewart drove the Ecurie Ecosse entry in the 'W Lyons' Trophy race at Snetterton, a race open only to XK 120s. As *Autosport* commented, there was no snarl of open exhausts in this race, but instead the shrieks of protesting tyres, markedly audible above the smooth hum of the engines. Unfortunately, the Scottish entry was very off-colour in this unique race; Hugh Howarth, Roy Salvadori and Michael Head took the first three places and Stewart failed to feature in the results.

Ian Stewart was entered with the team's shining, brand-new C-type Jaguar, registered JWS 353, in the Jersey International road race held over the very fast 3.2-mile St Helier road circuit on 10th July. Two of the team's XK 120s were entered for Dobson and Scott-Douglas and the opposition included works Aston Martin DB3s entrusted to George Abecassis and Reg Parnell. Stewart cantered away from the opposition in his 10-lap qualifying heat and in the final scored a magnificent victory at an average of 87.82 mph from Ken Wharton (Frazer Nash) and the two works Astons; the Ecuria Ecosse XK 120s finished fifth and sixth, Dobson heading Scott-Douglas across the line. Although the team continued to race the XK 120s during the remainder of the 1952 season, their efforts were concentrated on the C-type with which Ian Stewart scored a whole string of successes. On 27th July, Stewart won a sports car race at Charterhall and at the same meeting the team's new Cooper-Bristol single-seater made its debut.

The next race, however, proved disastrous; in the 100-mile race held at Boreham on 2nd August on a streaming wet track, Stewart went off the road on the first lap, slithered out of control across the grass and mowed down a group of spectators, none of whom, by great fortune, was badly injured. Thereafter the team's fine record speaks for itself, and Stewart and the C-type scored victories at Crimond in Scotland (9th August), Turnberry (23rd August), the Wakefield Trophy in Eire (6th September) and Charterhall again (11th October).

For 1953 Ecurie Ecosse retained JWS 353 and acquired three new production C-type cars. The team was planning to compete in a number of long-distance races to facilitate identification of the cars from the pits the later very famous white chevrons were painted across the noses of the cars; JWS 353 was the Lance-Corporal (single-stripe), KSF 181 the Corporal (two stripes) and KSF 182 the Sergeant (three stripes). MCV 630, which was delivered later in the season, was raced in a plain blue colour finish. The team also acquired another single-seater for 1953, a Formula Two Connaught, but neither of Ecurie Ecosse's racing cars achieved much in the way of success. The team's first outing of the season was at a Club Charterhall meeting at which Ian Stewart (with JWS 353) and Jimmy Stewart (with KSF 181) took the first two places in the sports car race. The two Stewarts were unrelated, but Jimmy Stewart was recent World Champion Jackie's older brother.

At Ibsley in Hampshire on 18th April, Ian Stewart and Jimmy Stewart took first and third places in the over-3000 cc sports car race, sandwiching Sydney Allard's new Cadillac-powered 'Le Mans' J2R Allard. In the Production Sports Car race at Silverstone the 4.1-litre Ferraris of Mike Hawthorn and Tom Cole took the first two places, the Ecurie Ecosse C-types were right out of the picture in the face of very strong opposition, and Ian and Jimmy finished ninth and twelfth. At Charterhall on 24th May, Ninian Sanderson and Jimmy Stewart were beaten into second and third places by Reg Parnell with the prototype Aston Martin DB3S which was making its race debut, and two days later, at Thruxton in Hampshire, Jimmy Stewart won the unlimited capacity events for both sports and racing cars. The following weekend the team was in action at Snetterton where Ian and Jimmy took first and third places in the 5-lap sports car race. At the end of June, Ecurie Ecosse entered C-types for Jimmy Stewart and Ninian Sanderson in the British Empire Trophy in the Isle of Man. In 1953 this race was held in class heats and a handicap final and Reg Parnell scored the Aston Martin DB3S's first important victory ahead of Wharton (Frazer Nash), Hans Ruesch (Ferrari 4.1) and Stirling Moss (works C-type Jaguar). With opposition of this calibre the Ecurie Ecosse team was a little outclassed, but

Sanderson and Stewart brought their cars across the line in fifth and sixth places.

The second 'W Lyons' Trophy for XK 120 Jaguars was held at the Snetterton circuit at the end of June. This year C-types were admitted, but had to face a handicap of 1 min 15 sec compared with the ordinary 'XKs'. The full Ecurie Ecosse team ran in this 10-lap race and Ian Stewart, Jock Lawrence and Jimmy Stewart finished first, third and fourth. Ian also set a new sports car lap record of 1 min 55 sec (84.52 mph) and won a 5-lap sports car race held later in the day.

Ecurie Ecosse made their first overseas entry in the 1953 Reims 12 Hours race, a single C-type for Scott-Douglas and Sanderson. The Jaguar works had just made history by bringing a complete team of C-type cars home in first, second and fourth places in the Le Mans 24 Hours race and at Reims contented themselves with a single entry for Stirling Moss and Peter Whitehead. On this very fast circuit the Coventry cars were outpaced by both the 4.5-litre works Ferrari of Maglioli/Carini and the American Cunningham entries. It was a lucky race for Jaguar, however; the leading Ferrari was disqualified for a number of infringements of the race regulations, including turning off its side-lights before the permitted hour (the Reims race started at midnight), and John Fitch crashed the fastest Cunningham. The works Jaguar went on to win the race at 105.52 mph and the Ecurie Ecosse C-type finished fourth behind the Talbot of Rosier/Giraud-Cabantous and the Cunningham of Cunningham/Johnston. It should be stressed that in this race the aim of the Scottish team had been to gain experience in long-distance racing and to finish rather than to chase after an improbable outright victory.

A week later Ecurie Ecosse was in action again in the Leinster Trophy race held on the Wicklow circuit in Eire and although they were handicapped too stiffly to score a victory, the Jaguars won the team prize and Ian Stewart was classified fifth. At the British Grand Prix meeting at Silverstone the works Aston Martin DB3Ss took the first three places, Bill Spear was fourth with a 4.1-litre Ferrari entered by Briggs Cunningham, Ian Stewart finished fifth with a works C-type Jaguar and Jimmy drove a good race to bring his Ecurie Ecosse car across the line in sixth position.

Ecurie Ecosse's greatest achievements in 1953 were yet to come and in the three months that remained before the end of the European season the team established a fine reputation in long-distance racing. In the 24 Hours race at Spa-Francorchamps at the end of July, Sir James Scott-Douglas partnered by Guy Gale brought MVC 630 across the line in second place behind the ailing works 4.5-litre Ferrari of Hawthorn and Farina; admittedly the entry had been weak and several of the faster cars had retired, but the watchword in endurance racing is consistency and Ecurie Ecosse had shown that it had learned a great deal from its entry at the Reims race earlier in the month.

A minor victory for Jimmy Stewart followed at Snetterton the next weekend and at Charterhall on 15th August, Ian and Jimmy Stewart finished second and third to Parnell with a works DB3S Aston. Then the team made a determined entry of two cars in the Goodwood Nine Hours race in which the opposition included the works Jaguar and Aston Martin teams. The works Jaguars were plagued by mechanical problems, two of the disc-braked Coventry cars retired and the Aston Martin team took the first two places. The surviving works C-type of Peter Whitehead and Ian Stewart was nursed home into third place. The Ecurie Ecosse drivers could not match the speed of the works entries, nor did they try to, but motored with their customary consistency and reliability to finish fourth (Jimmy Stewart/Dickson) and fifth (Lawrence/Curtiss).

Ecurie Ecosse was next in action again in another long-distance race, the first Nürburgring 1000 Kilometres event, and here three cars were entered. In practice Scott-Douglas had the misfortune to roll his C-type; it was far too badly damaged to run in the race and his road-going XK 120 was hastily substituted. The opposition in this race included a single 4.5-litre Ferrari which was driven to victory by Ascari and Farina, and teams of 3 and 3.3-litre Lancias and 2-litre Maseratis. The complete Lancia team was eliminated – two of the cars because of battery failure – and after the engine of the Giletti/Marimon Maserati had seized up on the last lap of the race, the Scottish-entered C-type of Ian Stewart and Roy Salvadori moved up into second place; Lawrence and Jimmy Stewart were classified sixth and Scott-Douglas and Sanderson brought the standard XK 120 across the line in tenth place. Ecurie Ecosse also took the first two places in the class for Production Sports Cars of over 2000 cc and won the team prize.

At the end of the year the C-types were sold and there was no difficulty in finding buyers for such successful and competitive machinery; JWS 353 was bought by Dutch driver Hans David, MCV 630 by Berwyn Baxter and KFS 182 went to John Keeling. The three 1953 works C-types with lighter bodywork and chassis tubing, triple Weber carburetters (in place of the SUs of the earlier cars), Dunlop disc brakes and rubber flexible fuel tanks were acquired by the Scottish team and were registered LSF 420 (Sergeant), LFS

671 (Corporal) and LFS 672 (Lance-Corporal). The fourth works disc-braked car, the Coventry team's spare, was registered OVC 915 and sold to Duncan Hamilton. The works team was now racing the very aerodynamic, monocoque D-type cars, but these did not appear until the Le Mans race in June.

The first round in the 1954 Sports Car Championship was the Buenos Aires 1000 Kilometres race and the Scottish team made the long trek out to the Argentine to compete with two of the C-types. The results were dominated by Ferraris which took the first two places ahead of the works Aston of Collins/Griffith, but Sanderson and Scott-Douglas, despite delays caused by misaligned wheels, did well to bring their C-type across the line in fourth place. The second entry was eliminated when Ian Stewart hit the retaining wall at one of the bends head-on and wrecked the front of the car.

Back in Britain, Ecurie Ecosse continued to compete in a large number of minor events and achieved a fair measure of success. The British Empire Trophy race was now held at the Oulton Park circuit in Cheshire, but the handicapping still favoured the smaller cars; Cooper-Bristol and Maserati took the first two places ahead of an MG-powered Lotus. The quickest of the larger-capacity cars was Duncan Hamilton's C-type which finished fourth and this Jaguar was followed across the line by the Ecurie Ecosse entries of Ninian Sanderson and Jimmy Stewart.

Jimmy Stewart and Sanderson took the first two places in the sports car race at the April Ibsley meeting, but at the May Silverstone race run in the wet and dominated by Gonzalez (4.9-litre Ferrari) the team's best was a fourth place by Jimmy Stewart. Stewart was third at Aintree, beaten by Hamilton and American Carroll Shelby with a DB3S Aston and Stewart and Sanderson took the first two places in the 21-lap Johnson Challenge Trophy at Goodwood on Whit Monday (this race was sponsored by the Johnson Wax company). The following weekend young Irish driver Desmond Titterington (a David Murray 'find') won the unlimited Sports Car race at Oulton Park from team-mate Ninian Sanderson. The works Aston Martins took the first three places in the Sports Car race at the British Grand Prix meeting at Silverstone, followed home by the V-12 Lagonda from the same stable, and the highest placed Ecurie Ecosse entry was Titterington in sixth place.

Ecurie Ecosse's first overseas outing in 1954 was not until the International sports car meeting at Zandvoort in Holland on 15th August. After what had so far proved a somewhat disappointing season, the team's luck returned and Ninian Sanderson and Sir James Scott-Douglas took the first two places ahead of a trio of Continental-entered C-types. Salvadori and Sanderson took the first two places for the team at Charterhall in September and these same two drivers finished second and third behind Picard's private Ferrari Monza 3-litre in the Penya Rhin Cup race preceding the Spanish Grand Prix at Barcelona in October.

At the end of 1954 two of the Ecurie Ecosse C-types were sold, LFS 671 to Hunter (to be driven by Lawrence) and LFS 672 to Peter Blond; the third car was retained by the team pending delivery of the first of its D-types and was advertised in *Autosport* for 25th March 1955 under the heading 'Sports Cars' as follows: 'The famous Jaguar XK 120C sports car which won the 24 Hours race at Le Mans in 1953. All the works improvements. "Wilkie" tuned and ECURIE ECOSSE maintained. Immaculate condition and ready for competition work about 11th April . . .'. After Ninian Sanderson had raced it in the British Empire Trophy at Oulton Park, LSF 420 was sold to young Bill Smith.

The 1954 works Jaguar D-types had been sold to Duncan Hamilton (OKV 1 and OKV 3) and to Johnny Broadhead (OKV 2) and Ecurie Ecosse had ordered two of the production D-types which had been announced at the 1954 London Motor Show. These cars, registered MWS 301 (Lance-Corporal) and MWS 302 (Corporal), were not delivered until just before the *Daily Express* meeting at Silverstone in May 1955; Jimmy Stewart crashed one of the new cars in practice and in the race the best that Titterington could manage was a poor sixth. Shortly afterwards the young Irishman finished second on handicap in the Ulster Trophy race held on the Dundrod circuit (the winner was Smith with LSF 420!). At the British Grand Prix meeting, held in 1955 at Aintree, Ecurie Ecosse was again out of luck and was rapidly discovering that the D-type was a far from suitable car for short-distance races; the works Astons took the first four places, trailed by Hawthorn with a works D-type, and Sanderson finished sixth for the Scottish team.

At Charterhall in August, Desmond Titterington drove MWS 301 to victory in the *Newcastle Journal* Sports Car Trophy and a week later won the sports car race at Snetterton with the same car. Titterington also contested the Formule Libre race over 25 laps of the Norfolk circuit and did well to finish third behind the Formula One cars of Peter Walker (Connaught) and Roy Salvadori (Maserati). The Aston Martin team won the Goodwood Nine Hours race for the third successive time, but in the absence of the works

Jaguars, Ecurie Ecosse upheld Coventry's prestige by taking second place with MWS 301 driven by Titterington and Sanderson. In September, Sanderson and Titterington took the first two places in the Sports Car race at Aintree. Titterington was a driver of outstanding ability, ability not unnoticed by works teams, and during 1955 he also drove for Jaguar at Le Mans and in the Tourist Trophy and for Mercedes-Benz in the Targa Florio in Sicily.

The 1955 season had proved one of the least encouraging in the history of the team from Merchiston Mews, but, fortunately, Murray was not too dismayed by the paucity of victories and for 1956 added to the stable a third production D-type, registered MWS 303 and with Sergeant's stripes. The coming season was to prove the most successful so far enjoyed by Ecurie Ecosse.

Ron Flockhart started the season well for the team with a win at the wheel of the new car at Snetterton, but Ecurie Ecosse was right out of the picture both at the Easter Goodwood meeting and in the British Empire Trophy. At Aintree, Titterington was beaten into second place by Roy Salvadori with a DB3S Aston. After this string of mediocre performances near-disaster struck the team at the *Daily Express* Trophy at Silverstone. Desmond Titterington, at the wheel of a works D-type with an experimental de Dion rear axle, spun on the first lap, was rammed by Peter Collins (works DB3S Aston), and Reg Parnell (DB3S) and Sanderson (Ecosse D-type) were both forced to take hasty evasive action; Parnell's car finished up in a ditch and the D-type was perched precariously on the top of an earth bank. Other DB3S entries driven by Salvadori and Moss took the first two places ahead of Bob Berry (Broadhead's D-type) and Alan Brown (Ecurie Ecosse D-type).

So far 1956 had proved an abortive season for Ecurie Ecosse, but the team's fortunes looked up at the 105-mile Production Sports Car race at Spa-Francorchamps in Belgium on 13th May and Sanderson won from Parnell (Aston Martin) and Frère (Ferrari), while Titterington, who retired, broke the Sports Car lap record which had stood to the credit of Farina's 4.5-litre Ferrari for nearly three years. The team returned to England for the racing over the Whitsun weekend and, at Goodwood, Titterington won a Formule Libre race and Flockhart and Titterington took second and third places in the main sports car race of the day.

Ecurie Ecosse returned to endurance racing at the Reims 12 Hours event, held on a fast, smooth circuit that was well suited to the D-type's excellent top-end performance and placed none too great a strain on its rather limited roadholding qualities. The works D-types took the first three places and the Ecurie Ecosse car driven by Flockhart and Sanderson played an excellent 'back-up' role to take a sound fourth place. A very interesting race held in 1956 was the 200-mile Rouen Grand Prix which was a sports car event with a capacity limit of 3000 cc; for this race 'Wilkie' produced a special 3-litre version of the D-type engine. This D-type, driven by Titterington, was no match for either the Astons or the Italian Ferraris and Maseratis over this fast course with its succession of difficult, high-speed bends and the Irishman finished a poor seventh. At the Grand Prix meeting at Silverstone the team performed rather better than usual in this sort of race and Titterington took third place behind Moss (3-litre Maserati) and Salvadori (Aston Martin DB3S).

In 1956 Ecurie Ecosse entered the Le Mans 24 Hours race for the first time. Le Mans was postponed until the end of July because of circuit improvements following the 1955 disaster and prototypes were limited in capacity to 2500 cc. There were a number of rather odd regulations including a fuel consumption limit (a maximum fuel capacity of 29 gallons and a permitted maximum of approximately 26½ gallons to be taken on at 34-lap intervals, working out at 11 mpg) and the requirements of a full-width windscreen and flexible tonneau cover. The D-type Jaguar and DB3S Aston Martin were admitted as production cars, but the organisers did not regard the 3-litre Ferrari Monza as falling into this category and so Maranello concocted some special prototypes that combined their new 2-litre 'Testa Rossa' production chassis with the 2.5-litre 4-cylinder engines that had powered Ferrari Grand Prix cars in 1954-5.

The works Jaguar team was put out of contention for victory almost as soon as the race had started. On only the second lap Paul Frère lost control of one of the works D-types at the Esses, slid broad-sided across the road and Fairman with another works car hit the bank in his efforts to avoid his stricken team-mate; de Portago's Ferrari collided with Fairman's Jaguar and all three cars were out of the race. Four laps later the surviving works D-type of Hawthorn and Bueb, the 1955 winners, was in the pits with fuel-feed problems; this car only rejoined the race seriously after several stops and the loss of 21 laps to the leaders. Now the Ecurie Ecosse D-type of Flockhart and Sanderson led from the Aston Martin of Moss and Collins. The Aston then went ahead on the streaming wet roads and Moss built up a good lead. When the rain stopped and the roads began to dry out, the Jaguar closed the gap again and by midnight had regained the lead and held a

40-second advantage. Just before dawn the Aston went in front again, but by 5 am the Scottish blue D-type had forged back into first place and it stayed ahead until 4 pm to win by the margin of one lap. This was the greatest triumph in Murray's racing career, it was the first victory at the circuit by two Scottish drivers and the first win by a private entrant since 1949. By the end of the 24 Hours race the Hawthorn/Bueb works D-type had climbed back to sixth place and had set fastest lap.

In August the Ecurie Ecosse team entered the *Daily Herald* Trophy race at Oulton Park. Race-day proved wet and stormy, shortly before the start the track was almost awash with water and Murray, deciding that conditions were too dangerous for racing, withdrew the two D-types. It was an unpopular decision; it was also a brave decision, but whether it was a wise one is a different matter. The 40-lap race was incident-free and the works Astons took the first four places.

By the middle of 1956 Ecurie Ecosse had agreed to buy two of the works 'long-nose' D-type Jaguars (registered RSF 301 and RSF 302) and as early as 27th July had advertised the existing team cars for sale in *Autosport.* In fact only two of the existing cars were sold and the team retained MWS 301. The works Coventry team had now withdrawn from racing and so an even greater responsibility rested on David Murray's broad shoulders.

At the beginning of 1957 Ecurie Ecosse took the long voyage to the Argentine to compete in the Buenos Aires 1000 Km race, the first round in the Sports Car Championship. Two D-types were entered, but in practice Ron Flockhart lost control and slid sideways into a concrete lamp standard and so only one of the Edinburgh cars, driven by Ninian Sanderson and Roberto Mieres, started the race. The finishing order was Ferrari-Maserati-Ferrari and these Italian cars were followed across the line in fourth place by the Scottish-entered Jaguar. Ecurie Ecosse had entered the Sebring 12 Hours race held in Florida in March, but the entries were scratched (probably for financial reasons) and at this race Jaguar fortunes rested with Briggs Cunningham, one of whose D-types with a new, enlarged 3781 cc engine was driven into third place by Hawthorn and Bueb.

Ecurie Ecosse was now limiting its entries to only the more important races and next entered the Mille Miglia and the Spa Grand Prix, which were held the same weekend. Ron Flockhart drove faithful old MWS 301 in the 1000-mile race and, despite the fact that the car was totally unsuitable for a road race of this nature and that there was an immensely strong Ferrari entry, rose to seventh place before the D-type succumbed to a broken chassis member at round half-distance. At Spa the Scottish D-types were no match for the latest Aston Martin DBR1s which took the first two places; Henry Taylor's private D-type was third and the best Ecurie Ecosse performance was sixth place by Jock Lawrence. In this race young Max Trimble wrote off his ex-Ecurie Ecosse D-type (MWS 303). Next on the calendar for the Scottish team was the Nürburgring 1000 Kilometres race, an event which the works Jaguar team had contested without success in 1956. The D-types simply lacked the roadholding qualities to do well on such a tortuous and arduous circuit, but the full team of three cars finished the race in eighth, eleventh and sixteenth places in the order Flockhart/Fairman, Bueb/Lawrence and Sanderson/Steed.

The team returned to Le Mans in 1957 with two 3781 cc long-nose D-types driven by Flockhart/Bueb and Sanderson/Lawrence. Despite strong entries from Ferrari, Maserati and Aston Martin, the D-types combined speed with reliability to take the first two places; and other Jaguar D-types finished third, fourth and sixth. One of the most remarkable aspects of Ecurie Ecosse's performances was that the team possessed only the three cars which had to be painstakingly rebuilt between races, and on very limited financial resources. Most of the other leading entrants had a much larger 'fleet' from which to choose and for them a write-off or major mechanical failure was no serious blow.

A fascinating event in 1957 was the Two Worlds Trophy held on the banked track at Monza and intended to provide a battle between the leading European contenders and the best of the United States Auto- mobile Club drivers with Indianapolis-type cars. Unfortunately most of the European drivers boycotted the race on the grounds that it was too dangerous (ie the 'ante' was not high enough), but a very courageous entry was a trio of cars from Ecurie Ecosse. The race was run in three heats and although American cars took the first three places, many of them proved hopelessly unreliable, the D-types were (in comparison) disappointingly slow but the epitome of consistency and reliability, and Jack Fairman, Jock Lawrence and Ninian Sanderson were classified fourth, fifth and sixth.

At the Swedish Grand Prix, held over 1000 kilometres at Kristianstad in August, the blue D-types were outpaced by the Ferrari and Maserati opposition. Lawrence and Scott-Brown (the latter was usually seen at the wheel of the works Lister-Jaguar) were in third place with their 3.8-litre fuel injection Jaguar with two-thirds of the race completed, and were closing on the second-place Ferrari when Scott-Brown made two off-course excursions and dropped to fourth; near the end of the race the car stopped because of a broken oil pipe and at the finish it was classified eighth. The second D-type driven by Sanderson and Fairman was never in the picture and was classified a rather hopeless tenth.

The following weekend Ecurie Ecosse was in action in the Belgian Grand Sports Car Grand Prix at Spa. Cars were entered for Fairman, Lawrence (both of whom retired) and, deputising for Ron Flockhart who had been injured in the French Grand Prix, young German driver Wolfgang Seidel who brought his D-type across the line in eighth place. This three-hour race was won by Tony Brooks with an Aston Martin DBR1. Ron Flockhart had recovered from his injuries by the *Daily Express* Trophy meeting at Silverstone in September (postponed from its usual May date because of the petrol rationing following the Suez crisis), but he spun his Ecurie Ecosse D-type on the first lap of the over-1500 cc sports car race. This was the Scottish team's last race of the 1957 season.

For 1958 a 3000 cc capacity limit was imposed in World Championship Sports Car races and the Jaguar factory responded by producing a 2986 cc (83 × 92 mm) version of the famous 6-cylinder engine and this was claimed to develop 254 bhp. David Murray realised that the D-type chassis was far too long in the tooth and inadequate in the roadholding department for road races and acquired one example of each of two new *marques* which used Jaguar engines, the Lister and the Tojeiro. The Lister, which in the hands of Scott-Brown had proved the sensation of British sports car races in 1957, had a de Dion rear axle, while the Tojeiro featured fully independent suspension; both cars were much lighter than the old D-types (which continued to be raced) and had vastly superior handling qualities. Neither, however, achieved much success, primarily because of the lack of reliability of the new 3-litre Jaguar engine and Ecurie Ecosse was now on the decline as a force in sports car racing.

For the first time Ecurie Ecosse contested the Sebring 12 Hours race in 1958, but both D-types retired with cylinder head problems caused by overweight valve springs. The Ecurie Ecosse Lister made its debut in 3.8-litre form at Aintree in April and at the Liverpool circuit it was driven by American Masten Gregory; Gregory drove a fine race to finish third behind Scott-Brown (works Lister) and Salvadori (Aston Martin DBR2). Gregory followed up this success with a win in the sports car race at the *Daily Express* meeting at Silverstone in May, defeating Scott-Brown with the works Lister, and won the Sports Car Grand Prix at Spa-Francorchamps a fortnight later.

This was a tragic race, for Scott-Brown crashed the works Lister-Jaguar which caught fire and he perished in the ensuing inferno.

A team of three D-types was entered in the Nürburgring 1000 Kilometres race and the car driven by Fairman-Lawrence, which was fitted with a 3-litre unit developed by 'Wilkie' as opposed to the works engine, finished seventh. The Bueb/Sanderson car retired with a blown radiator core plug and Gregory, whose long racing career was chequered by a series of lurid crashes, lapped faster than any D-type driver previously at the 'ring (9 min 58 sec) before spinning off at the North Turn. At Le Mans the team relied on the D-types, but in 1958 the Scottish Jaguars were out of luck and both retired with piston failure within thirty minutes of the start of the race. Ecurie Ecosse again contested the Two Worlds Trophy at Monza in 1958 with a pair of D-types and a specially built single-seater version of the Lister-Jaguar. It was hoped that the Lister would fare better than the sports cars, but it proved no faster and the team had to settle for ninth, eleventh and twelfth places on aggregate in the order Bueb (3.4-litre D-type), Fairman (Lister) and Gregory (3.8-litre D-type). This Lister was subsequently rebuilt for Phil Scragg to drive in hill climbs.

Ivor Bueb drove the Ecurie Ecosse Tojeiro on its debut at Silverstone in July and finished fourth behind Moss's Lister and a pair of Lotus Fifteens. In 1958 the Tourist Trophy race (a round in the Sports Car Championship) was revived at the Goodwood circuit. Ecurie Ecosse entered the Tojeiro and a D-type, but the new car was withdrawn after the first day's practice; only the D-type driven by Masten Gregory and Innes Ireland started the race and this finished fifth behind a trio of Aston Martin DBR1 cars and the Porsche of Behra and Barth.

Despite their waning fortunes Ecurie Ecosse persevered with their mixed bag of Jaguars, Lister and Tojeiro. The team's first race of the 1959 season was at Snetterton in March and here Flockhart won the sports car race with the Lister in 3.8-litre form. Gregory was sixth with the Lister at the Easter Goodwood meeting and shortly afterwards, at Aintree, Gregory with the Lister and Flockhart with the Tojeiro took third and fourth places in a 17-lap sports car race. At Silverstone in May Gregory ran out of brakes while trying to pass two slower cars into Becketts corner, and jumped off the tail of the Lister just before it wrapped itself round the retaining wall. Ron Flockhart scored the Tojeiro's only race victory at the Whitsun Goodwood meeting and Peter Blond, who was driving for Ecurie Ecosse for the first time, brought the rebuilt Lister across the line in third place. Gregory crashed the Lister yet again in the Nürburgring 1000 Kilometres race, apparently because of rear suspension failure, and Flockhart went off the road with the Tojeiro while trying to avoid a slower car that had crossed his line. At Le Mans the team entered a D-type and the Tojeiro, but neither car made it to the finish.

More trouble for the team followed at the British Grand Prix meeting at Aintree. In the sports car race Peter Blond spun and overturned the blue Lister and as it rolled, the Lister collided with the team's Tojerio driven by Flockhart. The team faced another serious loss at the Tourist Trophy at Goodwood. Masten Gregory was at the wheel of the Tojeiro when the brakes failed on the approach to Woodcote corner; the American performed his favourite trick of standing on the tail and jumped clear just before the car wrote itself off against the bank, but on this occasion he was flung over the bank, suffering a broken rib and dislocated shoulder. Jim Clark co-drove the Tojeiro with Gregory in this race.

For 1960 Ecurie Ecosse retained only one of the D-types for long-distance racing and severely restricted the number of races in which it competed. For 1960 the D-type had to be fitted with a high full-width windscreen and a large bulge on the tail forming a luggage container to comply with the latest Sports Car regulations. At Le Mans this car was driven by Ron Flockhart and Bruce Halford and, although on this circuit it was still very competitive and a potential winner, it succumbed to engine trouble during the early hours of the Sunday morning, while holding fourth place. This was the last appearance (and the seventh successive appearance) of a D-type in the Le Mans 24 Hours race.

In 1960 Ecurie Ecosse had taken delivery of a Cooper Monaco, a 2500 cc Coventry-Climax-powered rear-engined sports car based on the Cooper Grand Prix car. This was raced regularly – and with success – in British races, but the team's long International racing career was over. David Murray was, however, as enthusiastic about racing as ever, but simply lacked a suitable car. This was the situation that Murray remedied in 1962 by commissioning John Tojeiro to build the team two new Grand Touring Prototypes for long-distance racing. The new cars featured a multi-tubular space-frame, double wishbone independent front suspension and independent rear suspension by double wishbones and links. The fuel was carried in two separate tanks mounted on either side of the car, outboard of the driving compartment, and the body was a neat but rather ugly fast-back coupé. Originally it had been intended that the cars should be powered by

4-cylinder 2.7-litre Coventry-Climax engines and be fitted with Cooper gearboxes. It was later decided that these engines would not be reliable enough for long-distance racing and the team switched to a much-developed V-8 American Buick engine used in conjunction with modified Chevrolet Corvair transmission. This change resulted in the development of the cars being greatly delayed and they were not raced until the Charterhall meeting in July 1963. Here they were driven by Jackie Stewart and Tom Dickson and took the first two places in the race for Grand Touring cars over 1300 cc.

The team persevered with the Tojeiros in improved form in 1964, with Jackie Stewart as number one driver; the occasional victory was scored in minor races, but the team could no longer afford to contest major overseas racing and development of the coupés was expensive and protracted. The Tojeiro coupé was an inspired and advanced design, but the team simply lacked the resources to develop it to the point at which it would become a major race-winner. Another Ecurie Ecosse project was the Ecosse-Imp, a small, light single-seater built for racing at the Ingliston circuit neat Edinburgh. The Ecosse-Imp achieved a fair measure of success, but by 1966 David Murray had lost all interest in racing and wound up the team. His business affairs had been steadily deteriorating and eventually he fled to Majorca to avoid the public examination into his bankruptcy. As one journalist commented, this was the only cowardly act which Murray was ever known to commit. He was a large jovial man, a great Scottish Nationalist who assumed a humorous, shallow pretence of disliking the English. He died in Majorca in 1973.

15

Spa-Francorchamps:

The Fastest Road Circuit In The World

Familiarly known as 'Spa', more properly called Le Circuit National de Francorchamps, this 8.716-mile course running through lush countryside in the pine-clad foothills of the Ardennes mountains in Eastern Belgium, not far from the frontier with Germany, is the fastest and most exciting road circuit in the world. It is also one of the most demanding and exacting ever used for modern Grand Prix racing.

Spa was first used for racing in 1924 (and for the Belgian Grand Prix in 1925) and despite the fact that lap speeds have almost doubled since then, the course has remained substantially unchanged and only two important modifications have been made to it. Over the years, however, the road has gradually been widened and the surface is incomparably smoother. In essence the circuit consists of two public roads, the one leading from the town of Stavelot to Francorchamps and the other leading from Francorchamps through the village of Burnenville back to Stavelot. In fact the town of Spa is not situated on the circuit.

The fastest section of the course is the famed Masta straight on which the cars achieve speeds of over 180 mph and the slowest part is La Source hairpin, just before the pits, a really tight corner which is negotiated at little over 30 mph. The lap record at Spa stands to the credit of the late Jo Siffert who lapped at 162.087 mph with a 5-litre Porsche 917 in the 1971 Spa 1000 Km sports car race.

The first major modification to the circuit was made in 1938. Just beyond L'Eau Rouge bridge, only a hundred yards or so from the start/finish line the present very steep, long curve of irregular radius, known as the Raidillon and climbing towards Burnenville, replaced a hairpin corner (and incidentally vastly improved the spectators' view from the Grandstands opposite the pits). In 1950 the old Stavelot hairpin was by-passed by a very fast, very long curve. Together these two changes made a substantial contribution to the dramatic increase in lap speeds. A third, albeit temporary, major alteration to the circuit was adopted for the 1970 Belgian Grand Prix, the last of the series to be held at Spa. A chicane was installed at Malmedy corner, just over two miles from the start, so that the drivers were forced to brake very hard instead of taking this corner at around 150 mph.

The first important race to be held at Spa was the 1924 Belgian 24 Hours Touring Car Grand Prix which was won by a French Bignan 2-litre car at an average of 48.70 mph. Subsequent winners in this long-lived event were the French Chenard-Walcker and Peugeot (in 1925 and 1926 respectively), the Belgian Excelsior (1927) and, inevitably in pre-war long-distance racing, Alfa Romeo; cars from the Milan works won the race in 1928-30, 1932-3, 1936 and 1938. A Mercedes-Benz was the victor in 1931, a Bugatti in 1934 and there was no race in 1937. Later Belgian 24 Hours events were for sports as opposed to Touring cars proper and a pre-war British Aston Martin in the hands of St John Horsfall and Leslie Johnson won the race in 1948. The last two Belgian 24 Hours Sports Car races were in 1948 and 1953 and in both years a Ferrari was the winner. After an interval of eleven years the 24 Hours race was revived as a Touring Car event in 1964 and in recent years has been dominated by Ford Capris from Cologne and BMWs.

From 1954 onwards Spa was the scene of a number of sports races run over much shorter distances under the name 'Spa Grand Prix'. British cars, especially the *marque* Aston Martin, were well to the fore in these races. The 1954-7 races were limited to production cars, a term that was interpreted very loosely, and in 1955 Paul Frère won with an Aston Martin DB3S (a model of which only twenty production versions were built); Tony Brooks repeated this victory with a DB3S two years later. Another Aston Martin victory was scored in the Royal Automobile Club of Belgium's 3-hour Sports Car Grand Prix at the circuit in 1957; the winner was again Tony Brooks, but this time he was at the wheel of a DBR1 car (the model that won the Sports Car World Championship in 1959).

From 1963 onwards Spa was the scene of a 500-kilometre race for Grand Touring cars,. Prototypes were admitted in 1965 and from 1966 onwards the race length was increased to 1000 kilometres. Since 1967 the Spa 1000 Kilometres event has been a round in the Sports Car World Championship. The results of the races held since 1966 illustrate dramatically the rapid increase in lap speeds up until the demise of the 5-litre Porsche 917s and Ferrari 512s at the end of the 1971 season:—

1966:	M Parkes/L Scarfiotti (Ferrari P3 4-litre)	126.43 mph
1967:	J Ickx/R Thompson (Mirage/Ford 5.7-litre)	120.48 mph*
1968:	J Ickx/B Redman (Ford GT40 4.7-litre)	122.11 mph*
1969:	J Siffert/B Redman (Porsche 908 3-litre)	141.20 mph
1970:	J Siffert/B Redman (Porsche 917 5-litre)	149.42 mph
1971:	P Rodriguez/J Oliver (Porsche 917 5-litre)	154.77 mph
1972:	B Redman/A Merzario (Ferrari 312P 3-litre)	145.05 mph
1973:	D Bell/M Hailwood (Gulf-Mirage 3-litre)	151.89 mph
1974:	J Ickx/J-P Jarier (Matra-Simca 670C 3-litre)	148.20 mph
1975:	D Bell/H Pescarolo (Alfa Romeo Tipo 33TT12)	133.40 mph

* Wet track

Although Spa has become a mecca for high-speed sports car racing, this has primarily arisen from the reluctance of the modern school of Grand Prix drivers to compete there because of the circuit's inherent dangers; this reluctance culminated in a ban on the circuit by the Grand Prix Drivers' Association and the Spa was last used for Formula One racing in 1970, forty-five years after it had first served as a venue for the Belgian Grand Prix.

The first Belgian Grand Prix was one of the most boring *Grandes Epreuves* that has ever been staged. Only two teams were entered in this 503-mile race, Alfa Romeo and Delage. Because of engine trouble, the complete Delage team retired and Brilli-Perdi's Alfa Romeo was eliminated by a broken spring. The Belgian crowd, understandably seeking some relief from the boredom of watching two cars lapping this long circuit, demonstrated against the Alfa Romeo team's easy domination of the race. By way of retaliation Vittorio Jano called the Alfa drivers, Antonio Ascari and Giuseppe Campari, into the pits; while the cars were cleaned and polished during a five-minute stop, the drivers sat down at a table to partake of an impromptu picnic!

Five years elapsed before Spa was the scene of another Grand Prix and in 1930 the 373-mile race at the Ardennes circuit was given the title of 'European Grand Prix'; Bugatti's Type 35C 2.3-litre cars driven by Chiron, Bouriat and Divo took the first three places in this race which was run nominally at least to a fuel consumption formula. By 1931 the length of Grands Prix had been extended to ten hours and this year's race produced a good fight between the improved Bugatti Type 51 cars and the Alfa Romeo

Monzas; Williams and Conelli won the race for Molsheim from the Alfas of Nuvolari/Borzacchini and Minoia/Minozzi. The Belgian Grand Prix was still not regarded as a regular annual event and two years elapsed before the next single-seater race at Spa. In 1933 the winner was Tazio Nuvolari, driving for the first time that season as a private entrant with a Maserati, and he averaged 89.23 mph, leading home the Bugatti Type 51s of Varzi and Dreyfus.

Bugatti won the race in 1934, the first year of the new 750 Kilogramme Formula (the car was the Type 59 and René Dreyfus was at the wheel), but the remaining pre-war races were dominated by the Mercedes-Benz and Auto Union teams. Caracciola won for Stuttgart in 1935 at 97.87 mph, there was no race in 1936 and the following year it was Zwickau's turn. The Auto Unions of Rudi Hasse and Hans Stuck led home Lang's Mercedes. The year 1938 was yet another in which there was no Belgian Grand Prix and the 1939 race highlighted only too vividly and tragically the dangers of this high-speed circuit. By 1937 lap speeds were topping 100 mph (the winner averaged 104.07 mph) and the succession of fast curves and the great speed variations between the 180 mph-plus Masta straight and the 30 mph hairpin bends tested a driver's ability to the limit, with very little margin for recovery if he made an error.

The 1939 race was run in appalling conditions, with persistent heavy rain that swept across the circuit and severely limited visibility. At the start Giuseppe Farina (Alfa Romeo) screamed into the lead, but the Italian's advantage was short-lived and the strong German contingent had soon forged past the red Alfa Romeo; one by one, Müller (Auto Union), Lang (Mercedes), Carracciola (Mercedes), Dick Seaman (Mercedes) and Nuvolari (Auto Union) splashed past in a great sea of spray. The sheer impossibility of the conditions came home to any doubter on lap 9 when Rudolf Caracciola, the *Regenmesiter* who so often in the past had driven brilliantly on wet circuits, went off the track at La Source hairpin and was out of the race.

At this time the hero of British motor racing enthusiasts was Dick Seaman, one of the finest British drivers of all time who had proved his worth beyond doubt by his choice as a Mercedes-Benz works driver and by his victory with a Mercedes in the 1938 German Grand Prix. Seaman was much criticised for joining the Mercedes team when Nazi power was reaching its zenith and although the technical and racing achievements of the German teams in the 'thirties have always been greatly admired, Seaman's image has always been slightly tarnished by his Teutonic associations.

Dick's attitude was that his interest was motor racing and not politics, a view that was either naïve or self-deceptive.

In 1939 Seaman was maturing as an outstanding driver by any reckoning and he was in magnificent form at Spa. The Englishman moved up into second place and then passed Müller to take the lead. On lap 22 of this 35-lap race disaster struck. It seems that he took the left-hand bend before La Source hairpin too fast, was on the wrong line for the hairpin itself, went off the road and collided with a tree. Poor Seaman was rendered unconscious and perished in the fire that started from the ruptured fuel tank. Hermann Lang won the race from Hasse and von Brauchitsch (Mercedes). What can be said of Seaman's death? It was a terrible blow to British motor racing enthusiasts and to the Mercedes team (his was the first death at the wheel of a Stuttgart car since the team had re-entered racing in 1934), but there was the consolation, albeit a small one, that Seaman had died in pursuit of the sport which he loved more than anything else.

The Belgian Grand Prix was revived in 1947 by when the Grand Prix Formula had changed and the capacity of supercharged cars was limited to 1500 cc. During these early post-war years racing was dominated by the works Alfa Romeo 158s, cars that were basically unchanged since 1939, and the serious opposition was limited to the unblown 4500 cc French Lago-Talbots and the rather disorganised and inefficient private Maserati entrants. The 1947 race produced the expected result and the 158s of Jean-Pierre Wimille, Achille Varzi and Count Felice Trossi took the first three places. In 1948 there was no Belgian Grand Prix and by the following year the Alfa Romeo team had withdrawn from racing, albeit for the one season only. It had been expected that 1949 Grands Prix would be dominated by Enzo Ferrari's team of 1500 cc V-12 cars that had made their debut at Turin in September 1948. The Belgian race marked the first appearance of the works Formula One Ferraris in 1949 and two cars were entered for Alberto Ascari and Luigi Villoresi. Certainly the Ferraris looked and sounded formidable and they dominated the early laps of the race. But the heavy tyre and fuel consumption of the wearers of the 'prancing horse' proved their downfall and while the Ferraris loitered in the pits, Louis Rosier and his big, blue, bulky unblown Lago-Talbot forged into a lead that he never lost. Rosier averaged 96.95 mph and the first of the Ferraris, Villoresi at the wheel, trailed across the line fifty seconds in arrears.

Alfa Romeo returned to racing in 1950 with a strong team that consisted of Giuseppe Farina, Juan Fangio and Luigi Fagioli. At Spa two Ferraris were entered, one supercharged car and one of the prototype unsupercharged cars; neither proved a match for the Alfa Romeo opposition. Perhaps the most remarkable aspect of this race was the fact that Raymond Sommer at the wheel of a Lago-Talbot built up a lead of 26 seconds on lap 15 while all three Alfas were in the pits refuelling, but it was a short-lived lead and five laps later the French car was out of the race with a broken engine. Farina's Alfa later succumbed to gearbox problems which caused it to drop well down the field, and at the chequered flag the 158s of Fangio and Fagioli crossed the line ahead of Louis Rosier's Lago-Talbot.

By the early part of the 1951 season the battle for supremacy in Grand Prix racing was reaching an exciting climax. The battle was in fact waged between only two serious contenders, both Italian, and it was between the old, established competitor Alfa Romeo and the new, exciting *marque* from Maranello; it was also a conflict of design philosophies, the highly stressed, voraciously thirsty, supercharged 159s designed by Giaocchino Colombo against the much more lightly stressed, much more economical V-12 Ferraris which were the work of Aurelio Lampredi. It was also a tremendous contest between personalities. In pre-war days Enzo Ferrari had of course entered the works Alfa Romeos under the banner of Scuderia Ferrari. Giaocchino Colombo had designed the 158 in pre-war days and joined Ferrari after the cease of hostilities. Originally Lampredi had been Colombo's assistant at Ferrari, but Lampredi's persistence in advocating unblown engines for Grand Prix racing had won Ferrari's support and precipitated the downfall of Colombo who returned to Alfa Romeo to refine his original design.

At Spa in 1951 there were only thirteen entries, composed of three different makes. Alfa Romeo 159s were driven by Fangio, Farina and Sanesi and 4.5-litre Ferraris by Ascari, Villoresi and Taruffi; the remainder of the entry consisted of unblown French Lago-Talbot cars. Fangio drove the latest version of the 159 Alfa with a de Dion rear axle and with cockpit fuel tanks each side of the driver extending forward to the bulkhead, a tank on top of the scuttle and a further tank under the exhaust manifold. Farina's car had similar tanks apart from that on the scuttle. The race distance was 315 miles and it was marginal whether or not the Alfas could get through the race with only one refuelling stop (the Alfa fuel, which was 98% methanol, was consumed at the rate of 1.6 mpg). At this stage in their career the Ferraris were still slower than the Alfas, but they would definitely need only one fuel stop. The results of the race could, therefore, be determined purely on the time spent in the pits.

Villoresi's Ferrari roared into the lead at the start, and by the end of the first lap the order was Villoresi – Farina – Ascari – Fangio – Taruffi. Farina went into the lead on the third lap, Ascari passed Villoresi and then Fangio passed them both to hold second place behind his team-mate. In the early laps Farina had progressively improved on the lap record but, after a slow start, Fangio was motoring faster and faster and on lap 9 he finally reduced the record to 4 min 22.1 sec (120.51 mph). While Farina and Fangio roared away from the opposition the Ferraris were soon in trouble. On lap 10 Villoresi stopped at the pits for attention to a loose oil pipe and on the next lap Taruffi was out of the race with a broken back axle.

One by one the Alfas were called into the pits for their first refuelling stop. Sanesi came in on lap 12 and was stationary for 1 min 52 sec (but retired on his first lap after leaving the pits with overheating problems); Farina stopped on lap 15 and was away with fuel and new rear tyres in only 57 seconds; now it was Fangio's turn and he stopped on lap 17. Despite frantic hammering, pulling and shoving by the mechanics, the left-hand rear wheel of Fangio's 159 proved immovable. The cause of the trouble was that a spoke head had forced its way behind the hub-splines. After five minutes of frantic but vain effort, team-manager Guidotti directed the mechanics to remove the complete wheel, hub and brake-drum from the half-shaft. Still the hub could not be levered off and eventually the old tyre was removed from the rim, a new tyre fitted and blown up.

To quote *Autocourse,* 'During this seemingly interminable pit stop Fangio gave a unique display of sportsmanship. He stood silently watching the proceedings without displaying any emotions whatsoever. He knew that the possibility of repeating his victory of last year had vanished. He saw precious points in the Championship of the World disappearing as Farina passed four times, yet he was outwardly unperturbed.' After almost a quarter of an hour Fangio rejoined the race in tenth and last place and at the end of the 36 laps was classified ninth and last, four laps behind the winner. Farina was unnassailable in the lead and despite a second pit stop lasting 39 seconds, he won the race from Ascari's Ferrari by the comfortable margin of 2 min 50 sec. Ferrari came close to defeating Alfa Romeo a few weeks later in the French Grand Prix at Reims, but Maranello did not execute the *coup de grâce* until the British Grand Prix where Gonzalez beat Fangio into second place and another Ferrari driven by Villoresi finished third.

Following Alfa Romeo's withdrawal from racing at the end of 1951, all Championship Grands Prix in 1952-3 were held to Formula Two 2000 cc unsupercharged rules pending the introduction of a new Formula for 1954. In both years the winner was Alberto Ascari with a Ferrari, but in 1953 Fangio and Gonzalez (Maseratis) put up a strong fight and led the Ferraris until engine trouble intervened. The first two years of the 2500 cc Grand Prix Formula of 1954 onwards proved a Mercedes-Benz benefit, but the silver straight-eights from Stuttgart did not appear until the French Grand Prix in July 1954 and that year's Belgian Grand Prix was won by a Maserati driven by Juan Fangio. The great Argentinian won the Belgian race for Mercedes the following year and was leading with a Lancia-Ferrari in 1956 when transmission trouble forced his retirement; the 1956 race was won by Fangio's Ferrari team-mate, young Peter Collins, who enjoyed a brilliantly successful year which also included a victory in the French race.

There was no Belgian Grand Prix in 1957 and the Grand Prix circus next appeared at Spa-Francorchamps in 1958. There had been many changes in racing during the preceding two years; both Fangio and Maserati had withdrawn from racing (the Argentinian made a final appearance with the 'piccolo' lightweight Maserati at Reims a few weeks later) and the main battle for supremacy centred round Tony Vandervell's green Vanwalls and the Ferrari Dino V-6 cars. At this point in the 1958 season the Vanwalls were at the peak of their form and the Ferrari team was still struggling to find more speed. Stirling Moss retired his Vanwall on the first lap when he missed a gear-change and over-revved and his team-mates Tony Brooks and Stuart Lewis-Evans finished first and third, sandwiching Hawthorn's Ferrari Dino. Interestingly enough, even if Fangio was missing at this race, the 'piccolo' Maserati was present, but its appearance was limited to a few practice laps with American Masten Gregory at the wheel.

Two more years elapsed before the Belgian Grand Prix was again held and the 1960 race was an especially unhappy event. By this time racing had undergone yet another transformation and was now dominated by the rear-engined Cooper and Lotus-Climax cars, while the traditional front-engined Ferraris were poor also-rans. In practice there were two bad crashes; Stirling Moss suffered broken ribs, a fractured nose and leg injuries in a 100 mph crash caused by his Lotus shedding its left-hand rear wheel, and amateur driver Michael Taylor was critically injured when the steering on his Lotus broke at speed, and his car went out of control. In the race works Lotus driver Alan Stacey was hit in the face by a bird, lost control of his car, hit a bank and overturned; the Lotus caught fire and Stacey perished in the inferno. And poor Chris Bristow, an up-and-coming young driver, died when he lost control of his Yeoman Credit-entered Cooper at Burnenville in a fierce duel with Mairesse's Ferrari (the Englishman had been lured into driving beyond his ability). All in all, it was one of the unhappiest Grands Prix of recent years and Jack Brabham (Cooper) scored a victory from which he can have derived very little pleasure.

The 2500 cc Grand Prix Formula came to an end in 1960 and in 1961 the 1500 cc Ferrari V-6 cars reigned supreme. At Spa that year the Maranello entries of Phil Hill, Wolfgang von Trips, Richie Ginther and Olivier Gendebien took the first four places. For the next four years the Belgian Grand Prix was a Jim Clark benefit. Because of engine trouble, Clark was able to get in very little practice at Spa in 1962, but it was a race in which he displayed the mastery for which he was to become renowned. He took the lead on lap 9 from team-mate Trevor Taylor and maintained his advantage for the remaining 23 laps to win by a margin of 44 seconds from Graham Hill (BRM). This was another Belgian Grand Prix marred by an unpleasant accident. For lap after lap Trevor Taylor had been clinging on to second place, fighting off the efforts of local driver Willy Mairesse to force his way by with his Ferrari. On lap 18 Mairesse was hot on Taylor's exhausts when the Lotus suddenly jumped out of gear, slewed sideways and shot off the road into a telegraph pole; Mairesse had no opportunity to take evasive action, the Ferrari struck the tail of the Lotus and overturned. Taylor scrambled from the wreckage of the Lotus, while Mairesse crawled from underneath the burning Ferrari. Neither driver was hurt, but, hardly surprisingly, both were suffering from shock.

Clark completely dominated the 1963 Belgian Grand Prix, leading from start to finish. The last seven laps of the race were run in a torrential thunderstorm, the drivers were almost blinded by the beating rain and heavy mist blanketing the circuit reduced visibility to a few yards. In this miserable and processional race Clark averaged 114.10 mph with an unsupercharged 1500 cc car, almost exactly the same speed as Farina's in the 1951 race with a blown 1500 cc car (114.32 mph), but over 17 mph slower than his own average in the dry in 1962.

Although Clark achieved a Spa hat-trick in 1964, his third victory was fortuitous. On lap 28 of this 32-lap race the order was Gurney (Brabham), Hill (BRM), Clark (Lotus), McLaren (Cooper) and Brabham (Brabham). At the end of this lap Jim Clark made a brief pit stop to take on extra water and lost third place to McLaren. Dan Gurney had driven magnificently and was heading for what would have been the *marque* Brabham's first-ever Championship race victory. However, on the next lap the Brabham's engine began to cut out because of fuel surge, Graham Hill came past in the lead and when Gurney arrived in second place, he headed straight into the pits to take on extra fuel. Almost incredibly there was none available in the Brabham pit, but Dan was assured that he had sufficient to cover the remaining two laps to the finish and he was sent back into the race.

Gurney ran out of fuel completely just before Stavelot on lap 32; Hill had stopped at Stavelot, not because he was out of fuel, but because of a fault in the fuel feed system; and McLaren also had insufficient fuel to complete the course, but he succeeded in coasting the last few hundred yards. As McLaren crawled along towards La Source hairpin at little more than walking pace, Clark swept by to take the chequered flag, not realising that he had won the race. To add further confusion to an already confused situation the Lotus ran out of fuel at Stavelot on its slowing-down lap. Errors in calculating the amount of fuel required to complete a race are rare indeed, but it was a situation that was to repeat itself at Spa in 1968. Poor Gurney been especially unlucky, for he would have still won had the Brabham pit taken the obvious precaution of having a quantity of fuel ready just in case. The Californian's consolation came with a fine win shortly afterwards in the French Grand Prix at Rouen.

In 1965, the last year of the 1500 cc Formula, the race was again run on a rain-soaked course, but Jim Clark was master of the conditions and brought his Lotus, powered by the new 32-valve Coventry-Climax engine, across the line at an average of 117.16 mph. Jackie Stewart (BRM) took second place, a magnificent performance in his first season of Formula One racing and one which he repeated at Clermont-Ferrand (where he was again second behind Clark and thoroughly trounced BRM team-mate Graham Hill).

At the 1966 Belgian Grand Prix there occured a series of accidents that were destined to result in the death of Spa as a venue for Grand Prix racing. When the cars were assembled on the dummy grid shortly before the start of the race, dark, storm-threatening clouds lowered overhead but the track was dry. At this moment rain was falling at Stavelot, but the drivers were unaware of this as they accelerated away at the fall of the flag. By the time the drivers reached Malmedy, so had the rain and the track was lethally slippery. Surtees (Ferrari) was leading from Stewart (BRM 2-litre) and Rindt (Cooper-Maserati); the leaders safely negotiated Malmedy, but Jo Bonnier spun his red Cooper-Maserati, Mike Spence (Lotus-BRM) collided with the Surbiton car, and both shot off the track. Hulme (Brabham-Climax) and Jo Siffert (Cooper-Maserati) collided and both were out of the race. Along the Matra straight, Surtees' Ferrari, running on Dunlop wet-weather tyres, retained its lead, but Stewart's BRM spun off just before the start of the straight and Rindt spun his Cooper on the straight, gyrating for a hundred yards before regaining control and carrying on at reduced speed. Graham Hill spun his BRM off and Bob Bondurant rolled his private BRM on the grass. Neither of these drivers was hurt and Hill could have rejoined the race, but both rushed to aid Stewart whose car had overturned in a gulley, trapping the driver; the Scot lay with cracked ribs and broken collar-bone, and fuel from the ruptured tank was leaking through his overalls and searing his skin until Hill succeeded in removing the BRM's steering wheel so that Stewart could be extricated. Clark had retired his Lotus with engine trouble shortly after the start of that first lap and there were now only seven runners. Rindt came through to take the lead in a blinding cloud of spray, but as conditions improved in the later stages of the race, Surtees pushed Ferrari in front again and won by a margin of forty seconds.

Largely as a result of their experiences in the 1966 race most of the Grand Prix drivers, and Stewart in particular, formed an ever-increasing dislike of Spa. They disliked its unpredictable weather; one minute the circuit would be bathed in warm sunshine, the next it would be drenched by a cloudburst. They hated even more the fact that one part of the circuit could be bone-dry, while a couple of miles away the track could be treacherously wet. Spa's days as a Grand Prix circuit were numbered.

Despite his antipathy towards Spa, Jackie Stewart took the lead with his H-16 BRM in the 1967 race but, because of gearbox problems that meant he had to steer with one hand and hold the car in gear with the other, he was passed by Dan Gurney (Eagle) who scored the Anglo-American *marque*'s sole Championship race victory. In 1968 the winner was Bruce McLaren with one of the Ford-powered cars bearing his own name, but it was something of a hollow victory. History had repeated itself, for race-leader Jackie Stewart at the wheel of the new Matra-Ford ran out of fuel on the penultimate lap and lost a certain victory; Matra International boss Ken Tyrrell had calculated the fuel consumption at 7 mpg, but the Matra consumed fuel at Spa at the rate of 6.6 mpg. There was yet another unpleasant accident in this race when Brian Redman's Cooper-BRM went off the road following a suspension breakage, crashed through a safety barrier and hit a line of parked cars.

The car caught fire and Redman was lucky to escape with a broken arm and burned hands.

Because of opposition from the Grand Prix Drivers' Association, there was no Belgian Grand Prix in 1969. With some reluctance the drivers agreed to race at Spa in 1970, but they insisted that it should be lined throughout with Armco barriers, and a chicane was installed at Malmedy. The result provided an unexpected victory for Pedro Rodriguez and BRM – Pedro's second Championship race win (the first was with a Cooper-Maserati in the 1967 South African race) and BRM's first since Monaco in 1966. Chris Amon took second place with a works March.

The Belgian Grand Prix was not held at Spa again and in 1972, the next occasion on which the race was run, it was staged at the dull, uninteresting, flat, characterless Nivelles circuit, some twenty-five miles to the south of Brussels. Despite the dislike of most drivers for Spa, the finest and fastest road circuit, a few, notably Jacky Ickx, Pedro Rodriguez and Jo Siffert, revelled in its fast, difficult curves, its slow hairpin, its bumpy straight, its variety and its challenge. For two seasons, 1970-1, they were able to extract the utmost satisfaction from its difficulties and give the crowd a most exciting spectacle with the 5-litre Ferrari and Porsche competition sports cars; their battles are described in the next chapter.

16

The Giants of Sports Car Racing:

Pedro Rodriguez and Jo Siffert

In the history of sports car racing there has been a small number of drivers whose consistent and persistent successes have placed them well above their rivals: Phil Hill, winner at Le Mans on three occasions between 1958 and 1962 with Ferrari cars and still winning in 1966 at the Nürburgring and at Brands Hatch in 1967 at the wheel of Chaparral cars; Olivier Gendebien, who won at Le Mans for Ferrari on four occasions; Brian Redman, victor of four Spa 1000 Kilometres races. All these drivers possessed outstanding skill at the wheel coupled with great endurance and concentration over long periods, great consistency and a cool, calm, unflappable approach to racing.

Pedro Rodriguez and Jo Siffert have achieved equal fame in sports car racing, but both were fiery, thrusting, determined drivers liable to react in the heat of the moment, respond to an immediate challenge and throw caution and restrain to the winds in their pursuit of success – characteristics better suited to the cut and thrust of Grand Prix racing (in which they also achieved considerable success) than to the regularity and consistency of Sports Car racing.

For much of their careers Pedro and Jo drove for opposing teams, but in 1970 both were members of the Gulf-Porsche team which dominated that year's Sports Car Championship and each played a leading role in the presentation of one of the most exciting eras of Sports Car racing ever seen; both remained with Gulf-Porsche in 1971 and that year both were members of the BRM team which seemed to be going through a revival in its fortunes. And in that sad year both lost their lives in minor, unimportant races.

The son of a wealthy contractor, Pedro Rodriguez was born in Mexico

City on 18th January 1940. At the age of twelve he started racing with a 125 cc Adler motor cycle and by the time he was fifteen he had graduated to a Jaguar XK 120 sports car, the racing of which he shared with his younger brother Ricardo. In 1957 Pedro was given a drive with a Ferrari at Riverside Raceway in California by the North American Racing Team and the following year he made his European debut at Le Mans. He continued to drive Ferrari sports cars during the next three years; together with brother Ricardo he was third at Sebring and second at the Nürburgring in 1961 and won the Paris 1000 Kilometres race at Montlhéry in both 1961 and 1962. Although Pedro had a brilliant – and remarkably youthful – start to his racing career, at this time younger brother Ricardo was regarded as having the greater potential and was given a regular drive in the works Ferrari Grand Prix team in 1962. Ferrari did not contest the newly inaugurated, non-Championship Mexican race at the end of the 1962 season and here Ricardo was offered a drive in a Lotus-Climax by Rob Walker. The circuit was brand new and untried; Ricardo was only too keen to start practice on his home ground and rushed out on to the track at the earliest opportunity. Shortly after starting to practice, he lost control, hit the railings at the top of the banking and suffered injuries to which he succumbed shortly afterwards.

Pedro was completely distraught at his brother's death and his initial reaction was to give up racing. On reflection he realised that he loved racing too deeply to retire and returned to the circuits again in 1963, usually still at the wheel of North American Racing Team Ferraris. He won the 3-hour Daytona Continental race at the wheel of a Grand Touring Ferrari 250 GTO belonging to Mamie Spears Reynolds (a tobacco heiress), finished third at Sebring co-driving a NART-entered 'Testa Rossa' Ferrari with Graham Hill and won the Canadian Sports Car Grand Prix with a Ferrari 250 P belonging to NART; he also drove this car to a couple of second places during the Nassau Speed Week.

In 1964 Pedro's racing career followed a very similar pattern; he shared the winning 250 GTO Ferrari at Daytona with Phil Hill and with a 250 LM car, again entered by NART, won the inaugural race on the Mont Tremblant circuit in Canada. Second places were gained in the Bridgehampton Double 500 race on Long Island (driving a 250 P) and in the Paris 1000 Kilometres race (in which he co-drove a GTO with Jo Schlesser). Pedro's greatest encouragement in an otherwise rather bleak season was the drive in a works Ferrari, albeit an obsolescent V-6 model, in the Mexican Grand

Prix. Pedro made the most of the opportunity and drove a steady race to take sixth place and win his first ever World Championship point.

The young Mexican's best performance during 1965 was a win with Jean Guichet at the wheel of a 365 P2 Ferrari entered by NART in the Reims 12 Hours race and a third place in the Canadian Sports Car Grand Prix. Ferrari again offered him a drive in a works Grand Prix car at the end of the 1965 season, but this year the offer embraced two races and the car was the latest flat-12 model, albeit a model that was no real match for the British V-8 opposition. Pedro finished fifth in the United States Grand Prix at Watkins Glen and took seventh place at Mexico City. The following year poor Rodriguez was completely out of luck and his best performances were a fourth at Daytona co-driving a 365 P2 Ferrari with Mario Andretti and a third place with a Ferrari Dino (and Richie Ginther as co-driver) at the Nürburgring. At Le Mans Rodriguez and Ginther drove a works 4-litre Ferrari Prototype; they were the fastest Ferrari drivers in practice, but retired during the eleventh hour of the race with gearbox trouble.

Pedro's first real break in several years of racing came when Cooper team manager Roy Salvadori offered him a drive with a Cooper-Maserati in the 1967 South African Grand Prix. Pedro won the race, mainly because all the faster opposition retired, and he was offered a place in the works team alongside Jochen Rindt for the remainder of the season. As the year progressed, it became only too obvious just how uncompetitive the Cooper-Maserati was, but by dint of steady, restrained driving Pedro succeeded in gaining fifth places in the Monaco and British Grands Prix and sixth in the French race. He continued to race sports cars and also handled a Protos-Cosworth Formula Two car for Ron Harris.

For 1968 Pedro was offered a place in the works BRM team which he accepted with alacrity. BRM had just abandoned the hopelessly unreliable and over-complex H-16 model in favour of their new V-12 design. The V-12 was not really competitive and the year's Grand Prix racing was largely dominated by the Ford-engined cars of Lotus, Matra and McLaren. Nevertheless Pedro achieved as much, if not more, than could be reasonably expected of him and turned in a whole series of good placings: second in the Race of Champions and Belgian Grand Prix, third in the Dutch and Canadian Grands Prix, fourth in the Mexican and sixth in the German.

Pedro's outings in long-distance Sports Car races were few and far between, but he was given a drive in a John Wyer Ford GT40 at Le Mans in place of Jacky Ickx who had broken his leg in a practice crash with his Ferrari at the Canadian Grand Prix. Pedro and co-driver Lucien Bianchi turned in a magnificent performance at the Sarthe circuit and won the 24 Hours race at an average of 115.29 mph. The following year Rodriguez drove works Ferrari 312P Prototypes and for the first time he was seen battling it out regularly in long-distance racing with Porsche driver Jo Siffert.

Josef Siffert, known in later years as 'Jo' or 'Seppi', was born at Fribourg in Switzerland on 7th July 1936. Siffert came from a much more modest background than Pedro Rodriguez (his father was a motor dealer) and in his racing career he lacked any financial support from his family. Jo started in 1958 by racing motor cycles and his first machine was a 125 cc Gilera. Three years later Siffert moved on to four-wheel racing and during 1960 he competed in Formula Junior racing with both Lotus 18 rear-engined and Stanguellini front-engined cars. He infinitely preferred the Lotus and for the following season he acquired a new Lotus 20; during 1961 he scored seven wins, took a large number of good places and ended the season as joint European Junior Champion with Tony Maggs.

For 1962 Siffert received sponsorship from the wealthy Swiss Scuderia Filipinetti and he raced both a Formula Junior Lotus 22 and a Formula One Lotus; the Formula One car was a 1961-model 21 with a 4-cylinder Climax engine and Colotti 5-speed gearbox. Later in the year the Filipinetti team bought a new Lotus 24 for him to race with a V-8 BRM engine, a very competitive piece of machinery which, unfortunately, proved far less reliable than anticipated. During 1963 'Seppi' continued to race the Lotus-BRM with rather greater success; he was second at Imola and won the Syracuse Grand Prix. Siffert was usually especially successful in Sicilian races and once, when asked why, replied that the Sicilians never checked the engine size of the winning car and he was able to get away with using a 2-litre engine!

At the end of the season Siffert broke away from Scuderia Filipinetti and in 1964 raced a new Brabham chassis with BRM engine as an independent. The chances of an independent driver achieving much success against the might of the works teams is slim indeed, but Siffert finished fourth in the German Grand Prix and won the Mediterranean Grand Prix, a non-Championship race at Enna in Sicily. As the opposition at Enna included World Champion Jim Clark who was outpaced by the Swiss privateer, some people began to *believe* that 'Seppi' was using an oversize engine. Rob Walker took over Siffert's entries for the last two Championship races of the season and at Watkins Glen Jo finished a brilliant third behind Graham Hill (BRM) and John Surtees (Ferrari).

During 1965 Rob Walker, one of the greatest and most successful of all private entrants, ran a two-car team for Joakim Bonnier and Jo Siffert, the latter still with his familiar Brabham-BRM. Siffert took sixth places in the Monaco and French Grands Prix, was fourth at Mexico City and repeated his victory at Enna where the opposition again included Jim Clark.

As his experience increased, so Jo was improving in skill and ability; at this stage in his career, he seemed a sound, reliable driver but without apparent Champion potential. Rob Walker continued to support Siffert in 1966, the first year of the new 3000 cc Grand Prix Formula, and ordered a new Cooper-Maserati for the Swiss to drive. On paper the Cooper had seemed an excellent proposition and a potential race-winner, but in practice the handling was unsatisfactory and the V-12 Maserati engines were both down on power and unreliable. At the beginning of the year he drove the old Brabham-BRM into second place in the South African Grand Prix (a non-Championship race in that one year only), but the best that he could manage with the Cooper was a fourth place in the United States Grand Prix. During 1967 Walker and Siffert struggled on with the now uncompetitive Cooper, but no success was gained.

It was in 1966 that Siffert's career turned towards the category of racing in which he was to achieve his greatest successes. He made a few appearances at the wheel of works Porsche 906 Sports Cars and in 1967 finished second co-driving with Hans Herrmann at Spa and third with Bruce McLaren in the BOAC '500' race at Brands Hatch.

For the 1968 season Rob Walker bought an ex-works Lotus 49, but on the car's outing in unofficial practice at Brands Hatch Jo lost control and hit the bank; the car was returned to Walker's workshop at Dorking for repairs, and was destroyed overnight by fire. Walker replaced the burned-out Lotus with another ex-works car. During the early part of the season Siffert and the dark blue and white Lotus were completely out of luck; then, in the British Grand Prix at Brands Hatch, the team's fortunes changed. Jo was in third place behind the works Lotus 49s of Graham Hill and Jack Oliver and when these red, white and gold cars retired with transmission problems, he assumed a lead that he retained for the remainder of this 212-mile race and he scored his first Championship race victory ahead of the Ferraris of Chris Amon and Jacky Ickx. During the remainder of the season his only finishes were a fifth at Watkins Glen and a sixth at Mexico City.

During 1968 Siffert had emerged as one of the most successful drivers in the Porsche team and his string of successes included second place with Herrmann at Daytona (and a turn at the wheel of the winning car) and wins with Hermann at Sebring, with Elford at the Nürburgring and a solo drive to victory in the 500-kilometre Austrian Grand Prix at Zeltweg.

While Siffert persevered with Walker's Lotus 49 in 1969 Grands Prix, managing only a fourth in the South African race and a third place at Monaco, Pedro Rodriguez had been dropped by the works BRM team and signed up to drive a private BRM for the Reg Parnell Racing Team managed by Tim Parnell. By July the works BRM team was in a state of complete disarray having achieved no success whatsoever during the early part of the season. The team scratched from the French Grand Prix, sacked long-serving chief engineer and team manager Tony Rudd and appointed Tim Parnell as team manager in his place. Pedro Rodriguez was now without a Formula One drive and a one-off drive for Ferrari at the British Grand Prix ended in retirement with engine failure. Pedro next appeared in Formula One at the Italian Grand Prix where he drove the sole Ferrari into sixth place. Ferrari had been hoping to have his new flat-12 car ready by the latter part of the season, but it was suffering from development problems. Rather than race the now outdated and uncompetitive V-12 in the remaining three events on the Eastern side of the Atlantic, he loaned one of these cars to the North American Racing Team. NART engaged Rodriguez to drive the V-12 and the Mexican finished fifth in the United States race and seventh at Mexico City.

In Sports Car racing Jo Siffert was still the leading member of the works Porsche team, but Zuffenhausen had failed at both Daytona (where the winner was a private Lola) and Sebring (where a John Wyer Ford had won) and 'Seppi's' first sports car victory of the season was in the BOAC '500' race at Brands Hatch where his co-driver was Brian Redman.

Ferrari had re-entered Sports Car racing in 1969 after a year's absence with the new 312P Prototype powered by the team's Grand Prix engine. The new Ferrari appeared first at Sebring where it was driven into second place by Chris Amon and Mario Andretti despite overheating problems. At Brands Hatch Amon's co-driver was Pedro Rodriguez, but the Ferrari was delayed by a puncture and then lost much of its speed as the result of a stretched throttle cable. Ferrari had no hopes of victory in this race and the Maranello drivers did well to struggle across the line in fourth position.

Next on the calendar was the Monza 1000 Kilometres race where Ferrari made a determined effort by entering two of the 312Ps for Andretti/Amon and Rodriguez/Schetty. From Porsche a full team of four 908 Long-tail coupés was driven by Siffert/Redman, Herrmann/Ahrens, Elford/Attwood and Schütz/Mitter. At the start of the race the two open, very compact Ferraris screamed into the lead ahead of Siffert's sleek white coupé. By the end of that first lap Siffert had forged by Andretti into second place behind Rodriguez and already it was clear that Ferrari had made the major tactical error of committing both 312Ps to the battle for the lead instead of holding one car back at a more restrained pace.

For lap after lap, corner after corner, Jo battled furiously with Pedro's red Ferrari, and the second Ferrari with Mario Andretti at the wheel dogged Siffert's wheel-tracks. Siffert passed the Ferrari briefly on lap 12, Rodriguez was soon in front again, but on that lap Andretti suddenly slowed off and crawled back to the pits for a punctured tyre to be changed; the second Ferrari rejoined the race in sixth place. Just after quarter race-distance race-leader Rodriguez came into the pits to refuel and hand over to team-mate Peter Schetty; Schetty was soon in the race, lapping faster than Siffert's co-driver Brian Redman and steadily drawing away from the Porsche; Andretti now repassed Elford's Porsche to regain third place.

The impression that the Ferraris were going to trounce the German opposition was not sustained for long. On lap 37 Schetty was forced to stop at the pits for a wheel-change and when he tried to restart the car, the engine refused to fire. By the time Schetty was back in the race, he had lost over a lap and Redman led from Chris Amon who had relieved Andretti at the wheel of the second Ferrari. Just before he was due to stop at the pits to refuel, Amon swept past Redman to regain the lead for Maranello. When Chris rejoined the race after the refuelling stop, he was in fourth place behind Redman, Attwood (both with 908s) and team-mate Schetty and his Ferrari completed less than a lap before the engine blew up.

Schetty had steadily been catching up with the two leading 908s. He moved up into second place when Attwood stopped for attention to his Porsche's fan driving-belt and was closing rapidly on Redman's leading 908 when the Ferrari suffered yet another puncture. All the Ferrari drivers' efforts had been completely wasted, but when Rodriguez, relieving Schetty, rejoined the race, he was in a very determined mood and anxious to catch the leading Porsche 908s if humanly possible. Trying just a little too hard, 'Mexican Pete' lost control of the Ferrari Prototype at the Parabolica curve while avoiding a slower car, spun wildly and shattered the glass-fibre nose and tail of the 312P against the guard-rail.

Pedro roared back into the Ferrari pit without offering any explanation, fretted and fumed while a new wheel was fitted and rushed back into the race again. He was closing up on the second-place 908 and travelling at close to 170 mph when, as a direct result of the earlier accident, the tail-section of the Ferrari disintegrated. Completely out of control, the Ferrari spun wildly down the track, hit the guard-rail backwards smashing its rear suspension and hurtled on for four hundred yards before coming to rest. Pedro jumped out of the wreckage, a little shaken but otherwise unhurt. For Pedro this was what motor racing was all about!

Jo Siffert and Brian Redman won this race for Porsche at 128.39 mph and, just under a fortnight later, Porsche scored another victory in the Targa Florio in Sicily. Ferrari was not entered in this race and Siffert was missing from the Porsche team because the Sicilian event clashed with the Spanish Grand Prix. Pedro and Jo next met up in Sports Car Racing at the Spa 1000 Kilometres event where Porsche were again out in force and Ferrari was content with entering a single car for Rodriguez and David Piper (Chris Amon was out of the race because of illness). Jo Siffert was in magnificent form at this Belgian race and although he and Pedro battled furiously for the lead in the opening laps, the Ferrari lost time in the pits for attention to its bodywork after a minor collision – the offending Porsche 907 that had got in Pedro's way was pushed off the road and wrecked itself against an advertisement hoarding – and David Piper was unable to maintain the pace set by his team-mate. The Ferrari finished second, three and a half minutes in arrears.

At the Nürburgring still only one Ferrari, driven by Amon and Rodriguez, faced a veritable horde of Porsche 908 *Spyders.* Again Siffert dominated the race, setting a new Sports Car record on the first lap and he and co-driver Redman pulled further and further away from the rest of the field to win by a comfortable margin of four minutes. It was an unhappy race for the Ferrari team, and although Amon eventually set the fastest lap of the race, the 312P expired out on the circuit with electrical trouble. Both teams were out of luck at Le Mans where the winner was a John Wyer-entered Ford GT40 driven by Jacky Ickx and Jack Oliver. Most of the armada of Porsche 908s and 917s retired, including the very swift, superbly handling 908 *Spyder* of Jo Siffert and Brian Redman which expired with transmission problems. On this circuit where such high speeds are attained it was interesting that Jo should choose the *Spyder* version of the 908 which had been designed for use on slower circuits. The Swiss driver was, however, convinced that the superior handling, braking and acceleration of the *Spyder* more than compensated for its lower maximum speed. Of the two Ferraris entered (both fitted for this race with very handsome coupé bodies), one car, driven by Amon and Schetty, was eliminated on the first lap when it ran into the blazing fuel tank from Woolfe's crashed Porsche 917 and the car shared by Pedro and David Piper retired during the night because of transmission trouble without ever having mixed it with the leaders.

Ferrari did not contest the last two rounds of the Sports Car Championship at Watkins Glen and the Österreichring and both races were dominated by Porsche – and by Jo Siffert. The brilliant Swiss driver won the Watkins Glen Six Hours with a 908 *Spyder* co-driven by Redman and the Austrian 1000 Km race with a 4.5-litre 917 Porsche co-driven by Kurt Ahrens. Of the ten rounds in the Championship Jo had won a grand total of six, a performance that was unique in itself.

For 1970 the Porsche team and John Wyer's J W Automotive concern entered into an agreement whereby the works 917 cars were entered by Wyer in the Gulf Oil Corporation's pale blue and orange colour scheme and were known as 'Gulf-Porsches'. With the exception of Le Mans, where a third car was entered, J W Automotive Engineering fielded two cars in each round of the Championship and these were handled by a formidable team of drivers. Jo Siffert, who in fact remained under contract to Porsche of Stuttgart, was usually partnered by Brian Redman and to drive the second team car Wyer signed up Pedro Rodriguez and the comparatively inexperienced Finnish driver Leo Kinnunen. At the beginning of the year there was a great deal of speculation as to whether even strict disciplinarian Wyer and Yorke would be able to control a team that included two firebrands like Siffert and Rodriguez, both of whom would be pushing for victory every inch of the way. In fact both 'Seppi' and Pedro were kept in rein, but at times by only the narrowest of margins! Throughout 1970 the Gulf-Porsche team faced strong opposition from Ferrari's new 5-litre 512S Sports Cars with a team of drivers headed by Jacky Ickx. The season soon revealed that, although the Ferraris came so very close to matching the performance of the Porsche 917s, Maranello standards of preparation and team organisation were no match for Wyer wizardry.

At the first round of the Championship, the Daytona 24 Hours race, Rodriguez and Kinnunen enjoyed a completely troublefree race and scored a convincing victory at 114.87 mph. Neither the second Gulf car nor the Ferrari team was so lucky. All the Ferraris ran into trouble of one sort or another and the Siffert/Redman 917 lost second place and eighty minutes while the complete clutch unit was changed. 'Seppi' and his 917 joined the race in fourth place and the Swiss driver indulged in one of the most exciting and inspired drives in his career, hurling the Porsche round the Daytona circuit at tremendous speed, almost as if he was determined to prove what most people already believed, that he was the world's fastest sports car driver. Siffert snatched third place when the Parkes/Posey Ferrari stopped for bodywork repairs, but with six hours to go to the finish he still had 41 laps to make on the second-place Ferrari of Ickx/Andretti. The task seemed impossible until the Ferrari came into the pits for repairs to a broken chassis member; the 512S spent a total of 77 minutes in the pits and when it rejoined the race, 'Seppi' and Redman were only five laps in arrears. Redman gained another lap on the ailing Ferrari and then handed the 917 back to Siffert. In the excitement of the chase for second place, the timekeepers succeeded in losing count of the number of laps covered by the Ferrari and its blue and orange pursuer. Two hours from the finish Siffert was credited with regaining second place and he stopped to hand the 917 back to his team-mate who promptly scraped a wall, stopped at the pits for repairs and lost the hard-won second place. Siffert resumed at the wheel back in third place and officially a lap behind the Ferrari. Round and round Daytona Siffert screamed the 917 in pursuit of its red rival and on a circuit coated with oil and rubber from nearly twenty-four hours of racing he was credited with setting a new unofficial lap record of 1 min 48.7 sec (no official fastest lap was issued by the organisers at Daytona). Only four minutes before the chequered flag brought an end to this long and arduous race the Porsche surged by into second place again and, ironically enough, after the race was over the organisers confessed to a timekeeping error and admitted that Siffert was three laps ahead of Andretti at the fall of the flag!

At Sebring the 917s were plagued by mechanical problems and Ferrari scored their one and only victory of the season. The Gulf-Porsche team reasserted its superiority in the BOAC 1000 Kilometres race at Brands Hatch where Rodriguez and Kinnunen scored their second victory of the season. Again Siffert and Redman were out of luck; Redman, driving superbly on a rain-soaked track, was holding second place when a tyre burst and the Porsche shot off the track. One of the fastest races of the season was the Monza 1000 Kilometres race, a flat-out blind which was all over in not much more than four hours. At this race the Ferraris came very close to beating the Porsche opposition and the Maranello cars took second, third and fourth places behind the winning 917 of Rodriguez and Kinnunen. Siffert and Redman were right out of the picture after a long pit stop for repairs to damaged suspension and bodywork, the result of Siffert's spin into the guard-rail while trying to avoid a slower car that crossed his line.

The Porsche engineers at Zuffenhausen were well aware of the unsuitability of the large, immensely powerful 917 cars to the twists and turns of the 44.7-mile Little Madonie circuit used for the Targa Florio in Sicily. Specifically for this race Porsche had developed the 3-litre 908/03 car of very low weight and very compact dimensions. Because of their vast experience in entering the Targa Florio, the cars were managed at this race by Porsche and not Wyer staff (Porsche had won this race in 1963-4 and 1966-9) and Siffert and Redman were the winners at record speed. The real sensation of the race, however, was the single 512S Ferrari driven by Ignazio Giunti and local man Nino Vaccarella. Porsche confidence was badly shaken by the fact that at one stage the big, bulky Ferrari had actually led the race and it was only narrowly beaten into third place by Rodriguez/Kinnunen.

For Sports Car racing enthusiasts the race of the 1970 season was the Spa 1000 Kilometres, a race which was not only the fastest in the Championship series, but the most spectacular. No circuit (not even the Nürburgring) taxes more a driver's skill and courage and Rodriguez' and Siffert's control of the monstrous 917s at speeds of over 120 mph through Spa's bumpy and exacting curves was one of the outstanding feats of modern motor racing. While Siffert seared away from the opposition, steadily increasing his lead, Rodriguez kept at bay Jacky Ickx, the local maestro who knows Spa intimately. When Pedro was forced to stop for a wheel-change. Ickx moved up into second place and John Surtees, who relieved Ickx at the first round of pit stops, was actually out of the pits first ahead of Redman who had taken over from Siffert. Surtees, however, was unable to maintain the pace set by his Belgian team-mate, Redman had soon surged ahead and Rodriguez passed Surtees to take second place on lap 37.

At the next round of pit stops Ferrari team manager Mauro Forghieri made a tactical mistake that cost Ferrari the race. Ickx was fast enough round Spa to catch and pass both Kinnunen (who had relieved Rodriguez) and Redman, but Forghieri sent Surtees out for a second spell at the wheel. The probable reason for this decision was that Forghieri was trying to rest Ickx who had still not fully recovered from burns suffered in a crash in the

Spanish Grand Prix. Redman and Kinnunen were dominating the race, but the Finn's car retired with a seized gearbox and the Ickx/Surtees Ferrari moved up into second place again. Thirteen laps from the finish Siffert resumed at the wheel of the leading 917 and after four hours ten minutes of an exciting spectacle of speed and brilliant pit-work (at this race by both the Gulf-Porsche and Ferrari teams) the Swiss driver crossed the line to score his second victory of the season at 149.42 mph. Fastest lap in this race, a circuit record, was set by Pedro Rodriguez at an almost incredible 160.53 mph.

For the Nürburgring 1000 Kilometres race Porsche produced the 908/03 cars once more. It was not a Gulf race, both of the Wyer-entered cars retired and victory went to another 908/03 entered in the name of Porsche Konstruktionen (Porsche's Austrian subsidiary). It was on the Le Mans race that all Wyer's hopes were pinned and the team was anxious to repeat its 1969-70 victories. Once again, as at the Nürburgring, the Wyer team was destined to be disappointed. Two of the cars were eliminated by the most wretched bad luck and the third in circumstances that did not reflect well on the performance of the driver concerned. The pace was set in the opening laps of the race by Vic Elford with a special aerodynamic long-tail Porsche 917 entered by Porsche Konstruktionen, but during the second hour the Siffert/Redman blue and orange car pulled away into the lead, to a large extent because of the slickness of the Wyer pit-work. Already Rodriguez was out of the race because of a broken fan drive-shaft and not long afterwards in heavy rain Mike Hailwood crashed his Gulf 917 into a wrecked Alfa Romeo that was blocking the track.

Now the full responsibility for the success or failure of the Gulf team rested with Jo Siffert and Brian Redman and by midnight they had pulled out a comfortable lead of four laps. Now consistency and reliability would prove the ingredients of success. But 'Seppi' was a notoriously hard driver with precious little sympathy for the mechanics of his car and, despite the Gulf 917's substantial lead, he was still driving hard. Just after 3 am the inevitable happened and Siffert crawled into the Wyer pit with the 917's tachometer 'tell-tale' at an ominous 9600 rpm and oil pouring out of the exhausts. Siffert had missed a 'snatch' gear-change, the revs had soared and the engine had broken. Victory in the 24 Hours race went to the Porsche Konstruktionen-entered 917 of Dickie Attwood and veteran Porsche driver Hans Herrmann.

At the next round in the Championship at Watkins Glen team discipline was lost for the one and only time in two seasons of racing. The latent but fierce rivalry between Rodriguez and Siffert came into the open in this six hour race and they indulged in a physical conflict which jeopardised the team's chances of victory and for which Wyer blamed Pedro Rodriguez. At around quarter-distance in this six-hour race Rodriguez was leading the field, almost a lap ahead of Siffert in second place. When he caught Siffert, Pedro barged his way past without waiting for a suitable opportunity to lap his team-mate; the two cars collided and while Rodriguez, who had dented the cockpit of his car on the right-hand side, was able to roar away into the distance, Siffert was forced to stop at the pits for a wheel-change. Despite this altercation the Gulf-Porsche 917s took the first two places. The final round of the Championship was the Austrian 1000 Kilometres race in which Siffert and Redman were the winners.

Both Siffert and Rodriguez had enjoyed a brilliantly successful season in Sports Car racing and, as far as Pedro was concerned, it was the finest season in his career. In Formula One he had been driving for the BRM team and, although the V-12 cars from Bourne were by no means the fastest or most reliable of Grand Prix cars, he scored a fine victory in the Belgian Grand Prix, the last in the series to be held at Spa-Francorchamps, and finished second in the United States race. He would have won at Watkins Glen but for running out of fuel in the closing stages of the race; during the pit stop, while a few extra gallons were sloshed in the tank, he lost the lead to Emerson Fittipaldi's Lotus 72. For Jo Siffert the Formula One year could hardly have been more depressing. He had signed up to drive for the newly formed March team and in fact had been obliged to pay a considerable sum out of his own pocket to obtain his place in the team. In race after race throughout the year Siffert retired with engine trouble and he failed to finish in the first six at any circuit. Certainly Jo did suffer a great deal of bad luck during his year with the March team, but much of his misfortune could be attributed to his harsh, forceful, unsympathetic driving style.

Both Rodriguez and Siffert remained with the Gulf-Porsche team in 1971, but Kinnunen had been dropped by Wyer and Brian Redman had emigrated to South Africa (he remained there only a very short while). At most races Pedro was partnered by Jack Oliver and Jo by Derek Bell.

The first Championship race of the 1971 season was the Buenos Aires 1000 Kilometres, a race marred by the death of Ignazio Giunti, killed when his Ferrari collided with the Matra which Jean-Pierre Beltoise was pushing back to the pits after it had run out of fuel. Almost inevitably the race proved yet another Gulf-Porsche benefit; Siffert/Bell and

Rodriguez/Oliver took the first two places, leading home a duo of 3-litre Alfa Romeos. At Daytona the Siffert/Bell car was eliminated by a broken connecting rod, but Rodriguez and Oliver upheld the team's prestige and won at 109.20 mph, eleven laps clear of the second-place Ferrari.

At Sebring the Gulf-Porsche team was in all sorts of trouble. Siffert ran out of petrol just before his scheduled refuelling stop, lost nineteen laps while he went to the pits to fetch fuel and was penalised another four because he 'hitched' a ride on the pillion of a motor cycle back to the stricken 917. And Rodriguez succeeded in colliding with the Ferrari of Mark Donohue at the chicane to the detriment of both cars and to the anger of both drivers who blamed each other for the accident. The Rodriguez/Oliver Porsche rejoined the race with a cut-back right-hand front wing and jury-rigged headlamp and in the face of vociferous protests from Roger Penske, entrant of the Ferrari. Later in the race the Rodriguez/Oliver car was further delayed while a broken suspension wishbone was replaced. Victory went to the Martini Racing-entered 917 Porsche of Elford and Larrousse and the best that the Gulf-Porsche team could manage was fourth by Rodriguez/Oliver and fifth by Siffert/Bell.

Both of the Gulf-Porsche entries retired in the BOAC race at Brands Hatch and victory went to the Autodelta-entered Alfa Romeo Tipo 33/3 of Andrea de Adamich and Henri Pescarolo. Now that Ferrari had abandoned racing the 5-litre 512 cars after only one season, there was no serious opposition to the Gulf-Porsche 917s on the really fast circuits and the Wyer team completely dominated the Monza 1000 Kilometres race. Despite unscheduled pit stops for the windscreen to be cleaned (it was coated with fire extinguisher fluid accidentally sprayed on by marshalls dealing with the blazing wreckage of Jacky Ickx' crashed Ferrari) and to change a punctured tyre, 'Seppi' and Bell climbed through the field to finish second, three laps behind Rodriguez/Oliver.

In a repetition of the domination which they had displayed at Monza, Rodriguez and Siffert took the lead on the first lap of the Spa 1000 Kilometres race and were unchallenged throughout the 71 laps of this high-speed 'blind'. Certainly the performance of the Gulf 917s was brilliantly impressive and the 1971 1000 Kilometres was the last spectacular race to be held on the Spa circuit; but in the absence of a serious Ferrari challenge, the race lacked the excitement of the previous year's event. The winning pair, Rodriguez and Oliver, averaged 154.77 mph and Jo Siffert shattered the lap record with a speed of 162.09 mph, an almost unbelievable achievement on a circuit composed of public roads.

Three Porsche 908/03s were entered in the Targa Florio, one in the distinctive silver and blue colours of the Martini team, but all three retired; on the very first lap Brian Redman, brought back into the team for this one race, crashed the car he was sharing with Jo Siffert and Rodriguez wrecked the suspension of his car against a kerb. The Autodelta Alfa Romeos of Vaccarella/Hezemans and de Adamich/van Lennep took the first two places. Yet another defeat was suffered by the Wyer team at the Nürburgring. The new flat-12 Ferrari of Ickx/Regazzoni dominated the race until it retired with overheating problems; Siffert retired his Porsche with a broken chassis sub-frame and 'Seppi' was then switched to share with Rodriguez the car entered for the Mexican and Jack Oliver. This Porsche was handling atrociously and the Gulf drivers had to settle for a poor second place, soundly trounced by the similar Porsche 908/03 entered under the Martini banner for Vic Elford and Gérard Larrousse.

At Le Mans the Wyer team again entered a trio of 917s, two new long-tail cars for the usual pairs of drivers and a standard model for Richard Attwood (the 1970 winner) and Herbert Müller. Gulf-Porsche was passing through an unlucky patch and once again victory eluded the team. Rodriguez and Siffert held first and third places and after the first refuelling stop Siffert moved up into second place. Despite minor delays in the pits the two Gulf *Stromlinienwagen* continued to dominate the race and by 10 pm on the Saturday evening the third car of the team had moved up to form a solid Gulf-Porsche phalanx at the head of the field. In the early hours of Sunday morning mechanical trouble delayed the blue and orange cars; Rodriguez/Oliver lost ten minutes while a seized hub was sorted out and Müller/Attwood were delayed twenty minutes while the gearbox of their 917 was repaired. Then the Rodriguez/Oliver car dropped out of the race with engine failure; Bell retired the second long-tail 917 in a dense trail of oil smoke from a cracked gearbox casing and the surviving car of Attwood/Müller had dropped to second place behind the Martini-entered 917 of Marko/van Lennep, a position in which it remained until the chequered flag at 4 pm on the Sunday afternoon.

Jo Siffert made a rare mistake at the start of the Austrian 1000 Kilometres race at the Österreichring; he almost burnt out the clutch of his 917 and weakened it so badly that it failed completely early in the race when Jo tried to rejoin the race after a pit stop to change a wheel. While Siffert was throwing away his chances of success, Pedro Rodriguez was in the pits because of low fuel injection pressure, a fault traced to a flat battery. The stop cost Pedro three laps and resulted in a frantic chase after the 3-litre Ferrari which was only resolved when Regazzoni wrecked the Maranello entry against a guard-rail. Now Pedro had the race in the bag and he and teammate Dickie Attwood (who had replaced Oliver in the team) went on to win this race at 123.04 mph from the Alfa Romeo of Hezemans/Vaccarella.

Tragically, the Austrian 1000 Kilometres was Pedro Rodriguez' last drive for the Wyer team and on 11th July 1971 he was killed in an unimportant race at the Norisring circuit in Germany. The race was the Nuremberg 200, a round in the Interserie (a sort of European equivalent of Can-Am racing for Group 7 two-seater racing cars), and the car was a Ferrari 512M 5-litre belonging to Swiss driver and entrant Herbert Müller. Poor Pedro was leading the first heat of this race when the Ferrari went out of control, smashed into the barrier on the left-hand side of the track and ricocheted across into the barrier on the right-hand side. Although Pedro was still alive when he was rescued from the blazing wreckage, he was horribly burned and died soon afterwards.

Pedro Rodriguez was one of motor racing's natural fighters, always at his best when the odds were stacked against him and never admitting defeat; he was one of the very few drivers who could exploit the full potential of the monstrously powerful 917 and he was especially fast on a wet track. His death was a terrible blow to the Gulf team and there was no possibility of finding an adequate replacement. At the final round of the Championship, the 6 Hours race at Watkins Glen, Wyer entered two cars, for Siffert and Dutchman Gijs van Lennep and Bell/Attwood. Once again Gulf-Porsche was out of luck, both 917s were plagued by punctured tyres and, in the heavy rain that fell in the later stages of the race, they were slowed by bad engine misfires. Alfa Romeo scored their third victory of the season and the Tipo 33/3 of Ronnie Peterson/Andrea de Adamich led home the two Wyer-entered 917s.

After his disastrous 1970 season with the March team Jo Siffert was not slow to switch his allegiance in Formula One the following year and he joined Pedro Rodriguez in the BRM team. Although 1971 proved very much a Jackie Stewart and Tyrrell year, BRM, who had won only two Championship races in five years, enjoyed an improvement in their fortunes and seemed to be growing into a serious force in Grand Prix racing. After a fourth by Rodriguez at Barcelona and a second by the Mexican in the rain-soaked Dutch race, Jo Siffert began to find his form with the team; he finished fourth in the French race, drove his V-12 car painted in Yardley brown, white and gold colours to victory in Austria and took a very encouraging second place in the United States Grand Prix. In addition Peter Gethin, who had been brought into the Bourne team as a successor to Pedro Rodriguez, won the high-speed slip-streaming Monza 'sprint', a Grand Prix which lasted a mere hour and eighteen minutes.

The final Formula One race of the 1971 season was the Rothmans World Championships Victory Race, despite its grandiose title a short 40-lap race held at Brands Hatch at the end of October. This race, held as a sort of tribute to World Champions Stewart and Tyrrell, was marred by a ghastly accident when Jo Siffert's BRM went out of control just before Hawthorn corner, crashed into the bank at undiminished speed and exploded into a cloud of smoke and flames. There is little doubt that poor Jo was asphyxiated before the flames reached him. The cause of the accident was never satisfactorily explained.

The deaths of Pedro Rodriguez and Jo Siffert were a terrible blow to motor racing and to the John Wyer team. There was something ironic in the fact that they should both lose their lives towards the end of an era of Sports Car racing that they had immeasurably enriched by their flair and exciting driving. With the passing of these two great drivers and the demise of the Porsche 917 as a Championship sports car at the end of 1971 (open versions were developed for Can-Am racing) the chapter was closed on an important and exciting era of motor racing.

17

John Wyer, Team Manager Extraordinary

In the history of motor racing John Wyer has secured for himself a position that is almost unique, combining the roles of team manager and engineering director, and none has done it so successfully. Wyer has an unparalleled record of success in sports car racing with Aston Martin, Ford and Porsche cars and today he is still vigorously pursuing success with the Ford-powered Gulf Prototypes.

John Wyer's career of International motor racing success began with his appointment by David Brown in 1949 as Aston Martin Racing Manager. Behind him Wyer had a long career in the motor industry that had begun in 1927 when he joined Sunbeam of Wolverhampton as an apprentice, and had continued in post-war days with Monaco Engineering at Watford where he had developed special lightweight versions of the Singer-powered HRG sports cars. David Brown had spotted Wyer's great ability as a development engineer, his remarkable flair for diagnosing faults and suggesting remedies; his patient application in solving problems; his broad grasp of complex situations; and, very important qualities in a racing manager, his abilities to organise and to delegate with confidence.

David Brown had acquired the moribund Aston Martin and Lagonda concerns in 1947 and concentrated his car manufacturing and racing business on the old Aston Martin works at Feltham in Middlesex. Here Wyer undertook the development of the first successful David Brown model, the Aston Martin DB2, a remarkable hybrid which first appeared in 1949 and officially entered production in 1950; developments of this car were manufactured until 1959. The DB2 combined the 2.6-litre twin overhead camshaft engine which W O Bentley had designed for use in the post-war

Lagonda with a chassis that was basically of Aston Martin origins and a very handsome Italian-style coupé body.

The DB2 had won its class at Le Mans in 1950, finishing fifth and sixth overall, but it was considered that it was far too heavy for sports car racing. David Brown agreed to commission a new design purely for competition work and this was entrusted to former Auto Union engineer Doctor Eberan von Eberhorst. While von Eberhorst worked on the new design, Wyer prepared lightweight versions of the DB2 for the 1951 season. These DB2s, which were the first British cars to be fitted with Weber carburettors, finished third, fifth and seventh at Le Mans and dominated the 3-litre class.

Aston Martin had the first DB3 ready to race in the Tourist Trophy on the Dundrod circuit in Northern Ireland in September 1950. The new car featured a ladder-type tubular chassis, de Dion rear suspension, a 5-speed gearbox, sleek open bodywork and, in its original form, the 2.6-litre engine as fitted to the competition DB2s. In Ireland the new car was driven by Lance Macklin, but it was out of luck and retired because of a broken exhaust. By 1952 Aston Martin was racing a full team of DB3s and during that year Wyer introduced a 2922 cc engine developing 163 bhp. The DB3 was an unlucky car throughout its short career; the complete team of Astons retired at Le Mans that year and at the Goodwood Nine Hours race there was a disastrous fire in the pits which destroyed one of the team cars and badly burned Wyer and two mechanics. This was, however, one of the few races won by the DB3 and after the failure of the works Jaguars, another works 2.6-litre Aston Martin driven by Peter Collins and Pat Griffith came through to take the lead and score a fine victory at 75.42 mph.

Wyer was far from satisfied with the performance of the DB3, primarily because the car was only a hundred pounds lighter than the DB2s raced the previous year and over the winter of 1952-3 a complete redesign was put in hand. The 1953 car, the DB3S, was a vast improvement over its predecessors in every respect and it was constantly developed and raced by the works over the next four years. The DB3S featured a shorter wheelbase, lighter chassis, new body with much smaller frontal area (and of vastly improved appearance), a 4-speed gearbox and a more powerful engine developing 180 bhp at 5500 rpm. One of the most significant aspects of Wyer's work at Aston Martin was that the team used with great success an engine that had been designed as a modestly priced touring car unit and with no thought of competition work in the designer's mind. The success of Aston Martins powered by W O Bentley's Lagonda engine was a tribute both to the careful development work carried out under John Wyer supervision and to the basic qualities of the original design.

Until the DB3S was ready, the Aston Martin team continued to race the DB3 during the early part of the 1953 season and successes gained included a second place in the Sebring 12 Hours race and a fifth by Reg Parnell in the Mille Miglia (the latter a very fine performance in the face of overwhelmingly strong opposition). The DB3S made its debut in a minor race at the Charterhall circuit in May 1953 and a full team was entered at Le Mans where all the David Brown entries retired. After this disappointment the DB3S enjoyed a very successful season and wins later in the year included the Goodwood Nine Hours race and the Tourist Trophy. In both of these events Aston Martin defeated the works C-type Jaguars, but the Continental opposition was conspicuous by its absence.

For 1954 the team took a bold step in an effort to build a car that was as fast as the Continental opposition without sacrificing the fine roadholding qualities enjoyed by the DB3S. At the *Daily Express* Trophy meeting at Silverstone in May John Wyer unveiled the new V-12 4486 cc Lagonda, a car that aped Ferrari design practice and had an engine which was virtually a 'double-six' version of the familiar W O Bentley unit. Apart from increased dimensions the chassis was similar to that of the DB3S. Unfortunately the Lagonda proved a very expensive mistake; the chassis and engine were far too heavy and the claimed power output of 305 bhp erred on the optimistic side. The V-12 proved only marginally faster than the familiar 3-litre cars from the stable; at Le Mans in 1954, for example, the Lagonda was timed on the Mulsanne straight at 148.25 mph and turned in a fastest lap of 4 min 31.8 sec. In comparison the fastest DB3S achieved 144.23 mph through the flying kilometre and lapped in 4 min 42.5 sec. An experimental supercharged DB3S entered by the works in this race lapped *faster* than the Lagonda. Wyer persevered with the Lagonda until the end of 1955 (that year's car featured a new backbone-type chassis), but no success was achieved and this very ambitious and very expensive project was abandoned.

Fortunately Wyer had not pinned all his hopes on the V-12 cars and development work on the DB3S continued. In 1954 Aston Martin introduced a twin-plug cylinder head (in this form power output was boosted to 225 bhp at 6000 rpm) and a very interesting fixed head coupé which had been developed in conjunction with Vickers. Although the drag of the coupé was around 25% less than that of the open cars, for reasons which Wyer was unable to explain lap times were no quicker and, after the first two cars had been crashed at Le Mans, no further examples were built. 1954 was a poor year for Aston Martin; none of the five cars entered at Le Mans made it to the finish and the team's only worthwhile International success was a third place in the Buenos Aires 1000 Kilometres race held at the beginning of the year. The following year Aston Martin fortunes improved and the team's successes included a second place at Le Mans by Collins and Frère and a 'hat-trick' in the Goodwood Nine Hours race (this event had not been held in 1954). David Brown had been toying with entering Formula One and at the end of 1955 an experimental single-seater Aston with 2500 cc engine was sent out to New Zealand where it was raced by Reg Parnell.

Another second place was gained with the DB3S at Le Mans in 1956, but the significant event of the year was the appearance at the Sarthe circuit of a completely new Aston Martin sports car. The new car, typed the DBR1, incorporated all the many lessons learned with the DB3 and DB3S in four seasons of racing. There was a completely new, very stiff, very light multi-tubular space-frame, a new 'crash' 5-speed gearbox in unit with the final drive and a new magnesium-alloy body. After the expensive and abortive Lagonda project, David Brown's racing budget would not extend to the development of yet another new engine and the power unit of the DBR1 was still, basically, the old W O Bentley unit, but now with new crankshaft and con-rods (introduced on the DB3S in 1955), new cap-type bearings and dry sump lubrication. Because the 1956 Le Mans regulations limited the capacity of prototypes (as opposed to what the organisers accepted as production cars) to 2500 cc, the DBR1 first appeared with a short-stroke engine reducing capacity to within this limit. From early 1957, however, the DBR1s were raced with full 3-litre engines.

In 1957 John Wyer became Technical Director of Aston Martin Lagonda Ltd and Reg Parnell, whose active career as a racing driver had now come to an end, became Racing Manager. Wyer produced two new developments for 1957. An additional Aston Martin competition model was the DBR2, a 3670 cc car with a chassis of the backbone type evolved from that used for the Lagonda. Rather like its Lagonda predecessor, the DBR2 proved only marginally faster than the 3-litre cars and did not handle as well. For the DBR1 Wyer had developed a new cylinder with the valves at the much wider angle of 95 degrees; in this form the DBR1 developed 265 bhp and was a serious rival to most of the Continental sports/racing cars. Aston Martin successes in 1957 included first two places in the 132-mile Sports Car Grand

Prix at Spa-Francorchamps and a brilliant victory in the Nürburgring 1000 Kilometres race by Tony Brooks and Noel Cunningham-Reid.

For 1958 there was a capacity limit of 3000 cc in Sports Car Championship events, Maserati had now withdrawn from racing (Jaguar had retired at the end of 1956) and racing devolved into a duel between the 6-cylinder Aston Martins under the direction of John Wyer and the V-12 Ferrari 'Testa Rossa' cars under the management of Tavoni. Aston Martin won the Nürburgring 1000 Km race and the Tourist Trophy at Goodwood (no Ferraris were entered in the latter event) and took second place in the Sports Car Championship. Another Aston Martin development was seen in 1958; at the May Silverstone meeting Stirling Moss drove a variant of the sports car known as the DBR3 and powered by an engine of markedly oversquare dimensions permitting much higher revs than could be attained with the standard unit. The DBR3 was not raced again, but it provided much useful data in connection with the team's Grand Prix project that appeared the following year.

The battle between Aston Martin and Ferrari continued in 1959 and with victories at the Nürburgring (for the third year in succession), Le Mans (a race which Aston Martin had been struggling to win for ten years) and the Tourist Trophy the British *marque* succeeded in winning the Sports Car Championship, a magnificent triumph for Wyer after so many years of effort. In 1959 Aston Martin also contested Formula One with the DBR4 car, powered by what was basically the DBR1 6-cylinder engine. Unfortunately the DBR4 had been designed more than two years previously, it was front-engined at a time when racing was being dominated by the rear-engined Coopers and it was far too heavy to beat even its front-engined rivals. Aston Martin withdrew from sports car racing at the end of 1959 to concentrate their efforts solely on the single-seater category, but their chances of success were slimmer than ever; the existing 2500 cc Formula came to an end in 1960 and after a series of failures the team backed out of Formula One before the end of the season. To have entered Formula One was an unfortunate mistake and it seems that the decision was taken by David Brown against John Wyer's advice and judgment.

At the 1958 London Motor Show Aston Martin had announced their new DB4 production car with a 3.7-litre engine similar to that used in the DBR2 sports car. A year later there followed the lighter, faster DB4GT version and during 1962-3 these were raced by the works with limited success. David Brown had not altogether lost interest in the development of specialised competition cars and in 1962-3 the team raced new 4-litre Prototypes at Le Mans without success.

Although the Aston Martin competitions department was a pale shadow of its former self by 1963, John Wyer's brilliant development work and superb team management had established a reputation that was the envy of most of Aston's rivals. In August 1963 Wyer was invited to join Ford's new GT40 project and, now that development work at Aston Martin was stagnating, he was delighted to accept. Ford Advanced Vehicles was formed with new premises at Slough and John Wyer managed this organisation. Wyer was responsible for the management of the GT40's racing programme which included the Nürburgring, Le Mans and Reims races. Unfortunately the season was one of failure (the cars retired in all three races) and it was only too obvious that the GT40 still needed a great deal of development work before it would become reliable enough to prove a consistent race-winner. At the end of the year Ford decided to leave development of the GT40 in American hands and the racing programme was shared out between Carroll Shelby and Kar-Kraft, a new Ford racing subsidiary at Detroit.

For the time being at least Wyer was left out in the cold to develop the existing 4.7-litre car and to build production versions. A few relatively unimportant entries were made under the banner of Ford Advanced Vehicles in 1965, including the entry of an open version of the GT40 in the Targa Florio and at Le Mans a coupé sponsored by the *Weekend Telegraph.* For 1966 Wyer was given a contract by the Essex Wire Corporation to prepare their team of GT40s (the 4.7-litre model had now been homologated as a Competition Sports Car) and Wyer brought in David Yorke to manage the team. The tall slim Yorke had acted as Peter Whitehead's racing manager before joining the Vanwall team in 1955. Yorke had stayed with Tony Vandervell after he had withdrawn from serious racing at the end of 1958 and did not leave Vandervell's organisation until 1962.

In the later part of 1966 Detroit sold the Ford Advanced Vehicles set-up to John Wyer and Ford dealer John Willment at a very modest price. Wyer's fortunes were beginning to look up again, for in addition to assuming responsibility for the production of GT40s, Wyer's new company, known as J W Automotive Engineering Ltd, was asked to race a team of GT40s sponsored by the Gulf Oil Corporation. These cars were modified by Len Bailey (one of the original GT40 design team) and were raced with 4.7, 5 and, finally, 5.7-litre engines under the name 'Mirage'. The success of these blue and orange-painted cars included a win in the Spa 1000 Kilometres race.

New sports car regulations came into force for the 1968 season and these imposed a capacity limit of 5000 cc for Competition Sports Cars (which meant a minimum production of 50) and 3000 cc for Prototypes. The Gulf organisation continued to sponsor a team of J W Automotive-entered Ford GT40s and while these were being raced, financed the development of a completely new Mirage 3-litre Prototype to the design of Len Terry. During 1968 the Wyer-entered Fords won four rounds in the Sports Car Championship, including Le Mans, and scored a victory over Porsche in the Championship itself. Wyer relied on the faithful and very reliable Fords at Le Mans again in 1969 and these finished first and third. Ford's own very expensive racing programme during the years 1964-7 had netted two Le Mans victories and Wyer's team, operating on a very modest budget, had achieved as much success as the works!

The design of the new Mirage M2 coupé had been commissioned by Wyer in 1967 and designer Len Terry completed his drawings very quickly. J W were testing the first prototype by the summer of 1968, but development was badly set back when Robin Widdows crashed the first car at Snetterton in July. The first Mirage was tested, but not raced at Daytona in January 1969 and it made its competition debut in the BOAC '500' race at Brands Hatch in April, when it was already outdated. Since the design had been first conceived to comply with the 1968 regulations, these had been relaxed and the minimum windscreen height, ground clearance, cockpit width and all-up weight had all been dispensed with. These requirements had favoured the construction of a coupé, but for 1969's relaxed regulations an open car, as built by both Ferrari and Porsche, was more appropriate. Another handicap faced by the Mirage was that its V-12 BRM engine was lacking in sufficient power.

As the season progressed, Wyer endeavoured to overcome these weaknesses in the design of the Mirage. J W ordered a Ford DFV 3-litre Grand Prix engine and this was first used in one of the coupés at the Nürburgring 1000 Km race; by the Watkins Glen race in July the team had developed the new M3 *Spyder* Mirage which was much lighter and much more compact than the earlier M2 coupés. With Jacky Ickx at the wheel the M3 led the Austrian 1000 Km race before retiring with mechanical trouble and it scored a victory in the non-Championship Imola 500 Km race in September.

Despite the development work carried out on the Mirage during the 1969 season, Wyer had realised at the outset of the project that the chances of doing well in the face of strong Ferrari and Porsche opposition were slim. Porsche dominated racing in 1969 with their 908 3-litre cars raced in both *Spyder* and coupé forms, but this team had also produced another very exciting model that was as yet far from fully developed. The German team had laid down a batch of twenty-five flat-12 4.5-litre 917 cars (twenty-five was now the homologation minimum for admission as a Competition Sports Car in respect of which there was a 5-litre capacity limit) and had first raced the 917 at the Nürburgring 1000 Km event in May.

Wyer was the acknowledged master of the Sports Car scene in terms of organisation and the high standards of preparation work so essential for long-distance racing, but lacked a really competitive car and the means to develop one. Porsche were the leaders in racing technology and possessed the fastest and most successful cars, but recognised that their racing organisation was no match for Wyer's, their standards of preparation were inferior and their pit work slower and less efficient.

As early as March 1969 Porsche had made tentative approaches to Wyer to see whether he would be interested in running a full team of the 917s on behalf of the works during the two remaining years of the 5-litre formula. Certainly Wyer found the prospect alluring, but he realised that he would lose much of his independence through such an arrangement. In addition, as the season progressed, it became increasingly obvious that whilst the 917 was the fastest of all competing cars, it suffered serious handling problems and it was far from reliable. During 1969 the 917 scored only one victory, in the Austrian 1000 Kilometres race.

Eventually an agreement was worked out between Wyer, Porsche and the Gulf corporation whereby Wyer would enter the cars on behalf of the works and with Gulf sponsorship as Gulf-Porsche 917s. The cars were painted in Gulf pale blue and orange colours, all chassis maintenance was carried out at Wyer's works at Slough, but the Porsche factory retained responsibility for major engine work. Wyer's first problem was to solve the 917's handling troubles. His initial contact with the cars came at a test session at Zeltweg in Austria in October 1969 and he quickly realised that the trouble did not stem from the suspension, as believed by Porsche engineers, but from the aerodynamics. In its original form the 917 possessed a very smooth, aerodynamic nose and the choice of long or short tails with suspension-operated rear flaps. Wyer suggested a shorter, cutaway, uplifted tail and a squarer nose. At Zeltweg the modifications were improvised by using aluminium sheeting and they were subsequently adopted on a permanent basis.

During the next two seasons Sports Car racing achieved a zenith; the 4.5-litre (later 5-litre) blue and orange cars piloted by a magnificent team of drivers headed by Pedro Rodriguez and Jo Siffert provided a magnificent spectacle of speed and skill; throughout 1970 Gulf-Porsche battled with the new works 5-litre Ferrari 512S Competition Sports Cars and on occasions the conflict was close and furious. The 917 was marginally faster than its Maranello rival and Wyer's standards of preparation and organisation gave the 917s the extra edge needed to ensure victory. In 1970 Gulf-Porsche won at Daytona, Brands Hatch, Monza, Spa and the Österreichring, but sadly, failed at Le Mans where the winner was a Porsche 917 entered by the Porsche Salzburg team (Porsche's Austrian subsidiary). In the Targa Florio and at the Nürburgring Porsche used new and very light 3-litre cars and won both races. Ferrari's sole victory of the 1970 season was in the Sebring 12 Hours race.

Although not achieving such great success in 1971 the Gulf-Porsche team remained dominant. Ferrari had abandoned racing his 5-litre Sports Cars after one very expensive and disappointing season and instead concentrated his efforts on the 312P flat-12 Prototype, a car which was to dominate racing in 1972 when the 5-litre Sports Cars had been banned. The real threat to Gulf-Porsche supremacy in 1971 came from the Alfa Romeo Tipo 33/3 Prototypes which proved surprisingly fast and reliable; and mechanical failures on the 917s which spoiled the team's chances of victory in several races. The Gulf-Porsche 917s won at Buenos Aires, Daytona, Monza, Spa and the Österreichring. Once again the Wyer team failed at Le Mans where a Martini Racing Team-entered 917 was the winner.

With the ban on 5-litre Sports Cars from the end of 1971 John Wyer and the Gulf organisation were on their own once more; this was even more so because David Yorke had left to manage the Martini Racing Team which was involved in Formula One with the new flat-12 Tecno car and in the Grand Touring category with a team of Porsche Carrera cars. Another loss to the Wyer team was the departure of chief mechanic Ermanno Cuoghi, a Modenese by birth who had returned to his home town to work with the Ferrari Sports Car team. However John Horsman, Deputy Managing Director of J W Automotive, who had first met Wyer at Aston Martin in 1959 remained with the team and he and Wyer still made a formidable combination.

Already at the end of 1971 work was well advanced on a new Mirage, the 3-litre Ford-powered M6, designed by Len Bailey and this sleek blue and orange car made its debut at Sebring in 1972. The new car was entered under the banner of Gulf Research Racing. At its few races the Mirage was plagued by teething troubles, but it took a fourth in the Spa 1000 Kilometres race and at Nürburgring. Wyer decided to miss Le Mans and the Mirage next appeared at the Österreichring where it retired with an engine misfire. Two cars ran at Watkins Glen and that driven by Derek Bell and Carlos Pace finished third, the Wyer team's best performance of the 1972 season.

During 1972 the Ferrari opposition had been overwhelmingly strong, but Maranello efforts in Sports Car racing in 1973 were rather less intense, the French Matra team gradually gained the upper hand and Wyer found better opportunities for exploiting chinks in the armour of the Continental teams. After failures in the first four rounds of the Championship at Daytona, Vallelunga, Dijon and Monza, the Mirage M6s of Bell/Hailwood and Hailwood/Schuppan (Mike had a very busy day) took the first two places in the Spa 1000 Kilometres race. Gulf Racing Research did not run again until the Le Mans race where both entries retired. At the Österreichring the team's fortunes improved a little and the M6s, delayed by mechanical problems, finished fourth and fifth, positions that the team repeated in the final round of the Championship at Watkins Glen.

For the 1974 season the latest version of the Wyer-built Prototype was known as the Gulf GR7. By this time much of the public interest in Sports Car racing had been lost; the 3-litre Prototypes were far less exciting than their 5-litre predecessors, Ferrari had lost all interest in this classic of racing, the Alfa Romeo flat-12 cars had proved hopelessly unreliable in 1973 and, on paper at least, the only serious contenders were Matra and Gulf. The first event in the now much-reduced Championship calendar was the Monza race in April. Here the Alfa Romeos displayed a fine turn of speed coupled with new-found reliability and took the first three places ahead of the Gulf-Ford of Bell/Hailwood. At Spa Bell and Hailwood were second behind a Matra, and a Gulf shared by James Hunt, Vern Schuppan and Derek Bell finished fourth at the Nürburgring. The team missed the round of the Championship at Ifla to concentrate on preparation for Le Mans where Bell and Hailwood finished fourth. The Gulf team decided not to run at the sixth round of the Championship at Watkins Glen.

Once again in 1975 the Gulf team severely restricted its racing activities, but at Le Mans one of the Gulf GR8 cars driven by Jacky Ickx and Derek Bell scored a satisfying victory, albeit in the face of opposition that was far from strong. The second Gulf team car driven by Schuppan and Jaussaud finished in third place.

The tall, slightly stooping, taciturn, almost brooding Wyer has always run his teams with a firm hand. Discipline within the team has always been remarkably strong and firm. His organisation and attention to detail has been meticulous. The results of his administrative ability, his flair for development and organisation and his superb judgment in the choice of drivers has produced results that speak for themselves. Sports Car racing itself is now in a far from happy state, supported by only two important teams, Alfa Romeo and Alpine and with the Gulf team very severely restricting its racing programme. It is intended to introduce so-called 'Silhouette' Formula, a formula for cars that outwardly resemble production models but with almost unrestricted freedom to modify the mechanics. Any change that would result in an improvement in John Wyer's present mediocre fortunes and see him achieving the successes which his ability and experience merit will be welcomed by his many supporters.

18

The Rise of the Great American Drivers

Not a single Internationally recognised sport has a true world-wide following. Even football, that most widely played and widely watched of games, has only a limited, but admittedly rapidly growing following in the USA and, at a serious level, is almost completely lacking in support in such densely populated sub-continents as China and India. Motor racing however, is truly international and almost world-wide; its following bridges the Atlantic, Pacific and Indian oceans, although the level at which it takes place in Russia and other Eastern-block countries is little more than that of Club events. Grand Prix racing is held throughout Europe and in both North and South America – and an Australian round in the World Championship is likely to be added before long.

The true International flavour of Grand Prix racing has now been heightened by the appearance of two well financed, seriously organised Grand Prix teams from the United States whose first cars appeared towards the end of the 1974 season. In the 1974 Canadian Grand Prix the new Parnelli-Ford was driven into seventh place by Mario Andretti (a one-time member of the Ferrari team and winner of the 1971 South African Grand Prix) and the Penske-Ford was driven by Mark Donohue. Donohue, whose activities had been mainly restricted to United States racing events, made his Grand Prix debut in the 1971 Canadian Grand Prix in which he finished third at the wheel of a McLaren-Ford entered by Roger Penske.

With the appearance of two important new Grand Prix teams at a time when racing is flourishing (thanks largely to the sponsorship of cigarette manufacturers) and the battle for domination is being waged between six major teams, it is an appropriate moment to review briefly the early European Grand Prix efforts of American drivers, and to examine the careers of three leading American Grand Prix drivers whose successes and experience have done so much to encourage American interest in Formula One racing.

Doubtless the most successful American victory in pre-World War Two European racing came in the 1921 French Grand Prix held at Le Mans and here the victor was an American at the wheel of an American car. Four works Duesenbergs were entered, turned out in superb trim and in American blue and white colours; two of the cars were driven by Americans, Boyer and Murphy, and two by Frenchmen. The opposition came from teams of French Ballot and British (or, perhaps, more accurately Anglo-French) Talbots and Talbot-Darracqs. The surface at Le Mans was appalling, consisting in places of nothing more than loose stones, and the rate of tyre wear, especially on the British-entered cars, was phenomenal. Initially de Palma (Ballot) led the race, but then Murphy and his Duesenberg (the first Grand Prix model to be fitted with hydraulic brakes) went ahead on the second lap. Although Murphy retained the lead after his first pit stop, he was passed on the next lap by Chassagne (Ballot). The Frenchman's lead was short-lived, for after two laps the Ballot was out of the race with a burst fuel tank and Murphy's Duesenberg had an unassailable lead. He went on to win this 30-lap race by a margin of almost fifteen minutes from de Palma's Ballot. The other outstanding victory in Murphy's career was his win with a Duesenberg in the following year's Indianapolis 500 Miles race.

Ralph de Palma, the second-place man at Le Mans, was another successful American driver in European events and Peter de Paolo competed in Europe, finishing fifth with a works Alfa Romeo in the 1925 Italian Grand Prix, fifth with an American four-wheel-drive Miller at Tripoli in 1934 and crashing badly at the wheel of a Maserati at San Sebastian in 1935. It was not, however, until the late 'fifties that an American driver (North American that is, as opposed to South American) made a serious impact on the Grand Prix scene.

That American was Phil Hill, perhaps the most serious-minded and dedicated driver of his era and the only United States driver yet to win the World Championship. Phil Hill was a dedicated motoring enthusiast from childhood and was determined to go motor racing at the earliest possible moment. By the time he had reached the age of twenty-one the young Californian had abandoned a course in business studies at the University of California to work in a garage, and had saved enough money to buy an MG 'TC'. Phil's racing experiences killed his earlier ambitions to become a serious racing driver; he was convinced that he could never make the grade in serious racing and tried to convince himself that he was racing purely for fun. He had now joined the staff of an American importer of British cars and was sent to England for training courses at Jaguar and MG. Hill returned to the States with vastly increased knowledge and experience and a new Jaguar XK 120 which he raced regularly in 1950.

The following year the Jaguar was part-exchanged for a pre-war Alfa Romeo 8C-2900B and in 1952 the Alfa gave way to a new Ferrari 2.6-litre V-12. Probably Phil's best performance that year was a sixth place in the arduous Carrera Panamericana Mexico road race. By 1953 he was driving a new 3-litre V-12 Ferrari and, through the good offices of American Ferrari concessionaire Luigi Chinetti, made his European debut, driving an Osca at Le Mans and a Ferrari at Reims; he retired in both events. Richie Ginther was Hill's co-driver at Le Mans and he rode in the passenger seat of the Ferrari which Hill drove for Allen Guiberson in the Carrera Panamericana Mexico. This was a bad race for Hill, for the car went over a 100-foot drop and was completely written off, although both driver and passenger escaped largely unscathed.

Although Phil competed in the Buenos Aires 1000 Km race at the beginning of the 1954 season, he was forced to retire for the rest of the year because of serious stomach ulcer trouble. This enforced retirement served only to make Hill more determined to succeed as a racing driver and he returned to the sport in November 1954 by driving Guiberson's 4.5-litre Ferrari into second place in the Mexican road race.

Hill's racing career in 1955 continued with a series of drives in private owner's Ferraris and then in 1956, as a result of Luigi Chinetti's influence he had a works Ferrari drive in the 1956 Buenos Aires 1000 Kilometres race. His co-driver was Belgian long-distance sports car racing ace Olivier Gendenbien and they took second place to a Maserati. As a result of this fine performance Hill was invited to join the works Ferrari sports car team and his successes included a third at the Nürburgring (co-driving with de Portago) and a win in the 5-hour Messina Night race in Sicily. Hill remained with the Ferrari team in 1957, but his successes were limited to second places with Seidel in the Reims 12 Hours race and with Peter Collins in the Swedish Grand Prix and, at the end of the season, a win with Collins in the Venezuelan Grand Prix.

Throughout 1956 and 1957 Hill had been promised by Enzo Ferrari that he would be given a drive in a works Formula One car, but this failed to materialise. Hill remained with Ferrari for 1958 and his sports car successes included magnificent victories at Buenos Aires, Sebring and Le Mans. Still no Formula One drive was forthcoming and so Phil, thoroughly disillusioned by Ferrari's failure to provide a single-seater drive, hired an old Maserati 250F for the French Grand Prix and finished a satisfactory seventh.

In the French race Ferrari lost one of their leading drivers, Luigi Musso, who was killed when he crashed at a fast bend on the Reims course. Not only did Ferrari realise that he would lose Hill's services if he failed to provide him with a Grand Prix car, but he now needed the Californian in Maranello's Formula One team. After an outing in the German Grand Prix with a Formula Two Ferrari, Hill was entered at Monza with a Grand Prix Ferrari Dino; he drove magnificently, setting a new lap record and finishing third after a stop for a tyre-change. In the final race of the season, the Moroccan Grand Prix, he held second place to Moss's Vanwall for much of the distance, but then eased off to let Mike Hawthorn through to finish second and clinch the English driver's World Championship victory.

By 1959 the traditional front-engined Ferraris were no real match for the rear-engined Cooper-Climax cars of Jack Brabham and Stirling Moss; Phil enjoyed a mediocre season, achieving second places at Reims and Sebring (the latter circuit was the scene of the first United States Grand Prix) and a third in the German race on the high-speed Avus circuit. In 1960 Ferrari was still persevering with his front-engined Dino cars and Phil's only successes were a fourth in the Belgian Grand Prix at Spa and, in the absence of the British opposition which had boycotted the race, a rather hollow victory in the Italian Grand Prix held on the combined banked track and road circuit at Monza. Nevertheless the Monza victory was of great significance, for it was the first win in a European Grand Prix by an American driver since Murphy's victory with the Duesenberg at Le Mans.

Following the introduction of the 1500 cc Grand Prix Formula for 1961 onwards the Ferrari team enjoyed a season of almost complete domination of Grand Prix racing with their new rear-engined V-6 cars. Prior to the Monza race Hill's only victory of the year was in the Belgian Grand Prix in which the Maranello entries took the first four places. The World Championship was led at the time by fellow-Ferrari driver Wolfgang von Trips. Von Trips was killed in the Italian race in a collision with Jim Clark's Lotus, three other works Ferraris retired, and Hill with the surviving car went on to win the race and the Driver's World Championship.

At the end of 1961 Phil Hill was at the peak of his racing career. The following year the Ferraris proved no match for the new V-8-engined British opposition, Graham Hill with a BRM won the Drivers' Championship and Hill's best performance were a third in the Dutch race at Monza, a second at Monaco and another third at Spa. At the end of the year Hill and Ferrari parted company. Hill spent another two years in Grand Prix racing, neither of which proved successful. In 1963 he drove for the new ATS team whose cars proved slow and hopelessly unreliable and his sole Grand Prix finish was at Monza where he took a hopeless eleventh place. Phil signed up to drive for Cooper the following season, but Surbiton's star was waning, the Coopers were no match for the BRM, Lotus, or the now much improved Ferrari opposition, and his best finish was a poor sixth place in the British Grand Prix.

Phil Hill retired from Grand Prix racing at the end of 1964 with a distinguished record of three Grand Prix wins and a World Championship. He continued to take part in sports car racing, driving the new Ford GT40s in 1965, but switching to the American Chaparral team for 1967. He rounded off a fine career in International racing by co-driving with Mike Spence the winning Chaparral in the 1967 BOAC '500' race at Brands Hatch.

At the age of 39 and still a batchelor Hill returned to California and divided his time between working at races as a television commentator and running a business restoring and selling old cars. In 1971 Phil married Alma (who already had a child by a previous marriage) and the man whom everyone had believed to be a dedicated bachelor settled down to a comfortable family life; in November, 1972 the Hill's first baby, a daughter called Vanessa, was born. For Phil Hill motor racing is largely a memory from the past, but he appeared in the parade of *Anciens Pilotes* at Dijon in 1974 in commemoration of the fiftieth anniversary of the French Grand Prix.

A contemporary of Phil Hill – and a close friend – Richie Ginther was the second of the 'new wave' of American drivers to make a major impact on the European racing scene. After driving in American Club events Ginther competed with Aston Martin, Ferrari and Porsche cars for private owners in the United States. Ginther's first European drive was at Le Mans in 1957 where he handled a 2-litre Ferrari and held second place in his class until mechanical trouble compelled his retirement. Whilst continuing to race in American events, Ginther worked as manager of the Californian Ferrari agents and he did not become a full-time professional racing driver until he received an invitation to join the works Ferrari team for 1960.

The first race for the new member of the Scuderia was the Targa Florio held over the almost impossibly difficult 44.7-mile Little Madonie circuit and in this event Ginther crashed; the slight, freckle-faced Californian soon, however, proved his worth by driving the new Ferrari rear-engined Grand Prix prototype into fifth place at Monaco. Later in the year he finished second in the Italian Grand Prix. By the following season the determined, hard-driving Ginther was both Ferrari Chief Test Driver and a member of the Formula One team. He finished second at Monaco (where the winner was Stirling Moss with an outdated Lotus), third in the Belgian race and third in the British Grand Prix at Aintree; he took fifth place in the Drivers' World Championship.

For 1962 Richie Ginther switched his allegiance to the BRM team and for three seasons he proved a stalwart number two to BRM team-leader Graham Hill. Ginther's driving was always forceful and full of guts, even if he lacked the skill to make it to the top in Grand Prix racing. In his first year with the Bourne team he was plagued by series of unlucky accidents, but later in the year finished third in the French Grand Prix and second in the Italian race. 1963 proved a much more successful year for the Californian; on the strength of second place at Monaco, third at the Nürburgring and seconds at both Monza and Watkins Glen he took third place in the Drivers' Championship behind Jim Clark (Lotus) and team-mate Hill. Consistency was the watch-word of Ginther's performances in 1964 and he was the only driver to make it to the finish in every one of the year's Championship races. He was second at both Monaco and in the Austrian Grand Prix held on the Zeltweg airfield circuit and finished fourth equal in the Championship.

In the middle of the 1964 season the Japanese Honda team had entered racing with their new transversely mounted V-12-engined car and for the following year Ginther contracted to drive for the Japanese team. The Honda V-12s were immensely complex and hopelessly unreliable, but nevertheless Richie succeeded in winning the 1965 Mexican Grand Prix, his first Championship race victory and the last race to be held to the 1500 cc Formula. Honda returned to racing in 1966 with a new V-12 3-litre car to comply with the latest Grand Prix regulations. The new car was not ready at the beginning of the season and initially Ginther appeared at the wheel of a works Cooper-Maserati, finishing fifth in the Belgian Grand Prix. The new Honda made its debut in September 1966 at Monza and Ginther finished fourth with the new car in the final round of the World Championship at Mexico City. At the end of 1966 36-year-old Ginther decided to retire from racing, but he later reappeared as manager of a team of Porsche 911 cars and he drove the Porsche 908 camera car at Le Mans in 1970 for the making of the film starring Steve McQueen.

The third of the trio of great American drivers to break into European racing was Dan Gurney, another Californian who raced sports cars in the United States before receiving an invitation to drive for Ferrari in 1959. At the wheel of the front-engined Dino V-6 Grand Prix cars he finished second in the German Grand Prix, third in the Portuguese race and fourth in the Italian.

For 1960 the lanky American switched to BRM, but he was completely out of luck with the notoriously unsuccessful Bourne team and his sole success in Formula One racing that year was a second place in the Buenos Aires City Grand Prix. With the abandonment of the old 2500 cc Grand Prix Formula at the end of 1960 and the change to a 1500 cc Formula Dan Gurney joined the German Porsche team for whom he drove for two seasons. During 1961 Porsche raced their rather underpowered four-cylinder cars based on the previous year's Formula Two model and despite the fact that Dan was a notoriously hard driver with little sympathy for the mechanics of his car he drove with sufficient consistency to take second places in the French and Italian Grands Prix and to finish a joint third in the Drivers' Championship. By 1962 Porsche had their new and much improved flat-eight cars ready to race and Gurney enjoyed a successful season that embraced wins in the French and Solitude Grands Prix.

Porsche found the financial burden of Formula One racing too onerous and withdrew at the end of the 1962 season. Dan Gurney signed up with the Brabham team with whom he remained until the end of the 1500 cc Formula. Little fortune came the way of the turquoise cars in 1963, but in 1964 Gurney scored victories in the French and Mexican races and, almost heartbreakingly, was robbed of victory at Spa when his Brabham ran out of fuel while he was leading the race. Formula One victories eluded Gurney in 1965, but he enjoyed a relatively successful season with third places in the Dutch, German and Italian races and second places at Watkins Glen and Mexico City. At the end of 1965 Gurney quit the Brabham organisation to run his own team of Eagle Formula One cars. The fortunes – and misfortunes – of these beautifully finished blue and silver cars are discussed in an earlier chapter.

Following the retirement from racing of Dan Gurney, the last of this trio of great American drivers, at the end of the 1968 season there was an interregnum of several years before another North American racing driver rose to prominence in Formula One. Central and South American drivers in the persons of Pedro Rodriguez and Emerson Fittipaldi were beginning to make their mark, but it was not until 1972 that a United States *pilote* again became a consistent scorer of World Championship points.

That driver was New Yorker Peter Revson who had gained limited Formula One experience with a Lotus privately entered in 1964 by the Reg Parnell Racing Team. In the main Revson's experience had been gained in United States Automobile Club and Can-Am racing (he drove a Lola in 1970 and a works McLaren in this series in 1971), but he made a one-off appearance with a works Tyrrell in the 1971 United States Grand Prix; Revson was completely out of luck in this race and retired with clutch trouble at the end of the first lap.

Revson's drive with the Tyrrell led to speculation that he would be appearing regularly with one of the blue Elf-sponsored cars in 1972, but instead he signed up with the McLaren team and drove one of the Yardley-sponsored white, gold and brown cars alongside Denis Hulme. For a driver in his first full season of Formula One racing Revson performed magnificently and his successes included third places in the South African, British and Austrian Grands Prix and a fine second in Canada.

By 1974 Revson had matured considerably, although several of his critics felt that he was insufficiently ambitious and forceful to score an outright Grand Prix victory. The debonair 34-year old Revson convincingly proved them wrong; following a second place in the South African Grand Prix Revson went on to win the British Grand Prix (which was restarted after a multi-car crash at the start of the second lap) and the Canadian race (but because of time-keeping errors no one was certain who was the *real* winner at Mosport Park).

Whether Revson was World Champion material or not was as yet unproven, but he was a driver whose services were in great demand. He was now disillusioned by McLaren team politics and for 1974 decided to throw in his lot with the Shadow team, financed by the American Universal Oil Products Corporation, but British based. The Shadow had made little impression during its first season of Formula One in 1973, but the team was hoping for much better results with their new DN3 car. Revson retired in the Argentine and Brazil and then disaster struck during pre-race practice for the South African Grand Prix at Kyalami. As a result of front suspension failure Revson's Shadow collided with a steel barrier on the outside of a bend and the American was killed instantly.

Both of the new American teams that appeared at the 1974 Canadian Grand Prix were serious contenders for major honours. From Roger Penske, one of the most experienced and most able of American entrants, came the Penske PC1 sponsored by the First National City Bank and driven by Mark Donohue. Donohue was making a racing come-back and had last appeared in the 1973 Can-Am series which he had won with a turbocharged Porsche; his extensive experience included a season with the Sunoco-Ferrari 512M, a Sports Car Championship contender which had been completely rebuilt by Penske, and a one-off drive with a Penske-entered McLaren in the 1971 Canadian Grand Prix in which he had finished third.

The other new contender was the Parnelli VPJ4 entered by Vel's Parnelli Jones Racing and driven by Italian-born American-naturalised Mario Andretti. Andretti is one of the most experienced American racing drivers and his varied career has included extensive Formula One experience. Andretti had made his Grand Prix debut with a Lotus in the 1968 United States race (he had practised for the 1968 Italian race, but did not start) and not only did he take pole position in practice, but he led the race until the nose cowling began to disintegrate.

This brilliant driver drove a works four-wheel-drive Lotus in the 1969 German race and he re-appeared in 1970 with a new March car sponsored by Andy Granatelli's STP oil additive concern. Unfortunately the March failed to come up to expectations, the year's racing was dominated by Jochen Rindt with the Lotus 49B and Andretti's Grand Prix season came to an untimely end when he crashed the March heavily during the Austrian Grand Prix in August. Mario had driven for the Autodelta sports car team in 1969, but for 1971 he signed up for another Italian team, SEFAC Ferrari, but appeared in only those Grands Prix which his American racing commitments permitted. The new flat-12 Ferrari had shown great promise during 1970, but in the early part of 1971 it lost its competitive edge and Jackie Stewart and the Tyrrell soon emerged as the year's most successful driver/car combination. Nevertheless Andretti did well to win the South African Grand Prix (following Hulme's retirement in the closing laps of the race) and the non-Championship Questor Grand Prix at the Ontario Motor Speedway in California. Andretti stayed with the Ferrari team in 1972, but missed many of the year's races and achieved no success.

Neither Penske nor the Parnelli team were expecting immediate success;

although both were relying on the Ford-Cosworth V-8 engine and Hewland transmission that had powered every World Championship-winning car since 1968, the problems of developing a competitive chassis and evolving a team capable of coping with the pressures of Formula One racing were immense. Both teams were well satisfied that their cars finished in the 1974 Canadian race, albeit at the tail of the field, but both retired in the United States event. Nor did the early events of the 1975 season bring the American teams any success; but both Andretti and Donohue are drivers of outstanding ability, the teams that enter them painstaking and patient. A new era of American Grand Prix success has yet to arrive, but it is most certainly well on the way.